Shelf Life

Shelf Life

Reviews, Replies and Reminiscences

C. K. Stead

AUCKLAND
UNIVERSITY
PRESS

To my fellow poet-critics and friends of many years
Craig Raine in Oxford
and Mike Doyle in Victoria, BC

First published 2016

Auckland University Press
University of Auckland
Private Bag 92019
Auckland 1142
New Zealand
www.press.auckland.ac.nz

© C. K. Stead

ISBN 978 1 86940 849 7

Publication is kindly assisted by

creative*nz*
ARTS COUNCIL OF NEW ZEALAND TOI AOTEAROA

A catalogue record for this book is available from
the National Library of New Zealand

Cover design by Scott Crickett
Cover image: Gretchen Albrecht, *Small Winter Sunset*, acrylic and
acrylic staining on stretched cotton duck, 1972, The Rutherford
Trust Collection, The Wallace Arts Trust

Printed in China by 1010 Printing International Ltd

Contents

Introduction: Afternoon Work

Putting together a collection of this kind makes me more aware than I usually am of the categories in which I have worked – poetry, fiction, non-fiction – and how the last of these has divided between academic publication and varieties of literary journalism. I had always been a writer first and anything else second; but thirty years ago, when I left the university to become the writer full-time, I was nervous that working alone and lacking the pressures of a timetable, busy colleagues and eager students, I might find myself sitting about doing nothing. I had a wife, Kay, still working at the university library. Now I had to earn my living in a new way. I gave myself a five-day working week, and kept office hours, though of course I could and did work 'overtime'. My old friend and mentor, Frank Sargeson, used to require of himself 'a page a day' – handwritten, so possibly only 300 words. I was making up for lost time, and that would not have seemed enough. I worked very hard and consistently. I had worked hard as a university teacher too, but now it was at what I wanted to do rather than at what the timetable required.

My days began with a vigorous walk or a swim, and then the morning was devoted to the primary project of the moment – fiction at first; but later, once I had proved to myself that I really was a working novelist, I would switch for a period to 'poetry mode'. So there was soon an almost regular alternating pattern – a novel followed by a collection of poems, and then fiction again. Sometimes this work continued after lunch; but on the whole I tried to reserve the afternoons for the other side of my professional life – reviews, literary journalism, columns, occasional lectures, correspondence. For a time I reviewed fiction for the *Sydney Morning Herald*; at another period I wrote a column for *Metro*; for over fifteen years I wrote for Karl Miller's *London Review of Books*. And I wrote randomly for a number of literary journals and newspapers both local and overseas. My academic life did not quite stop either. I was still known for work on the poetry of twentieth-century Modernism, and invitations came to lecture, visit, supervise. My life fell into a pattern of nine or ten months at home working in Auckland, and two or three (very occasionally more) overseas. No year passed when I didn't cross the equator at least once.

Monetary rewards varied; but, given that the New Zealand market is small, I had what I needed to keep afloat as a professional writer – overseas publishers. Nothing of mine ever sold quite as well as my first critical book, *The New Poetic*, which was published on both sides of the Atlantic in a number of formats and editions, and has remained in print in Britain for half a century. I learned early that it is very important to be practical about money matters; but it is also true that the financial rewards seldom ran even approximately parallel with one's inner sense of achievement, and the inner sense was the one that mattered most. Money from advances, royalties, translation rights and movie options, local grants and awards, international prizes – any or all of these were welcome if and when they sent down a small, usually unscheduled, shower of gold. So were the annual authors' lending right payments for books in libraries, and grants from Creative New Zealand towards local publishers of poetry, and for travel to attend literary festivals. But the real rewards came when you knew, on your own internal scale of things, that you had written something not just good, but uniquely your own. A poem, a short story or chapter – even a page – of fiction; a witty review or an insightful paragraph of critical analysis: whatever it happened to be, if the internal monitor told you it was good, that was where true satisfaction, a sort of peace to the spirit, was to be found.

What ghost was being appeased? What wrong was being righted or sin atoned for? I didn't know. It was all, this writing business, and had been since it first began when I was still at school, mysterious, possibly even neurotic. I knew only that for a moment the world which 'out there' seemed so imperfect, so 'fallen', so much less than the heart desired, 'in here' had been called to order. Others might like what was pleasing me so much, or they might dislike, even deplore it; or (most probable) it would pass unnoticed – but one had struck gold of another kind, the kind that gave meaning to the whole project. In a very real sense I was in the business to please myself. If I set out to please others (and particularly something conceived of as 'the Market') that was a recipe for inauthenticity and failure.

My non-fiction prose writing has divided into three kinds. First, the academic – *The New Poetic*, and then the larger (and possibly better, though I have never re-read it since it appeared in 1986) *Pound, Yeats, Eliot and the Modernist Movement*. Second, my work specifically on New Zealand literature, gathered first in *In the Glass Case*, and expanded in *Kin of Place: Essays on 20 New Zealand Writers*. Third has come the afternoon work: reviews, essays, public lectures, columns, travel diaries, literary reminiscences – every kind of literary journalism, including the parts that spill over into politics, education, and reflections on language and the teaching of English in schools and universities. In this area I have quite often been involved in disputes, and have acquired a reputation which has meant the word 'controversial' is often attached to my name. This is not a designation I like much, but unavoidable I suppose given the kind of person I am, the kind of writer I have chosen to be, the nature of the New Zealand literary community, and the public matters I have tiptoed over or trespassed upon. Candour is welcome if you agree, unwelcome if you don't. It both clears the air and divides the room.

At intervals I have put together collections of this kind of writing. The first was called *Answering to the Language* (1989), the second *The Writer at Work* (2000), the third *Book Self* (2008). The present book is the fourth. Each has had an introduction intended to suggest the collection's general literary predisposition. The introduction to the 1989 collection was called 'At the Graves of Yeats' and described visiting (with W. B.'s son and daughter) the place where Yeats was first interred at Roquebrune; and then, alone this time, his final resting place in Ireland, the grave in Drumcliff churchyard, with the inscription he composed for it:

> Cast a cold eye
> On life, on death.
> Horseman, pass by!

I described asking myself, '*What* horseman? Why did Yeats not write "Motorist, pass by!"' And I went on, 'Because, of course, such an injection of reality would have interfered with the rhetoric of the occasion. Yeats was the kind of poet who could not leave even his obsequies to others.' I was presenting myself, I suppose, as a realist: 'All literature', I wrote, 'is grounded in language and in observation. Imagination, exalted by the Romantic movement, was never a vehicle of escape from reality but rather a mode of entry.'

In the introduction to my next collection of this kind, *The Writer at Work*, I described how, having in my writings marked myself out as a political liberal, I discovered that to then question any part of the liberal package could bring down on one's head the wrath reserved for the apostate.

Arrested in 1981 on Hamilton's Rugby Park [i.e. during protests against the South African tour of that year] I had felt like Daniel emerging from the lions' den. Now it was as if Daniel had demanded better working conditions for lions.

Central issues at this period included the Treaty of Waitangi as 'our nation's founding document', my part in the Labour Government's sesquicentenary gift to New Zealand writers of a flat in London, my critical rigour with two or three contemporaries, my conservatism about the teaching of English in schools and universities, and even perhaps my robust and undisguised scepticism in religious matters. Rejection of French (and consequently anglophone) literary theory as pointless obscurantism brought grumbles from the groves of academe while its fashion lasted. Feminists took offence at my novel *The Death of the Body*, which I still suspect might be, not my 'best', but my cleverest (always dangerous in 'Aotearoa/New Zealand').

But by the time I came to put together the next collection, *Book Self*, I knew there was a quite lively appetite here for intellectual and literary discussion that ranged wide in the world, and which, within our own borders, was not bound by, or too bothered about, 'proprieties'. Where pieties were anticipated, freshness was often received as a welcome surprise. My introduction to that collection took its title from a once famous essay by T. S. Eliot, 'The Function of Criticism', and was an attempt to place myself in time, a product of the mid-twentieth-century literary world dominated by T. S. Eliot, F. R. Leavis and the New Criticism, the same period or phase from which Martin Amis (though he was sixteen years my junior) saw himself as having emerged. I affirmed both Virginia Woolf's 'common reader', which recent critical theory had declared a meaningless term, and insisted on the life of the author in the text, also denied by the theorists. The literary nationalism with which I had begun, influenced by Curnow, Sargeson and the whole literary atmosphere of post-World War II New Zealand, no longer had its old attraction and was rejected; but I felt, nonetheless, that there was most often a strong regional element in poetry and fiction, which deserved, and rewarded, attention.

I saw myself still as a practising critic; and I was able to end with the same words that ended the first of these collections:

> If there is a specialist in every common reader there is also a common reader in every specialist, and it is to that person I address myself.
>
> For that reason I think there is no important difference in tone, in vocabulary, or in the demands they make, between my academic papers and my reviews for journals. I am not interested in arcane dialogue. I would like where possible to be understood.

The same is true of the present collection. There is less in it that challenges current orthodoxies and local pieties than in my earlier books of this kind. That is not, I think, because I am 'better behaved', though a certain mildness may have crept up on me with age and the recognition of how generously I have been treated by my country; but mainly, I think, because my attention during the past decade has been more purely literary. My academic work has been mostly to do with Mansfield, a result of the development of the Katherine Mansfield Society and its biannual conferences; and although I am not altogether happy at the thought of myself as one of several international angels dancing on the head of the Mansfield pin, her writing is a subject that continues to engage me. My reviewing has been as random as ever, resulting from whatever interests me and what I was asked to do. The interviews have become more numerous and more varied in tone and approach, and in putting some of them together here I have tried to edit out repetitions and overlaps.

In the fourth section I have added six pieces written since I became New Zealand's Poet Laureate for 2015–17 and posted as 'Laureate Blogs'. These are in part recollections and in part what F. R. Leavis long ago taught us to call 'revaluations', so sitting on the borderline between criticism and autobiography, a position I have in the past argued in favour of. Here the voice is neither academic nor abstract, not the voice of God nor of a committee, but of a writer whose confidence and competence come with a history and a name, and are always open to challenge.

★

The individual papers, journals and books in which these reviews and interviews first appeared, and the venues and conferences at which lectures were given, are acknowledged in the notes on the first page of each item. I am grateful to the editors and organisers of these for the invitations to contribute. Thanks also to various copyright holders for permission to quote from letters and poems. The essays in the fourth section of the book were written as part of a series of blogs I am writing as New Zealand Poet Laureate for 2015–2017. I am grateful to the National Library of New Zealand for this role; and also to the Alexander Turnbull Library for providing two pages of the Mansfield Urewera Notebook to illustrate points in the first of my Mansfield lectures.

C.K.S.
Auckland, February 2016

1.

The Mansfield File

Meetings with 'The Great Ghost'

My awareness of Katherine Mansfield began even before I'd read her. When I was at primary school during the Second World War there was a series of cards, 'Great New Zealanders', which came with the breakfast cereal Weet-Bix, and I still remember some of them. The great New Zealand scientist was (of course) Ernest Rutherford, the great athlete was Jack Lovelock, the All Black George Nepia, the tennis player Anthony Wilding, the statesman 'King Dick' Seddon, the soldier 'Tiny' Freyberg, the opera singer Oscar Natzke, the Maori leader Sir Peter Buck, and the writer Katherine Mansfield. There were others, but if my memory is right there was just one in each category. I'm sure Mansfield would have been chosen for one reason only – not because in New Zealand she was much read outside the literary community, but because she was known to have 'made it overseas'. These were still (though I would soon be resenting and rejecting the description)

A keynote address to an international conference on Katherine Mansfield held at Birkbeck College, University of London, in September 2008.

colonial times – but the Dominion (as it then was) was striving to shake itself loose, to see itself as an independent nation. What better measure (ordinary New Zealanders would have asked) that we were a nation in our own right than that some of ours could measure up against those of the homeland; could succeed and shine there?

Here, then, we have Mansfield figuring possibly as inspiration, possibly as burden; and the burden aspect, I'm sure, explains the irritation in the voice of Allen Curnow in the only spoken comment I recall him making on her. He and Denis Glover and I were on a literary panel in Auckland and her name came up. Curnow's response was to recall 'some fool' in the Christchurch of his youth writing that she was 'the only peacock in New Zealand's literary garden'. I interjected 'peahen', which Denis capped with 'Piha'; and if more was said I've forgotten it.

The undertone of irritation with Mansfield around this time among New Zealand writers trying to establish an indigenous literature was quite strong. Curnow, dismissing what he calls the 'awful archness' of Robin Hyde's lines on Mansfield, adds a gratuitous footnote quoting Geoffrey de Montalk on the subject.[1] Denis Glover disparages her as 'prissy' and says he gave up reading her long ago.[2] And Frank Sargeson warns the young Vincent O'Sullivan not to 'spend his life on the dreams of a Karori schoolgirl'.[3]

For myself, reading Mansfield began at secondary school and university. It was random, intermittent, the stories only (no letters or journals), and quite unrelated to formal courses. She was not 'taught', nor was 'New Zealand literature', but I was very conscious of her, and admiring – especially of a quality I would much later describe as 'an indefinable, all-pervasive freshness in her writing, as if each sentence had been struck off first thing on a brilliant morning'.

I think I was also soon aware that if you read more than a few stories you were likely to come upon some in which the wonderful sensibility deliquesced into mush, the sharp eye missed its target, the trick-cyclist fell off her bike. But these were only impressions, and

I never gave Mansfield focused critical attention until 1972 when, at the age of 39, I was awarded the (as it then was) Winn-Manson Menton Fellowship – so named to commemorate its primary bene-factor, Sheilah Winn, its founders, Celia and Cecil Manson, and the French town that honoured Mansfield with a memorial. By that time I was Professor of English at Auckland, my special field being twentieth-century Modernist poetry and criticism.

Before I come to that, however, I want to say a word more about Mansfield's reputation in New Zealand when I was young. The two men who influenced me most, and encouraged me as a poet during my student years, were Frank Sargeson and Allen Curnow. Curnow was my teacher at the university, Sargeson my literary friend and mentor outside it. I never heard either of them say much about Mansfield. There was the irritable Curnow remark about the peacock in our literary garden; and I do remember Frank once, in conversation, saying of something of hers I had admired that, 'Yes, OK, it was good', but it was *the kind of thing women can do*'. This rather odd idea (odd enough for the remark to stick in my memory) was one he had once tried to elevate into a critical principle, though I didn't know that until it appeared posthumously in a selection of his critical pieces.[4]

It was a radio talk he gave in 1948. His argument is that as a fiction writer Mansfield is 'in the *feminine* tradition'; and he hastens to add that this is not just another way of saying she's a woman. Others he lists as belonging to this tradition are Samuel Richardson, Jane Austen and E. M. Forster, all of whom he admires. But then he adds, seeming to contradict himself, that 'the feminine tradition is the *minor* tradition'. The tendency that characterises it is concern 'with the part rather than the whole – in other words a tendency to make your story depend for its effectiveness on isolated details and moments of life'. A writer of Jane Austen's stature can get away with it; but fiction of this kind, when it fails, fails very badly, 'because everything is so very tenuous – everything is, as it were, hanging by the finest of threads'.[5]

He then offers two examples of Mansfield stories: one, 'The Voyage', which succeeds; another, 'Her First Ball', where those tenuous threads break and the story is a failure. I should think it's not difficult to agree that 'The Voyage' is a success and 'Her First Ball' possibly a failure. And other points he makes about her work, positive and negative, are plausible. But the larger point seems more than anything an indicator of an anxiety about Mansfield and a wish to place her safely inside a box; to label her '*minor*'; to contain her and put her away on a shelf.

That was Sargeson in 1948. Twenty years later, towards the end of his career, he found an entirely different way of dealing with her. In an interview published in 1970, he brings up something H. Winston Rhodes has reported of a young woman student saying that there were two tragedies in New Zealand literature – one was Katherine Mansfield and the other Frank Sargeson. And he comments, 'This is a tremendous thing – I think it's very very good indeed – salutary, all sorts of things could be said about it.'

It becomes clear as the interview continues that Frank took this to mean that each of them, Mansfield and Sargeson, imposed a style which others felt it necessary to emulate. 'Mansfield, writing powerfully', he says, 'imposed a pattern on our writing so that everybody was impressed and hosts of young women wrote Mansfield stories'.[6] And then he quotes Dennis McEldowney saying that when he first read Sargeson he thought that *this* was New Zealand, and that Sargeson's was the only way to write about it.

There may be, or may have been, some broad truth in all this. But it strikes me, at this distance in time, as simultaneously a piece of self-promotion and of Mansfield-containment. It appears to be modest. 'Instead of opening something for New Zealand', he says, 'both Mansfield and myself have tended to be constricting influences'.[7] Modest, except that it puts him at a stroke alongside Mansfield, on a par with her. The twin tragedies of New Zealand literature! She can come out of her box so long as he can sit at her right hand.

I stress that my view of all this is affectionate, even admiring, because I see strategies of that kind as an inevitable outcome of writers at that time struggling to be noticed in their own country, competing with the name that was big with the New Zealand public, not because they read her, but because they knew people 'overseas' did.

Curnow's only serious comment on Mansfield is in the introduction to his 1960 *Penguin Book of New Zealand Verse*. What appeals to him in the poem 'To Stanislaw Wyspianski' is the unambiguous self-identification as a New Zealander, couched in terms which are more negative than positive. What Curnow is weary of, clearly, is the false clamour of nationhood, the glamorising of our collective identity, and the expectation that poetry should fly the flag. He lingers especially on the line 'I, a woman, with the taint of pioneer in my blood': 'the feeling', he comments, 'is something like shame for her country: for its childish clumsiness, its merely *physical* preoccupations [. . .], its ignorance of, or indifference to, "ghosts and unseen presences"'. And he goes on:

> Denial and acceptance are mixed in 'To Stanislaw Wyspianski', though the denial given to New Zealand is their argument. I think they express Katherine Mansfield's intuition that New Zealand's obstinate social hedonism, marching with the littleness and the isolation [. . .] stood between her and the knowledge of life (and death) she needed.[8]

This is among the clearest statements anywhere in the anthology's very long introduction of Curnow's own position – what might be called his 'negative nationalism'. Yes, the poets should speak for, as well as of, the nation; but they have a responsibility to represent the negatives as well as the positives; and in particular to articulate what he calls 'the New Zealand sadness (always there, however deeply buried)'.[9] The broader tradition Curnow is attaching himself to is the social realism of the 1930s that evolved partly out of the war poetry of 1914–18 and Wilfred Owen's dictum, 'The true Poets must be truthful'.[10] It's quite a weight for the young Mansfield's Whitmanesque windiness to carry, but he doesn't misrepresent her poem; and it does seem that, by 1960, he has grown beyond the resentment of her fame that was common two and three decades earlier, so that he can now call on the authority of her name to ratify something that for him is immensely important.

I come back now to myself in 1972, the second writer to receive what's called these days the New Zealand Post Katherine Mansfield Menton Prize.[11]

In Menton I set about writing what Allan Phillipson has referred to as my 'difficult second novel'.[12] In that chilly little memorial room under the Villa Isola Bella I worked very hard at the fiction; but the secondary task I set myself was to read everything of Mansfield's in print at that time, to read the biographies, and to form some sort of critical overview of her life and work.

My interest in her was still partly nationalistic – she was 'a New Zealand writer' and, whatever that means, so was I; and partly I saw reading her as a politeness, an acknowledgement of the fellowship that had brought me to the south of France. But neither of those motives would have kept me studying her for more than a few weeks if her work and her life had not engaged my mind and imagination as fully as they did. She was, quite simply, immensely rewarding; and it was in the course of that reading I conceived the idea of making a selection of her letters and journals which could be run together, arranged chronologically, with chapters and biographical notes.

I was in Menton for about eight months with my wife, Kay, and our children – then aged two, five and eight – after which we went on to London for the remaining five months of my sabbatical leave. There I put the letters and journals idea to Judith Burnley at Penguin/Allen Lane and received, in the right order, encouragement, the use of a Xerox machine, and a contract.[13]

I knew there were problems with the correctness or otherwise of the published texts, and that I should check them where possible; so for those months I worked in the British Museum, reading Mansfield and Bloomsbury material, and relevant manuscripts held there, checking texts of letters I'd chosen, and now and then adding passages, or whole letters, omitted from the published editions. It was there I came on her letter from Cornwall describing Lawrence chasing Frieda and beating her, while Katherine and Jack sat transfixed at the supper table, embarrassed and uncertain what they should do. That letter was published for the first time in my selection; and years later I made it a scene in my novel about her.

Back in New Zealand I was on a committee that took me to Wellington from time to time, and I made each visit an opportunity to work on manuscripts in the Alexander Turnbull Library. The letters that went into my selection were checked against the manuscripts, which didn't mean there would be no mistakes, but that there would be fewer.

But time was passing, and I knew that checking the journal entries as well would try my publisher's patience. I had met Margaret Scott in Wellington; and I remember she showed me (almost, it seemed, teased me with) copies of the published editions of the *Journal* and the *Scrapbook* (as Murry called them), annotated with her corrections. That might have been a short-cut to more dependable texts; but I didn't like to ask, it wasn't unambiguously offered, and if it had been, I would still have been dependent on someone else's transcriptions. So the texts derived from Murry's edition of the *Journal* were left uncorrected.

My edition was dedicated to Celia and Cecil Manson, the originators of the Menton fellowship. They deserved the acknowledgement and they were unambiguously pleased by it. A quarter of a century later, when the book had been re-issued for the last time in the United Kingdom and was being taken up by Random House New Zealand, the Mansons were dead, and I dedicated the new edition to Margaret

Scott – without, alas, first seeking her permission. Foolishly, I thought she would be pleased. She tried not to seem ungrateful; but she made it clear she was not happy to have her reputation for accuracy compromised by association with Murry's uncorrected journal texts. I'm glad to acknowledge here that the mistake was mine.

Of course this was never intended as an edition primarily for scholars; and one did, on the whole, get a very good sense of Mansfield from those early Murry transcriptions. Much of what he copied presented few problems; and where there were extreme difficulties (the *Urewera Notebook*, for example) no one was going to be infallible.

Sometime in the 1980s, after my selection was published, I spent a few days in the Turnbull Library doing a test transcription of some pages of the *Urewera Notebook* which I then compared with Ian Gordon's text, and have since compared with Margaret Scott's. I wanted to gauge how far the Murry text of her journal misrepresented her, and how much difference, if any, a further transcription would have made. Gordon's transcription is good, and Scott's better; but neither can be called perfect, because in many instances it's impossible to be certain. Here are two examples where, if you add mine to the others,[14] you get four different readings:

During the Rotorua visit Mansfield dashes down something which Murry transcribes (believing, apparently, that nga moni was a kind of sweet potato) as 'We pick nga-moni'. Gordon corrects this to 'We play nga maui', with a note explaining that 'nga maui' is a string game, otherwise known at cat's cradle. So Gordon's reading makes sense; but no one, looking at the verb, could possibly read it as 'play'. This is a wishful reading. Scott corrects it to 'We pluck nga maui'. 'Pluck' is closer to the look of the word on the page, which undoubtedly begins with 'pl', but it only makes sense, if at all, with difficulty; and it's very difficult to see a 'u' in what Gordon saw as an 'a'. What it is, I think, is an 'e' and an 'a' pushed together, and the word, as I read it, is 'pleach' – 'we pleach nga maui'; unusual, but it has the double advantage of making sense,[15] and matching the look of the letters on her page. 'Pick', 'play', 'pluck', or 'pleach' – the difficulties of Mansfield transcription could hardly be better illustrated!

A little further on Murry transcribes 'That evening – horrid', and doesn't even try to copy the next phrase. Ian Gordon has 'that evening – horrid the purple bowl'. Scott has 'that evening – horrid – the people – bores [?]'. Gordon's 'bowl' is almost right but his 'purple' is clearly wrong. Scott's 'people' is right but her 'bores [?]' I think is wrong. My transcript reads, 'that evening – horrid – the people – bowls'. Since there was, even in 1907, a bowling green in those Rotorua gardens, and since people who play bowls are the kind the young Mansfield would very likely describe as 'horrid', I think my transcript is probably right.

So it is, up to a point, a game anyone can play; and no one is going to score ten out of ten. But beyond question our chief debts are, first, to Murry, because he went first;[16] and second to Margaret Scott, because she has done the hard slog over so much material over so many years.

In my introduction to the selection I tried to do justice to Murry – not only as first transcriber of the manuscripts, but also as their preserver, and the one who kept the world interested in her and in them. Of course he profited by that. She had willed all her work to him, so that was his right. I was impatient with the view, quite widely encountered especially in the 1980s, and represented, for example, by that rather silly movie, *Leave All Fair*,[17] that Murry had sinned in not doing what she'd asked him to do; had not tidied up her 'camping ground' and '[left] all fair'. She had, I argued, given him impossible instructions: 'destroy all that you do not use', and 'destroy all [...] you do not wish to keep'.[18] The word 'use' surely suggests publication. And as to keeping or destroying: the same people who criticised him for preserving and publishing would have been merciless if he had destroyed so much as a single page.

My selection came out in hardcover from Allen Lane in September 1977, and simultaneously in the Penguin Modern Classics series, where it was re-issued and remained in print for more than twenty years. Among other things, it was the initial trigger and provider of material for Cathy Downes's one-person show, *The Case of Katherine Mansfield*, which was also revived often over many years.

Working with manuscripts, learning when and where they were written, produces a sense of closeness. Another source of that feeling is to meet survivors, as they seem, who were Katherine's friends. That happened to me only twice. The second and less significant occasion was in 1977 when A. S. Byatt suggested she and I should lunch with Claire Tomalin who was just beginning work on her Mansfield biography. I've forgotten where the lunch took place – somewhere in Bloomsbury – but a little old man who shuffled up to our table to greet Claire was introduced to me as Richard Murry, Jack's much younger brother. Katherine had been very fond of Richard, wrote him a number of good letters, and bequeathed him a pearl ring that he could give to his lover when he had one.

Much more significant was my meeting with Ida Baker in 1972.[19] I'd exchanged letters with her and she invited me to come to her cottage in the New Forest. It was a very amiable occasion, just the two of us; and I was surprised to find her quite a firm personality, not the dilly incompetent represented in Katherine's letters and notebooks – almost blind, but still able to cook lunch. And yet I could also see in her the quality of plodding, devoted literalness that Katherine had exploited while at the same time being driven mad by it – the 'ghoul' she dreamed of killing in Ospedaletti. And it seemed to me absolutely consistent with Katherine's portraits of Ida that she should explain to me that her door, opening not onto a road but what was hardly more than a track through the forest, had to be left open day and night because a bird (I think it was a swallow) was nesting in the beams of her ceiling and had to be free to come and go.[20]

A lot of what Ida Baker said had recently appeared in her book of memoirs – they were well-rehearsed stories, though better for being told in her own voice.[21] But now and then there were flashes which brought me suddenly closer to Mansfield's people – the slightly dreamy look when she said of Jack, 'Oh he was a *charming* boy'; and the sense of panic in her voice when she described Lawrence, with his flaming hair and beard, *pacing* up and down the room, hungry and impatient for the lunch it was her job to prepare.

By 1977 the selection was ready for publication and I was back in London as a visiting fellow in the English Department at University College London, where I was part of Karl Miller's team teaching the twentieth-century moderns paper. I was now working on what was to be my second book on that subject, so I lectured on Yeats, Eliot and

Auden; but I also included Mansfield in my part of the course, and an article based on my Mansfield lectures appeared that year in Ian Hamilton's *New Review*.

I was less inclined to be forgiving of Murry as Mansfield critic than I'd been of him as Mansfield editor. Murry had sentimentalised her and misrepresented her literary life, writing himself so determinedly into its centre that her fiction was shown as flowering when he and she were together-and-in-accord, and failing, or turning dark, when they were apart in fact and/or in feeling.

Most of the first draft of 'The Aloe', for example, had been written, not during their idyll together at Bandol, as Murry asserted, but when she was alone in Paris living in the apartment of her French lover Francis Carco.[22] Further, I was able to cite a letter by Murry to Sydney Schiff, which I'd come across in 1972 in the British Museum, to show that 'A Married Man's Story' was written at the Chalet des Sapins in August 1921. This not only contradicted Murry's subsequent placing of that story (and consequently everyone else's) as coming from her stay in Cornwall in 1918; it showed again the inaccuracy and wishfulness of his positive/negative pattern for how, when and why her best work was done.[23]

In my remaining years at the university my most serious academic work was completing my second book on Pound, Yeats and Eliot;[24] but in my New Zealand literature courses, Mansfield always had a place both at first year and MA levels, and from time to time I wrote about her work. I'd like to mention briefly now a mild spat that occurred in the early 1990s because I think it raises a question that still hangs over the figure of Mansfield.

In 1987 I reviewed Claire Tomalin's biography in the *London Review of Books*. It was a book I admired especially for confronting the subject of Mansfield's health in a way that hadn't happened before. But in an otherwise entirely favourable notice, I objected to the description of Mansfield as 'sexually ambiguous, with a husband, a wife, and lovers of both sexes'. This was, at the time, a fashionable view, but it seemed to me imprecise to the brink of inaccuracy and untruthfulness, and I suggested the author was 'letting the times do her thinking for her'. Tomalin made no complaint; but four years later, when someone in the *TLS* quoted what I had said, she wrote objecting, and an exchange followed.

There is, of course, no doubt that in the hothouse atmosphere of Queen's College, where girls had crushes not only on their male teachers but on one another, Mansfield embraced the ideas of Oscar Wilde as exciting, liberating, *avant garde*; and Vincent O'Sullivan has shown how these ideas led back to Pater as well,[25] and shaped some of her earliest and most enduring notions of the role of the artist, and of what constituted a work of art. No doubt, either, that when she recorded in her notebooks her one or two immature homosexual experiences (if that's what they were), 'Oscar' was invoked – not the figure of delicate mockery he later became for her, but a serious intellectual influence. Whether, or in what way, lying all night in Edie Bendall's arms was sexual, can't be determined. In retrospect Edie was sure it was not; at the time, or for the purposes of her journal, Katie chose to give the impression it was, and that 'Oscar' would be pleased with her.

My point, in the exchange with Tomalin, was that when Mansfield had emerged out of the turmoil of her teenage years, it didn't seem that any significant shred of sexual ambiguity remained. She could love both males and females, as we all can – and from time to time her love was gushingly expressed. That was the manner of the time, and it suited her temperament. But sex for the adult Mansfield, as far as I have ever been able to discover, was something that happened with males – and, while her health held up, it happened quite often. This is also the view of Margaret Scott who, in transcribing the letters and complete notebooks, must have spent more time in Mansfield's company than anyone else alive. 'As a teenager', Scott writes,

[Mansfield] had one or two crushes on girls or women, as do many girls who are incarcerated in single-sex schools away from men. But in her adult life there is simply no evidence of her sexual interest in any woman, though plenty of her interest in men.[26]

Is this a question that matters? I think we all feel some responsibility to get these things right as far as possible; not to overstate for dramatic or fashionable effect; and not to insist where no one can be sure. The writers we study, and whose work we teach, were people like ourselves, and would want us to be scrupulous. So when, for example, Tomalin says, 'None of her sexual relations with men appears to have given her happiness or even satisfaction',[27] I ask myself what this means precisely, and how it can be known. Does 'satisfaction' there go together with 'sexual' in the same sentence? Sexual satisfaction? Pleasure? Orgasm? Or simply enjoyment, emotional fulfilment? In the journal entry about her brief affair with Francis Carco, she writes so simply about undressing and getting into bed with him, without trying to make any particular impression (unlike those overheated teenage entries) – just a truthful record:

The act of love seemed somehow quite incidental, we talked so much. It was so warm & delicious, lying curled in each others arms, by the light of the tiny lamp [. . .], only the clock & the fire to be heard. A whole life passed in the night: other people other things, but we lay like 2 old people coughing faintly under the eiderdown, and laughing at each other and away we went to India, to South America, to Marseilles in the white boat & then we talked of Paris & sometimes I lost him in a crowd of people & it was dark and frightening, & then he was in my arms again & we were kissing.[28]

No happiness? No satisfaction? The effect is of drifting in and out of sleep, uncertain which is which – and it sounds pretty enjoyable to me. And what of her relations with Jack? Of course (as most such relationships between talented and high-energy people are), it was turbulent and often negative; but by what right do you pass over all the evidence of the positives in it, including that late letter in which she says, 'I think no two lovers walked the earth more joyfully – in spite of all'?[29]

O'Sullivan also describes Mansfield as 'bisexual', speaks more than once of her 'lesbianism',[30] and interprets 'Bertha's feeling for Pearl Fulton' in the story 'Bliss' as 'a lesbian one'. 'This may not be explicit', he writes, 'but it would be an obtuse reading of the story which overlooked it.' *Obtuse*? This is not at all, as it happens, how I read the story; but more important, even if it were, I would not feel it meant the story's author was correctly described as 'lesbian'.

This is a large subject, and I touch on it only because the dispute was part of my on-going engagement with Mansfield's life and work. It will at least explain why, when I represent her in my novel *Mansfield*, there is (or I hope there is) richness of personality, unpredictability, risk-taking, openness to whatever comes along; and she can *play the game* of bisexuality, as she does in one scene with Carrington at Garsington. But there is nothing to which the word 'lesbian' could properly attach itself.

I come back to my title, which derives from Damien Wilkins's description of Mansfield as 'the great ghost in New Zealand's cultural life'.[31] She has certainly been a ghost in mine, but not a difficult or oppressive one; and I think this does mark an historical change from writers like Curnow and Sargeson, born twenty and thirty years before me, for whom she was a decidedly mixed blessing and a problem requiring a strategy.

By 1972, my fortieth year, when I came to treat her work, not just as a reader but professionally, a lot had changed in the New Zealand literary scene, and those changes were continuing and accelerating. There was still (I detect, looking back) an element of slightly self-conscious nationalism in the way I went about my work – of 'laying claim' to her – but as a motivating factor that was insignif- icant, and soon absent altogether. What kept me at the task was the quality of mind, the superior literary intelligence and sensibil- ity, and the way the letters and journals, together with unfinished, or finished yet imperfect, stories opened the door on a writer's workshop. That Murry didn't 'leave all fair' was a great gift to Modernist and Post-modern generations, who valued the literary process as much as, and in some ways more than, the finished and perfect product. Mansfield was uneven (and how could it be oth- erwise? – she died at 34), but she was never boring. She loved the business of writing, loved to record it, reveal it, to be, and be seen to be, the writer at work.

But for myself a whole further aspect of my relationship with Mansfield was to develop, and I'll conclude by saying a little about that. I finally left the university altogether in 1986, but soon found that I had taken Mansfield with me. She drifted in and out of my con- sciousness, first in poems and then, quite decisively, in my 1992 novel *The End of the Century at the End of the World*.[32]

This is a novel in which the central character, Laura Barber, a 'mature student', is doing postgraduate work on a now-dead New Zealand writer, Hilda Tapler. Tapler had written, in the 1950s, a fictional account – or it has been assumed to be fiction – of meeting and interviewing Katherine Mansfield in Northland where she'd gone to live after faking her own death at the Gurdjeff Institute and taking the name of Katya Lawrence. Hilda Tapler's Mansfield fiction greatly interests Laura Barber, who begins to suspect, and even to find some evidence, that it might not be fiction at all.

This is metafiction of course, and by the end of the book the question of what happened 'really' and what was merely invented has become less important than, simply, the creation of a story: nar- rative as the structuring of experience necessary to the preservation of sanity; fiction as the recorder of social truths and human wisdom.

Nine years later Mansfield made another guest appearance, this time in my novel *The Secret History of Modernism*, where she's seen with T. S. Eliot, walking away from a dinner party in Hammersmith in 1917. That, in turn, gave me the idea of writing a whole novel about her; and this novel, called *Mansfield* and published in 2004, opens with the same event (one which indeed happened) – Eliot and Mansfield walking along the tow-path at Hammersmith, discussing the party they've just left where Robert Graves was still holding forth.

Mansfield came out of the recognition that here was a terrific story, full of incident and emotion, with an incomparably rich cast of ready-made characters, and that I might be as well-qualified as anyone to write it. I decided to confine myself to three years of her life during the First World War, the period that would include her affair with Francis Carco, Leslie's death, the rediscovery of her New Zealand subject matter, the Bandol idyll with Murry, the Cornwall fiasco with the Lawrences, a glimpse of Garsington and Lady Ottoline, and only at the end the first unmistakable intimation of tuberculosis. Much of what went into the novel was a filling in around, or building out beyond, what is already known.[33] But what you find when you write historical fiction is how huge the gaps are. The life we think we know so well is only a sketch. And the test is whether you can enter that sketch imaginatively, assume her voice, and fill the gaps.

---

1   Allen Curnow (ed.), *The Penguin Book of New Zealand Verse*, Penguin, 1960, p. 57.

2   Gordon Ogilvie, *Denis Glover: His Life*, Godwit, 1999, pp. 413 and 381.

3   Vincent O'Sullivan, 'Katherine Mansfield', *New Zealand Listener*, 5 July 2008, p. 14.

4   Frank Sargeson, 'Katherine Mansfield', in Kevin Cunningham (ed.), *Conversation in a Train and Other Critical Writing*, Auckland University Press / Oxford University Press, 1983, pp. 28–33.

5   This is a line taken also by T. S. Eliot in his subsequently suppressed lecture series published as *After Strange Gods: A Primer of Modern Heresy* (Faber and Faber, 1933), where he compares a Mansfield story with stories by Joyce and Lawrence, commends Mansfield's 'perfect [handling] of the *minimum* material', describes this as a 'feminine' quality and dismisses the story's 'moral implications' as 'negligible' (pp. 35–38).

6   'Conversation with Frank Sargeson: An Interview with Michael Beveridge', in *Conversation in a Train*, p. 153.

7 *Ibid.*, p. 154.
8 Curnow, p. 40.
9 *Ibid.*
10 E. Blunden (ed.), *The Poems of Wilfred Owen*, Chatto and Windus, 1955, p. 41.
11 And now, in 2016, the Katherine Mansfield Menton Fellowship. In 1972 it was worth NZ$1,750; it is now worth 'not less than' NZ$75,000.
12 I'm referring to an abstract of one of Phillipson's papers, entitled 'Menton Blues: C. K. Stead and the Difficult Second Novel', presented at the NZSA conference in Florence, 'New Zealand and the Mediterranean', 2–4 July 2008.
13 Judith Burnley, herself a fiction writer, published two novels, *The Wife*, 1977, and *Unrepentant Woman*, 1982.
14 These are not in fact passages that occur in my Penguin selection.
15 'Pleach – v. tr. To entwine or interlace (esp. branches to form a hedge)' (*Concise Oxford Dictionary*).
16 I'm speaking here of transcription and decipherment, not of editing and annotating of the kind done mostly by Vincent O'Sullivan.
17 *Leave All Fair* (1985), dir. John Reid. An interpretation of the life and relationships of Mansfield, starring John Gielgud, Jane Birkin, Feodor Atkine and Simon Ward.
18 Vincent O'Sullivan and Margaret Scott (eds), *The Collected Letters of Katherine Mansfield*, vol. V, Clarendon Press, 2008, pp. 234–5, letter dated 7 August 1922. (This volume hereafter referred to as *Letters* V.)
19 See 'Mansfield's F.O.' in my *The Writer at Work*, University of Otago Press, 2000, pp. 73–76.
20 Margaret Scott has many similar stories in *Recollecting Mansfield*, Godwit, 2001.
21 Ida Baker, *Katherine Mansfield: The Memories of LM*, Taplinger, 1972.
22 My 1977 *New Review* article can be found reprinted in *Kin of Place*, Auckland University Press, 2002, pp. 8–28. My correction to Murry's account of the writing of what became 'Prelude' was followed exactly by Vincent O'Sullivan in the introduction to his 1982 edition of *The Aloe with Prelude* (Port Nicholson Press).
23 Antony Alpers rejects my dating of the story in a footnote on pp. 339–40 of his *Life of Katherine Mansfield* (Viking/Cape, 1980), but in his collected edition, *The Stories of Katherine Mansfield* (Oxford University Press, 1984), he dates it as I had done, citing the same letter as his evidence, but without referring either to my article or to his own footnote.
24 C. K. Stead, *Pound, Yeats, Eliot and the Modernist Movement*, Macmillan / Rutgers University Press, 1986.
25 Vincent O'Sullivan, 'The Magnetic Chain: Notes and Approaches to K.M.', in *The Critical Response to Katherine Mansfield*, ed. J. Pilditch, Greenwood Press, 1996, pp. 129–54.
26 *Recollecting Mansfield*, p. 110.
27 Claire Tomalin, *Katherine Mansfield: A Secret Life*, Viking, 1988, p. 37.
28 Margaret Scott (ed.), *The Katherine Mansfield Notebooks*, vol. II, Lincoln University Press / Daphne Brasell Associates, 1997, p. 12.
29 *Letters*, V, pp. 234–5, 7 August 1922.
30 O'Sullivan, 'The Magnetic Chain', pp. 143 and 144.
31 Damien Wilkins, 'Katherine Mansfield: Short Story Moderniser', 11 April 2001, www.nzedge.com/heroes/mansfield.html#GREATGHOST (accessed 11 July 2010).
32 C. K. Stead, *The End of the Century at the End of the World*, Harvill, 1992.
33 The only really speculative thing I added, founded on known facts but going some significant way beyond them, was the brief affair with Frederick Goodyear.

Katherine Mansfield and the Fictions of Continental Europe

My first thought in approaching the subject of 'Katherine Mansfield and Continental Europe' was that most Mansfield scholars and critics take almost as a given that her New Zealand stories are her 'best' – but are they? The question should at least be reconsidered from time to time, because there has always been an element of literary nationalism in it, and national sentiment is, or should be, largely irrelevant to literary criticism. I had in mind that there are a few stories quite late in her short career which leave not only family and Wellington behind, but London too, and seem embedded in continental Europe; and that these perhaps promised a new path, a different flavour, a new sophistication – stories like 'Poison', and 'The Escape'. There is also, a little earlier, 'Je ne parle pas français' – technically very important in her development. And there's even the question of whether all of the *In a German*

A keynote address given at the Katherine Mansfield conference in Ružumberok, Slovakia, in June 2012.

Pension stories deserve their relegation to the second-class status she gave them. These are some of the thoughts and questions I began with, for what I intended should be essentially an old-fashioned literary-critical exercise.

Continental Europe first enters Mansfield's consciousness, and has a shaping effect on her sensibility, through music. She learns the cello and wants to be a musician. She sings well, likes to perform and to write songs. The Trowell family, all musicians, have a profound effect on her – she falls in love with one son, then the other. One of the only two pregnancies of her life comes from the relationship with Garnet Trowell. Her next love, and the cause of her second pregnancy, is a Pole with a notable singing voice. She writes stories about music lessons. Her first marriage is to a singing teacher. Moments of heightened consciousness in her stories often come through, or accompanied by, music. So – given the standard classical repertoire – music is her first, constant and most direct access to continental Europe.

French and German come to her both in the original language and through translation; and translations are especially important when her interest is aroused in the Russians and eastern Europeans.

Once she begins to write, continental Europe figures in two ways, leading to two kinds of story which sometimes remain distinct and sometimes conjoin: in one, Europe is a zone of sophistication and linguistic challenge – intellectual, literary, 'high-brow'; in the other, it's a zone of difficulty and danger in which a young English-speaking woman has to make her way carefully, even fearfully – where she's often threatened, sometimes a victim.

Mansfield has a double identity in this: on the one hand she is 'British' and thus removed from continental Europe; but she is also 'the little colonial', at one remove from true Britishness, and so twice removed from the Continent. Europe, then, is doubly distant, doubly 'foreign', doubly challenging and doubly exciting. Her arrivals in Germany, France, Italy are always full of vividness, drama, keenest observation and sharpest wit. They are often followed by disappointment, distress, even disgust. The contrast between her first impressions of the Casetta Deerholm at Ospedaletti and the black notebook entries she wrote there a few weeks later is only the most extreme example of the contradictions that characterise virtually all her accounts of living in Europe.

The book she called *In a German Pension* is a mixed bag, but with one or two stories almost as well worth preserving as any that came later. Some stories come direct out of her personal situation at Wörishofen, and only make complete sense if you take her pregnancy, which the story doesn't reveal, into account. Others, like 'A Birthday' and 'The Swing of the Pendulum', are really New Zealand stories in disguise. But some, including 'A Modern Soul', are truly European stories, and full of clever things. She had already absorbed so much of Europe, both literary and cultural – German society and language, Chekhov (from whom she made one notable 'borrowing', if it wasn't a theft); some French writers; even a Polish influence which led her to write the poem 'To Stanislaw Wyspianski' – all of these elements, in close conjunction with her disturbing personal circumstances, liberating a wit which has a character all its own.

> Sonia absorbed my outward and visible form with an inward and
> spiritual glance...

> On the appointed day the married ladies sailed about the pension
> dressed like upholstered chairs...

Lawrence likened Mansfield to Dickens because of her humour – the places where you almost hear the writer laughing at his own joke, and you laugh with him. In the scene in 'A Modern Soul' where our young protagonist meets Frau Godowska and her daughter, the 'sensitive soul' Fraulein Sonia, the dialogue, the non sequiturs and the timing are all perfect. And oddly, right here in this story which is entirely European in content and influence, there is one way in which you can detect the New Zealander. She's the detached *outsider*. She has no loyalty or allegiance to either side. When Frau Godowska recalls her late husband's opinion that England is 'an island of beef flesh swimming in a warm gulf sea of gravy', and offers her own view that the English are 'Fish-blooded. [. . .] Without soul, without heart, without grace. But you cannot equal their dress materials', the young narrator neither gives credence to these views, nor bridles at them on England's behalf. She simply looks on and represents; looks on and laughs.

This outsider's detachment is a point I will return to.

Staying for a moment with Lawrence's comparison: Dickens can be satirical, he can be angry, and he can be just 'funny'. Satire has a serious moral purpose, and when it turns to anger in Dickens (as in the death of little Jo the crossing sweeper in *Bleak House*) one respects the passion and salutes the cause. But sometimes what is *simply* comic, dependent on exact observation and clever re-enactment with no corrective intent, can seem wise, even profound, as a good joke can, because behind it is an acceptance of the human absurdity. Humour of that kind is what flashes intermittently in Mansfield when she's writing at her best. It reminds us that humans are the only animals that can talk *and* laugh; that language and laughter are the two things that make us distinct.

It's something like this I think Mansfield has in mind in a very early story when she writes (precociously) of 'people who are enlightened enough to understand laughter that has its wellspring in sympathy'.[1] Mansfield's laughter at its best has its wellspring in sympathy.

This is a truth she later forgets, or will no longer admit. She tries to repress comedy; she's embarrassed by it, afraid that it doesn't do justice to human suffering, afraid to be 'frivolous'. So her illness becomes not just the enemy of her life, but of her writing as well. Stories like 'Life of Ma Parker' and 'Miss Brill' always strike me as alien to her true talent. They are worthy in intent, but artistically inauthentic. The Mansfield of the one or two best *German Pension* stories is a freer spirit. There is suffering; but there's also buoyancy, a spring in the step of the prose.

There is now a sort of interlude in her writing life in which continental Europe figures either as a tourist destination (as in 'Journey to Bruges' and 'A Truthful Adventure') or as a place where a proper young woman is not safe from monsters (as in 'The Little Governess'). Even the story called 'An Indiscreet Journey', which relates the non-sexual half of her adventure in the war zone with Francis Carco, is hardly more than tourism.[2] The war which was to take her brother's life had not yet become entirely real to her. The adventure for her was as much as anything in getting past the old men in uniforms, and into the forbidden territory of the war zone to be with her new lover; and the value, or what might be called the return for this, was in excitement and heightened observation. It was *copy*.

But the meetings with her brother in London and their endless talk of childhood, as we all know, set in motion a return to New Zealand and her childhood for fictional subjects; and this was enormously reinforced by his death. So although she's in Paris when she begins what was to become 'Prelude', in Bandol when she takes it up again, and in London when she brings it to a conclusion, she's not writing about any of these places. In her head she's now thoroughly back in New Zealand.

In fact continental Europe doesn't figure again in her writing until 1917. This is in the two stories 'Feuille d'Album' and 'A Dill Pickle'. The first is set in Paris; the second is in London, but is all about an ambition – unfulfilled in the case of the central character, fulfilled in the case of her friend and former lover – to go to Russia. Both these stories have a Chekhovian delicacy of thought and phrase; they have the subtlety, refinement and cleverness of Mansfield at her best. They are, if you like, the beginnings of what might have become a new phase in her work.

'Je ne parle pas français' is a more substantial story, set in Paris and written in Bandol, the subject of much attention first by the author, then by Murry, and subsequently by others including myself. Many years ago I took Murry to task for his simple taxonomy of Mansfield stories, which divided them between up-beat affirmations of life and love when she and he were on good terms, and 'cries against corruption' when they were not. This was nonsense; and I traced the times and places in which major stories were written to show that, *au contraire*, she often wrote her best work when they were at odds and apart. In the same article I made a distinction between two new approaches to the writing of her fiction, each of which avoids a simple sequential narrative line. I called one 'aggregation' (the method of 'Prelude' and 'At the Bay') and the other 'circumlocution' (the method of 'Je ne parle pas français').[3] What I argued about 'Je ne parle pas français' was that Mansfield's own description of it as 'a cry against corruption', which Murry made the basis for one side of his Mansfield taxonomy, was written when she was only part way into the story, and that in the course of the writing she swung from a negative to a positive state of mind. Gradually she wrote herself not into admiring Raoul Duquette, but into enjoying *being* him – playing the part. The joke about the bosomy lady in the Metro with 'flowers on a balcony', and the one about the Englishman's whisky, tweed knickerbockers and ginger whiskers; Duquette's presentation of himself as Madame Butterfly hearing of the arrival of *ce cher Pinkerton*; his escape from the 'old spider' concierge with her soup ladle; his clowning in the taxi; his film noir imagining that Dick has shot himself ('rushed in, saw the body, head unharmed, small blue hole over temple') – in all of that and more the comic Mansfield is at work, excited and enjoying herself.

However, although it's true to say that this comic Raoul Duquette replaces the corrupt one, it's only partly true, because it doesn't take into account the bits that were clipped from the story before it was published in the form we have in *Bliss*, and in the old *Collected*

Stories. These cast a shadow over the comedy: elements of corruption are there right to the end.

Nor is it quite right to suggest that the method I called 'circumlocution' – the unfolding of the story from a centre, rather than in linear sequence – continues throughout. Mansfield creates the character of Duquette in that way; but in the end she has to tell a story and what emerges at this point is somewhat thin – only, alas, a variant of Mansfield and Murry in the guise of the beautiful delicate Mouse abandoned by her weak-willed mother-dominated partner to the evils of Paris.

Mouse has no large part to play in the story; but when she does get some lines, she speaks decisively. In her first scene she demands tea, '*Immediately!*' She sees Duquette feeling for cigarettes and indicates, while weeping quietly, that there are matches in the candlestick, demonstrating alertness – and perhaps false tears? When it becomes apparent that agonised Dick has run off back to his agonised mother, Mouse says the little she has to say clearly and in a 'cold, salty little voice'. And when Duquette asks whether she will go back to London and see Dick again she says, 'more coldly than ever', that she won't go back. She can't, she explains, because 'my friends think I am married'.

There seems general agreement that the description of Duquette, the little fox terrier Frenchman, plump, effeminate and self-regarding, is based on Francis Carco; and it's possible that the negative characterisation is revenge for his portrayal of her, in his novel *Les Innocents*, as the young writer avid for copy. But at least as relevant as the part Carco may have played in the story's conception, and equally pertinent to my subject here, is that it is another example of Mansfield's debt to Russian literature – not Chekhov this time but Dostoyevsky, and in particular his 'Memoirs from a Dark Cellar'.

One of the techniques she borrows from that story, that lends a sense of immediacy, is the speaker (or writer/narrator) commenting on his own performance. Here's Dostoyevsky:

Mind you, I never accepted any bribes, so that I had at least to find something to compensate myself for that. (A silly joke, but I shan't cross it out. I wrote it thinking it would sound very witty, but now that I have seen myself that I merely wanted to indulge in a bit of contemptible bragging, I shall let it stand [...]!)[4]

And here's Mansfield's Raoul Duquette after describing the waiter strewing the floor of the cafe with straw:

One would not have been surprised if the door had opened and the Virgin Mary had come in, riding upon an ass, her meek hands folded over her big belly ...

That's rather nice, don't you think, that bit about the Virgin? It comes from the pen so gently; it has such a 'dying fall'. I thought so at the time and decided to make a note of it. One never knows when a little tag like that won't come in useful to round off a paragraph.

Then there is the technique of question and answer, again giving a feeling of immediacy. Dostoyevsky's narrator:

By the way, what does a decent chap talk about with the greatest possible pleasure?

Answer: about himself.

Very well, so I will talk about myself.[5]

And Mansfield's:

Query: Why am I so bitter against Life? And why do I see her as a rag-picker on the American cinema, shuffling along wrapped in a filthy shawl with her old claws crooked over a stick?

Answer: The direct result of the American cinema acting upon a weak mind.

The dark cynical, self-accusing yet self-excusing, or anyway unrepentant, tone; the direct address to an audience as 'gentlemen' (or in Mansfield's case 'ladies and gentlemen') who are treated, not politely but with something close to contempt; the egotism and insistence on great sensitivity combined with emphasis on sordid detail – Mansfield's debt in all this is quite as clear as is her debt to Chekhov in other stories. She has a good ear, she's a natural mimic, and some of her funniest squibs for the *New Age* were parodies. The opening sections of 'Je ne parle pas français' are very close to pastiche. Yet there's a significant difference too. Dostoyevsky's character describes himself as spiteful, and there's an angry tone that gives his story an unpleasant flavour right from the start. Mansfield's touch is lighter. The comedian in her is uppermost. It's the same method but not so frantic, so *insistently* black, so *remorselessly* self-accusatory, so (almost you might say) *insane* as Dostoyevsky, and consequently more ingratiating. But it's unimaginable that the story could have been written without the prior example of the writer she and Jack referred to as 'Dosty'.

But after these introductions to the character, both she and Dostoyevsky have to get on and tell a story. Here they differ considerably; and I have to say on reflection that when I re-read what I wrote all those years ago about 'Je ne parle pas français' it seems to me I slid over its major weakness, which is simply the enormous implausibility of its central event – Dick's arriving in Paris with Mouse and luggage (including quantities of books), and then immediately walking out on her, not even telling her he's going, and leaving only a note by way of explanation. Technically, 'Je ne parle pas français' is a new development, even a breakthrough into a new mode. But as a story it's not entirely convincing.

On the other hand, when we look at some of her European fictions that might in one sense be called more successful, the response might be, 'Well yes, but are they as sophisticated or as interesting in terms of the development of fiction in the twentieth century?' Part of the difficulty is that our consideration of these later stories often gets entangled in facts about her health and personal circumstances.

'The Man Without a Temperament' is an example. It was written at Ospedaletti at the time of her darkest entries in her notebooks – entries so agonised, so despairing, you feel appalled reading them, as though you've been allowed a glance into the torture chamber of the human soul. Day after day she reads Shakespeare, thinks dark thoughts about Jack who visited and has now returned to London, and writes for each day a single, brief, very black note:

8 Thursday
BLACK. Wrote to Jinnie. A day spent in Hell. Unable to do anything.
Took brandy – determined not to weep – wept. Sense of isolation
frightful. I shall die if I don't escape. Nauseated, faint cold with misery.
Oh I <u>must</u> survive it somehow.[6]

The entry two days later finishes, 'Thought out The Exile. Appalling night of misery deciding that J. had no more need of our love.' And then the following day:

Worked from 9.30 a.m. to a quarter after midnight only stopping to eat.
Finished the story. Lay awake then till 5.30 too excited to sleep. In the
sea drowned souls sang all night. I thought of everything in my life and
it all came back so vividly – all is connected with this feeling that J. and I
are no longer as we were. I love him but he rejects my <u>living</u> love. This is
anguish. These are the worst days of my life.[7]

This then is the background to 'The Man Without a Temperament', which she first called 'The Exile'. How do you put all that out of your mind and read the story 'critically' – just as a story? The story and its provenance or its genesis, once you know them, are locked together.

One of the most surprising comments on the story occurs in a footnote of Alpers's second Mansfield biography:

Not a few have supposed – the present author being among them once – that this acute portrayal of a man whose wife is hopelessly ill on the Riviera was a picture of Murry himself [. . .] and a hostile one. That is not at all what he thought. After reading the author's previous biography in 1953 he said that its comment struck him as 'a quite fantastic misreading of the story,' and he added: 'If ever a character was drawn with loving admiration, Salesby was. I should be very well content to go down to posterity as his original.'[8]

I find this interesting because it seems to me both Murry and Alpers are partly right and seriously wrong. Alpers was quite wrong that the portrayal of Salesby is 'hostile'. Salesby is the attentive husband Mansfield longed for. But Murry was wrong too if he meant (and perhaps he didn't) that Salesby is himself as Mansfield saw him. Salesby is the husband he *failed* to be; and in that sense the character and the story are a profound reproach.

'Temperament' is not quite a neutral word. It often goes with an adjective like 'nervous' or 'artistic'. As an adjective, 'temperamental', the negative overtone becomes clearer. Mansfield has a number of stories at this time about women who are much like herself, 'temperamental', and her view of them is very often negative. Salesby is if you like a 'colonial's' view of a middle-class Englishman – faintly absurd of course, but nonetheless cool, detached, in control, able to dominate a social situation. His lack of 'temperament' is precisely what equips him to be the perfect guardian of an ailing and needful wife.

So if Murry's exchange with Alpers was meant to suggest that this story is another K.M. tribute to him and to their love that would have to be rejected. There are so many indicators in her letters and notebooks judging him a failure. Here's one, for example, written some months after the story: after an account of her frightful coughing, and the pain that went with it, she describes Jack '[hiding] his face with his fingers <u>as though</u> it were unendurable'. And she goes on, 'If he could only, for a minute, serve me, help me, give <u>himself</u> up!'[9] Salesby is the husband who does all that – serves, helps, forgets *himself* in favour of his invalid wife. This you might think, in personal terms, is not altogether fair to Murry; but I can't see that there's any ambiguity about it. The story is another one of those little surprises, those packages of hate which Linda Burnell imagined sending to Stanley.

Salesby is 'the exile', missing England, hardly enjoying himself in that hotel, but allowing himself to be ruled by his wife's illness and what it requires of him. His twisting of the ring on his finger is an image of entrapment if you like; but Mansfield makes it a signet ring, not a wedding ring. It's his own choice to be where he is; the choice has his own name on it. He acts decisively, always with her health and well-being in mind. He's mocked by the servant girl and by the two German sisters, 'the Topknots', and seems to be greatly disliked by the Countess and the General; but he's quite indifferent to that, as he is to the children when they seem to be frightened by his sudden appearance. '*Très* rum!' he says, making his wife laugh and think to herself how brilliant and learned and handsome he is, and yet he can delight her with something unexpected and funny like that. He's a man of few words, but very decisive, even commanding, with her no less than with the staff of the hotel. He makes sure that she has the wrap she needs out of doors, and that the lift doesn't keep her waiting; he's firm with the management; he kills the mosquito under her netting. And when she asks 'do you mind awfully being out here with me?' –

He bends down. He kisses her. He tucks her in, he smoothes the pillow.
'Rot!' he whispers.[10]

That's how the story ends, all vividly present tense.

If the story has a fault it's the same one you find in a story like 'Bliss': that the central characters exist on one level – of seriousness, of realism – while the peripheral ones are close to caricature.

40

The Two Topknots with their knitting; the American Woman with her atrocious anglophone French (her dog's name, Klaymongso, is clearly meant to represent her pronunciation of Clemenceau); Antonio with his funny English ('I made-a the postman give them for me'); the Countess with her lorgnette and the cawing General with the blanket over his knees – these are routine, almost panto-mime characters, quite different from the Salesbys, especially the proto-Mansfield ailing wife, whose prospects are so clearly signalled (or should I say so crudely symbolised) in the following:

> The sky is the colour of jade. There are a great many stars; an enormous white moon hangs over the garden. Far away lightning flutters – flutters like a wing – flutters like a broken bird that tries to fly and sinks again and again struggles.

I can't read that without imagining how Lawrence would have cringed and deplored its self-pitying note. I feel great compassion for Mansfield; but her illness is not serving her art well there.

There remain those two stories, 'Poison' and 'The Escape', which made me think perhaps here was a new direction for K.M. – a possible stepping-off point into a future she wasn't, as it turned out, going to have, where European stories might have been an advance on anything she'd done before. It's interesting that both the women at the centre of these stories are represented negatively, but in quite different ways. Beatrice in 'Poison' is entirely self-possessed and conscious of the fact that, metaphorically, she is poisoning her naive, inexperienced and younger lover whom she is about to leave for someone else. He tells the story himself, but he is seeing it all in retrospect, having attained the wisdom and/or cynicism he lacked at the time.

It's beautifully written, full of subtleties and ironies. The young man's romantic illusions are delicately represented, with a kind of nostalgia, so that although the account is essentially ironic, the beauty is not entirely lost or cancelled out. I see it as another example of Murry's inadequacy that he should have put K.M. off publishing it – though later, after her death, he would describe it as 'a little masterpiece'.

The woman in 'The Escape', on the other hand, lacks self-possession entirely. She is one of those neurotic, or neurasthenic, women (Monica Tyrell in 'Revelations' is another) who are like one aspect of Mansfield herself – like enough that they can appear to be acts of self-recognition and self-reproach. It's a female role that seems in those years to have been almost fashionable (like Victorian women's fainting fits, or the 'little girl' Marilyn Monroe voice in the 1940s and '50s), as if to be like that was considered especially and fetchingly 'feminine'.

The story was written in London but it happens on the Riviera and it's possible to see the setting as Menton or Roquebrune. The woman sees herself as the victim of her husband's incompetence and malice. Her suspicions of his motives are clearly groundless and her behaviour is unambiguously appalling, hysterical, solipsistic. We are left in no doubt what we should think of her. She's condemned out of her own mouth and her own thoughts. Now and then the point of view switches from her to the husband. The children she sees as 'horrid little monkeys' he sees as 'poor little mice'; he wants to give them money, she wants to drive them off. When the parasol she has thrown in a fit of pique on to the hood of the carriage falls off into the road, she sees this as a plot against her by the husband and the coachman, and insists on stopping the coach and walking back for it herself – 'For' (she says) 'if I don't escape from you for a minute I shall go mad.' The husband settles down in the sun to wait. At first he's depressed, as anyone would be dealing with such unreasonableness:

He felt himself, lying there, a hollow man, a parched, withered man, as it were of ashes. And the sea sounded, 'Hish, hish.'

Now I want to float an idea here that this fictional couple might have been partly based on T. S. Eliot's relations with his first wife, Vivienne, but transferred (so to speak) to the south of France, where Eliot was known to visit. It was a famously disastrous marriage from which Eliot later escaped. The story was written for K.M.'s new friend Violet Schiff, wife of the wealthy arts patron Sydney Schiff who also wrote fiction under the pseudonym 'Stephen Hudson'. Katherine had met this couple while she was living in Menton and liked them very much. Sydney was endlessly caring and considerate, and Violet delicate, sensitive and beautiful. On 2 May 1920, after her return to London, Katherine writes in a letter, 'Violet, I have nearly finished the story I wrote for you. I shall type it out and send it to you.'[11] On 10 May she writes that the new plan to include short fiction in the *Athenaeum* will 'begin with my story about your tree'.[12]

The Schiffs knew the Eliots and so did Mansfield and Murry. Katherine liked Tom Eliot but disliked Vivienne intensely. To Violet she wrote, after having them to dinner, '[Vivienne] really repels me. She makes me shiver with apprehension'; and she describes Vivienne's strange manner, her loud voice, and her insistent talking about her husband in his presence as if he weren't there. 'Mrs E's voice rises "Oh don't commiserate Tom. He's *quite* happy."'[13]

It seems to me that since Mansfield liked the Schiffs so much and was doing everything she could to please them, she must have known this negative account of Vivienne would be acceptable to them; and she might even have hoped, in a story written for Violet, that they would make the connection.

Eliot would almost certainly have read this story in the *Athenaeum* when it appeared in July of that year; or in *Bliss* when the collection was published in December. Could he have lingered on it long enough to have recognised the portrait, and even to take from it the title for his poem of a few years later, 'The Hollow Men'? (The story, you remember, has the protagonist recognise himself as 'a hollow man'.)[14] Could his recognition of Mansfield's feelings about Vivienne have been part of the reason for the apparently irrational way he took against her, telling Pound she was 'a dangerous WOMAN'?[15]

The story has an interesting and somewhat puzzling conclusion. While the 'hollow man' waits for the wife to return with her parasol, and the sea sounds 'Hish, hish', he experiences a kind of epiphany. He sees a beautiful tree (described in some detail – hence this being a story for Violet 'about' her tree), and then . . .

> As he looked at the tree he felt his breathing die away and he became part of the silence. It seemed to grow, it seemed to expand in the quivering heat until the great carved leaves hid the sky, and yet it was motionless. Then from within its depths or from beyond there came the sound of a woman's voice. A woman was singing. The warm untroubled voice floated upon the air, and it was all part of the silence as he was part of it. [. . .] What was happening to him? Something stirred in his breast. Something dark, something unbearable and dreadful pushed in his bosom, and like a great weed it floated, rocked . . . it was warm, stifling. He tried to struggle to tear at it, and at the same moment – all was over. Deep, deep, he sank into the silence, staring at the tree and waiting for the voice that came floating, falling, until he felt himself enfolded.

This is very strange, very intense, slightly over-written. Now there's a break in the narrative and we find ourselves on the train they were hurrying to catch. It's night-time, he's standing at the open window (I assume – the word used is 'door') of their carriage, and he can hear his wife's voice reassuring someone there's nothing to worry about – he likes to stand there, 'it is his habit'. He's happy travelling, likes 'roughing it'. It's like Mansfield's report of Vivienne Eliot saying, 'Oh don't commiserate Tom. He's *quite* happy.' And as the voices continue there's the repeated 'my husband . . .', 'My husband . . .'. Clearly she likes talking about him, this man she has treated so badly, and is glad to claim him. The story ends as follows:

The voices murmured, murmured. They were never still. But so
great was his heavenly happiness as he stood there he wished he might
live for ever.

This is connected to, I suppose a result of, the moment of communion with the beautiful tree. It would be interesting to hear what
Mansfield meant by this, but so far as I know she wrote nothing about
it, apart from telling Violet it was for her and about her tree. Perhaps
it's as well that we have no authorial 'explanation'. But it's clear this
sensitive male character with the neurotic and hectoring wife has an
intense inner life – the inner life of a poet, perhaps – which proceeds
without her; and equally clear, I think, in this final scene, that despite
her appalling way with him she loves and is proud of him.

To return where I began: I was not able to defend the idea that
the common description of Mansfield's New Zealand stories are her
'best' might be just a nationalist piety. 'Prelude', 'At the Bay', 'The
Doll's House', 'The Garden Party', these, together with miracu-
lously perfect little stories like 'The Wind Blows' and 'The Voyage',
and then the earlier outback or other-side-of-the-tracks stories,
'The Woman at the Store', 'Millie' and 'Ole Underwood' – all put
together would make a collection still unmatched in New Zealand
short fiction. You could make a very nice parallel selection of her best
European stories, but they would not be a match in quality.

And the reason for this, I think, is partly because the New Zealand
stories have precisely what some commentators – Frank O'Connor,
for example, and V. S. Pritchett – say they lack: a community.
Often her British and European stories are dependent on a single
consciousness, and what lies beyond, though vivid (especially
vivid because it's *foreign*), is seen largely from the outside. In the
New Zealand stories she can move about. She can become Linda,
become Beryl, become Our Else who 'seen the little lamp'; become
even the Pa-man Stanley, or the frustrated actor Jonathan Trout;
become the servant girl Alice talking to herself as she walks along

the empty beach at midday – any and all of these, with the confidence of having observed them closely enough to feel sure she knew what they were thinking and feeling, and knew the larger social contexts that contained them.

One obstacle to claiming more for a 'European' Mansfield is the effect of her illness on her temperament and consequently on her practice as a writer; and then of course her early death and the cutting short of her career. There are signs of developments in European directions, but only the beginnings of what might have been.

But even there, in the European stories, her 'New Zealandness' declares itself, and would have continued to declare itself. This brings me back to a point I made earlier about her detachment from either side – British or German – in the *German Pension* stories.

Writing in a recent issue of the *London Review of Books*,[16] Colm Tóibín considers the case of Flann O'Brien (author of *At Swim-Two-Birds*) and puts him alongside Jorge Luis Borges and Fernando Pessoa as writers whose circumstances removed them in some degree, geographically, culturally, linguistically (any of these in any combination) from their readers, or from the prime source of the languages they wrote in; and for whom, in consequence, there was 'no body of readers' that could be counted on. For such writers it is, he says, not possible 'to write with a reader in mind'. Because of this, Flann O'Brien, his prime example, was 'looking for [. . .] a way of breaking with standard narrative in fiction'.

I think the same might be said of Mansfield; and it is in this, rather than her 'subject matter', that her 'New Zealandness' would have remained a permanent part of her work. Though English was her mother tongue, and she was largely educated in England and tried to make her home there, Mansfield's relations with continental Europe were significantly different from those of British writers. Birth-nation, and the identity that goes along with it, can never be entirely omitted from the discussion, any more than they can, for example, from the case of Doris Lessing.

1   'A Truthful Adventure', *Collected Stories of Katherine Mansfield*, Constable, 1968, p. 545.
2   Though I have to add that Frank Sargeson's recently published *Letters*, selected and edited by Sarah Shieff (Random House, 2012), reveals that he read this story in 1954 and was enchanted, describing it as 'that very good fairy tale – *An Indiscreet Journey* which somehow I had always missed previously: it should be called *The Little Corporal*' (p. 176).
3   'Katherine Mansfield: The Art of Fiction', *Kin of Place: Essays on 20 New Zealand Writers*, Auckland University Press, 2002, pp. 8–28. The essay first appeared in *The New Review* in September 1977.
4   Fyodor Dostoevsky, 'Memoirs from a Dark Cellar', *A Gentle Creature and Other Stories*, translated by David Magarshak, John Lehmann, 1950, p. 104.
5   *Ibid.*, p. 106.
6   Margaret Scott (ed.), *The Katherine Mansfield Notebooks*, vol. II, Lincoln University Press / Daphne Brasell Associates, 1997 (this volume hereafter referred to as *Notebooks* II), p. 187.
7   *Ibid.*, p. 188.
8   Antony Alpers, *The Life of Katherine Mansfield*, Viking/Cape, 1980, p. 305.
9   *Notebooks* II, p. 219.
10 Vincent O'Sullivan, in 'What We Mostly Don't Say about Katherine Mansfield', *Katherine Mansfield's Men*, ed. Charles Ferrall and Jane Stafford, Steele Roberts, 2004, pp. 96–106, refers to the word 'rot' as 'the penetrating, bitter pun of its final line' – thus seeing the story as at one with 'Poison' for example, a bitter reflection on love and marriage. Again this seems to me a serious misreading, not taking into account the commonness and *neutrality*, in everyday middle-class discourse of Mansfield's time, of the word 'rot', used exactly as we would say 'rubbish', not meaning to evoke the realities of rubbish, but simply and emphatically 'No, that's not true', 'Certainly not', 'Not in the least'. So for example, in the last scene of 'At the Bay' you find '"Oh rot!" Harry Kember didn't believe her.' Or in 'The Young Girl' '"Why can't you leave me?" she said furiously. "What utter rot!"' Or in 'Brave Love', '"You've made an extraordinary impression on him," said Mildred. "I have? Oh rot!"'
    It isn't true, of course, despite Salesby's denial, that he doesn't mind being away from England. It's costing him a great deal. But in saying, and so emphatically ('Rot'), that he doesn't he's proving his commitment to love and marriage, not, as O'Sullivan seems to be suggesting, the reverse.
11 Vincent O'Sullivan and Margaret Scott (eds), *The Collected Letters of Katherine Mansfield*, vol. IV, Clarendon Press, 1996 (this volume hereafter referred to as *Letters* IV), p. 4. Note 2 identifies the story as 'Revelations' but this is incorrect. (See note 12 below.)
12 *Letters* IV, p. 10. Note 4 again wrongly identifies the story as 'Revelations' which (the note goes on) 'concluded with a quasi-mystical "epiphany" as the protagonist observes a remarkable tree. The Schiffs' home at Roquebrune was called "Big Tree Villa"'. But there is no such tree, nor such an 'epiphany', in 'Revelations'. The description here fits 'The Escape' which is clearly the story Mansfield is referring to.
13 *Letters* IV, p. 11, letter dated 14 May 1920. 'The Escape' appeared in the *Athenaeum* in July 1920, so clearly Mansfield was wrong, or there must have been a change of plan, when she said in May that it was to be the first in the *Athenaeum's* new regimen of stories. For my discussion of the relations between Eliot and Mansfield, see 'Tom & Viv and Murry & Mansfield', pp. 69–84 below.

14 Eliot himself in a letter to the *TLS*, 10 January 1935, says he believes he arrived at the title by combining the title of William Morris's romance, 'The Hollow Land' with that of Kipling's poem 'The Broken Men'. T. S. Eliot, *Inventions of the March Hare: Poems 1909–1917*, ed. Christopher Ricks, Faber & Faber, 1996, p. 395.
15 Valerie Eliot and Hugh Haughton (eds), *The Letters of T. S. Eliot*, vol. I, 1898–1922 (revised edition), Faber & Faber, 2009, p. 473, letter dated 3 July 1920, and reporting that K.M. is about to go back to the Riviera for the winter.
16 'Flann O'Brien's Lies', *London Review of Books*, 5 January 2012, pp. 32–33.

First Person as Third Person: Mansfield's Married Man

Three Mansfield stories are unusual in her oeuvre in that each is a significant work in itself, and each has a male first-person narrator: 'Je ne parle pas français' (February 1918), 'Poison' (December 1920), and 'A Married Man's Story' (August 1921). The three are connected in other ways as well: the theme of poisoning, real or symbolic, connects two – or one might argue all three; and each represents a male persona who is cynical, corrupted and/ or corrupting, and extremely self-conscious. Each of these men is about as far from innocence as it's possible to be. I offered some ideas about 'Poison' and 'Je ne parle pas français' in my paper on Mansfield and continental Europe. My subject today, to complete the trio, is the darkest of the three, the unnamed 'Married Man'.

Raoul Duquette, the first-person narrator of 'Je ne parle pas français', is Parisian – and even intended I suppose to represent

A keynote paper given at the Katherine Mansfield Society's international conference at the Université Sorbonne Nouvelle, Paris, in June 2014.

something in the French character. The 'I' of 'Poison' is probably English, but certainly at home in France where the story occurs – I think in a location one can recognise as Menton and even the Villa Isola Bella. But the 'Married Man' is of no specified nationality, and his household is located nowhere in particular.

A word now about the dating of this story. For a long time it was incorrectly dated (as a result of a confusions caused by John Middleton Murry's wanting to fit it into his self-serving narrative of his relations with Mansfield) but the correct date is established by a letter of 23 August 1921 in which Murry told Sydney Schiff that Katherine was writing 'the longest and last of her stories for the new book. It's to be called (I believe, though this is confidential) "A Married Man" and other stories. It's the married man she's in the middle of now. I think it's an amazing piece of work.'

What this means is that Mansfield must have set aside 'At the Bay' to write 'A Married Man's Story', and also, incidentally, to write the story called 'The Voyage', and then returned to complete 'At the Bay'. This not only contradicted a previously accepted idea, affirmed by Alpers and repeated by others, that 'A Married Man's Story' was the piece she had been working on in Cornwall in 1918 – it also seemed, on the face of it, unlikely; even impossible. As Alpers wrote in a footnote hastily added to his 1980 *Life*: 'Katherine could hardly have *begun* a story of this character while in the midst of *At the Bay*, let alone complete five thousand words.'[1]

Four years later, however, Alpers published *The Stories of Katherine Mansfield*, ordered according to their chronology of composition, and now 'A Married Man's Story' was placed with 'At the Bay' and 'The Voyage' as dating from Switzerland in 1921. The accompanying note says simply, 'Not written or begun at Looe in 1918, as argued in the *Life*, but wholly written at the Chalet des Sapins in late August 1921, as a third interruption to the writing of "At the Bay".'

One would think that was the end of the matter – and perhaps it is. But there is still that footnote on pages 339–40 of the Alpers

Life; and perhaps as a consequence, and despite Alpers's later and very clear '*Not* written *or begun* in Cornwall' (my italics), we still find it misplaced from time to time. Patrick Morrow's 1993 book dates it as 'written shortly after Mansfield married Murry',[2] which means 1918. In his 2002 revised biography Jeffrey Meyers dates it to 1923 (with no clear reason for that – it must be a mistake);[3] and in Kathleen Jones's 2010 biography we find Mansfield bringing back from Cornwall 'a number of notebook sketches and the complex and bitter "A Married Man's Story" about a man who poisons his wife'.[4]

The story is not strictly about 'a man who poisons his wife'; it's about a man who believes his father poisoned his mother – though it's true that at least symbolically he has begun to repeat his father's real or imagined crime. But what is most significant about it, most puzzling and in need, if not of explanation, at least of enquiry, is that it should have been written entirely in 'one hit', as part of the very same burst of new work that included 'At the Bay'.

From Alpers's account of the manuscripts – which came after his biography, and by now he has the chronology right – it seems 'Marriage à la Mode', 'The Voyage' and 'A Married Man's Story' were all written in the same notebook.[5] Alpers thinks he sees signs of 'tension' rather than 'lively excitement' in the writing of the first of these, while the next two proceed with speed and confidence even though one remains possibly unfinished. Discontent in 'Marriage à la Mode' and confidence in the others is certainly what one might expect to find, since 'Marriage à la Mode' seems such an inferior, even rather shoddy and obvious, piece of work – one of a number of magazine stories written for Clement Shorter at *The Sphere*, of a kind Alpers suggests 'did lasting damage to Mansfield's reputation'.[6] By contrast he describes 'The Voyage' as 'a flawless little New Zealand story', and 'A Married Man's Story' as 'an unbroken spate of writing, done under firm control from the start to the breaking off'.[7]

Let me take a moment here to remind you what kind of a fiction 'A Married Man's Story' is, and how different from the stories written at the same time. Alpers writes:

> Its self-centred narrator, the son of a chemist who has poisoned his wife, is a new invention. The child's recollections of the dying mother's visit to his bed, of a battered harlot lurching into the shop for his father's famous pick-me-up, and the domestic scene of frozen hatred in which the tale itself is written – all are signs of an intention to strike out in new directions.[8]

To that I would add that there's a ferocious *cool* about this story – a steadiness and bitterness of tone, new in Mansfield. The narrator has something in common with Raoul Duquette of 'Je ne parle pas français', but less buoyancy, less sense of fun. There is a much more dangerous feel about him. He is scarier, colder, harder, darker. If you were ever in doubt that this was a writer who deserved serious attention, if you were ever inclined, like Katherine's cousin Elizabeth, to condescend to her as the author of 'a pretty little story' called 'At the Bay', this would pull you up short and make you pay serious attention. So it's doubly mysterious – first that it should have come up in the midst of the writing of 'At the Bay', like a volcanic eruption out of a tranquil landscape; and second that it should be so good, so strong, so full of promise, and yet remain unfinished.

We have, then, Mansfield at this point in her career in unprecedented full spate, writing always fluently, often brilliantly, and now and then just for money; writing in what might be called her best established vein of 'Prelude'; and simultaneously in a mode that has only one imperfect precedent in 'Je ne parle pas français'. And at the same time she is writing some of her very best and happiest letters.

The letters are full of joy in the mountains, in the birds, the squirrels and other wildlife, which she watches through binoculars;

and pleasure in a domestic life lived for once at peace, and even at times joyfully, with Jack. They go on picnics in the woods. They make plans for the future, for building their own house there in the Swiss Alps. Enjoying one another's conversation, they have to try to discipline themselves against talking in bed. And then the resolve breaks, they talk, get excited, can't sleep, and so get up for a feast of cake at midnight. She concludes a letter to Violet Schiff, 'Im writing late at night. Murry is asleep. He looks about 16. I must turn out the light.' When she signs off, 'My fondest love to you',[9] one feels it is her fondest love to Murry as well.

She is selling her stories easily at this time, for good prices and negotiating confidently with an agent. She summons 'the F.O.', Ida Baker, 'the Faithful One', to come and manage the house while she and Jack get on with their writing. Ida brings the cat, Wingley, from London and it becomes again part of Katherine's life. Their neighbour, her cousin Elizabeth whom previously she didn't entirely trust, she begins to admire and love; and K.M. writes brilliantly both to and about her. To Dorothy Brett she writes:

[Elizabeth] appeared today behind a bouquet – never smaller woman carried bigger bouquets. She looks like a garden walking – of asters, late sweet peas, stocks, & always petunias. She herself wore a frock like a spider's web, a hat like a berry and gloves that reminded me of thistles in seed. Oh, how I love the appearance of people – how I delight in it if I love them. [. . .] And then when she smiles a ravishing wrinkle appears on her nose – and never have I seen more exquisite hands. [. . .] The point about her is that one loves her and is proud of her. [. . .] Read her last book if you can get hold of it. It's called *Vera* & published by Macmillan. It's amazingly good.[10]

A few days later, when Elizabeth calls and makes that 'pretty little story' remark about 'At the Bay', she's described as 'fascinating in her black suit; something between a Bishop and a Fly'.[11]

Elements of the surreal enter the letters. There's a fantasy in which Wingley is imagined writing his memoirs, which will be bound in mouse leather. He's dictating them to Katherine, who figures in them as Grandma Jaegar, while Jack is MasteranMan (one word), Ida is Fostermonger, and their servant Emmeline is The Swede. 'He has rather a contempt for her.'[12] Wingley is also 'to have lessons on the fiddle'. 'All the BEST cats can play at least Hey diddle diddle. He *must* learn.'[13] Katherine and Jack are both knitting, and she tells Elizabeth,

> [it] becomes almost frenzied at times. We may be sober in our
> lives – but we shall be garish in our shrouds and flamboyant in our
> coffins if this goes on. John now *mixes* his wools thereby gaining
> what *he* calls 'a *superb* astrackhan effect'. Chi lo sa! I softly murmur
> over my needles . . .[14]

If you'd received one of these letters you would have concluded all was going well *chez* Mansfield-Murry. And Murry's taxonomy of her fiction would now, in retrospect, seem to be confirmed by this picture if only 'A Married Man's Story' *had* been written in Cornwall three years earlier. But here it is, the almost perfect case of her old 'cry against corruption', right alongside, even intertwined with, K.M. at her most affirmative in 'The Voyage' and 'At the Bay'. She was happy with Jack for the moment, happy enough, or could keep her discontents out of sight. And the writing was going well – that was what mattered. All of that seems true; and 'Which came first, the happiness or the fluency?' is a 'chicken and egg' question. The processes of creativity are mysterious – more mysterious and more complex than that foolish and self-serving 'she loves me / she loves me not' scenario Jack proposed to explain them after her death.

I've mentioned the importance of her cousin Elizabeth as a neighbour during this Swiss period, and the publication of Elizabeth's new novel, *Vera*, in 1921. Elizabeth was already famous as the Countess von Arnim, author of *Elizabeth and her German Garden*. The Count von Arnim had died and Elizabeth had been in the public eye more recently as the wife of Earl Russell (elder brother of Bertrand).[15] There had been an ugly divorce from the Earl, and the new novel was said to be an exposure of Russell as Elizabeth perceived him, a monster of selfishness and solipsism. So a certain amount of scandal was attaching itself to the publication.

The character based on the Earl is Everard Wemyss, a sulky, petulant, domineering fellow, described by the novelist variously as 'a great cross schoolboy' and 'a pathetic human being, blindly bent on ruining his own happiness'.[16] Katherine, who might have had reservations about Elizabeth's earlier work, admired this novel; in particular she admired the way it was 'carried through' to its dark and unsentimental end. The reader hopes for, and expects, Wemyss to receive his punishment, and that his poor victim Lucy will be saved, but this doesn't happen, and K.M. especially admired the novelist's resoluteness in not giving herself and her readers an easy 'out' that would have made it a more popular and sentimental book. 'Wasn't the *end* extraordinarily good', she asks Brett. 'It would have been so easy to miss it; she carried it right through. I admired the end most, I think.'[17]

In a letter to her sister she writes, 'I think its by far the most brilliant book she has ever written.' It has had 'rather a mixed reception' and Katherine says she can 'quite understand' this. Readers have said the character of Wemyss is too extreme; but surely 'there are few men who have not a touch of Wemyss'.[18]

She makes the same point to Brett, who was inclined at first to be dismissive: 'You are so very superior, Miss', she responds. 'Have you ever known a Wemyss? Oh my dear, they are *very* plentiful! Few men are without a touch.' Of Lucy, the recently bereaved girl misled about Wemyss and persuaded to fall in love with him, she says, 'Not that I can stand the Wemyss "brand". No. But I can perfectly comprehend Lucy standing it.'[19]

But there's a franker and darker comment in another letter written directly to the novel's author. Katherine's sisters have sent a copy of the novel to their father, 'Which makes me gasp', she tells Elizabeth. 'But I expect he will admire Wemyss tremendously and agree with every thought and every feeling and shut the book with an extraordinary sense of satisfaction before climbing the stairs to my stepmother.'[20]

This is I'm sure unfair. Harold Beauchamp may not have been subtle but he was not stupid, and you would have to be stupid to see Wemyss as anything but self-deceived and unpleasant. But that 'climbing the stairs to my stepmother' makes the bad feeling, and its source, plain. Katherine's mother had died, her father had married again, and she resented it.

But that was not the view she wanted uppermost in 'At the Bay'. The story was to be an affirmation of love. Stanley could be shown as boastful and childish, even absurd; Jonathan Trout could be sadly, histrionically defeated by domestic and suburban life; but neither could be a Wemyss. They had each to be somehow innocent, worthy of love, and capable of it. The story required that of her; and that meant, it seems, a certain amount of dross and darkness had to be filtered out of her imagination. This, I'm suggesting, must have been a function of the writing of 'A Married Man's Story', and why it had to come when it did. It was like the draining of that tubercular abscess that Katherine had to endure at intervals during this period.

I've said the picture those letters paint of life in the mountains is joyful and affirmative; but was it the *whole* picture? Letters, for a writer as self-conscious and deliberate as Mansfield, were semi-public documents, geared to their recipients, and destined for 'keeps'. But they leave out all the details, all the horror, of her physical condition – the coughing, shortness of breath, racing heart, soreness of the lung and pain in the limbs, lack of sleep, and the inability to climb stairs or walk any distance without distress. These facts are simply banished from the letters of that period. They were borne with fortitude; and along with them went fear, a sense of impending doom and a longing for a miracle. In other words it was partly a game she and Jack were playing there in the mountains; partly a pretence.

Furthermore, when you go hunting you find there are glimpses in the notebooks not just of the circumstances of illness, but of other darknesses that were not allowed into the letters, and were no doubt meant to be part of the 'camping ground' Jack was supposed to 'clean up' and 'make fair' after her death.[21] In November, for example, after the new book has gone off, and a new story, 'The Doll's House', has been written, she has a dead spell. She has new ideas, and prays to 'be found worthy to do [them]!'[22]

And then the woman who lodges upstairs catches her waiting for Jack to come home, and rebukes her for it. (This is in one of the notebooks.)

> She simply – rounded on me – there's no other word for it. Told me I ought to be ashamed of myself for waiting up for him, that it served me right if he came in later and later, that she'd be ashamed at my age, not to know better.

And then Katherine reflects:

> It's a long time now since he started going out every evening. I can't stop him – I've tried everything but it is useless – out he goes. And the horrible thing is I don't know where it is he goes to – who is he with? It's all such a mystery, that's what makes it so hard to bear. Where have you been. I've asked him and asked him that. But never a word, never a sign. I sometimes think he likes to torture me.
>
> But then I've got nobody else. I suppose that sounds strange. But I can say as truly as a girl in love: He is all the world to me.[23]

Momentarily, here, she seems to be picturing herself as Elizabeth's Lucy, helpless in the emotional grip of her Wemyss. And in the light of those ebullient letters, those copious pictures of contentment together, this seemed, when I came upon it (going from the letters to the notebook), such an improbable turnaround that I wondered for a moment had she slipped from journal into fiction. But no; straight afterwards, on the same page, comes another dark entry, this time about '[t]he deep grudge that L.M. has for me' and how '[s]he keeps it under for a long time at a stretch but oh – how it is there! Tonight, for instance, in the salon we hated each other – really hated in a queer way. I felt I wanted her out of my sight; she felt that she must insult me before she went.'

The Katherine who stares out of that entry about Jack's mysterious evening absences is Katherine without the mask – and without the mask she says should be under the mask. She's like the woman in 'A Married Man's Story', 'staring into the dark with those trustful, bewildered eyes'.[24]

And what *was* Jack up to? My first thought was that he was having an affair down the hill with cousin Elizabeth. Unlikely, you might think, given how much older she was than him; but around that time she'd been having an affair with an even younger man; and Katherine describes her as '[looking] about 35 – not a day more, runs up the hills, climbs, laughs, just like a girl'. In the same letter she says 'Jack loves this place and the life here'.[25] An affair would not have been out of character for either of them. Nor, of course, would it have been for Katherine herself in her days of good health and high spirits. One can only speculate, and pass on. But why Jack's refusal to answer K.M.'s questions? Why not the truth – or alternatively a big fat lie? It's as though he's teasing her with the 'honesty' of his silence. As she says, 'I sometimes think he likes to torture me.'

So no; there was always darkness in her somewhere, and in her life, even without invoking her early love for Garnet Trowell, and the abandonment, the necessary but unwanted marriage and the lost baby. No special explanation is needed for the fact of it. She is never entirely separated from the words written at the end of the MS of her story 'Six Years After', in which the Pa-man's insensitivity is so patent he might well have been borrowed directly from Elizabeth's novel: 'Oh my *hatred*!' she wrote.[26]

But she could make separate parcels of her feelings – as Linda in 'Prelude' imagined sending Stanley different parcels of hers, and the last one would be a little packet of her hate, 'for a surprise'.[27] Perhaps it's not too glib and speculative to suggest that in August 1921 Mansfield had gone back and forth between the parcels of love that were 'At the Bay' and 'The Voyage', and the parcel of hate that was 'A Married Man's Story'.

★

'A Married Man's Story' opens with a domestic scene in which the man describes his own emotional detachment from his wife and child.[28] 'A queer thing is I can't connect him with my wife and myself – I've never accepted him as ours.' He adds that his wife doesn't seem to him a natural mother. 'Where is that . . . animal ease and playfulness, that quick kissing and cuddling one has been taught to expect of young mothers?' He admits he may be wrong, but feels it isn't there. She is 'like an aunt and not a mother'.

He understands his wife, at least well enough to know how to make her unhappy. He's keenly aware, for example, of her lack of confidence about her appearance, and plays on that cruelly. But he is more interested in himself as a writer than he is in her as a suffering human being. Within the first few pages he has begun to comment on his own performance in the piece we are reading. For example, he imagines his wife standing in the cold kitchen knowing that 'nobody is going to come behind her, to take her in his arms, to kiss her soft hair, to lead her to the fire and to rub [her] hands warm again'.

> And she knows it. And yet, being a woman, deep down, deep down, she really does expect the miracle to happen; she really could embrace that dark, dark deceit, rather than live – like this.

But now, instead of experiencing to the full the recognition and sympathy invoked there as a kind of knowledge – knowledge of the wife, whom he will soon describe as '*a broken-hearted woman*' (K.M.'s italics) – he is distracted by his own turn of phrase:

> To live like this . . . . I write those words, very carefully, very beautifully. For some reason I feel inclined to sign them, or to write underneath – Trying a New Pen.

This is precisely the method used in 'Je ne parle pas français', and borrowed direct from Dostoyevsky's 'Memoirs from a Dark Cellar'.

These narrations are written as if to be spoken aloud, addressed directly to the reader; but not in a tone to win approval. Rather, the writer in each case is showing off, pleased with himself and proud of his own clever and shameless display of bad faith, insincerity and malice. Each seems so detached, even from himself, that he treats himself as a third person. As my title suggests, this is a technique of 'first person as third person'. Raoul Duquette gets some pleasure from it. He laughs at his own jokes and enjoys his own high spirits. There is a little of that with the Married Man, but much less; he is darker and more like Dostoyevsky's narrator, who specialises in displays of bitterness and self-contempt. 'Oh that was base of me!' the Married Man exclaims, offering yet another example of his own insensitivity, his conscious cruelty to the poor suffering wife described as having the 'trustful, bewildered eyes [. . .] of a cow that is being driven along a road'.

He is a lone wolf; but having reached that acknowledgement, he's bothered by the phrase that comes into his head, making the wolves his 'fleet grey brothers'. 'Fleet' seems false – 'a word I never use',[29] he says – and that distracts him from the recognition of self. So he drifts into another reflection on how difficult it is to write well, and to a statement of literary aspiration worthy of Mansfield in her juvenile Oscar Wilde phase when she made lists of such *bons mots*: 'That is how I long to write. No fine effects – no bravuras. But just the plain truth, as only a liar can tell it.'

My feeling is that this technical borrowing from Dostoyevsky, with its extreme and deliberate self-consciousness and self-contempt, did not quite match what Mansfield wanted; or rather, it's not where she felt the piece should finish, and the overall impression she wanted it to make. So she moves away from it; away also from the wife as victim, to the Married Man's own life story – and here the narrative gets its own 'pick-me-up'. Already she has struck the necessary note – subtle, dark, dangerous, but with just an edge of a smile. It's a sinister smile, almost illegible, but it's there. Tone is everything here. It has us listening, eager and apprehensive: what's going to happen?

We're told that the narrator's mother never emerged from her bedroom, lived all her life there during his childhood, until the night of her death when she came to his room and told him his father had poisoned her – and next morning she was dead. But he's uncertain whether this event really happened or was a dream. He has always been an outsider, disliked and shunned at school, given the nickname Gregory Powder because the smell of his father's chemist shop is on him, feeling like a plant kept in a cupboard and only allowed out now and then into the light. His sinister father, whom he secretly names 'old DP' – deadly poison – dispenses green pick-me-ups for his female customers who are mostly disreputable, probably prostitutes, and with whom he consorts late into the night.

This is the background from which the narrator has emerged to become the Married Man of our story, very briefly happy with his wife – though even on their wedding day, he remembers, there was a moment of cruelty when she looked for reassurance about her appearance and he pretended not to hear. But something happened 'last Autumn', and as a consequence, happiness is gone; they are estranged. He sees her as alien and, while seeming almost to pity her, he quite consciously torments her.

If there is anything we are actually offered by the story that could have been the event of 'last Autumn', it must be the birth of their child. This, I suggest, was the point at which he had to see himself as the father, and therefore possibly as the poisoner. But there is something else. In a narrative sequence that is by no means clear, he tells us he is like the child of myth, suckled by a wolf; and now finally he has been accepted into the lupine fraternity. And the story concludes with these extraordinarily constructed sentences: 'I was taken, I was accepted, claimed. I did not consciously turn away from the world of human beings; I had never known it; but I from that night did beyond words consciously turn towards my silent brothers...'

The awkward precision of that last sentence seems to me weird and perfect. It's as though he's slipping finally 'beyond words', beyond human language into the world of the wolves, his brothers.

There are some sentences by the Canadian poet Anne Carson which, when I first read them, made me think at once of the Mansfield story. Carson is writing about 'a poem of radical loneliness' by a seventh-century Greek poet, Alkaios. He has set up his household 'all alone' where 'wolves and women have replaced "the fathers of my fathers"'. Carson goes on:

> The wolf is a conventional symbol of marginality in Greek poetry.
> The wolf is an outlaw. He lives beyond the boundary of usefully culti-
> vated and inhabited space marked off as the *polis*, in that blank no man's
> land called the *apeiron* (the unbounded).[30]

Mansfield is experimenting here, stepping outside the boundaries of the social, within which fiction normally functions, and which is very much the region of 'At the Bay' and 'the Voyage' – the two stories she set aside to write this one. 'At the Bay' in particular is about bonding, interdependency, marriage, family and love. 'A Married Man's Story' is about (as the narrator puts it) the 'relish [. . .] in the very best of us [. . .] that leaps up and cries "A-ahh!" for joy at the thought' of a marriage destroyed.

And yet there is something that holds it all together and makes it compelling, and even almost coherent. That something is style, is tone, is what? – a particular quality in the writing that I think is quite distinct; that you don't find, not exactly as it is here, in her previous work, and I suspect it comes from her late reading of James Joyce. Mansfield was only ever a 'young writer' and consequently always in some degree derivative. Everything she writes has her fingerprints, her DNA; and yet the debts are obvious in a way they tend not to be in an older writer with a more formed identity. In this story I think we see her moving from Dostoyevsky to Joyce.

Here's the Mansfield:

Outside it is raining. I like to think of that cold drenched window behind the blind, and beyond, the dark bushes in the garden, their broad leaves bright with rain, and beyond the fence, the gleaming road with the two hoarse little gutters singing against each other, and the wavering reflections of the lamps, like fishes' tails . . . . While I am here, I am there, lifting my face to the dim sky, and it seems to me it must be raining all over the world – that the whole earth is drenched [. . .] And all at one and the same moment I am arriving in a strange city, slipping under the hood of the cab while the driver whips the cover off . . .

And now here's her contemporary, Joyce:

Yes, the newspapers were right: snow was general all over Ireland. It was falling on every part of the dark central plain, on the treeless hills, falling softly upon the Bog of Allen and, further westward, softly falling into the dark mutinous Shannon waves. It was falling, too, upon every part of the lonely churchyard on the hill where Michael Furey lay buried. It lay thickly drifted on the crooked crosses and headstones, on the spears of the little gate, on the barren thorns. His soul swooned slowly as he heard the snow falling faintly through the universe and faintly falling, like the descent of their last end, upon all the living and the dead.[31]

Joyce's 'The Dead' is one of the great short stories in the language, and what I'm suggesting is that there's a tonal similarity, and a debt – and not only in those parallel images of universality, the rain in Mansfield that 'must be [falling] all over the world', and the snow in Joyce 'falling faintly through the universe'.

Virginia Woolf recalls Mansfield's first encounter with *Ulysses*, in a typescript at the Hogarth Press, reading some sentences, beginning to mock and then checking herself, recognising the *quality* in the writing – a moment, Woolf suggests 'that should figure [...] in the history of literature'.[32]

After that historic moment of recognition, Mansfield said a number of contradictory things about Joyce, and was never quite at ease with his realism, which of course offended her quite highly developed sense of Protestant middle-class propriety. Just a month or two after the great burst of writing I've been speaking about she told Sydney Schiff she had *re*-read *Portrait of the Artist as a Young Man*, which she described as 'awfully *good*', and insisted Joyce was 'immensely important'. Of her aversion to Joyce's realism she added, 'it seems to me the *new novel* [...] is so by far and away the most important thing that one must conquer all minor aversions. They are unworthy.'[33]

We also know that the following year she and Murry met Joyce. She reported that he 'was rather – difficile', and that the two men 'simply sailed away out of my depth. I felt almost stupefied'. Murry might have been showing off and probably didn't understand *Ulysses* as well as he pretended, because Joyce reported that Mrs Murry seemed to understand the book better than her husband did.[34]

Alpers says there is no evidence Mansfield ever read *Dubliners*, which contained the story Joyce called 'The Dead'. But there would be no evidence either that she'd read *Portrait of the Artist* if she hadn't happened to mention *re*-reading it. Although *Dubliners* was, as Alpers says, 'a neglected book in 1920',[35] Joyce was constantly talked about in literary circles; and I think it's significant that Mansfield's great friend, Fred Goodyear, asked his parents to send him a copy just before he was killed in France.

There's a marked similarity between 'The Dead' and Mansfield's 'The Stranger', written in Menton just before the 1921 Swiss efflorescence. These two stories are different in detail, but each ends with a husband feeling excluded, shut out from a moment of intense emotion between his greatly loved wife and a man now dead. Here's the sad husband in Joyce's story:

> The tears gathered more thickly in his eyes and in the partial darkness he imagined he saw the form of a young man standing under a dripping tree. Other forms were near. His soul had approached that region where dwell the vast hosts of the dead.[36]

And now Mansfield's:

> Janey was silent. But her words, so light, so soft, so chill, seemed to hover in the air, to rain into his breast like snow.
>   The fire had gone red. Now it fell in with a sharp sound and the room was colder. Cold crept up his arms. The room was huge, immense, glittering. It filled his whole world.[37]

You see how the grief in each case seems to expand into an image of something vast, inexpressible. The intrusive Other has escaped into death, taking with him whatever passed between him and the wife.

Alpers sees the similarity in idea between these two stories, and refers to 'The Dead' as 'Joyce's cognate masterpiece'.[38] 'Cognate' suggests a common source rather than influence of one upon the other; but he offers no suggestion what that might be, and my own preference is for direct influence, Joyce on Mansfield. It's true 'The Stranger' is based on something that happened to, and between, her parents; but I think the idea of using that event in fiction came from thinking about the Joyce story, seeing the parallel and making use of it. So Joyce is there in the idea for 'The Stranger'; but also, I would say he is there in the tone and stylistic imprint of significant passages of 'A Married Man's Story'.

My suggestion is that Mansfield did much more than 'conquer all minor aversions' to Joyce's work. She found in it a new path, a direction she didn't live long enough to explore.

Is 'A Married Man's Story' (as it's usually described) 'unfinished'? Or should it be seen as an exercise in twentieth-century Modernism – as many words long as it needed to be to achieve its effect and leave our imaginations to do the rest? I come back to those peculiar and marvellous sentences on which it ends in its present form. Writing them would have pulled her up short. Where could she go from there – and did she need to go anywhere? They *are* an ending; and if she'd wanted to write more, I feel the extra material would have to have been placed *before* them, so they still constituted 'the End'. Further, she liked the story so much while writing it that Murry was able to report in that letter to Schiff it was to be the title story of the new collection.

But she had interrupted the writing of 'At the Bay' to write this one, and she now goes back to, and completes, 'At the Bay' – the story that (along with 'Prelude') would be her signature piece, marking her indelibly as 'the New Zealand writer, Katherine Mansfield'. She had not much more than a year to live, and never returned to 'A Married Man's Story' to make final decisions and revisions.

See it, then, as 'unfinished' or as mysteriously complete: either way, the story of the story is fascinating – its strange place in the sequence of her writing, the influence of Dostoyevsky displaced by the shadowy presence of Joyce, its seeming function as the release of certain 'dark matter' clearing a path for 'The Voyage' and 'At the Bay' – all of that itself makes a narrative within the larger story that is 'Katherine Mansfield'.

1   Antony Alpers, *The Life of Katherine Mansfield*, Viking, 1980, pp. 339–40.

2   Patrick Morrow, *Katherine Mansfield's Fiction*, Bowling Green State University Popular Press, 1993, p. 94.

3   Jeffrey Meyers, *Katherine Mansfield: A Darker View*, Cooper Square Press, 2002, p. 69.

4   Kathleen Jones, *Katherine Mansfield: The Story-teller*, Penguin/Viking, 2010, p. 356.

5   Antony Alpers, *The Stories of Katherine Mansfield*, Oxford University Press, 1984, p. 571.

6   Alpers, *The Life*, p. 338

7   Alpers, *The Stories*, p. 571–2.

8   Alpers, *The Life*, p. 282.

9   Vincent O'Sullivan and Margaret Scott (eds), *The Collected Letters of Katherine Mansfield*, vol. IV, Clarendon Press, 1996 (hereafter referred to as *Letters* IV), p. 303.

10 *Letters* IV, p. 287

11 Margaret Scott (ed.), *The Katherine Mansfield Notebooks*, vol. II, Lincoln University Press, 1997 (hereafter referred to as *Notebooks* II), p. 315.

12 *Letters* IV, p. 311.

13 Vincent O'Sullivan and Margaret Scott (eds), *The Collected Letters of Katherine Mansfield*, vol. V, Clarendon Press, 2008 (hereafter referred to as *Letters* V), p. 23.

14 *Letters* IV, p. 301.

15 Bertrand succeeded to the title in 1931.

16 Elizabeth von Arnim, *Vera*, Virago, 1983, pp. 301 and 307.

17 *Letters* IV, p. 346.

18 *Letters* IV, p. 309.

19 *Letters* IV, p. 346.

20 *Letters* IV, p. 300.

21 *Letters* V, pp. 234–5 and n.

22 *Notebooks* II, p. 290.

23 *Notebooks* II, pp. 290–1.

24 Gerri Kimber and Vincent O'Sullivan (eds), *The Collected Fiction of Katherine Mansfield*, vol. II, *1916–1922*, Edinburgh University Press, 2012 (hereafter referred to as *Collected Fiction* II), p. 384.

25 *Letters* IV, p. 309.

26 Alpers, *The Life*, p. 350, n.

27 *Collected Fiction* II, p. 88.

28 *Collected Fiction* II, p. 379–90.

29 In fact the phrase 'my fleet grey brothers' seems effective; but Mansfield would have associated it negatively with the song she uses in 'The Singing Lesson', with the lines 'Fleetly! Ah fleetly Mu-u-sic's gay measure / Passes away from the listening ear.'

30 Anne Carson, *Glass, Irony and God*, New Directions, 1995, p. 124.

31 James Joyce, *Dubliners*, Cape, 1952, pp. 255–6.

32 *The Diary of Virginia Woolf*, vol. V, ed. Anne Olivier Bell and Andrew McNeillie, Hogarth Press, 1984, p. 353.

33 *Letters* IV, p. 352.

34 Alpers, *The Life*, pp. 357–8.

35 Alpers, *The Life*, p. 330.

36 Joyce, *Dubliners*, p. 255

37 *Collected Fiction* II, p. 249. The sentence about the snow is the one Mansfield reproached Murry for not singling out for praise. See *Letters* IV, p. 114 and n. Possibly in an earlier version of the story the phrase was 'into his breast like the first snow'.

38 Alpers, *The Life*, p. 329.

Tom & Viv and Murry & Mansfield

The release last year of the first two volumes of T. S. Eliot's letters,[1] and the year before of the final volume of Katherine Mansfield's,[2] raises interesting questions about the relationship of these two and of their respective spouses, Vivienne Eliot and John Middleton Murry. Why was Eliot distrustful, and even apprehensive, of Mansfield? What was Murry's relationship with Vivienne – and indeed with Eliot himself? Why were Vivienne's feelings about Murry so tortured – and was Mansfield jealous of her? The fact that the editors of the Eliot volumes have included a significant number of letters to him by Vivienne, his family, friends and associates, helps fill out the larger context of his life in the 1920s.

There can be no doubt that Eliot was deeply suspicious of Mansfield, and there is plenty of evidence that she observed him closely and accurately. According to Clive Bell a number of the Bloomsbury set first heard Eliot's 'The Love Song of J. Alfred Prufrock' in Mansfield's reading of it in 1916 at Garsington, where,

First published in the *London Review of Books*, vol. 33, no. 5, 3 March 2011.

he reports, it 'caused a stir, much discussion, some perplexity'. A short time later the two, Eliot and Mansfield, met at a dinner party in Hammersmith (Robert Graves was also present) where, she reports, Eliot 'grew paler and paler and more and more silent' while their host (whom she likened to a butcher) 'cut up, trimmed and smacked into shape America and the Americans'.[3] The two, he lacking his wife Vivienne, she lacking Murry with whom she was living as yet unmarried, left the party together, and her description of their walk seems to owe as much to the cityscape of his early poetry as to reality.

Mansfield's letters in the next few years occasionally echo his poems, or reflect on his criticism; but there is no significant overlap of their lives until 1920. In April of that year Eliot writes to thank John Middleton Murry *very much* for 'your thought of me'. What Murry is being thanked for here is not clear, but the year before he had offered Eliot the deputy editorship of the *Athenaeum* and though Eliot declined he took the offer (and reported it to his mother) as another sign that 'there is a small and select public which regards me as the best living critic, as well as the best living poet, in England'.[4] In the letter to Murry he says he and his wife Vivienne 'are looking forward to seeing Katherine'.

Katherine's report on their dinner party is waspish about Vivienne, but gives, with momentary vividness, a revealing snapshot of the Eliots as a couple:

The Eliots [*sic*] have dined with us tonight. They are just gone – and the whole room is *quivering*. John has gone downstairs to see them off. Mrs E's voice rises 'Oh dont commiserate Tom; he's *quite* happy.' I know its extravagant ... but I dislike her so *immensely*. She really repels me. She makes me shiver with apprehension ... I don't dare to think of what she is 'seeing'. From the moment that John dropped a spoon & she cried: 'I say you are noisy tonight – whats wrong' – to the moment when she came into my room & lay on the sofa offering idly: 'This room's changed since the last time I was here.' To think she had been here *before*. [. . .] And Elliot, leaning towards her, admiring, listening, making the most of her – really minding whether she disliked the country or not . . . .

I am so fond of Elliot [. . . .] But this teashop creature.

M. comes up after they are gone, and he defends her. He tells me of a party he gave here & how she came & was friends with him & how he drank to get over the state of nerves she had thrown him into. 'I like her; and would do the same again.' I feel as tho' Ive been stabbed.[5]

Perhaps Eliot was aware of this critical eye; and perhaps Vivienne was too. In any case it is only a few weeks later that Eliot is writing to Pound, mocking Murry's exaggeration (as he sees it) of Mansfield's talent, and adding 'I believe her to be a dangerous WOMAN; and of course', he goes on about the Murrys, 'two sentimentalists together are more than two times as noxious as one' (473).

This impression of Mansfield as in some way powerful and a threat is echoed soon after in a letter in which, signing herself 'Yr most adoring', Vivienne urges Tom, *'Write to Schiff* – very nicely. Must not let him fall into K.M.'s hands' (492).

Eliot's professional life remained intertwined with Murry's, but the degree to which his largely concealed dislike could rise is revealed in a letter to his mother in January 1921:

I and Murry have fallen apart completely. I consider his verse quite negligible, and I don't like his prose style; his articles seem to me to become more and more windy, verbose and meaningless. Personally, I think him a man of weak character and great vanity, and I do not trust him . . . (535–6)

This negative feeling about Murry seems to spill over into his view of Mansfield, who is all the more suspect because Murry is indiscreet in promoting her work; so one can take it as a reflection back of Eliot's own view when Scofield Thayer, in a letter to Eliot, refers to Murry as 'this sparse husband of England's latest short story prima donna' (632).

But it is in 1922, at the time of establishing his new literary periodical, *The Criterion*, sponsored by Lady Rothermere, that Eliot's distrust of Mansfield reaches a peak. The first sign of the crisis comes in a letter from Vivienne to Ezra Pound in which she says Lady Rothermere has written 'three offensive letters' to Tom 'about the *Criterion*'.

> . . . if when she sees T. she behaves in the same way as her letters I don't see that he can do anything but throw up the *Criterion – and I believe that is what she wants.* She is unhinged – one of those beastly raving women who are most dangerous. She is now in that asylum for the insane called La Prieuré [i.e. Gurdjieff's 'Institute for the Harmonious Development of Man' at Fontainbleau] where she does religious dances naked with Katherine Mansfield. 'K.M.', she says in every letter – 'is *the most intelligent* woman I have *ever* met.' K.M. is pouring poison in her ear (of course) for K.M. hates T. more than anyone. (770)

There appear to be no grounds for this suspicion (and the naked dancing is surely a fantasy). Mansfield did not hate Eliot; she quite liked him in fact, but viewed him with a certain amused detachment. In February 1922, for example, she wrote to the Hon. Dorothy Brett:

> Yes he is an attractive creature; he is pathetic. He suffers from his feelings of powerlessness, He knows it. He feels weak. Its all disguise. That slow manner, that hesitation, side long glances and so on are *painful*. And the pity is he is too serious about himself, even a little bit absurd. But its natural; it's the fault of London, that. He wants kindly laughing at and setting free.[6]

In August of the same year she writes to another friend that she has seen *The Criterion* 'advertised to appear shortly. It looks very full of rich plums'.[7] But it is clear that Eliot shared his wife's suspicion, and blamed Mansfield for Lady Rothermere's negative response to the first issue.

Pound's contribution to this discussion is typically peculiar, original and not altogether unhelpful. Lady Rothermere has thought the magazine dull. He thinks so too, but believes (and seems to expect Eliot to confirm) this is deliberate – that Eliot as editor is playing 'possum', intending to sneak radical stuff in under a cover of dullness. And he suggests that Eliot 'conciliate the K.M. faction' by including something of hers in the journal. He also asks whether Eliot is sure Lady Rothermere 'is being *intentionally* offensive'; and suggests that 'in your present exhausted and enerve condition . . . perhaps a slight magnification takes place' (772–3).

There is nothing to suggest that anyone had asked, or even hinted, that work by Mansfield should be included in *The Criterion*. In fact at this time Katherine was too preoccupied with health, physical and psychic, to be giving much thought (apart from retrospective dissatisfaction) to her literary career; but Eliot replies to Pound as if agreeing reluctantly that such a bargain needs to be struck, and that he will 'suggest to Lady R. that she should secure a story from K. Mansfield'. 'I myself', he goes on,

> should much prefer to have something from Murry; he is at least in every way preferable to his wife. The latter is not by any means the most intelligent woman Lady R. has ever met. She is simply one of the most persistent and thickskinned toadies and one of the vulgarest women Lady R. has ever met and is also a sentimental crank. (775)

Mansfield could evoke strong reactions, positive and negative, in the literary community of the time; but this is surely the most extravagant on record, and the one least founded on anything except insecurity and a paranoid imagination. Lady Rothermere, though she found (without help, I'm sure) the first issue dull, and disliked its format, was not about to cut off funds or curb her editor's freedom, and the fuss soon died down.

Katherine Mansfield died on 9 January 1923. Two days later, still not knowing of her death, Vivienne wrote to Tom (whom she addressed as 'Dearest darling Wing') responding to a letter in which he must have reported that Mansfield's illness was serious:

> Funnily – I have had Katherine M. perpetually in my mind the last two
> days – *and*, last night I dreamed of her *all night*! This a.m. when I read
> yr. letter that she was v. ill I felt that there is indeed something psychic
> going on. I think [Lady] Rother[mere] shd. be blamed if anything
> happens to K.M. for if she was not mad and irresponsible she wd. not
> have allowed K.M. to stay in the bug-house [Gurdjieff's Institute again].
> And <u>Murry</u> – !!⁸

Nine days later Eliot writes the necessary (somewhat Jamesian) letter of condolence:

> Dear John,
> Forgive me for writing to you at all, but one must express oneself if only
> by a sheet of paper. There is, of course, nothing that I can say, except
> to remind you that I feel very very deeply, and that this has hardly left
> my thoughts for ten days, and that my sympathy with your suffering is
> something that cannot be written.
> Yours always,
> Tom (17)

A postscript promises 'a critical article on K's work'; and a letter on 26 January assures Murry 'I constantly think of you' (24).

Eliot's anxieties at this time are enormous and complicated. Vivienne is constantly ill. Pound is attempting, through the fund he called 'Bel Esprit', to free Eliot from his employment in Lloyds Bank. Eliot is cautious, secretive, manipulative, and not entirely honest about his own financial affairs, denying that he has received any money from the Bel Esprit fund when in fact he has, and not making clear to Pound and other contributors that he is receiving income from his family's brick-manufacturing business.

He continues to labour and complain. Even the ever loyal Vivienne, who is by now (mid-1920s) helping him with his editing of *The Criterion*, and writing for it in an unmistakably Mansfield manner, records in her diary, 'One waits, sympathises, but it is dreary work. [Tom] is like a person about to break down – infinitely scrupulous, tautologous, & cautious'; and Virginia Woolf in hers that he is 'peevish, plaintive, egotistical'. The question of whether he will or won't leave the bank is intolerably protracted, the drama of ill health (his own, but more especially Vivienne's) seems as if it will never reach a fifth act – it is a weary and unrelenting story. As editor Eliot is industrious, capable of waspishness but also of diplomacy, particularly when dealing with his difficult and favoured colleagues, Pound and Wyndham Lewis.

As a husband he displays, for the most part, agonised patience, and both sympathy for and understanding of Vivienne's suffering. Her talent is also acknowledged and her work published in *The Criterion* under various pseudonyms, all with the initials F.M. The debt her writing owes to Mansfield is never mentioned, but is clearly not held against her. Mansfield herself, however, is not forgotten, and when a new collection of her stories is published Eliot writes to Richard Aldington asking him to review it. 'I think her inflated reputation ought to be dealt with.' (167)

There is now a peculiar tone in letters to Murry, one or two of which are almost like love letters.

Thanks, dear John, for your adorable letter. Will you wire me please, what you are going to do and where you are to be each day of this week, and give me a chance to reply by wire. Vivien is so dangerously ill that there is a fresh consultation of doctors every day to decide whether she can be moved to London in a closed car.

I feel a kind of dependence on you, and it will be a great comfort to know every day where you are. You are the only person I want to be in touch with. (110–1)

This was April 1923. In June of that year Vivienne writes to Murry in terms which seem to need an explanation the present editors are unable or unwilling to offer. After praising his 'beautiful cottage' and saying the bedrooms 'particularly touched me', she goes on:

To speak the truth to you – and you must take this please as my answer to what you tell me of your feelings about me and Tom – since coming back to London I have been in despair. I mean real despair, which isolates and freezes one. [. . .]

In addition, I am trying to come to a decision. It is an old indecision, really, but the conclusion becomes always more urgent. My despair is paralysing me. There, John, there is no-one else in this world today to whom I would make an explanation.

So I can't see you just now, my dear. But if you are what you *must* be, you will let me call on you the moment I smash a chair or two, and will come then quickly, before I have time to get re-bound. (170)

This is surely something to do with a crisis in the marriage, otherwise intimated but not directly recorded during the mid-1920s. Something is referred to as understood between them; and this, or something similar, recurs in a letter from Vivienne to Murry in August 1925:

Up till now, it has seemed to me impossible that you would care to hear that I have thought about you constantly for the last month. And that I have had what has happened incessantly in my mind.

Perhaps we may meet some day, and be able to talk.

I am afraid Tom's terrific life takes all my energy, and I can only lie still and wait for it to end.

With all my thoughts and wishes for you

Vivien Eliot. (714)

Shortly afterwards she writes to him again, a letter which includes the following:

I am beginning to believe now that I have really got a little niche in your thoughts, and that's what I want. When things are *extra* bad I shall always write and ask you to give me as much of your attention as you have time for. [. . .]

Really John I think of you for ever, constantly, and I know, by thinking, lots of little things about you that it seems to me nobody else knows now. (718)

Eliot's own feelings towards Murry veer about, and in April 1924 he declines an invitation to Murry's wedding in a letter that doesn't sound altogether unlike the tone of a jilted lover:

My dear John,

You know it is impossible for me to come to your wedding, as I am in a bank and cannot get away at such an hour. I am sure that you have done the best thing for yourself in marrying again, but you know that it has always been impossible for me to understand any of your actions.

Ever yours,

T.S.E. (380)

Eliot's underlying and ongoing distaste (expressed in that early letter to his mother) was given public expression in his 1923 essay 'The Function of Criticism', in which he takes Murry to task for his idea that the 'English writer, the English divine, the English

76

statesman, inherit no rules from their forebears; they inherit only this: a sense that in the last resort they must depend upon the inner voice'.

'The possessors of the inner voice', Eliot responds, 'ride ten in a compartment to a football match at Swansea, listening to the inner voice, which breathes the eternal message of vanity, fear and lust.'[9]

This distaste must have been refreshed when he learned that Murry was at work on a life of Jesus, and it finds expression in his reply to a letter telling him that his friend was coming to London from the country. Murry, it seems, had rejoiced that for himself 'the time of stony places' was over. Eliot's response to this was extraordinarily sniffy, pompous and insulting:

> If you are going to be in London, you will probably find a great many 'friends' to welcome you. [...]
>   But do you really consider it a good sign that 'the time of stony places is over'? If so, you are luckier than the Saviour, who found things pretty stony to the last [....] I do not suppose that I share any other characteristic of the Founder of Christianity, but at least I have nothing but stony places to look forward to. This isolates me, of course, from those who can pass in and out of stony places with practised ease. (554)

But before Eliot could relax into a settled hate for this proponent of the human Jesus and 'the inner voice', Murry had done him a great favour. Having just given the Clark Lectures at Cambridge, Murry suggested to the university that Eliot might give the next series. It came just when Eliot was feeling most insecure. 'You must have *realised*', he wrote, 'that your proposal of my name, and the hope of this job, would come as a ray of hope at the *blackest moment in my life*'. And in a subsequent letter:

> And now I am inclined to retract my views about *friendship*. Other people have offered things, gifts, but no one, except you, has ever come with them exactly at *the* right moment. What is this except friendship?

You came once with the *Athenaeum* – and I have since felt that this was a *gran rifiuto* on my part [. . . .] I shan't make that mistake again. (592)

So it is not surprising that when the Eliots' marital problems reached some kind of new crisis in April (again the cruellest month) 1925, Murry was one of three men to whom he wrote seeking help and guidance. (The others were Bertrand Russell and Leonard Woolf.) The first of two letters to Murry is peculiar; either it is incomplete, or perhaps it was attached to the second dated 12 April 1925. It begins without preliminary, and has something of the flavour of a statement to the police:

In the last ten years [i.e. since meeting and marrying Vivienne] – gradually, but deliberately – I have made myself into a *machine*. I have done it deliberately – in order to endure, in order not to feel – *but it has killed* V. In leaving the bank I hope to become less a machine – but yet I am frightened – because I don't know what it will do to me – and to V. – should I come alive again. I have deliberately killed my senses – I have deliberately died – in order to go on with the outward form of living – This I did in 1915. What will happen if I live again? 'I am I' but with what feelings, with what results to *others* – Have I the right to be I – But the dilemma – to kill another person by being dead, or to kill them by being alive? Is it best to make oneself a machine, and kill them by not giving nourishment, or to be alive, and kill them by wanting something that one *cannot* get from that person? Does it happen that two persons' lives are absolutely hostile? Is it true that sometimes one can only live by another's dying? (627)

One wonders what is being talked about, whether it is sex, or something less tangible. Stephen Spender once said that, in conversation, when Eliot got on to some unpropitious subject – the weather, or sales of poetry – he might pursue it remorselessly 'like a tram going through a slum'; and anyone who has read a number of the editorial commentaries in *The Criterion* will know what Spender meant. In the year before her death Mansfield had noticed the same painful, treadmill quality when she wrote to Violet Schiff from Switzerland about his 'London Letter' in the October 1921 issue of the *Dial*:

> Poor Eliot sounds tired to death. His London letter is all a maze of words. One feels the awful effort behind it – as though he were being tortured.[10]

There is the same feeling, in the statement to Murry, of the mental engine turning over – abstractly self-tormenting – and with the same preoccupation, and the same circularity, that would surface in the Sweeney poems:

> Any man has to, needs to, wants to
> Once in a lifetime, do a girl in.
> [...]
> He didn't know if he was alive
> and the girl was dead
> He didn't know if the girl was alive
> and he was dead
> He didn't know if they both were alive
> or both were dead
> If he was alive then the milkman wasn't
> and the rent-collector wasn't
> And if they were alive then he was dead.

It was, however, the kind of flattering invitation to be wise that was grist to the Murry mill, especially when Eliot added that he sought John's advice 'because I know that in many ways – spiritually, you are much wiser than I'.

'Of one thing I am convinced', Murry pontificated:

That it is your duty *absolutely* to come alive again. Absolutely, – this
without regard to what might be the consequences for V. [. . .] You have
done a great wrong to yourself, and a great wrong has been done to her.
You are involved in a vicious circle, which thinking only tightens: you
must break it [. . . .]

I know the consequences of this *may* be awful for V. I don't know that
they will be. But I am sure nothing but harm can come of your trying to
kill yourself to keep her alive. [. . .]

Oh, Tom, I am almost afraid to say these things [. . . .] But I think I
know this. There is a point at which the choice really is: she may die,
I must die. Then you must say: I will not die.

That sounds terrible: it is terrible, but not in the way it sounds
terrible. When you take your stand: 'I will not die', then indeed you do
die – to all that you were. That is a self-sacrifice of the deepest.

Live, and let come what may. One of you two must go forward. It can't
be V. She can only go forward by bodily death, in the state she is in now.
And anyhow going forward is the man's job. [. . .] But try not to think
about the future. You can't know what will be. And I am sure there is no
other way of helping her. (631–2)

Murry here seems to be laying a claim for himself as the man who
bravely chose life, even at the expense of his wife's survival, and the
falseness of tone puts me in mind of a letter in which Mansfield took
him to task for some of his critical writing:

Now Ill be franker still. There are still traces of what I call your sham
personality in this book & they mar it. [. . .] Can't you see what a *farce*
it makes of your preaching the good Life. The good Life indeed,
rowing about in your little boat with the worm eaten ship & chaos!
Look here! How *can* you! How can you lay up your sweat in a phial
for future generations! I dont ask for false courage from anyone, but I
do think that even if you are shivering it is your duty as an artist and a
man *not* to shiver.[11]

How clean and fresh Mansfield's comments sound when compared with either Murry's or Eliot's! A dose of that kind of salt might have been more salutary than Murry's maundering. But Murry's reply had given Eliot a problem more immediate and more mundane than that of living or dying or killing his wife. In his next letter he explains that he *thinks* he understands Murry's advice; but that Vivienne knows he has written for help, and she will want to see the reply. The present reply can't be shown to her, so will Murry please write an edited version? Murry obliges of course, beginning with the news of the birth of his first child – to be named Katherine.

Towards the end of 1925 (where volume II of the *Letters* ends), Eliot's financial position has been secured by a directorship on the board of Faber and Gwyer, his editing of *The Criterion* seems secure, and his Clark Lectures are in preparation. *Tout va bien.* A breakthrough has been made in the understanding of Vivienne's illnesses (she had been almost starved to death by 'specialists' who claimed to understand her case), but her state of mind is worse, and she appears to be complaining of some kind of confinement and of Eliot absent and ignoring her (a foretaste of the worse to come).

Murry recedes from the picture. Mansfield's 'inflated reputation' has not been 'dealt with' in *The Criterion*; but in his 1933 lectures, published as *After Strange Gods* and subsequently suppressed, Eliot was to use her story 'Bliss' as one of three examples of the modern short story, the others being D. H. Lawrence's 'The Shadow in the Rose Garden' and James Joyce's 'The Dead'. The three make an interesting combination in that each is about a painful revelation in a marriage that a loved spouse has had or is having an association of some emotional intensity with another person. Mansfield's story Eliot describes as 'brief, poignant and, in the best sense, slight' – which shows Mansfield's great skill in handling 'perfectly the *minimum* material' – a skill that defines her work as 'feminine'. Lawrence's story, Eliot considers, has 'an alarming strain of cruelty' and 'an absence of any moral or social sense'. Joyce may have lost the

Catholic faith of his boyhood but his sensibility remains 'orthodox', and this is demonstrated by the fact that the suffering husband at the end of the story feels that 'His soul had approached that region where dwell the vast hosts of the dead'.

Eliot gave these lectures in America, and used the trip as an occasion to escape permanently from Vivienne. She was notified only through his lawyer, and he never returned to her, hiding from her until, some years later, she was incarcerated in a hospital for the insane, where she died in 1947. By 1931 Murry's second wife (who had modelled herself on Mansfield, did her hair in the same way, and wrote short stories) had died – like Mansfield of tuberculosis. In the same year Murry married for a third time. The new wife, Betty Cockbayne, inflicted numerous physical assaults on him until he escaped, ultimately into a fourth, and this time happy, marriage. He died in 1957, the year before Eliot married his second wife, Valerie, co-editor of these new volumes of his letters. Murry's gravestone bears the inscription:

John Middleton Murry
author and farmer

'Ripeness is all'

1   Valerie Eliot and Hugh Haughton (eds), *The Letters of T. S. Eliot*, vol. I, 1898–1922
    (revised edition), and vol. II, 1923–1925, Faber & Faber, 2009. Page numbers in brackets
    will refer to this volume.
2   Vincent O'Sullivan and Margaret Scott (eds), *The Collected Letters of Katherine
    Mansfield*, vol. V, Clarendon Press, 2008.
3   O'Sullivan and Scott (eds), *The Collected Letters of Katherine Mansfield*, vol. I,
    Clarendon Press, 1984, p. 318.
4   Eliot and Haughton (eds), *The Letters of T. S. Eliot*, vol. I, p. 331. Page references which
    follow in the text are to this volume unless otherwise indicated.
5   O'Sullivan and Scott (eds), *The Collected Letters of Katherine Mansfield*, vol. IV,
    Clarendon Press, 1996, p. 11.
6   O'Sullivan and Scott (eds), *The Collected Letters of Katherine Mansfield*, vol. V,
    Clarendon Press, 2008, p. 75.
7   *Ibid.*, p. 256.
8   Eliot and Haughton (eds), *The Letters of T. S. Eliot*, vol. II, p. 9. Further page numbers in
    the text refer to this volume unless otherwise indicated.
9   T. S. Eliot, *Selected Essays*, Faber & Faber, 1999, p. 27.
10 O'Sullivan and Scott (eds), *The Collected Letters of Katherine Mansfield*, vol. IV, p. 303.
11 *Ibid.*, p. 140.

A Note on Larkin on Mansfield

In his *Selected Letters* Philip Larkin had already been revealed as
an admirer of Katherine Mansfield, though with a kind of butch
embarrassment, as if it had to be explained to his male friends,
and excused. Several things surprised me about the man revealed
in the recently published *Letters to Monica*, selected and helpfully
edited by Anthony Thwaite. The first was how genial Larkin could
seem, how little there was of the famous reactionary (he is hardly
political at all); and though there is something of the curmudgeon,
he is more eccentric than that description suggests, always having
difficulty doing ordinary things, worried about where his talent for
fiction has gone and where his next poem is coming from; anxious,
apprehensive, unable to make up his mind. But he is reading all the
time, and commenting on his reading with uncommon keenness,
indifference to accepted views and high intelligence. And one of
the admirations he shared with his friend and lover of many years,

Contributed to *Katherine Mansfield Studies*, vol. 4, 2012, after reading
Letters to Monica, edited by Anthony Thwaite (Faber, 2010).

Monica Jones, was of Mansfield. In fact Monica seems to admit to using Mansfield sometimes to get him to write to her: 'I'm touched and amused to see how, always, a little of KM shakes a letter out of you to me – it does, doesn't it?' (p. 127, n. 1)

Early on he has been reading *Mrs Dalloway*, and quotes Mansfield writing to Woolf: 'You write so well, Virginia, so *damned* well'. 'Well, yes', Larkin says, 'but there is so much wooden & dead in V.W.' (16) – and those who know what Mansfield really thought know that she was not being quite honest with Virginia, and that she would have agreed with him. In the same letter he goes on to say Woolf lacks the 'depth' of Mansfield.

> The difference between V.W. and K.M. is the difference between E.M.F. and D.H.L. It is discouraging to reflect on KM's experience & apprehension of pain & suffering & to reflect how little she has become 'known' by it – I mean to say 'Mansfield!' suddenly brings to mind a bright Russian-doll-childish person, not the lonely Shakespeare-annotating invalid of the *Letters*. You – or rather the *Sunday Times* – would never call her a mistress of the human heart, so little did all she 'went through' express itself in full. (16–17)

That was October 1950. About a year later, in a new job in Belfast, he writes 'Just as two years ago at Birmingham, [so here] my comfort and stay is K.M.'s letters'. But the effect on him then, in Birmingham, 'was visionary: the world glowed with imparted radiance'. Now the effect is different. He is reading, one guesses, the volume of letters to Murry, and instead of getting 'a series of brilliant "sketches"' he is finding complete love letters, and feels he is 'inhibited [...] by knowing that it's J.M.M. who is the recipient [...] alas there *is* something suspect about it – it's perfect, & therefore untrue, of the imagination only' (57–58).

A few weeks later he is complaining about a review in the *New Statesman* of the same volume of letters, which spoke about Mansfield's 'hate & rancour'.

The review made me quite angry: surely KM was only a simple case of passionate imaginative energy & love, damaged by a typical disease and by 'loving' (not to enquire into that word more than necessary) a slippery emotional character like Murry, who played up to her all-for-love two-children-holding-hands line of talk but was quite content to live apart from her & indeed found actual cohabitation with her a bit of a strain. It takes her a long time to realise this discrepancy but when she does she immediately starts to shorten her lines, to be independent, & this entails *curing* herself [i.e. of Murry]. (62)

A few years on and he is reading the new enhanced version of what Murry called her *Journal*:

and it has done me good – I mean I feel more sensitive, more receptive, happier, than before. O, I daresay there'll be a few jeering reviews [...] I do think that she is one of the few people (Hardy is another) who set things moving, swinging, quietly, harmoniously, inside one, as if some thaw was taking place. And again it makes you dreadfully miserable, since you apprehend life more keenly, and since you know (or I know) that she's so far ahead in unselfish observation and transcription.

He then quotes some of his favourites among her *bons mots*: 'Be not afeared, the house is full of blankets'; 'Why hath the Lord not made *bun* trees?'; (of a cat) 'his whole little life side by side with ours'; 'Every umbrella hides a warm bud of life' (124); and the joke that Forster's Helen Schlegel must have been got with child by Leonard Bast's umbrella. The *Journal* causes him to ask himself a series of semi-comic but searching questions about his own progress in life, and to see himself as 'just drifting', achieving little.

[...] my point about K.M. [is] that she is enormously dedicated, from page 1 ('I mean this year to try and be a different person...') in 1904, to p. 334 ('to be rooted in life...') in 1922, she was enormously aware of things unquestionably more pure, more significant, more beautiful than she was herself & of the problem of translating them by means of art, by catching hold of their tiny significant manifestations ('Charles sat darning socks ... When he took up the scissors, the cat squeezed up its eyes as if to say "That's quite right", and when he put the scissors down it just put out its paw as if to straighten them ...'). This seems to me to depend enormously on the fact that she did not distinguish between life and art [. . . .] Art is good insofar as it catches life, and, really, the opposite is true too, in K.M. (125)

He wrestles with this for a while and then pulls himself up:

If you don't believe art is better than ... no, wait a minute, that isn't what KM thought. If you *don't* believe that good art is better than bad life, then bugger off, there's plenty of room for your sort in the civil service. If you *do* believe it, then stay and try to convert *the whole of life into art*, until the smallest action is a ritual, an *auto da fe*, rejecting what you can't transmute. (125)

Less than a week later he is at her again.

Do you see what struck me? The incessant harping on the conviction that the *aperçus* in which 'life' seemed most piercingly summarised (e.g. 'On the wall of the kitchen there was a shadow, shaped like a little mask with two gold slits for eyes. It danced up and down') put on her not only an artistic obligation to record them, but a moral obligation to 'live up to' them. This is stressed again & again & again. *I* think (but of course I've never been a girl) you do her less than justice in implying that 'wanting to be a different person' was only self-dramatisation. In its numerous contexts it reads to me more like the ordinary reaction of any person who sees anything beautiful – a wish to return thanks, or to – this is more like it – to struggle towards a state of mind in which such percep-tions would be more common, and in which they wd be of some practical use. [. . .] I only bother about this idea because her noticings (is that the English equivalent?) are so extraordinary. I am quite sure nobody has ever written to touch her, not even Lawrence. That sentence, or pair of sentences, about the shadow on the wall, seems to me to contain such a lot: the suggestion of gaiety, sinister because heartless, at the very centre of life – yet only a mask! What looks through it is still a mystery. (126)

He admits that 'there is a lot about her I don't care for', and mentions 'the childish racket', the 'fits of temperament', the 'self will', though he finds excuses for each of these in her illness, as he does for what he calls the 'crankiness & mystic notions & dramatics' (126). He acknowledges that the stories don't measure up to the quality of the literary mind found in the letters and journals. But what we find in this correspondence with Monica Jones is a notable literary intelligence *engaging* with Mansfield, thinking it out as he goes, and relating what he finds there to his own life and his work as a writer.

How does this fit with the current received notion of Larkin? To me it came as a very pleasant surprise, a bonus in a book which has, of course, a great deal else to admire and enjoy.

Janet Bites the Hand . . .

The latest publication in what has become a virtual campaign by Janet Frame's literary executors to keep her name alive and her reputation bright before the public is a novel, *In the Memorial Room*, written in 1974 while Frame was holding what was then called the Winn-Manson Katherine Mansfield Fellowship in Menton. An unsigned Foreword tells us that Frame was awarded the Fellowship in 1973, and that she spent the following year in Menton on the Côte d'Azur. This award is associated with the Memorial Room beneath the Villa Isola Bella, where Mansfield lived and wrote for a time – 'a small stone room' the Foreword explains, 'commemorating her work and given to the Mansfield Fellow as a place to write.'

Though she struggled to work in the difficult conditions of the Memorial Room – with no running water or toilet facilities and delays in receiving her fellowship payment – it was in Menton that Janet Frame wrote *In*

A review of Janet Frame, *In the Memorial Room* (Text Publishing, 2013), published in *Katherine Mansfield Studies*, vol. 6, 2014, now slightly revised, and with the addition of the poem at the end.

the Memorial Room, the story of Harry Gill, writer and recipient of the Watercress-Armstrong Fellowship.

Frame, we are told, did not allow publication of the manuscript during her lifetime. She worried that 'certain people' might 'see themselves in the characters portrayed and, finding unflattering portraits, be offended.' But we are assured she always intended the novel to be published posthumously, 'at the right time'. It had been put aside to be looked at later, while in the meantime she moved on to the writing of *Living in the Maniototo*, a novel interlaced with some of the same characters, events and places.

Now, almost forty years after Janet Frame wrote *In the Memorial Room*, on her second-hand typewriter, the wait is over.

This strangely ringing Foreword seems to suggest that the Menton Fellowship was less a favour to Frame than another set of difficulties to overcome, obstacles to be surmounted – slow remittances, no running water or toilet, second-hand typewriter. But now, for us, her readers, 'the wait is over'.

I was the holder of the Fellowship in 1972, two years before Frame, and I remember how disconcerted I was when the poet Anton Vogt, who had left New Zealand in a huff over I've forgotten what, vowing never to return, and who had taken up residence in Menton, wrote a scathing piece on Frame's behalf in the *New Zealand Listener*, condemning whoever was responsible for providing for her so inadequately during her tenure. I knew there was a struggle to keep the Fellowship going (it has continued almost year by year right up to the present), and this was the kind of publicity which could only have an adverse effect on its chances of survival. I wrote a piece, in effect an answer, for the same journal, explaining that one was not obliged to use the room as a work place; that having three small children I had chosen to use it and had found it not without its charms and advantages; that there were plans to improve it; that meanwhile there was a public loo in the little Garavan railway station only two minutes' walk away – and so on.

Vogt had in fact provided Frame with accommodation in a villa attached to his own house; and he and his wife would have found themselves unflatteringly portrayed in this novel, as would several of the members of the Watercress-Armstrong (i.e. Winn-Manson) fellowship committee, whose naive enthusiasm for the work of the writer they commemorated, Margaret Rose Hurndell (i.e. Katherine Mansfield), is mocked. Celia and Cecil Manson and their son Bill, in particular, are cruelly lampooned and would have been deeply hurt. Frank Sargeson, posthumously celebrated for the help he gave Frame at a crucial time in her life, used to say that helping Janet was a risky business: you were as likely as not to be punished for it in her fiction – and those who awarded her the Menton Fellowship would have had cause to agree.

As for the poet Margaret Rose Hurndell, whose work is commemorated by the Watercress-Armstrong award: we are offered a couple of brief clips of her poems which seem (and Frame surely intends they should) pretentious and opaque. Harry Gill, the narrator and recipient of the award, reflects that Hurndell's poetry would probably be forgotten in a few years, and that the Watercress-Armstrong 'memorial gesture' might be destined for oblivion. It was a strange idea indeed to make the tenure of a literary fellowship the subject of a fiction written while holding a similar one in the same town; and all the more so when it offers 'a horrifying vision' of the creators of the fellowship 'feeding on the death' of the writer commemorated, 'nourishing themselves with the power of permanence which death has and which they so much desire'.

But none of this would matter too much if the novel, only now publicly revealed, were indeed, as the jacket blurb announces, 'a funny, nuanced and brilliantly witty masterpiece . . . Frame at her sparkling best'. Do we care if a brilliant novel or poem unfairly skewers some innocent and worthy victim? Think of Lawrence's fictional version of Lady Ottoline Morrell, Huxley's of Middleton Murry, Mansfield's of Francis Carco; or (this has a long history) Dryden's of Shadwell and Catullus's of Caesar. It's a matter of interest; something to be noted by scholars; a reason for tut-tutting and sympathy sometimes. But if the work is successful and important, the circumstances and people who occasioned it are not of primary concern – less and less so as time goes by.

In this case, however, the claims made for the novel are grossly exaggerated. It arouses interest because anything by Frame does. It certainly deserved preservation, and attention by scholars and critics. But I seriously doubt it was wise, or will serve her public reputation well, to have put it out in the commercial marketplace promoted in these extravagant terms.

★

Harry Gill is a 33-year-old writer who has been awarded the Watercress-Armstrong Fellowship in Menton. Differences between this fellowship and its recipient on the one hand, and the originals in real life on the other, are clear. Gill is male and younger than Frame was when she received the award; and the writer commemorated is a poet whose dates are quite a lot later than Mansfield's. Beyond those details, however, there is not a lot of space between the fiction and the reality.

Harry is met in Menton by Connie and Max Watercress, their son Michael, and other members of the Welcoming Committee. He represents himself as personally insignificant and is made to feel his work is unimportant and that he doesn't look or behave like 'a real writer'. The Watercress son, Michael, on the other hand, with a big beard, great confidence and early signs of literary talent, exactly matches Connie and Max's idea of a perfect recipient of their award. At a reception the mayor supposes Michael *is* the Fellow, and has his photograph taken for next day's *Nice-Matin* shaking his hand. At a restaurant Michael is again mistaken for the Fellow and given free champagne, while Harry is overlooked. Later in the novel, when Harry goes deaf overnight, Connie and Max will attempt to persuade him to give up the fellowship in Michael's favour.

The senior Watercress pair are both unsuccessful writers. 'Somehow their writing life had been separated from their ambition'; but the death and fame of Margaret Rose Hurndell had allowed them 'to bask [. . .] in the reflected glory. They flourished in her fame.' This reverence is another cause for Harry's sense of his own inadequacy. The key to the Memorial Room is handed over to him with much emotion, and when he goes there alone, the room (unmistakably modelled on the Mansfield memorial close to the little Menton-Garavan station) is described as 'another grave for her, to keep alive her death rather than her work'. It is, Harry reflects bitterly, a 'unique memorial, to pay a writer to work within a tomb!'

One of the problems throughout this novel is that it is at times a non-realist work of symbol and fable, at others a literal recounting of Frame's experience of the Fellowship and a vehicle for her personal grumbles and deeper anxieties. So immediately after the sentences quoted above come complaints about the 'sheer physical discomfort', the lack of 'running water or toilet, little light and little warmth', the 'roar of the construction machinery [. . .] and the constant close passing of the trains'. Gill is not pleased, and neither was Janet Frame.

At quite another level of reality (or unreality/symbolism) Harry tells us he is going blind. When he informs the local GP, Dr Rumor, of this he is told his eyesight is perfect and that he is displaying 'incipient signs of intentional invisibility'. 'You are trying to make yourself invisible [. . . .] Like a child who shuts his eyes and thinks no one can see him.' Dr Rumor reminds him of the recent history of 'annihilation of races' and adds, 'There's another form of annihilation, obliteration, if you will, of a psychological nature, practised by human being upon human being.' And he goes on that Harry is co-operating with his assassins, and may be about to vanish altogether.

Harry rejects this at first, but then seems to accept it as fitting his case. 'I found myself thinking again and again of psychological annihilation.' His 'habitual method of dealing with his life', has been one of 'passive submission'; and in such a case 'a storm of unusual force, a combination of aggressive personalities', might indeed result in his destruction. It would be 'like wolves descending from the mountains upon the timid sheep'. We are clearly in Frame territory here, and it's difficult to see this quite as 'fiction' – rather a moment of more than half-serious self-inspection by Frame in her own person.

Harry has found himself a dingy, smelly one-room apartment – all he could afford on the 'rather meagre Fellowship'; but Elizabeth and Dorset Foster, members of the Welcoming Committee, now rescue him from this and set him up in their spare villa next door (as the Vogts did for Frame). The opportunity seems to exist for the mood of the novel to lift; but soon, from feeling overlooked and slighted, Harry finds himself swamped with attention, including further offers of accommodation he now doesn't need. Feeling patronised, and armed with Dr Rumor's warning that he may be in danger of psychological annihilation, he begins to suspect and resent the attention even more than the previous neglect. The Watercresses are regularly 'claiming' him, 'for a journey, for a visit, for a meal'. He feels they are enlisting 'my co-operation in their annihilation of me and their replacement of me by their son'. Once he has brought this to consciousness he is no longer afraid of them. 'The Fosters were more to be feared.' And unfortunately they have him trapped in the little house in direct view of theirs. He feels he is a captive. 'And so they descended upon me. Where could I, Harry Gill, hide?'

Elizabeth Foster is the older sister of Margaret Rose Hurndell (they were named after the royal princesses of Frame's childhood) and is part of the Committee which includes Liz Lee and her husband George, an Englishman whose speech is so astonishingly unintelligible that each time he says something, what Harry hears is 'Angela will be livid'. As the novel goes on, and Harry gets to know him better, this becomes 'Angela will be livid. Old, retired'. This is the novel's best, and most characteristic, Frame joke – based on language, and with a delicate nuance of Kiwi versus posh-Pom antipathy.

Though he now has a place to live and write, the excess of attention impedes progress with his work – and with Frame's too, it seems. There is no narrative momentum – indeed hardly any movement at all; and it's here that Frame/Harry introduces a new experiment. Harry has been reflecting on the idea, prevalent in Menton, of 'retirement', and how 'human beings' (Frame novels are prone to pronouncements of this kind) 'live their lives in a prison of images', trapped by 'the appalling deceit of language', in particular the metaphor of the journey. Harry has heard of an Englishman, an expert on Shakespeare, who retired to Menton vowing to speak only in nouns and verbs. 'All references to emotion were excluded because they could not be described accurately. There was no reference to things of the spirit: no abstract words [. . . .] No thoughts.' His intention was to '[strip] his mind of the corruption of language'.

This is an idea that appeals to Harry. Wanting to hide from the Hurndellites who are besetting him,

> I retreated into my novel, I became the retired professor, and if you want to find me, you must look there, and [. . .] you will find Harry Gill, living his pure life, unadjectived, unadverbed, fully nouned and verbed, and numbered; and you will read of the consequences of his decision: '*Quick now, here, now, always* – '. In the next chapter.

This introduces what I'm sure must have been an accidental ambiguity about whether what we are reading has become the novel Harry is writing, or continues to be, as it began, only an account derived from the journal of his 'tenure'. That question apart (and I think it would be fruitless to labour it), the effect of this decision, which carries on through chapter eight and on into nine, has to be seen at some length for its full effect to be felt. On me it struck a seriously false note, somewhere between free-wheeling vacancy and pretentiousness. For example:

> They asked me was the heater working. I said yes the heater was
> working. The heater was a radiator with thirteen panels, filled with
> oil which heated when the heater was plugged into the electricity.
> The switch could be adjusted on a scale from one to ten, with a wattage
> from seven hundred and fifty to one thousand, a medium warmth. It was
> grey, with small grey rubber wheels making it portable as far as its flex
> of two metres would stretch without pulling the plug from the power
> point set five centimetres from the passageway into the hall upon a
> yellow-painted skirting board.

And so on – and on – at great length. This experiment in literalness, which is perhaps (who knows?) intended to illustrate the unsatisfactoriness, the deadly-dullness, of realist fiction – in other words that there is no escape from 'the deceit' of metaphor, symbol, fable, myth – runs on for a dozen dire pages, but breaks down when Louise says to Harry, 'Your time is your own.'

'It isn't, you know', Harry says, and his 'three thousand words without adjectives, without judgment, feeling, thinking' have been derailed by a 'time-image from within the convention of the myth'.

The novel ambles on now with further lucubration on time, retirement, the discontents of Menton's inhabitants, the ferocious competitiveness of Margaret Rose Hurndell's devotees and the necessary 'emptiness' of the novelist, whose consciousness must make space for his characters. By chapter thirteen Harry is able to describe his state in Menton as 'settled'; but the Fosters, keen to look after him even better, decide improvements must be made to the house, all for his benefit, and once again he is beset everywhere by noise and activity.

Harry is anxious about his larger role as writer: 'My fellow writers have called me a man of straw. I do not write political articles. I do not march in demonstrations. I do not make my voice heard against tyranny, injustice. In private life I turn the other cheek as I murmur, *I understand the motive.*' This may well have been an anxiety of Frame's, though I don't think any of her fellow writers ever called her a woman of straw, because it was always accepted that she'd had a rough ride in her early years and was, so to speak, exempt from kitchen duties.

Just over two thirds of the way through the novel, Harry's encroaching blindness is abandoned, or set aside, in favour of a new disability. He wakes to find himself stone deaf – a significant shift in the narrative's underlying metaphor; and the consequences of this disaster will account for the very little, in terms of action or event, that follows. Dr Rumor, to whom Harry now returns, describes his condition as 'Auditory Retaliation. [. . .] A sealing-off, a closure. Auditory hibernation.' After a few more (written) questions from Harry he replies (also in writing), 'everything is favourable for your obliteration. You have been stifled, muffled, silenced. You cannot cry out because you cannot hear the cries of others.' He recommends that Harry 'Just wait and see. I think your condition will cure itself.'

So the ending of the novel occurs like a slow loss of vital functions, but with the following momentary snap to attention: 'Whatever the explanation I accepted my deafness with a passivity which, before the age of the raging clitoris, would have been looked on as feminine!'

Harry refuses to see a specialist and tells everyone (always in writing) that the condition is permanent and incurable. He does however resist the attempt of the Watercress parents to wrest the Fellowship away from him for their son, even discovering a kind of confidence, not so much in himself as in, or through, the comparison with Michael, and the latter's lack of true literary substance:

What a paragon of a writer he was! I simply couldn't deny it [. . . .] and although I did feel a sneaking jealousy of his ability to play the role in costume of a writer [. . .] his talent did not match his appearance [. . . .] His thoughts and the thoughts of others were constantly on what he would achieve, on what he would become. [. . .] Poor chap, I thought. He's already going to seed. Destroyed by his promising future. A man without a past or present.

Dialogue is now confined to what can be written on scraps of paper. There is a lack of conviction in the writing, and of substance in the story. One feels Frame's reluctance to continue and her resorting to what reads sometimes like vacuous self-imitation:

I had not realized until then that we own the words we speak as we own the food we swallow or reject; we own the words, command them, shift them, re-emphasise them; they, powerful, have little power over our speaking them; the loneliness that came over me was caused, I think, by the degradation of the words, their descent from the pampered sheltered ones to the homeless outcasts that could not be spared an inflexion or a morsel of emphasis or a loving hesitation.

She has lost the confidence that there is any story to sustain, and is only going through the motions. The novel concludes with variations of 'last words' of the kind put at the end of a letter, repeated over and over; and then passages that seem to be copied from a manual of 'rules for good writing', six or seven pages of them, going wearily nowhere, saying nothing.

This is a looking-in-darkly rather than a looking-out-bravely novel, with an exceptionally unappealing and self-disliking central character. It is also fiction which makes surprisingly little, nothing in fact, of the visual lift offered by its Côte d'Azur setting.

★

Half way through the novel Margaret Rose Hurndell's sister explains to Harry, 'I'm here – we're here – more or less to guard Rose's interests, not in a material way, in a memorial way.' There is certainly an irony in the fact that a novel about the memorialising of a dead writer, which is in part a satire on such pieties, should be posthumously published as itself an act of memorialisation of (as the jacket reminds us) 'one of New Zealand's greatest writers'. I find it very difficult to believe Frame could have thought the novel was finished, or that she would have wanted it published in this unsatisfactory state – but her executors are clear it was so.

The joke about the man whose every statement is heard as 'Angela will be livid' was for me a small flashing reminder of what good company Frame could be, how clever and funny as well as serious – both in person and on the page. Of course there is intermittent but clear evidence of her great talent, and sometimes just the unmistakable ring of authentic Frame sentences. But there is too much unfiltered resentment and malice, too much self-pity, unevenness of tone and uncertainty of direction – and in the end, no shape.

From the example of Mansfield and many others we know that the enthusiastic heirs of a writer's copyright, the 'keepers of the flame', as Ian Hamilton called them in his book on the subject, are not always the best or wisest servers and preservers of a literary reputation. Much that has happened since Frame's death has repeated the lesson.

'The memorial room'

Janet Frame in Menton

This blue sky

                blue sea

           she seems to have seen

neither

              attuned only

to her own
inner
                culture of complaint

blind to orange roofs
and ochre walls
                and the transparencies
                        of a sea
with so many
memories

                deaf to the gulls
that when the wind is up
                cry all night
and the daylong
twitter of swifts

        neglected when none will help
        put upon when help is offered

is this ingratitude
                        or only
                the solipsist's
sad and solo cantata?

                            Menton, June 2014

Margaret Scott, 1928–2014

I first knew Margaret Scott as the wife of Harry Scott, a noted lecturer in psychology at the University of Auckland, and as the sister of Jonathan Bennett who, with Robert Chapman, co-edited the 1956 *Anthology of New Zealand Verse*. Harry Scott was killed climbing in the mountains of the Southern Alps early in 1961 when Margaret was pregnant with their third child. Margaret moved south to be near her parents in Christchurch and I lost sight of her until she began to emerge as the Turnbull Library's Mansfield expert and the chief transcriber of that famously difficult handwriting. In between had come her years alone with three children, facing more than the usual difficulties of a woman looking for secure employment equal to her talents.

It is worth mentioning here that of those three children, Jonathan is now Professor of History at the University of Auckland, Rachel was a few years back appointed head of Otago University Press, and

An obituary contributed to the Katherine Mansfield Society's *Newsletter*, December 2014.

Kate (named Katherine after K.M.) is Professor of Psychological Medicine at Otago University – an extraordinary and brilliant group, and a tribute to their solo mother as well as to their own genes and character.

One person who helped Margaret through those middle years was Charles Brasch, New Zealand poet, founder, and for some years editor, of New Zealand's most important literary journal, *Landfall*. Brasch had been deeply attached to Harry, and Margaret was to become, in recent years, the transcriber of Brasch's journals as they were prepared for publication. So, late in life, Margaret was able to read with benign amusement Brasch's first impressions of herself, and descriptions of her marriage to Harry. At this time she and I were in irregular email correspondence, so I would hear of her latest discoveries about Brasch and his agonies about his own sexuality. She was also reading there about herself in the 1960s, and her own love affair with Brasch, apparently his first.

In 1971 Margaret was the first recipient of the Winn-Manson Mansfield Fellowship to Menton, and there is an account of this in her book *Recollecting Mansfield* (2001), which also offers a description of her work on Mansfield at and beyond the Turnbull Library, and of her association with Brasch. I received the Fellowship the following year, 1972, and Margaret gave me and my wife Kay a briefing about what to expect there and some advice (not all of it wise, I have to say) on 'how to deal with the French'. My own first work on Mansfield followed from that Fellowship, and so I was always aware of, and often in touch with, Margaret as a major figure in the field, someone whose intelligence I admired, and whom I thought of always as one who could be 'temperamental', but generous, sensitive, herself a stylist of refinement, an entirely appropriate person to be dealing with K.M.

She wrote to me frankly about periods of depression, and sent me a memoir which included this: 'In those days I used to drink too much. I treated my depression with alcohol although I was aware the anti-depressant effect was always extremely brief and always followed by an intensification of the depression.' Though she had the intelligence, the dedication and the resources at hand for Mansfield scholarship at the highest level, she lacked confidence, and it was for this reason that a co-editor (Vincent O'Sullivan) had to be found for the letters she was transcribing. The two-volume *Notebooks*, which she did alone, are notable transcriptions, very useful in correcting impressions given by those Middleton Murry compilations which he called 'The Journal' and 'The Scrapbook' of Katherine Mansfield, and essential in themselves to any Mansfield scholar; but they need further scholarly work, and are being re-edited by Claire Davison and Gerri Kimber for the collected works coming from Edinburgh University Press. Margaret was very generous in granting permission for the re-use of her work as a transcriber, and a significant number of stories and fragments in the new *Collected Stories* are likewise taken direct from her transcriptions of the notebooks.

We are all in Margaret's debt for her transcriptions, and as a source of information. Her book *Recollecting Mansfield* is both entertaining and informative, and includes colourful recollections of L.M. (Ida Baker) and others. I remember Margaret with fondness as a notable co-worker in the field of Mansfield studies, an elegant, witty and intelligent writer, and one whose e-messages I have sadly missed since the shades of dementia began to close around her two or three years ago.

Some Railway Journeys in
New Zealand Literature

New Zealand, like Italy, is a long thin country with many mountains. Unlike Italy, however, it is also sparsely populated. This meant that before air travel became common, rail was very important. It also meant that there was never enough public money to build the kind of rail network the country really needed. Also significant is the fact that very early in our history a decision was made that we should have a narrow gauge railway – I suppose for cheapness – and as a consequence the developments possible in modern times have been limited. Finally, and possibly worst of all, in the 1980s a government infected by Reaganomics, Thatcherism and the Friedmanite fashion for 'user pays' and the privatisation of public assets sold the national railway to an overseas company which promptly engaged in cutting staff and services, closing branch lines and general asset-stripping. At present it's hard to see how New Zealand rail services can ever recover from

This invited paper was presented at VIII Convegno Internazionale Da Ulisse a . . . Il viaggio in treno tra storia e memoria ('The railway train in literature and memoirs'), Imperia, on 2 October 2007.

the damage that was done during those few years of self-defeating economic puritanism.

When I was young, which as you will see at a glance was a long time ago, I lived in Auckland, the largest city. When, as a student, I went south to the capital, Wellington, either to, or on my way to, a winter tournament, or to do my military service, I always travelled second-class on the night train, which left Auckland around six in the evening and pulled into Wellington twelve or thirteen hours later in the early morning. This hellish journey has an almost exact equivalent for me now when the second leg of my journey home from London is the twelve-hour night flight from Los Angeles to Auckland, which gets in at around 5 in the morning. The difference is that in the past I covered 800 kilometres in the twelve hours; now I cover about 10,000 kilometres in the same time.

One thing I noticed when I thought about my brief for today was that the examples that occurred to me all suggest travelling by rail in New Zealand involved slow speeds, open windows and a great deal of stopping – time for the fiction writer to look out, think, take in a scene and try to make sense of it. It's as if rail travel was a window on a world requiring interpretation, and therefore imagination. Here's the 19-year-old Katherine Mansfield, exactly one hundred years ago (November 1907):

> There is something inexpressibly charming to me in railway traveling. I lean out of the window, the breeze blows, buffeting and friendly, against my face, and the child spirit, hidden away under a hundred and one grey city wrappings, bursts its bonds, and exults within me. I watch the long succession of brown paddocks, beautiful, with here a thick spreading of buttercups, there a white sweetness of arum lilies. And there are valleys, lit with a swaying light of broom blossom.

There's more of that – teenage literary musing as she and her carriage drift through the landscape. And then she records, 'At Kaitoke the train stopped for "morning lunch"' – and she describes what she calls the 'saloon' on the platform:

> . . . a great counter was piled high with ham sandwiches, and cups and saucers, soda cake and great billys of milk. We didn't want to eat and walked to the end of the platform, and looked into the valley. Below us lay a shivering mass of white native blossom – a little tree touched with scarlet – a clump of *toi toi* waving in the wind, looking for all the world like a family of little girls drying their hair.[1]

This is clearly rail travel of an existential kind, where the journey is more important than the destination. The young Mansfield, back home with her 'boring family' (as she called them) after three years being schooled in London, is burning to get away again. Meanwhile she experiences rail travel up into the central North Island as freedom, escape. She becomes a tourist in her own land. Everything seen is relished, and tends to beauty.

In a story called 'Chapter' by Maurice Duggan, another New Zealand writer noted especially for short fiction, you find the same sense of rail travel as something slow-paced, even static, providing a window on a life other than one's own. But Duggan's temperament, much darker and more brooding than the young Mansfield's, determines that what is seen is neither happy nor beautiful. The story begins:

> The train slowed and came to a stop; the fleeting country settled and was still. Out of an empty sky the sun beat down on the stationary carriages and the iron roof over the platform. The single line of the railway ran up past the bright hot shed of the station and went on away from it, not turning, until it was lost in the horizon. A few withering weeds grew between the ties and except for a bright strip in the centre the rails were dark with rust.
>
> Harry had fallen asleep. [. . .]

He woke now, hot bemused and uncomfortable, swimming from
sleep into a still thick lifeless world that burned and smoked; a silent
world from which he was insulated by the thick glass of the window as
from a painting in umber and yellow-green and grey over which was
imposed his own reflection [. . .]

Whereas Mansfield feels liberated by what she sees, and in imagination enters the world beyond the train, Duggan feels shut out
from it. He sees his own reflection in the glass superimposed on the
scene; and so his own dark mood determines how he reads what's
visible beyond.

As the story continues, and the train remains stationary, he sees a
Maori woman in a shed close to the line. She has a child with her and
he can see that she's weeping. Her distress is like a projection of his
own. He has a fleeting feeling that he can communicate with her, but
at that moment the train moves off. The passage concludes:

Something intimate had been shown him, something much more,
he felt, than a woman weeping. He could not believe that it had been
shown too to those passengers in other carriages; it was [. . .] part of a
nightmarish world created by himself over the years and made apparent
only by this journey.[2]

In my own novel, *The Singing Whakapapa*, the principal character,
Hugo Grady, lives a rather boring childhood in Auckland from which
the escape is north at holiday times to stay on the farm of his relatives, the Beaumonts. So, as with Mansfield, the rail link represents
escape into a desired world; and the slowness of the journey is, to the
boy, part of the pleasure.

The railway took you through the western suburbs, west of the upper
harbour, through Swanson and Waitakere, and then on north through
Taupaki, Kumeu, Huapai, Waimauku, Rewiti, Woodhill, Wharepapa,

Helensville, Kaukapakapa, Kanohi, Tahekeroa, Ahuroa, Woodcocks,
Kaipara Flats, Hoteo, Wellsford, Te Hana, Topuni and Kaiwaka. These
words, run together by young Hugo Grady, made up a romantic sentence
which, loosely translated, meant 'It's summer, school's over, and I'm
on my way to the Beaumont farm.' But in those days the sentence was
always articulated slowly. Those trains, pulling goods and passengers
together, seemed to stop at every shed-sized station (attached, most
of them, to nothing but a name, a dusty road and an empty landscape),
sometimes to shunt into a siding and wait, fuming, while a man walked
up and down the line hitting the big metal wheels with a hammer to see
that each was properly tuned for the next movement. Five hours sometimes, for sixty miles, like an opera by Wagner, and as Hugo's mother
would say of an opera by Wagner, never too long.[3]

One of the most interesting New Zealand examples of a rail
journey as part of a narrative construction is the one Frank Sargeson
uses in the third of his three-volume autobiography with the wonderful sequence of titles, *Once is Enough, More than Enough* and
Never Enough. I knew Sargeson well, and I remember him telling me,
while he was writing that third volume, how pleased he was with the
way he had constructed it around the image of two journeys north
of Auckland, separated by fifty years – the first early in the book,
the second right at the end. He spoke of this as you would speak of
a novel – much less concerned whether the events had happened
'really', or happened precisely as they were made to happen in the
book, than in their usefulness in giving it a structure, the quality of a
work of art.

So the second chapter of *Never Enough* begins with Sargeson per-
suading a young male friend that they should take their summer
holiday together. He writes of the pleasure he's had from 'slow train
journeys' south to his uncle's farm in the King Country. But, he goes
on, 'the line [north] right through to the Bay of Islands had now been
opened' and that was where he and his friend would go, taking a tent

for camping. And he concludes that opening paragraph of the second chapter with this remark:

> And so it all turned out. Also, for reasons I shall try to explain, I have had to live a long lifetime in order to see that rail journey as memorable beyond anything I could have been likely to imagine.[4]

That 1924 journey, as he records it, is notable especially for a moment when the train has slowed, his friend is looking to show him his first sight of nikau and kauri,[5] and Sargeson's eye fixes on the sight of the green valley with pasture, cows, a farm house and a stand of nikau. A great deal of emotion is attached to this visionary moment. In fact we are told that this glimpse of the distinctive northern New Zealand landscape 'had become to me instantaneous paradise [and] was too intoxicating'. It was to be the high point of his holiday, after which everything was anti-climax and disappointment.

Why the disappointment? This is not explained. We are simply left with the promise that at some point in the narrative we will learn why that moment was to become, in retrospect, 'memorable beyond anything I could have imagined'.

In the final chapter of the book, when Harry Doyle, his friend of many years (in fact his homosexual partner, though he doesn't say so) has died, Sargeson is making a new friend in old age, a man he refers to only as M. M. invites him to visit his property near Kaukapakapa (one of the little stations passed through by my Hugo Grady on his trip north to Kaiwaka and the Beaumont farm) and there Sargeson has his second revelation. He recognises that this valley is the one he saw fifty years before from the passing train.

> The sun was beginning to shine into the valley from the far end (as I would in another few minutes remember I had seen it do fifty years previously); [. . . .] And yet it was not at that moment that I remembered [. . . .] M helped me with [. . .] parcels and my loaded rucksack, and

immediately we were beyond the persimmon tree I saw the gable at the righthand end of the much decayed verandah. And I don't know why but it was the gable that did it. I abruptly dropped my share of the load, turned and walked back through the demented dogs and out beyond blackberry and stinkweed until I could look down onto the pasture and across to the railway line and beyond.

M had followed me.

'What happened to the nikaus?' I asked him.

And matter-of-fact, he replied that years ago he had cut them out, along with a lot of cabbage trees that had become too much for the good of the grass. But as for nikaus, there were plenty in the bush.

And there it was. The man I stood beside had been the ten-year-old boy I hadn't seen (but could have, it was only a question of timing), that fifty-year ago Christmas Day, when with my brother-in-law to be I had gone by crawling train along that railway line, and on up onto the gumland plateaus – to arrive in the evening at the Bay of Islands.[6]

What makes these passages more interesting, I think, is to recognise the complex strategy Sargeson is engaging in. He was a man for whom homosexual relationships were the centre of his emotional life, but who had been traumatised – first by a puritan upbringing, with strict views of sin and punishment, and then by the shame of an early conviction for a homosexual offence, an event which put a stop to the professional life he had embarked upon as lawyer and civil servant. I think as a consequence of all this, and also of the times, which were still repressive, Sargeson tried to write books with undertones, codes, signals not recognised by conventional, 'proper' people but visible to more sophisticated readers, and especially to fellow homosexuals who would recognise the emotional core of his narratives.

So why was that first trip north in the end disappointing? He doesn't say. But one might have guessed, and if one reads his posthumous biography by Michael King this guess is confirmed. It was disappointing because he had been deeply in love with the young man he took with him on holiday, but this friend was to prove heterosexual, and in fact would subsequently marry Sargeson's sister.

And why was the vision of that green valley with its single kauri and its stand of nikau so pregnant with significance? Because it was, though unrecognised at the time, a promise of fulfilment in old age with his new friend M., who was already living there as a ten-year-old boy. And all of this meaning and significance proceeds out of the use he has made of a view caught from a slow-moving train, travelling north in 1924 – a fiction writer's strategy applied to what purports to be autobiography.

A paper on this topic, random and incomplete as it must be, can hardly avoid a brief mention of Janet Frame. This is not because she writes particularly about rail journeys (though if I checked I might find there are examples). It's because she was the daughter of a railway man, and her own autobiography is full of images of her father the engine driver, and of the railway houses they occupied.

Early in her narrative the family moves into a series of huts, which she describes in some detail, with bunk beds for Janet, Myrtle and 'Bruddie', and a bedroom hut for Mum and Dad and baby Isabel. Each of these huts was about 6 feet by 8 feet; the kitchen/living-room hut was slightly larger, with a stove with a tin chimney poking through the roof. There was a deep-hole loo which they called the 'dumpy'. Lighting was by candle and kerosene. 'It seemed to be always snowing with the snow lying deep around the huts and in the central courtyard.'

Soon after this the family move into a proper house in what Frame calls 'the heart of our railway country'.[7]

There was a time when it was rumoured from Stockholm that Frame was seriously in the running for the Nobel Prize; and in the few months before her death in 2004 these surfaced again. She was suffering a kind of blood cancer, kept alive only by regular blood transfusions; but this didn't stop a journalist from phoning to ask what she would do if she won all that money. She replied at once (remembering that sad Friedmanite sale to North American asset-strippers), 'I'd buy back the New Zealand railways.'

But I have to say that when I thought about New Zealand writers and trains, the one who I'm quite sure exceeds all the rest in the number and copiousness of her accounts of such journeys is Katherine Mansfield; and all of these (apart from the one I've already offered) occur in England and Europe. Her life, after she left home, was full of drama and tragedy, often involving movement from place to place – especially, during her last years (she died aged 34), to and fro between London and the Mediterranean where she went in the hope of escaping the effects of the northern winter on her tubercular lungs. (These places of escape included, briefly, Ospedaletti, very near Imperia, where we're meeting today.)

There are, of course, quite a number of Mansfield's European rail journeys recorded in her letters and notebooks. But instead of giving you one of those, I'm going to finish with a scene from the novel I wrote about her, called *Mansfield*.[8] So although my final example is not set in New Zealand, it does involve the hand of two New Zealand writers – Mansfield, who recorded the events, and Stead who borrowed them and converted them back from fact into fiction.

> Then came Marseilles, the effort of it, the gathering of her luggage, the long queues, getting her visa stamped again, the uncertainty about where from, and when, the train to Bandol would leave, the bruising rushes with the crowd as announcements and contradictions sent it surging from one platform to another…
>
> Simply to be on board, seated, with a compartment all to herself, as it turned out to be, and to hear the doors banging shut and the whistle blowing, was such a relief it almost cancelled the disappointment she felt at having eight Serbian officers and their two dogs push in with her at the last moment.

'Madame does not object?' one asked in French, bowing and baring a set of exceptionally white teeth under his black moustache.

She felt it would not have made any difference if Madame had; and in any case they were handsome animals, all ten of them, and, ill or not, this side of death she was not going to be indifferent to manly good looks. 'Not at all,' she assured him. 'More bodies means more warmth, *n'est-ce pas*?'

In their own language they discussed what this meant, seemed to come to an understanding, and all smiled at her together. Even the dogs smiled. She felt she had recruited a palace guard. It was a piece of good fortune. The train was not moving, despite a second whistle-blast from the guard and a wave of his flag. Out there on the platform a contingent of French soldiers were holding up the departure, demanding places on the train. The shouting grew louder. All at once they attacked. It was no outburst of good-humoured high jinks. These were angry men just back from the war zone around Verdun, bitter at what they had been put through while these civilians had sat at home. Why did people need to travel while there was a war on? Were they going on holiday?

They burst into the train, shouting, dragging passengers, men and women, old and young, man-handling them out on to the platform and taking their places. The Serbians were ordered out but refused. They too were fighting men, they insisted. They had been fighting for France, and had earned their places in blood. Coriolanus-like, they uncovered their scars. They were staunch, determined. Also, they were armed.

'Well, *she* must go,' a French soldier said, grabbing Katherine and dragging her towards the door.

The Serbian who had first spoken to her intervened, holding the Frenchman by the shoulder, towering over him. '*Non, Monsieur. Elle est ma femme.*'

The Frenchman, who smelled strongly of wine, tobacco and stale sweat, hesitated, then let her go. He didn't know whether to believe it, but it might be true (she was a foreigner), and clearly it would have been folly to intervene between such a large man and his wife. The Serbians eased him out of the compartment and secured the door with their dogs' leather collars. As the train began to move she could see civilians, some weeping, others angry and bruised, some with their luggage and some with nothing, all helpless on the platform. Up and down the train the French soldiers burst into a triumphant 'Marseillaise'.

She had been frowning hard, concentrating on the thought that whatever happened she must not cry. Now she smiled at her protector.

'Thank you,' she said. '*Merci beaucoup, Monsieur. Danke schön.*' And then, searching among the bits and pieces of several languages she'd learned in Germany, she added, not feeling quite sure it was the word she wanted, '*Hvala!*'

They laughed and applauded. 'My wife is a linguist,' he said in French. 'Madame is welcome. Now she will have a small brandy and a cigarette?'

1   These quotations come from *The Letters and Journals of Katherine Mansfield: A Selection*, ed. C. K. Stead, Allen Lane, 1977, pp. 27–28.
2   Maurice Duggan, *Collected Stories*, ed. C. K. Stead, Auckland University Press / Oxford University Press, 1981, pp. 99–102.
3   C. K. Stead, *The Singing Whakapapa*, Penguin, 1991, pp. 46–47.
4   Frank Sargeson, *Never Enough! Places and People Mainly*, A.H. & A.W. Reed, 1977, p. 16.
5   The nikau is a sort of sub-tropical palm, and the kauri a native pine that grows to enormous size. Both grow only in the northern parts of the North Island.
6   Sargeson, *Never Enough!*, pp. 143–4.
7   Janet Frame, *To the Is-Land*, George Braziller, 1982, pp. 29 and 31.
8   C. K. Stead, *Mansfield*, Harvill Press, 2004, pp. 235–7.

The Murry–Mansfield Muddle

T his is the first full biography written since the publication of the two-volume edition of Mansfield's *Notebooks*, transcribed by Margaret Scott, and the final (fifth) volume of her *Collected Letters*, edited by Scott and Vincent O'Sullivan. It also draws on all the previous scholarly work, including especially biographers Antony Alpers and Claire Tomalin, and further back the work of Ruth Mantz, Mansfield's friend Ida Baker and her husband and first editor John Middleton Murry. A huge amount of the work had been done, but much of it was scattered. What was needed was diligence in pulling it all together, and Kathleen Jones has been diligent.

She has a problem, however. Like every Mansfield scholar she faces the question of what to do about Murry, and Murry's subsequent families who lived, in one way or another, in Mansfield's shadow and with her ghost. Four of these (Murry himself, his son Colin and daughter Katherine from his second marriage, and his

A review of Kathleen Jones, *Katherine Mansfield: The Story-teller* (Penguin/Viking, 2010), published in *Canvas* magazine, the *New Zealand Herald*, 27 November 2010, p. 37.

fourth wife Mary) all wrote personal memoirs. Colin and Katherine suffered lifelong consequences of being, so to speak, inheritors of the Mansfield legend, or the Mansfield curse. So, no doubt, did the two children of Murry's third marriage; but one of these died young and the other has remained silent. Murry's second marriage, to Violet le Maistre, who modelled herself on Mansfield in dress and hair-style, wrote similar short stories and died young of TB, is like a bad dream; his third marriage, to an extremely jealous, angry and violent woman, Betty Cockbayne, is a nightmare. After all of that the fourth marriage, though peculiar, had to be idyllic, if only because it was peaceful; and that – idyllic – is how he and Mary both represented it.

This, then, is the scope of the present book's material – not only the 34 years from Mansfield's birth until her death in 1923, but (with strange mathematical symmetry) a further 34 until Murry's death in 1957. It is, therefore, quite wrongly named. Insofar as its subject is Mansfield, it is about her not only as 'story-teller' but as ghost. It is about a figure who meant no harm to those who came after, but who was sufficiently a force to be an occasional blessing and a frequent curse in their lives. Murry she made prosperous but left obsessed. She also made him publicly conspicuous. Without her in his life it's likely he would have been quickly forgotten, and the records he kept of his own life forgotten too. As the beneficiary and promoter of her literary remains, however, he has been exposed in all his ghastly well-meaning duplicity, weakness, woolly idealism and self-deception.

How to organise all this material in one book? If it had been arranged chronologically a good third of the book would have happened after Mansfield's death and the post-mortem tail might have seemed to be the life of the dog. The tail at the very least would have had the long last word. The method Jones uses to avoid this is odd, and not, I think, completely successful. The Mansfield story, the one which many of us, to some greater or lesser degree, know, is told in the present tense; while the Murry (and Murry family) story is told as a series of past-tense interludes in the gaps between sections of the main story. I suppose the intention of the present tense narrative is to represent it as somehow the foreground, the principal story, more vivid and immediate than the Murry story which is background and less important.

At times the continuous present tense creates verbal difficulties, even for an experienced writer such as Jones undoubtedly is; and the chronological leaps produce strange unintended effects – so that, for example, Murry's death in 1957 comes before the account of Mansfield's final moments in 1923.

There are details which scholars will quarrel over. Jones decides that the diagnosis of gonorrhoea, which Claire Tomalin made so much of, is wrong and that the symptoms which were taken to indicate it can all be explained by tuberculosis. Her dating of one or two items is contentious, and one is wrong. She follows fashion in making too much of Mansfield's teenage devotion to Wilde with its consequent girl-crush raptures in her notebooks. But the Mansfield story is all there, and for the most part it is well-told, vivid in representing her life, with its wide swings between hope and despair, principally in her own words.

Giving Murry such a large part in the story, however, has the effect of making it all seem grimier than it need have been. As I read the book I felt that Mansfield's heroism and literary brilliance were being needlessly tarnished by association.

2.

Book Talk:
Sixteen Reviews

An Important Modern Critic

I f Hugh Kenner's best book, *The Pound Era*, had had some other and more palatable poet at its centre it might have been recognised, as it deserves to be, as one of the great critical books of the twentieth century. That's not to say it is faultless, or without its bad habits, and it is Kenner's bad habits I should discuss first, one of which he defends in *Historical Fictions* as follows:

> Some years ago Donald Sutherland wrote a book about Gertrude Stein which among its other brilliances brilliantly employed an adaptation of Miss Stein's famous style. That was astute of him. Part of a writer's labor is to develop just the configuration of language that will serve a personal vision, and the critic who is going to write about that vision should have the sense to glean hints on how to do it from the writer.

We can be grateful that so few critics have followed this course, and that Kenner himself has not followed it consistently.

A review of Hugh Kenner, *Historical Fictions: Essays* (North Point Press, 1990) published in the *Times Literary Supplement*, 25 January 1991.

His worse weakness is for schools, programmes, wronged greats. I, too, see Pound as a major historical figure, a writer whose erratic genius deserves more intelligent celebration than for the most part it has received; but to make out a case for Pound which doesn't fully acknowledge his errors, follies and failures seems the least persuasive way to proceed.

Sometimes one has had the feeling that Kenner's confidence has become complacency, with a consequent casualness about the means of persuasion, as when, in *A Sinking Island*, he gave a context to his announcement that Charles Tomlinson (who probably doesn't deserve to be so onerously encumbered) was 'England's chief living poet', by discussing, not Craig Raine's and Andrew Motion's poetry, but the fact that one, as Faber's poetry editor, presides over 'a nest of sinking bards', and that the other, then poetry editor for Chatto, had been described in a newspaper as having a 'consumptive frame' and 'unquestionably sensitive' looks.

Discussing C. David Heymann's *Ezra Pound: The Last Rower* in the present book, Kenner suggests that there may be some unacknowledged critical and scholarly debts. Heymann's book is thus, if not discredited, at least depreciated, before we get to its central argument, which does not, however, depend on borrowed material. For a few sentences it appears that Kenner is going to face up to Pound's idiot conjunction of economic theory and anti-Semitism: 'The lure of false clarities, not to mention the Puritan susceptibility to devil-theories, helps to explain his vulnerability to anti-Semitism.' But then we are advised that Heymann (himself a Jew) would have been able to understand all this better if he had had the advantage of knowing 'that remarkable woman' Dorothy Pound, from whom the anti-Semitism derived, and who was merely exercising, 'with no malice whatever', something that used to be 'normal in British professional classes'.

After that perhaps one isn't altogether astonished to be told that Pound's 'angry lines about "kikery"' which interrupt the 'continuously sustained paradisaic vision' of Canto 91, 'are meant to record the manner in which vision is dispelled by upwelling frenzy'. Here is a part of the passage which Kenner refers to but doesn't quote:

> *Democracies electing their sewage*
> *till there is no clear thought about holiness*
> *a dung flow from 1913*
> *and, in this, their kikery functioned, Marx, Freud*
> *and the American beaneries*
> *Filth under filth . . .*

In these lines, which you or I might read as yet another, and late, explosion of the old deplorable spleen, Kenner discovers 'a moving, humiliating confession'. To read this kind of special pleading and insist that Kenner is a great critic poses the same kind of difficulty as reading the Pound passage and insisting that Pound is a great poet. Nevertheless, it is something I would want to affirm in both cases.

Critics of literature are not unlike mechanics with car engines or doctors with human bodies: they are seen at their best when they have to probe and explain what has gone wrong under the bonnet. Kenner's account of Saul Bellow's path towards the writing of *The Dean's December* brilliantly charts a decline from the dramatic ('presentative', Pound would have called it) to the ruminative. 'No writer has more authority with the feel of place'; but 'along the way Bellow has acquired an alter ego named Herzog . . . a Leopold Bloom with a PhD', who 'prides himself on the cogency of his moral reflections'. Worse, the Dean of the title is stranded in communist Romania: 'So his plight – killing time in limbo – is rather close to the plight of his author, who must fill a book with sheer inaction, and has consequently piped in . . . the Herzogian vitality to be gotten from *opinions.*' To make his point finally, Kenner goes back to early Bellow, and to the kind of 'comic epiphany that can salvage all'. 'Devoid of reflections', he concludes, 'it prompts them'.

His book is full of such concentrated intelligence. There is, of course, a kind of modern writer who engages his full heart and mind – Wallace Stevens, W. C. Williams, Robert Duncan, for example, among the poets; among fiction writers, Beckett, Nabokov, Flann O'Brien, Wyndham Lewis – all of whom figure in these essays. They are all intuitive innovators, and Kenner is impatient with the middle-of-the-road commercial style which he sees as always and only repetitive, doing 'mindlessly what was done yesterday'.

Yesterday's literary invention becomes today's conventional picture of 'reality'. The mould has constantly to be broken, the 'other' re-invented. This is the principle of 'make it new', by which the Larkin-icon must always (and would prefer to) fail. And it is here that the transatlantic differences become abrasive.

Kenner's writing has a personal voice. He has the civility to be himself – not to pretend to be nobody; or God. His criticism is demanding, yet it is also open and available, without needless and pretentious obscurity. It moves fast, engaging the literary intelligence on the run. It is a form of high scholarly entertainment, spiked with small pertinent narratives and with off-beat facts. He is the most readable of living critics, the one I should least like to be without.

Kiwi Kevin

Kevin Ireland is my age and a fellow Aucklander. I have known him on and off since we played on opposing sides (Mt Albert Grammar v Takapuna Grammar) in a soccer match when a leg (neither his nor mine) was broken and the crack echoed horribly around the Auckland Domain. We must have been, for the brief time (1951–52) when he was enrolled there, fellow students at Auckland University College – though I notice neither appears in the other's memoir of that period. In 1957, after I left New Zealand, and before he changed his surname from Jowsey to Ireland, Kevin used to visit Frank Sargeson, who sometimes wrote me news of him. Kevin and I both acknowledge a debt to Frank: if we are not 'sons of Sargeson' then perhaps grandsons. There has always been an affinity, though it has been at times a cagey one. Very recently we found ourselves in sixth-floor rooms of a cheap Paris hotel, looking out of our adjoining windows under the slope of the mansard roof, and agreeing that 'in

A review of Kevin Ireland, *Selected Poems, 1963–2013* (Steele Roberts, 2013) and *Feeding the Birds* (Steele Roberts, 2014), published in *Landfall* 228, Spring 2014.

the event of' a fire on the stairs no fireman's ladder from the street could reach us – the angle would make it impossible. It's the kind of thing that might figure in one of his poems.

The jacket shows the many faces of Kevin over the years, and I thought at first one might say that, by contrast with these several faces, the poems show just one – but that's not quite true. There is a predominant persona; but in fact there are, in the poems, two distinct Kevins. The best known, the most public and prominent, is the bluff hearty affable commonsense fellow with the moustache, with a glass of wine (always red), a broad grin, and a story full of bluster and exaggeration – self-deprecating if it's about himself, excoriating if it's about one of the (largely mythic however) Rulers of our Roost. In this role he's a latter-day Denis Glover, but always stopping, as Denis did not, short of self-immolation; and indeed there's a poem in celebration of Glover that seems unequivocal, but slyly, and *accurately*, slips in the qualifier: 'a great heart half-used'.

But the other Kevin, the one less well-known, hardly recognised behind all the noise and panache of his loud counterpart, is the sensitive, watchful, curly-headed, rather beautiful young man centre-page on the cover, who reminded me of something I wrote back in the 1970s – a long poem, 'Walking Westward' (a 'process poem' I think was the fashionable term), which ranged about autobiographically in time and place and, touching down briefly in London in the late 1950s, remembered

> Calamari in a Chelsea basement
> Shadbolt worrying about his lungs
> Kevin Ireland
>   lost child with a long nose
> sadly sketching

I didn't know Kevin well at the time I wrote those lines, which must have been fifteen years after that London encounter happened, and

I knew nothing of his personal and family circumstances. He was living overseas – and I would not see him again for possibly another ten. Yet the lines came as a memory, vivid enough to push themselves into the poem at that point – and what they recorded was not the jolly Kevin his public knows now, but a sensitive sad 'lost child', who might have gone underground but has never entirely gone away. He is the aesthete, the monitor, the stylist, even the 'soul' of these poems. He is there at almost every stage, largely hidden, but an extension of the range, an element the collection would be poorer without.

I wouldn't like to make too much of this, but I find myself connecting this Kevin with the boy whose mother, we now know, walked out on the parental marriage when he was nine, and whom he did not see again (and then only briefly, at his grandfather's funeral) until he was almost twenty. He writes about her in his autobiography, *Under the Bridge and Over the Moon*, rather distantly, honouring her achievements, admiring her as a woman, not as a – or as *his* – mother. There is a poem about her in the present collection, 'A volatile fluid'. The tone is uncomplaining, factual, and ends with the taste of the drink she pours him on that meeting after ten years, which tasted, he says, 'of mothballs and gasoline'. In the autobiography he quotes this line and says, 'though I felt I had to add "Or perhaps I imagined that"'. He says that this is 'a taste or general impression I sometimes can't get out of my mouth when I think of her. It's the flavour of a whole set of memories. Stale but still flammable.'

In the new book the poem appears again, with the qualifier line slightly revised: 'I couldn't have invented that' – but I think it still might not catch the feeling he wanted to convey, or not the full blast of it. To be abandoned by a mother who then made a success of her life must be more galling than if you found her later a wreck, a failure, someone you could pity. Yet Kevin himself is too worldly-wise to grumble about the hand life dealt him. Another poem in this group begins 'The hardest poem / is the one you write / about your mother' – which then goes on to illustrate how hard the task is by tying itself in a knot of images ending with the womb as 'a secret tomb / where serpents are fed / milk and roses'. The radical equivocation is there again, and not really resolved because it can't be. But it is surely the same child's deep resentment that arrives obliquely in a poem about something quite other – the US bomber pilot who named his superfortress 'Enola Gay', after his mother, before dropping from it the A-bomb that destroyed Hiroshima – the name 'a touching / good-boy sign of mother-love'. That, I guess, is the true voice of feeling.

His mother makes a much later appearance, old, incontinent and weeping in a hospital bed, conjoined in a villanelle with her son's dog, Daisy. The mother must unwillingly 'persevere', while the son was free to shoot the dog; and the poem ends

> I shot old Daisy in the head.
> My dog is dead.

But if there is *odi et amo* for the mother, the father – neither poet, aesthete nor stylist – is the practical man so frequently met in the fathers of New Zealand poets and writers, well-meaning though bewildered by the puzzling, possibly bewitched infant he has begotten. Kevin's father was serious and disciplined about catching fish, and there's a poem about how he worked at it, how it was not to be treated as fun or recreation, and how difficulties like bad weather and blistered hands were hardships rewarded by a good catch and the pleasures of cooking and eating it. 'Our fathers exist', he concludes, 'to uphold the law, not to make sense.' And perhaps there's a hint that catching fish and catching poems are not, after all, unrelated. An earlier poem, 'Skinning the fish', is first an almost technical manual for skinning and filleting, and then becomes a source of tropes for 'getting through', and so a manual for living.

There's a kind of shrewdness about a typical Ireland poem – 'Cloud', for example, which begins by describing the many things this particular cloud appeared to be, including

It was like nothing much at all
one minute, then the next
was quite definitely something.

One moment it was yellow
then in half a tick, I tell you
it was black and white, or red.

And it was silent, of course,
except when its guts rumbled
or it cracked its knuckles.

For a moment we might think here's a pictorial and picturesque sequence being worked up to go nowhere. But that 'in half a tick' reminds us this is not the poet so much as a character speaking – and soon it becomes clear he's telling a girl about the cloud because that's what she missed when she went 'off / on the pillion of that fellow / with the 1000 cc bike'. He's telling her he's sorry for her. Imagine roaring off on a fast bike when you could have been looking at the cloud! It's a small representative enactment of the sufferer of an ordinary ego-defeat soothing his pain.

Irony is one of his chief modes or tones of voice, unmistakable in his *Tiberius at the Beehive* collection, but a tendency throughout. He describes scenes brilliantly, reflects on them, charms, and then surprises with back-handed wisdom, or winners down the side-line. Or he's content simply to entertain. How would you give a poem called 'The protocol of laughter' a meaning to match the ring of that wonderful title? It's about one of those dreams where you meet the Queen – but in this one she's with her sister Princess Margaret on

Devonport wharf. Kevin suggests tea at the Esplanade hotel across the street. H.M. asks how you can drink tea in a dream – and they laugh so hard the poet falls out of bed.

Another called 'The extraordinary power of love' succeeds, not by irony at all but because it doesn't welsh on its hyperboles. There's a certain daring in that, and it works because the language tells you it was honestly felt.

Ten years ago when Kevin was the second recipient of the $60,000 Prime Minister's Award for Literary Achievement in poetry there were grumbles that others should have had it ahead of him; that his limitation was a lack of clarity about how 'seriously' he wanted to be taken (Murray Edmond); that he turned away from anything too dark and troubling and refused to dig deep (Iain Sharp). These statements of limitation might have been right or wrong; but at this distance, after another decade of Kevin simply being himself, making his mark in his own way, they seem irrelevant – one of the many bad side-effects of literary awards, which skew the market, confuse the critics, create envy and upset almost everyone except the winner, his or her family and their literary claque. With the passage of time, and the command that comes simply by long and consistent practice, a poet like Ireland earns – has earned – the right to be himself.

★

Taken together with Kevin Ireland, three of his closest contemporaries, Fleur Adcock, Peter Bland and Mike Doyle, tell a generational story of to and fro movement between 'here' and 'there', identity and anxiety. Adcock, with New Zealand parents, spent early childhood in England, returned and grew up here, became a poet, married and had two children all in New Zealand, and then, still young (perhaps thirty) scarpered to England where she established herself firmly and remains. Bland grew up in England, came to New Zealand as a young immigrant, established himself here as poet and actor, and since then has gone to and fro between New Zealand and the United Kingdom, each time buying a house ('a nomad in my own back yard') and announcing that journeying is over and 'home' has been found. Doyle, of an Irish family, grew up in London and was, like Bland, a 1950s (probably £10) immigrant. He made his start as a poet in Wellington and, after a stint as lecturer in Auckland, travelled to North America and settled in Canada where he has remained since the late 1960s, Professor of English at UBC Victoria, now retired. Finally Ireland, growing up in Auckland, left for Europe at the end of the 1950s and remained away thirty years, but retained always his literary connection with New Zealand, publishing his books here. It was in particular Robin Dudding who kept his reputation alive during those years – to such an extent I used to joke that the always late but high-quality literary journal Dudding edited, *Islands*, should be renamed *Ireland's*.

So when Kevin returned it was to a seat kept warm for him at the literary fireside. I don't know whether he ever tried to publish in the UK – probably not, or not very hard – and if he did it seems it was without success. Bland found an outlet there with Alan Ross and the *London Magazine*, and latterly Carcanet, as well as acting work in London theatres. Fleur Adcock of course has flourished in England, elected Fellow of the Royal Society of Literature and winning the Queen's Gold Medal for Poetry, the latter something also achieved only by Curnow among our poets.

Doyle's work belongs clearly in the literary history of twentieth-century Modernism and experiment, which has its own self-sustaining reach in academic studies. He has a family in Canada and a life he enjoys there; but his poetry, with its interesting history of experiment, and associated published work on William Carlos Williams and poetics seems to exist apart from all that, somewhere out in space. He has Canadian publishers but has not quite achieved recognition as a Canadian poet; and says or implies somewhere that he feels he escaped from New Zealand literary nationalism only to fall foul of the Canadian variety.

Bland, since the death of his New Zealand-born wife of many years, has finally, after quite absurd and surely needless difficulties with New Zealand immigration authorities, been permitted to come back to be with his children. His poems are as adroit as ever, but he has more the air of an actor without a stage than of a poet without an audience.

★

After I had begun writing this piece a new collection of Ireland's work, *Feeding the Birds*, was launched at the Depot in Devonport. We might have done without its publisher, Roger Steele, telling us that there were lines in this book that 'Yeats would have given his left hand for' – but I was struck by how at ease Kevin was among this big homely crowd of readers and well-wishers; and it's true that the lines Roger Steele quoted were a good example of a kind of eloquence that has the particular Ireland stamp upon it:

> Sometimes when the tide hangs low and flat
> against the rocks, and the massive fronds of weed
> waver from the deep towards the mirrored sky
> the sea becomes like love: soundless, rich, substantial,
> with questions far beyond all asking, a mystery of tones
> and shadows welling softly from the waters.

These late decades of his return to New Zealand (not altered by a recent third marriage that has had him commuting between Auckland and Oxford) have been a prodigal's return.

Curnow's literary nationalism, though 'of its time', was something of a mistake, especially in his later years when he clung to it like a dog with a favourite stick. Nationalism is tribal – something genetic which, in the world as it is now, we need to unlearn, or at the very least confine to sport and other non-lethal areas. But it is nonetheless true that poetry, and the language of poetry, do always, and innocently, tend to be regional; to signal 'belonging', 'our place', 'our words and our subjects'. This is not a rule but a general literary truth, and it's where Kevin Ireland's strength lies. Whatever the word 'Kiwi' means in the popular mind, it is a meaning that includes him, and is to be celebrated there.

Roddick is Back – A Celebration

As a poet slightly older than Alan Roddick I was very much aware of his presence on the literary scene in the early 1960s, and later as the author of a remarkable collection, *The Eye Corrects*, published in 1967. By that time I knew him personally, and from time to time we exchanged poems, and political arguments about current matters like the war in Vietnam. I was a great admirer of the economy and the quiet, sharp wit of his writing, especially effective in his reading of his own work, which his accent (more Scots to my ear than Northern Irish, though I think he grew up in Belfast) suited so well. Re-reading the few survivors from that first book reprinted here I'm reminded of the best qualities of our poetry in the 1950s and early '60s, the discipline that went into it then, the care and attention to form that became almost unfashionable as the 1960s rushed on into the '70s and '80s, when so much of poetry was given over to (or perhaps flowered-powered into)

An advance review of Alan Roddick, *Getting It Right: Poems 1968–2015* (Otago University Press, forthcoming 2016).

'self-expression', confession, and even self-therapy. Every age looks back on the previous one as in some way 'a mistake'; but the truth is that any mode can be well or badly done; any fashion can feed genius or its absence. Those early Roddick poems are among the best of their time.

I continued to look out for and admire new poems in periodicals subsequent to that first book, but they appeared less and less frequently, and finally not at all, though he continued to figure on the literary scene, author of a very good monograph on the poetry of Allen Curnow, member of the Literary Fund Advisory Committee and, after 1973, literary executor to the estate of Charles Brasch. It seemed his profession as a dentist finally prevailed over that of writer and (as he puts it in the introduction to the present collection) 'my muse and I seemed agreed I was not going to have a second book any time soon'. This was especially regrettable because some of the poems from that middle period – 'And the Swan?', 'Of Helen, in Hospital', 'Winter Pruning' – seemed to be taking him into new territory.

What a special pleasure then that from 2007 that distinct and authoritative poet-voice has begun to be heard again, with the same qualities of compression and exactness, tight form, high intelligence and keen wit. The new work, it seems, began with a residency in Fiordland and (going by the author's note) put him on board a ship somewhere in southern New Zealand waters in the company of other poets and artists. This experience must have set him researching and writing poems about Cook's second expedition.

Always a problem for a poet, 'starting up again' after a long break, is material (and modesty) – what have I to write about that anyone could possibly be interested in? One can see that this research into the Cook voyage gave him his material; and the poems he wrote, focusing on those historical subjects, in turn gave him confidence that his talent had not deserted him.

So from those big subjects out of our past Roddick could turn again to the day-to-day, the moments insignificant in themselves which it is poetry's job to make known and make important. 'Know that Bird' is a good example, when the poet forgets for a moment, or remembers wrongly, the name of piwakawaka (the fantail), harbinger of death, the poem ending when the bird flies off saying sinisterly, 'next time, *remember* me!' Or there is the very small poem about a toddler's very small shoe left in the rain, now filled with 'a foot of rainwater'. You have to attend to detail in these poems, as he does. In a poem about a family football match, in the line 'we do our best, to make it a draw' the midway comma makes the sense subtly different from what it would be without punctuation. In a clever poem seen from a child's perspective, the line 'the grown-ups are holding their drinks' means one thing to the literal child but much more to the adult reader. The poem 'Kevin, Still Talking', commemorating ten years since the death of Kevin Cunningham, contrives to be also a memorial of Charles Brasch, and to catch with exactness something – something quite different – about the two writers. 'A Musical Incident' recounts a performance of a Beethoven quartet in which the poet, 'all eyes as I listen / all ears as I watch', sees one of the performers, losing his place in the music, turn the pages back and forth in confusion until he finds the right one and the trio becomes a quartet again. It's as much action as idea that is caught here – as it is also, and more obviously, in 'Ashore on Anchor Island':

> You step
>
>   over
> (unhook your boot from)
> duck
>   (under)
> each loop or trailing
> tangle of cable:
> real bush wiring!

where the syntax enacts movement and forces the reader's mind to enact it.

Among the 'material' found lying about for processing into poems are, of course, memories of childhood, including his proximity to Seamus Heaney, whose accent (the Catholic one) Alan's Protestant father 'banned'. There are nice historical ironies here. When the father had to beat him for a misdemeanour it was always with the 'LDV belt', kept in a filing cabinet along with 'silk regalia for a secret Order'. LDV stood for Local Defence Volunteers – and no doubt the secret order would have been the Orange Lodge. Among these poems come the memories of 1946–47 visits to relatives in Scotland, a lovely group of poems that appeared recently in the prestigious *Scottish Review of Books*.

Sometimes it's no more than the precise cool placing of clearly remembered facts that give his poems their ironic flavour. Here is the boy Roddick visiting their Unitarian minister:

> I went once to see him and
> his three white goats
> and his two Welsh sisters.
> They gave me fried onions for lunch ...

Roddick is a 'cool' poet, a temperament that seems reserved, controlled, decent, funny and intelligent; a craftsman not a showman, with a fine musical ear, whose work is dependable and of the highest order. And as well as witty and clever work, there are poems that catch moments of deep feeling; and equally of exhilaration, such as the ten-year-old Alan standing up on the seat, his head through the sun roof of his father's car that is cruising downhill 'pushing 40' with the engine off to save petrol, 'drunk with the scent of heather and whin, / that airy silence ...'

The language can at times be rich and 'chewy' – you feel its texture as you read or speak it:

for I too was growing to know
your horse-powered harvests, the *crex-crex*

of corncrakes among the stooks,
the stench of retting flax

over crannog and souterrain
and The Twelfth of July's bullying

yammer of Lambeg drums.

Such richness, transported over so many years, and so many miles, to find its home here: it is for us all gain.

Roddick is writing as well as any New Zealand poet currently at work on the scene. It is wonderful to have him back – something to celebrate!

Virginia Woolf's Nightmare?

It is 27 January 1866 in the gold-rush town of Hokitika in New Zealand's South Island when a handsome stranger, Walter Moody, shaken by something terrible he has seen – dying man or ghastly apparition – on board the barque *Godspeed* from which he has just come ashore, disturbs a secret conclave of twelve assorted townsmen in the smoking room of the Crown Hotel. The men soon give up the pretence that they are unconnected and acknowledge their common purpose.

Thomas Balfour acts as spokesman, and with help from them all, tells Moody the events that have brought them together. A couple of weeks earlier three significant things occurred. The town's 'wealthiest man', having spent the night with a whore, disappeared. The whore was found almost dead of a drug overdose, and with no recollection of what happened. And a hermit landowner was found dead, apparently of natural causes, in his remote cabin which contained a fortune in gold.

A review of Eleanor Catton, *The Luminaries* (Granta, 2013), published in the *Financial Times*, 7 September 2013. The *Financial Times*'s heading, 'All that Glistens', was theirs, not mine. The book shortly afterwards won the Man Booker Prize.

Involved in the interlocking stories that follow there is a Jewish newspaper editor, an Irish Free Methodist chaplain, a dapper Norwegian merchant, a brilliantly quick-tongued Frenchman, two Chinese men (one a goldsmith, the other a prospector and opium addict), a grumpy but noble Maori prospector for pounamu (jade), a 'blackguard' sea-captain (who figures largely but doesn't appear until page 400), a fascinating whore, a pallid banker, a vicious jailer, a wicked widow, a publicly flamboyant, privately peevish politician ... and more, including bluff boring Balfour, a shipping agent. Finally there is the missing 'wealthiest' townsman, on whose absence the story pivots, and who emerges after 600 pages, and not altogether consistently with what has gone before, as a golden-haired, golden-hearted, truth-telling youth.

Each of these characters is developed over many pages. They are 'stock', but it is good stock. The reader comes to know and enjoy them. The mysteries and the melodrama multiply, each story seeming to lead into another. The tone is cool, the telling clear, almost hard-headed, except in one late aspect where it slides towards sentimentality.

It is related with exceptional detail and verisimilitude, and frequent moral/psychological observation: 'When a restless spirit is commissioned, under influence, to solve a riddle of another man, his energies are, at first, readily and faithfully applied. But Thomas Balfour's energies tended to span a very short duration, if the project to which he was assigned was not a project of his own devising. His imagination gave way to impatience, and his optimism to an extravagant ...'

And so on, at great length. I assume we have 'tended to span a very short duration' rather than 'did not last long', and the deletable repetitions of 'energies' and 'project' – and the chintzy upholstered tone of it all – in the interest of a pastiche of the nineteenth-century novel. Why else (for example) would the word 'damned' be spelled 'd__ned' whenever it occurs; along with 'b__er', and 'f__ing'? Even the 'wisdom' reads like pastiche. There is a feeling of precocious imitation – the literary equivalent, I sometimes felt, of unearned income.

Every episode has its setting, décor, clothing, its period bric-à-brac, its slightly formal but often sharp dialogue. This is costume drama. It is conventional fiction, but with the attention to fact and connection which the mechanical (cross-checking, keeping track and online research) facilities of the modern computer permit. That apart, only the author's cultural sensitivity in dealing with Maori and Chinese characters, and an occasional anachronistic word or phrase in the dialogue ('paranoid', 'serendipitous') locate authorship in the present.

The history of literary fiction in the twentieth century was a struggle, never entirely successful, to escape from this kind of writing. It is the mode of the novel in its Victorian heyday, with something also of the twentieth-century murder mystery which was always indifferent to literary Modernism. It is, you might say, Virginia Woolf's nightmare of how many steps back a woman might take the form if given her head and a room of her own.

All of this massive narrative has an astrological structure which I have allowed myself to pass over.

Exhaustively 'authentic', the story is also shamelessly implausible – in its particular events but more, in their fortuitous combinations. I discover my own limits here – those of the impatient realist. My difficulty is similar to one I have with much of Peter Carey's work (and Catton is quite his equal): that it doesn't allow me to forget, even for a moment, that *this is fiction* – the novel as game, played brilliantly, but at such length and so elaborately I couldn't entirely overcome that impatience. Ingenuity outruns admiration and becomes tedious. I finished the novel acknowledging enormous talent, but feeling the demands made on time and attention offered insufficient human or intellectual return.

There is also the problem that such a conventional 'story' requires a conventional rounding off and bowing out; but so many hares, false and real, have been set running, no tidy resolution is possible, and *The Luminaries* tails off in an untidy tangle of loose ends.

Colm Tóibín's Mary

In the few exchanges between Jesus and his mother in the Gospels, he shows her little feeling other than the irritation of a man who has important work to do. She figures as the Virgin only in the first of the Gospels, and is present at the crucifixion only in the fourth. But in works of art she has been represented frequently and movingly, both as the innocent recipient of the angel's inseminating light-shaft, and as the grieving mother nursing her executed son. Throughout its history the Catholic Church has enlarged on these narrative fragments. By Papal Bull it was decreed in 1854 that Mary was herself 'immaculately' conceived; and in 1950 that upon her death she was assumed bodily into heaven. If you can believe in the Virgin birth, why not these as well? But for Colm Tóibín, despite, or more likely because of, a Catholic upbringing, Mariolatry is absurd, and the story needed retelling.

In fact his Mary, a natural woman and not in the least virginal, is not pleased with her son nor with the company he has been keeping.

A review of Colm Tóibín, *The Testament of Mary* (Viking, 2012), published in the *New Zealand Listener*, 22–28 December 2012, p. 35.

His followers are earnest sycophants in whose presence Jesus (never named) has become a peddler of his own greatness, and of the wisdom of riddles – 'his voice all false and his tone all stilted'. 'I could not bear him, it was like something grinding and it set my teeth on edge.' Since his death his followers have become sinister manipulators of the truth, and of Mary herself.

The crucifixion is represented in its full horror, and Tóibín speaks through Mary when he sees it, not only as fact, but as symbol of the religion to come: 'foul and frightening', an 'unspeakable image'.

When I wrote my own version of the Jesus story, *My Name was Judas*, I wanted only to represent the known (or supposed) events in a way that a modern, educated and rational person could readily believe. That meant miracles and supra-natural events would have to be explained as appearances and misapprehensions, tricks even, rather than facts. That seems to have been part of Tóibín's intention too; but there is perhaps an element of ambiguity.

Mary, late in life, is being pressured to confirm what is becoming the authorised version – that she was present at the death, washed the body, saw the empty tomb and the risen Christ. None of this is true, and she rejects it; but she knows it is what the world will be told. But had Jesus performed miracles? It seems, at least in the case of Lazarus (though she has it only by hearsay), he may have.

Here I think Tóibín wants to show that, imagined as a reality, the idea of resurrection is a horror. Lazarus, deprived of the natural state of being dead, is represented as howling in anguish and pain. Christianity's central symbol, then, is either untrue or repellent; and Mary has abandoned her Jewish faith in favour, not of her son and his redeeming death, but of the temple of Artemis, goddess of childbirth and of life.

I'm surprised at the tone of UK reviews I've seen – 'beguiling and deeply intelligent', 'moving', 'lyrical', 'a poem in prose'. The prose is indeed lyrical, perhaps in parts too soft for my taste; but the message is diamond hard and uncompromising. Intellectually I understand

Tóibín's impatience: faced with the scientific realities of the twenty-first century, and the beauties of the natural world, why, except for its history, would anyone persist with this stuff? But only someone who grew up right inside it could reject it with such vehemence and disgust.

Not Part of the
Entertainment Industry

James Wood has been widely admired as the most knowledgeable, entertaining and demanding fiction reviewer of the moment. In this short, densely written book, different in style from his reviews, he offers a survey of the development of the novel as a European form. What interests him especially is what has happened in (relatively) 'modern' times – since Flaubert, whom he credits with the invention of what he calls 'the free indirect style', where the author both inhabits the mind of a character, yet remains detached, subtly signalling, even in first-person narrative, how readers might react to what they are seeing and hearing.

But his discussion takes him back further, tracing a line from Denis Diderot through Stendhal and on to Dostoyevsky, Proust, Knut Hamsun, Henry James, Ford Madox Ford, Joseph Conrad and the twentieth-century Modernists who learned from them.

A review of James Wood, *How Fiction Works* (Cape, 2008), published in the *New Zealand Listener*, 7 March 2009.

What is refreshing about Wood's book is that, in an unassertive but unapologetic manner, he has invoked what used to be called the Great Tradition, reminding us that fiction is an art, not a part of the entertainment industry, and that, like all the arts, it has a history which its best practitioners of necessity learn from and draw upon. Ignorance will not get you far – or not for long. Popularity belongs to the moment, not to the art. Among his heroes in this book few did very well commercially in their own lifetimes, and some, like Henry James, did appallingly badly; but they have lasted because there is a grace in the language and a depth in the psychology that survives changes in fashion and continues to speak to the intelligence and imagination of serious readers.

Learning from past writers, however, doesn't mean simply copying their methods. Literary innovation soon freezes into convention. Renewal has to be constant. Iris Murdoch's limitation is 'a Fielding-like devotion to excessive plot-making'. John Le Carré, and even Graham Greene, are capable of 'nice writing'; they are 'efficient' story-tellers, often 'elegant'; but their prose is 'a clever coffin of dead conventions'. They are masters of 'commercial realism', 'the most powerful brand in fiction', a set of 'mannerisms and often pretty lifeless techniques' which are 'economically produced, over and over again' for the marketplace.

Wood wrestles with the term 'realism' in relation to fiction. 'Seen broadly' it means 'truthfulness to the way things are'. That is the novelist's responsibility. But it is not enough. 'All the great realists', he insists, 'from Austen to Alice Munro, are at the same time great formalists.' They are concerned with the art, the artifice, of fiction; with the novel as literary form; with technique.

Though he rates Flaubert so high, he also blames him for his ambition to write 'a novel about nothing'; for his tendency to elevate the prose (*'le mot juste'*) above what it means. 'Detail', 'good observing', which Flaubert insists upon, are indeed crucial in fiction; but super stylists – Nabokov and Updike for example – 'at times freeze detail into a cult of itself'. At the end of this, the wrong path out of Flaubert, lies, in the realm of theory, the Barthesian notion that all that happens in fiction is writing, '*écriture*'; and in practice, the static, impenetrable, precious fictions of Robbe-Grillet and Nathalie Sarraute. Something richer, stranger, more demanding, more innovative than the conventions of commercial fiction, is called for. But the alternative is not prose for its own sake and the novel about nothing. It's a fine line, a big ask, a tough call – but why not? This man is serious, and I agree with him.

Wood is in some quarters disliked for reviews which were frank and, worse, persuasive, about what he saw as the weaknesses of some of the stars of contemporary fiction – Don DeLillo, John Updike, Salman Rushdie, Zadie Smith, Jonathan Franzen and others. In this book we hear little or nothing of those popular favourites; but we see the foundation of literary-historical knowledge and critical analysis which has given his reviews their confidence, coherence and authority.

Much as I admired the book, however, I thought it was more like a guidebook for writers than for readers; and that Wood's finest critical writing has come from his tough engagements *as a reader* with those famous novelists of the present day whose commercial tendencies he will not forgive.

Golding's Booker

An eighteenth-century-built ship on a nineteenth-century voyage to the Antipodes: this is such a perfect location for a Golding novel it's surprising it took him so long to think of it. Confinement, established social priorities against 'natural' pre-eminence, the drama of this played out in the 'wooden world' of a ship surrounded by the inimical element – perfect! And Golding was himself a peacetime sailor and in war a naval man who could describe the heave of the decks underfoot in a way that tells you he had experienced it, and its internal consequences. He was also a writer interested in the larger philosophical and moral questions of man's place in the universe and the notion of God. So his ship's captain, Anderson (it is probably intended we should think of Ahab), an angry tyrant, is also anti-clerical, and will not allow a clergy-man as any official part of the crew. Among the passengers there is Mr Prettiman, an atheist and 'inveterate foe of every superstition',

This was contributed to the survey in *Areté* 45, Winter 2014, of Booker Prize winners. William Golding's *Rites of Passage* won the prize in 1980.

who will soon be patrolling the decks with a borrowed blunderbuss, hoping to shoot an albatross to show that the idea behind Coleridge's poem is tosh. Even our first-person narrator admits, as they approach the equator, 'how much I had enjoyed these few weeks of freedom from the whole paraphernalia of Established Religion'. Before the journey is over Captain Anderson will have let his attack dogs, the seamen, loose on the passenger clergyman, the poor little Rev. Colley.

The story is told first in the form of a journal kept by the snobbish and self-important Edmund Talbot, whose ambition, now that his 'foot is on the ladder', he tells us is 'boundless!' The journal is kept for, and addressed to, his noble godfather, brother of the Governor of Van Diemen's Land (Tasmania) in whose service Talbot is going to be engaged. The godfather has secured this posting, and is thanked profusely at intervals. He has instructed that the journal should leave out nothing: 'Did you not say "Tell all"? You said, "Let me live again in you!"'

So when Talbot is involved in a sexual skirmish with Zenobia, one of a brace of 'doxies' travelling with Mr Brocklebank who passes her off as his daughter, and whose 'magnificent but foolish bosom' at dramatic moments 'heaves', we get as detailed an account of it as an eighteenth-century novel would permit: unambiguous, frank, but not by modern standards full. This, the novel's comic entertainment, is where the sense of pastiche is strongest – and it is sceptical Mr Prettiman's first shot with the blunderbuss that triggers Talbot's premature climax with Zenobia.

On the first page Talbot establishes his literary credentials and stylistic preferences. Noting that his parents had wept over him at the moment of departure and that, though moved himself, it had taken him only the length of the drive and a short way beyond to recover, he thinks his godfather will approve of this as 'manly', and remarks, 'We have, I believe, paid more attention to sentimental Goldsmith and Richardson than to lively old Fielding and Smollett!'

Later there will be references to Sterne and Defoe. So in placing his character, Golding places himself: these are his stylistic models; and though he won't be excessive or slavish in imitation, and we will not forget that we are reading a novel by a twentieth-century practitioner, those names establish compass points for stylistic navigation. The 'liveliness' of Fielding, Sterne and Smollett is what he aims for. This will be a comic novel, but – since its author is Golding – it must be qualified as tragic-comic.

Equally, Talbot's mention that he sleeps with Falconer's *Marine Dictionary* by his pillow signals that Golding, like his subject, intends to 'speak the tarry language as perfectly as any of these rolling fellows'; and in the pages before and after this statement we see, italicised, that rather than copper-bottomed their ship is *pitched within and without*, that they are lying to the hawser *in the good old way*, that Talbot's chests are *struck down below*, that the canvas bowl in his cabin has shifted in its *gimbals*, that the cannon are *bowsed down*, and so on – sea-language that gets into the dialogue too when the ordinary seamen are involved:

> The gunner nudged him. 'Wake up, Shiner. You wasn't even in the ship. We hadn't hardly come out of ordinary.'
>
> 'Ordinary,' said Mr Gibbs. 'That's the life, that is. No nasty sea. Lying up a creek snug in a trot with the pick of the admirals' cabins and a woman on the books to do the galley work.'

Talbot is shocked to discover that the Royal Navy crew is not an integrated unit but has been knocked together only days or weeks before sailing, and that its officers are not, as they should be, all gentlemen. When one such, Summers, whom Talbot considers 'the person of all this ship who does His Majesty's Service most credit', admits that he began as a 'common sailor' and got to be an officer only by '*coming aft through the hawsehole*', Talbot absorbs this and records that his reply was 'as dextrous as the occasion demanded, though perhaps spoken with a too magisterial aplomb'.

'Well, Summers', I said. 'Allow me to congratulate you on imitating to perfection the manners and speech of a somewhat higher station in life than the one you was born to.'

Summers will later remind him of this lordly reply, causing Talbot, learning as he goes, to apologise handsomely: 'I ask your pardon Mr Summers. It was – insufferable.' They discuss how hard it is in England to 'translate a person wholly out of one class into another', and are able to agree that the Rev. Colley is a case where the 'translation' has not been a success. His lowly origins are apparent 'in his physique, his speech, and what I can only call his habit of subordination'.

At this point in their conversation they know that Colley, for reasons of class and even more because he is a clergyman, has been the victim of the captain's bullying. The full details of this, the novel's central event, are not at this point known to Talbot, but he knows that Colley has been permitted to hold a religious service, and that he has appeared 'in a positive delirium of ecclesiastical finery!' Passengers and crew have been drinking, and Mr Prettiman is decrying this 'survival of barbaric finery'; but Colley is unaware of anything but the wonder of this ecclesiastical opportunity:

> . . . the sight of a parson not so much walking into such a place as processing into it – for there had been about him that movement, that air, which would suppose about it a choir, a handful of canons and a dean at least – this sight I say at once amused and impressed me. He lacked the natural authority of a gentleman and had absurdly overdone the dignity of his calling.

Some part of the action happens out of sight of our narrator. But what he next hears is applause, then Summers appealing to the Captain that the men are drunk and should be restrained. When Colley is seen again all his finery has gone; he is drunk, singing, wearing some kind of canvas garment.

His legs had no calves, but dame Nature in a frivolous mood had furnished him with great feet and knots of knees that betrayed their
peasant origin. [. . .] Then, as if seeing his audience for the first time,
he [. . .] flung out his arms as if to embrace us all.

'Joy! Joy! Joy!'

Then his face became thoughtful. He turned to his right, walked
slowly and carefully to the bulwark and pissed against it.

So Colley's shame before the whole ship's company is total. He is
helped legless to his cabin and refuses to move from his bed, except
to hide a letter he had been writing at intervals to his sister, an
account of his voyage. After a few days he is dead, seeming to have
willed himself to die, but the letter remains with Talbot, who finds it.
That letter, amounting to about a quarter of the whole narrative, is
pastiche in a style different from Talbot's journal. Colley's sentences
can ring with deep emotion, particularly on the subject of young
sailors stripped to the waist, and of the sight of Talbot sleeping; but
it is for the most part the plain style of its time, with trimmings of
Christian piety.

We hear essentially the same story Talbot has told, but from the
other side. We see Colley's misreading of Talbot, and recognise, as
he does not, that his too keen interest in the young sailors (one in
particular) has a strong homo-erotic element. He is revealed as good
but simple-hearted, well-intentioned, naive, honestly devout and
wholly misguided, the perfect victim for bored sailors who don't
lack encouragement from their captain. More detail is revealed,
especially of the grossness of the 'crossing the line' initiation inflicted
on him, and an apology from the Captain that followed it.

With Colley dead we return to Talbot's narration. There is an
official enquiry into the death, and what emerges first is the suspicion that Colley, having been more or less forced into drunkenness,
has 'suffered a criminal assault' by one or several of the seamen.
One of these, the splendid Billy Rogers, foretopman (reminding us

of Billy Budd, also a foretopman), is called. He is told that 'Mr Colley suffered an outrage' in the fo'castle, and asked, 'Who did it?'

He says he knows 'nothing at all' about this.

Making the question clear the Captain shouts: 'Buggery, Rogers, that's what he means. Buggery. [. . .] Come along, man! We cannot sit here all day!' So Rogers is being required either to admit guilt, or name others.

'Aye aye, sir', he replies. And then, after a moment's thought, 'Shall I begin with the officers, sir?'

This had not been anticipated, and it puts an end to the questioning, and to the enquiry. 'Very well Rogers, that will be all. You may return to your duties.'

Colley is buried at sea and Talbot promises he will write a letter to the sister that will be 'all lies' to soften the loss. But Talbot, regaining his good spirits and completing the account for his noble godfather, reviews the evidence again and concludes that Colley was indeed tormented outrageously but suffered no sexual assault. To the contrary, what happened in the fo'castle was an act of fellatio; Colley, all caution obliterated by rum, 'gave Rogers a chew'. This was the final shame, worse even than the public humiliation he had suffered, and it was this which caused him to lie face down in his bunk gripping the ring-bolt and refusing to move, or to be moved, until he died.

The novel sets in opposition the rational and the religious. Neither is ratified; but there is at least greater sympathy for the man of faith than for the men of reason. It is skilfully engineered so that we see the truth emerging bit by bit in three parts – Talbot's diary, Colley's letter, and then Talbot again as he discovers further facts and deduces beyond them. There is a fair amount of contrivance in all this, and some loss of credibility. How far the reader suspends disbelief will vary; but there are rewards for doing so.

However one might have thought *Rites of Passage* rated against the competition at the time, it probably looked an entirely worthy

Booker winner. Whether it reads now as the work of a man who only a few years later would win the Nobel Prize is more debatable. Probably the Nobel Committee would have seen Golding primarily as the author of *Lord of the Flies*, and to them *Rites of Passage* would have seemed a novel sustaining that bleak view of how cruel and brutal the group can be to the individual who, by whatever means, becomes separate and 'different'. To me it is not a novel that has any one of the qualities – great originality, exceptional vision, stylistic purity, intellectual brilliance, dangerous political integrity, risk – that one feels ought to define the winner of such a global prize. But the works of only a few Nobel laureates do. Literary prizes are for the most part a nonsense, at one level a critical distraction and at another simply a distortion of the market.

Author Obsession

1. Frank and Janet – Fictioned Again

This is a very strange novel. Its three principal characters, Frank Sargeson, Janet Frame and Harry Doyle, are the three who variously occupied 14 Esmonde Road (which Frank always spelled Esmond, insisting that this, and not the street sign, was right) during 1955–56. People, place and time all have undeniable foundation in fact; and although a note by the author insists 'this is a novel', they are all very close to the real thing. Evans's fictional Sargeson is already acknowledged as a sort of founding father among New Zealand writers. Doyle is his horse-racing trainer friend, the love of his life, who keeps him on his toes with uncertainty and laconic wit. Frame is the writer just at the beginning of her career, writing her first novel while she occupies the army hut in his back garden.

A review of Patrick Evans, *Gifted* (Victoria University Press, 2010), published in *Metro*, December 2010; followed by a review of Patrick Evans, *The Back of his Head* (Victoria University Press, 2015), published in *The Spinoff* (http://thespinoff.co.nz), October 2015.

Peripheral characters bear various resemblances to people who knew Sargeson at the time (Lawrence and Margaret Guigan in particular are very close to Maurice and Barbara Duggan), but have fictional names so there are no grounds for complaint – except of course that they are not the people who would in reality have been in and out of the Sargeson house.

One effect of this is that when what is central to the novel departs in any way at all from the 'facts', a reader who knows them feels that Evans has 'got it wrong'. For example, the famous hedge was not macrocarpa. Sargeson did not compose straight on to the typewriter – his first drafts were always by hand. Frank grew up in Hamilton not South Auckland. Harry was never in extended residence while Janet was there. Frank knew that Janet, who was brought to him by her sister, not by a friend, had spent most of the previous decade in psychiatric hospitals. (In the novel he doesn't know, and the fact is only hinted at.) The famous hole in the hedge developed much later and in 1955 was just a normal gate gap. There was never any 'lawn', not even the merest hint of grass, on the Sargeson section. I don't believe there were peaches or nectarines in the garden. When Frank ate Chinese in town in those years it was at the Golden Dragon in Grey's Avenue, not the Peking in Wellesley Street which opened later ...

And so on. But this is 'a work of fiction', isn't it? Yes and no; because Evans has gone to great lengths to get things 'right' and to make us conscious of their foundation in fact. (He thanks someone who helped him with Takapuna details.) The problem for me is that the book is neither consistently fact nor fiction; and there's a feeling that the novelist himself is often uncertain where the boundary lies between them, and when and whether he has crossed it.

For example, I think he has tried very hard to get both characters 'right'. The Sargeson is an excellent likeness, partly because the first-person narrative style is so closely modelled – a pastiche in fact – on Frank's autobiographies, and the twists and turns and peculiarities of that style mirror so well the character of its author. The Frame on the other hand is not right. She is a much more formed character than the 31-year-old Janet was in reality. She confronts Frank, asserts her own will, is clear about what she wants, and makes it clear. She has theories about language, and explains mysterious events to Frank in accordance with these. None of this matches the Janet Frame of 1955–56 (or of any year probably). Her only way of asserting herself at that time was to take to her bed, to be waited on and worried over. She was a terrified mouse, with a great sense of humour, and special talent on the page. Manipulative – yes, probably; but obliquely, stealthily, even inadvertently. Evans represents her as shy and often silent, but a woman of considerable presence and force of character.

So for me the centre of this novel is not the relationship of Frank and Janet, but rather that of Frank and Harry, which I think is not so much what happened in reality between the two men, but is, rather, like a reading of that relationship as it existed in Frank's imagination. This is the novel's great strength and its emotional centre. It is the product of close reading of all of Sargeson's work, fiction and non-fiction, and a projection from that back into 'reality' – a 'might have been' rather than a 'was' reality. It is very well written, imbued with Evans's considerable intelligence, and fuelled by a fine, penetrating imagination.

The Frame part of the narrative, on the other hand, though it's certainly good enough to do its part and keep the interest alive, reads to me like a product of the intelligence, an idea or set of ideas (partly about the relations of language and reality), without the same emotional resonance. In fact it's perhaps an accidental measure of these two writers, Sargeson and Frame, that though Frame seems always so much more brilliant, she doesn't feed Evans's flame in the way Sargeson does.

This is a novel for novelists: literature for the literate and the literary. It is a feature of the 'mandarin' style (as Sargeson used to call it) that you don't use ten words if twenty can be found to do the job. I don't recall that this lack of economy ever bothered me in Sargeson's autobiographies; but there were passages in *Gifted* when I did feel Evans had parked the car overnight with the engine running, going nowhere. Some brisk editing could, I think, have improved the outcome. But this is clearly a labour of love, and the editor would have been resisted. In any case we must take what we get and be grateful. This is a stranger and more interesting fish than commonly caught in our waters.

They say orange roughy has to be down at some considerable depth for many decades before it's of an age and size to be caught and eaten. This is that kind of fish. Give it a try!

2. The Author as Monster

Patrick Evans's last novel was a clever piece of ventriloquism. This new one takes the theme, or subject, or obsession, one stage further and beyond 'the facts'. New Zealand (Canterbury) novelist Raymond Thomas Lawrence has won the Nobel Prize for Literature. A Trust of four of his friends/associates has been set up to run his literary estate, protect his copyright, and manage the Residence which is now a museum. The principal among these, Peter Orr, the nephew he adopted as his son, is first narrator of the story, though at intervals it is taken up by Thom Ham, not one of the Trust but an unliterary body-builder engaged in the later part of the great man's life to work for him, act as chauffeur, and when necessary to man-handle him in and out of bed and the shower. Thom talks his part of the story into a tape recorder.

We begin after Lawrence's death, but are taken back in time, and this story-telling, tale-shifting, unfolding truths about the writer and his relations with the Trust members, is skilfully managed, so there are constant revelations, with hints of more (and usually worse) to come. Of the Trustees, Peter Orr is (or at first appears to be) reverent about Lawrence's greatness. Robert Semple, on the other hand, a failed and bitter poet, describes him as 'a great arsehole'. Marjorie Ursula Swindells, who was his mistress for a time, has published just one novel, *Unravel Me*, successful because it 'told all' about the love affair. She has been unable to find an equal attachment with anyone else, or write another book, and continues ambiguous and confused about Raymond who used to spank her which she disliked herself for liking. Julian Yuile, the fourth of the quartet, a rather mild-mannered printer of beautiful books, expresses no opinion about Raymond until late in the novel when he hears an account from Peter about how uncle and nephew have interacted, and advises Peter, 'You need to get away from him.' He argues that Raymond keeps hold of Peter by seeming to reject him. 'He's a fucking monster! He manipulates everyone like that.'

The picture of the great man gradually and remorselessly darkens. Julian discovers evidence that many of the most striking ideas in his work come from the writings or the doings of others. There are even passages he has borrowed and re-written – 'improved' often – but not his own. By the time this discovery is made the Nobel Prize has been awarded and the great writer has died. To avoid the scandal which would certainly follow revelations of plagiarism, and of misappropriation of the experience of others, Peter and Julian destroy the evidence – a hoard of materials Raymond has kept and from which things have been imported into his own books.

Raymond's worst manipulation is of Peter. That he has abused him sexually in boyhood is hinted at but never made quite clear; but he has certainly enslaved him emotionally, destroyed his early ambition to be a writer, and left him a poor shadow of a man, fighting to be free of the attachment, but in the end captured by it, loving his role as the heir to greatness:

I came to understand that if I hadn't accepted the things he made me do and the things he did to me when I first came into his life, I would never have walked with the gods. We all did, the four who have become the Trust. *Look where he took us, I tell them. He took us to Stockholm –*

The power of Raymond's personality, and his ability to control those around him, is exemplified even by the non-literary body-builder Thom. When Thom is being considered for the job Peter objects, 'But he's an idiot.' Raymond's reply is, 'I don't need someone to sit with me under a travelling rug. I want a *follower*.' And a follower is what he gets. The 'idiot' attests to the power merely of his smile: 'I'd have followed him into hell. Shit it was powerful. *You are mine* it was like he said that to me.'

Because of the importance of the Nobel award others than the four are after the great writer's story. There is an academic, Geneva Trott, who writes one inaccurate and unsatisfactory book about him and is keen to write another – even to become his official biographer. She has tapes, possibly of Raymond talking about himself, and Peter believes she is threatening to use these if she is not given the role she wants. The Trust consider what they should do – should they kill her for example? Two of them steal the tapes but then they are acciden-tally dropped into a lavatory and spoiled before they can be listened to. This, and indeed the whole Geneva Trott sub-plot, is not the only episode where Evans seems to go part way down a narrative path and then abandon it in a way that makes it seem pointless. The 'point', I suppose, is fun – amusement, comedy – but then the work resounds throughout with a note so dark it makes 'fun' seem off-key.

Thom's recorded narrative is being done for someone else, addressed as 'Patrick' (Evans, we are no doubt meant to guess), who also wants to write a book about Raymond Lawrence. This, I suppose, is the novel we are reading.

The darkest parts of the novel relate to Raymond's fiction, and how he used those about him, particularly Peter, to create it. This is especially so where the subject is North Africa, the Algerian war of independence, and an Arab boy who is both loved, and slowly, sadistically murdered by a narrator who is a figure for Raymond himself. How much of this is based on reality is unclear. I think one is probably meant to conclude very little, despite the fact that Peter Orr seems in the end to believe it all, even that Raymond fought in the Algerian war. But Peter is the one Raymond has 'mined' to create his 'Arab boy' – used and loved, loved and destroyed.

Raymond is a literary monster of a kind that seems familiar, conventional, suggesting something out of the wardrobe department or dress-up box of John Fowles, or perhaps Iris Murdoch. When he wins the Nobel he says to his 'bum-boy' Peter, 'I've made it. Now watch me I'm going to fuck it up.' He surprises his retainers by making a good speech in Stockholm, but his next, at home, is a shocker, accompanied by outrages which are never specified. His subsequent novel is also an outrage and produces consternation and disgust. He is now completely out of control, an embarrassment – and his final act is one of destruction, taking himself along with the school of creative writing which has been named to honour him, and seven of its students – not a bad joke in itself, but once again confusing as to the tone of the whole.

The novel ends with a new mystery concerning a child in a wheelchair, and the narrator, Peter Orr, saying, 'I think I am beginning to understand.' Perhaps by now impatience had set in and I was reading too fast, because I did not understand at all.

★

So I went back to the end and looked again. The woman, Jennifer, whose child is in the wheelchair, refers to Peter Orr as 'Mr Lawrence'. Well, he is the adopted son of the writer, Raymond Lawrence, but I think she is hinting he is in fact the natural son – something which has been hinted at along the way. And she wants him to see the wheelchair boy's back. Peter looks and recognises why, without telling us quite what he has seen.

Peter himself suffers from scoliosis, and this has been explained in the course of the novel as caused by the administration of hormones, which Raymond persuaded the young Peter to take to advance puberty; and it is even suggested, once, by Marjorie, that it was caused by a physical attack Raymond made on Peter. Now I think we must be expected to guess that the child in the chair is suffering from the same condition – and that this is because Peter and the child are half-brothers, the mysterious woman, Jennifer, having had a child to Raymond, and Peter's mother likewise while she was still married to Raymond's brother.

If that is not the explanation then I am still in the dark. But it is also slightly embarrassing to spell all this out. There is something so dingy about it.

The cover blurb calls the book 'a hilarious and troubling satire'. It is troubling, but the tone is too uncertain, too various, too all-over-the place to be either comic or, really, satiric.

The Man who Wished to be Other

It must have been forty years ago that Bill Pearson told me an anecdote about his first days at school. When he reached the school on foot in the mornings he had still to walk the length of what seemed to the five-year-old a long fence to a gate, and then back the same distance to the primers' classroom. One day, as he completed this walk, a teacher picked him up and popped him back over the fence so he had to do it again. I'm sure I remember this decades later because at the time it struck me as representing Bill, and even (why else did he remember and repeat it?) his image of himself – facing the usual obstacles, but *twice over*, and unfairly.

From so many years of working with Bill on a daily basis in the English Department of Auckland University, and also on the committee of the University Press, I retain (though without our ever having been really close) an indelible impression of him, something that seems when I reflect on it a quite profound knowledge of his

A review of Paul Millar, *No Fretful Sleeper: A Life of Bill Pearson* (Auckland University Press, 2010), published in *New Zealand Books*, Winter 2010.

character; so although there is a great deal in this very good biography I didn't know (for example, that late in his life Bill seriously
damaged relations with his long-term partner Donald Stenhouse by
falling in love with inveterate hetero Andrew Sharp), there is nothing
in it that really surprises me, and little that conflicts with my sense
of the man I knew. Bill grinned rather than smiled, chuckled rather
than laughed. He was a dour West Coaster with a dark secret; but the
grin and the chuckle were infectious, and he could be jolly company.
Physically he was a slightly comic figure, walking always with his
arms out from his body, outriggers on either side, and swaying,
especially after a few beers. He was serious, scrupulous, an exact
scholar, precise in his choice of words, but not fluent on his feet, and
in lectures incapable of meeting the collective eye of his class which
he avoided by a sweep from the lower left corner of the floor all the
way to the upper right of the ceiling. One of his most notable characteristics in the English Department was truculence, especially in his
working relationship with the equally truculent Elizabeth Sheppard.
There were periods of harmony, but each became the other's *bête
noire*; and Millar mentions a letter in which Bill, after opening his
eyes in hospital in London (this was a period of leave) to find 'Betty'
in the chair by his bed, wrote to a friend that he thought for a moment
he had died and woken in hell.

But the big sad story this biography tells is of Bill's unhappy discovery of his homosexuality, his wish to be other, his attempts and
failures to be 'normal', and the consequences for his writing, particularly of *Coal Flat*, where the hero Paul Rogers, an ur-Bill Pearson, had
to be one or the other, 'straight' or 'gay', an alternative which seemed
to represent either inauthenticity or exposure. For a time he con-
templated what would have been in artistic terms a disaster – that
Paul's homosexuality would be revealed, and then 'cured'. Since Bill
himself had tried more than once to achieve heterosexuality, this is
only mildly surprising. But there was and is no 'cure' for something
that occurs, like blue eyes or baldness, in the genes. Bill had to live

with his own sexuality, and chose for many years to conceal it, so it had to be concealed also in his fictional hero.

Before I ever met Bill Pearson I knew him from the pages of *Landfall*. His essay 'Fretful Sleepers' made a strong impression when I was a student. I and my friends read it, talked about it, cited it. It was a rare example (Fairburn's 'We New Zealanders' was another) of an essay which generalised New Zealand society, intellectualised it, analysing and criticising. Popular attitudes and moral reflexes were exposed; but then the intellectual and literary community, who might have been expecting praise, or at least absolution, were blasted equally, leaving Bill dancing (as I've said elsewhere) not on the head of a pin but on its point. It was Bill's '*J'accuse*', much of it springing, not frankly but none the less directly, from his distress at finding himself a sensitive and romantic young man inclined to fall in love with other young men, in a society which deplored and mocked such tendencies, and criminalised their physical expression. Homosexuality, then, was the *raison d'être* for 'Fretful Sleepers'; but it was hardly mentioned, so it could be said that those of us who were excited by the essay also missed its point.

Millar records (deriving the fact from Pearson's own unpublished account) that Bill cried a lot as a child. It was, he said, his resort, and continued far beyond the point where such behaviour is normally given up in favour of manly stoicism. It occurs to me that Bill would have heard himself described as a 'fretful' child – so he turned the tables on us all with his title. We were 'fretful sleepers', crying in our sleep and not knowing why, not conscious of the threats that might cause us to wake one day and find ourselves under the control of a dictator. (The *Smith's Dream* scenario clearly owes a lot to Pearson.)

But 'fretful' is what Bill was and continued to be throughout his life. I have seldom known a man so beset by imaginary threats, or so prone to interpret neutral behaviour negatively. Every slight, real or imagined, was remembered. And it is in this that I take slight issue with his biographer. Millar is scholarly, scrupulous, thorough,* while always (and appropriately) taking his subject's side, defending and protecting him. Everything is put down to Bill's homosexuality, his distress at this discovery about himself, the dangers it exposed him to, and his consequent fears and sensitivity to slight and insult. I don't for a moment minimise the difficulties such men as Bill faced, or the pain they suffered. But not every gay man of those times made the heavy weather of it Bill did. He began life (we learn) as a religious prig, trying to 'save' beautiful boys whose language and behaviour were an offence to God, while remaining indifferent to the ugly and dirty ones for whom hell was probably the right place. Self-discovery, then, was bound to be painful. Bill was mature before he accepted his sexuality and stopped looking for that 'cure'; and he was an old man before making any move to 'come out'. He was all the good and sad and deserving things Millar says he was; but he was also one of those temperaments suspicious even when the sun shines, because *why is it creating all these shadows?*

He was ten years my senior but we were both products of a traditional university Eng. Lit. education of the time. There was a professional (almost a moral) obligation to 'evaluate' works of literature, and to explain your r/evaluation by what I. A. Richards called 'practical criticism'. In addition, as New Zealanders we were literary nationalists, both somewhat equivocal (sometimes just sad) about what had been left behind in England where our postgraduate work had been done. When my first substantial piece of fiction, 'A Race Apart', whose narrator is a middle-class Englishwoman, was published, Bill told me he 'couldn't see its point'. I was disappointed, but also faintly guilty. What *was* its point? Did it have one? *Should* it have one? It was a work of art, wasn't it? – but I knew that was an

---

* Not infallible, however. New Zealand House in the London of the 1950s was in the Strand, not, as now, in the Haymarket (p. 196).

insufficient answer. On the other hand when I wrote to him explaining why I thought two of his stories, from which he hoped I might select one to put into the second Oxford *New Zealand Short Stories* I was editing, didn't work, he wrote back thanking me. 'It is the first tangible criticism I have had of them.' Later I found and admired his story 'At the Leicesters" and included it in the collection.

Bill reviewed the first novel of our colleague Mike Joseph (whom, Millar explains, he considered to be a homophobe) unfavourably, and was paid back (or believed he was) by being mocked in Joseph's second as an 'unpublished novelist' who danced absurdly at pretentious parties. He took Maurice Shadbolt's first book, *The New Zealanders*, to task and subsequently believed (on good evidence, Millar suggests) that Shadbolt had a considerable hand in publishers' rejections of *Coal Flat*.

No doubt it was naive (a naiveté I shared) to think critical candour would go unpunished in such a small literary community. This was a time when our colleague Allen Curnow was in fierce conflict with Wellington poets (Baxter, Johnson, Campbell, Bland) who succeeded in delaying, and very nearly scuppered, his *Penguin Book of New Zealand Verse*. The Penguin finally emerged in 1960, and *Coal Flat* in 1963; but the fractious early 1960s were not productive years for either man. In the longer term Curnow simply out-lived and/or out-wrote and out-classed his adversaries of that time; but Pearson seemed to get bogged down in it, increasingly paranoid, writing memos and corrections 'for the record' rather than new work.

Millar's chapter on Pearson's relationship with Frank Sargeson focuses first on a review I wrote of Michael King's Sargeson biography in which I suggested King had been too ready to accept an account Bill had put on record in the Turnbull Library of Sargeson falling in love with him. Certain relevant letters and their carbons had been destroyed at Bill's request, 'to save embarrassment'. Later, Bill had had second thoughts and created his own record, including the opinion that Frank had been 'indulging himself, combing his hair before the mirror, as it were, admiring himself in love'. It needs to be understood that this correspondence, only some of which survives, was taking place between Frank in Auckland and Bill on leave in London. My suggestion that under these strange circumstances (first having the record destroyed, then recreating it, in effect putting words into Frank's mouth) Pearson's account 'should have been treated with some scepticism' caused Bill such distress he felt compelled to put yet another document on the record.

Millar makes his way as best he can through this thicket, agrees that 'Pearson's account [. . .] should be treated sceptically'; but concludes that 'Sargeson was certainly in love, and his feelings were deep and genuine'. This would not be worth pursuing except that I believe Pearson did not understand what Sargeson was about, and neither does his biographer.

Central to all this is the fact that Bill had had an extraordinary period of productivity in London during which he wrote not only his PhD thesis but also his most notable essay, 'Fretful Sleepers', his only novel, *Coal Flat*, and a handful of short stories. Without that burst of creativity there would hardly be a subject for this biography – yet it came and went. We were all looking for what would follow. Nothing followed; or nothing of such quality. By his early forties Bill was a writer with a past, and with almost another forty years to live.

When Sargeson waxed eloquent about Bill's 'suffering', his 'agony', as he did from time to time in conversation, I used to think he was overdoing it; but I now believe that, although he didn't know Bill well, he understood him (I suppose by analogy with his own history) better than anyone did. What he wanted was that Bill should 'unwrap' himself, free himself into new work. This was not quite the same as 'coming out'. 'Gay liberation' came too late for Frank. But he wanted the writer in Bill freed into new work; and he thought what Bill needed was to be loved. I don't mean that Frank was pretending. I'm sure he did love Bill, even if it was largely a Bill created in his head and at a distance. But there was an element of therapy in it.

Frank believed beyond everything in literature. He wanted to give Bill a longer literary life.

Bill was at once flattered and terrified. He thought (to put it vulgarly) that Frank was 'coming on to him' – and this is accepted by Millar, who then explains to us that a relationship between these two was not possible because Bill only ever fell in love with men younger than himself. He forgets, or ignores, the well-established fact that Frank could only fall for men older than himself (he used to call himself a 'gerontophile'). Bill was not being propositioned by Frank; but he thought he was.

In a letter to Frank quoted by Millar, Bill wrote 'It is flattering to have your love'; but he went on 'It is a pity your energy and your thoughts and your feelings are wasted this way on someone who doesn't reciprocate.' Not surprisingly Frank gave up. To Janet Frame he wrote, 'I realize [Bill . . .] has gone on wrapping himself in protective layers (within which the ego has thinned out) until there's no one left at all. There's nobody home.'

Bill Pearson will remain notable as the author of what must be our one major regional/realist novel. As an academic he had a very large hand in establishing New Zealand literature as a serious part of university courses. He also created a role for himself helping to make a more secure place for Maori in the university. For a time the Auckland University Maori Club became his haven, a place of warmth, welcome and acceptance. In the English Department, especially in examiners' meetings, Maori and Polynesian students always had a special advocate in Bill. It is interesting to learn that among his protégés (before Maori activism began to make him feel, as a Pakeha, less welcome in the Maori Club) was the young Pita Sharples, whose education for a short time he funded out of his own pocket.

In Paul Millar Pearson found a biographer he felt he could trust. The trust was not misplaced.

'Moss'

When I was young New Zealand fiction had three Maurices. Duggan ('Maurice') was the maestro, Gee ('Moss') the dependable tradesman, and Shadbolt ('Morrie') the showman. The maestro wrote mostly very slowly and with difficulty; the tradesman was more fluent and produced new work with what appeared to be near regularity; the showman was always ahead of the pack, prolific and catching the public eye, but was felt by some to be a bit of a sham. All three were in varying degrees neurotic – to be a writer in the '50s, you had to be. If you were male you were supposed to have a trade or profession. Especially if there was going to be a wife and family you needed employment – lawyer, doctor, plumber, builder. But what was a 'writer'? It was no more than a claim for yourself. Even now, a product of my time, I can't fill in 'Occupation: writer' (though I do) without it seeming to look back at me saying, 'Occupation: bullshit'. We were also trying to escape from colonial

---

A review of Rachel Barrowman, *Maurice Gee: Life and Work* (Victoria University Press, 2015), published in *New Zealand Books*, Summer 2015.

dependence, and consequently were caught on the hook of literary nationalism – Curnow's 'the New Zealand thing, the regional thing, the *real* thing'. We wanted to make it happen *here*, but (lacking cheap jet-travel and instant communication) were always aware of the inconceivably distant *there*, and of the range of opportunities it offered. All three Maurices went *there* (the long way, by sea) for a brief time; all three came back (by sea).

My friend Rob Dyer and I were the first to publish Gee – in the Auckland University literary annual *Kiwi* in 1955. Shadbolt was the first to find himself a London publisher – Gollancz. A few years later Gee, Duggan and I found one in Hutchinson's collection, *Short Story One*, along with Diana Athill, latterly famous as an autobiographer-editor. This led on to the publication of Gee's first two novels with the same firm.

In 1965 Maurice, Moss and Morrie went (and I with them) into Oxford's *New Zealand Short Stories* (2nd series). I wrote a sonnet, parodying the famous *Macbeth* 'Tomorrow and tomorrow...' speech, which began

> To Maurice and to Maurice and to Maurice
> Duggan, Shadbolt, Gee, how they load us down with fictions

> And all our yesterdays maybe have lighted fools
> The way to Dostoevski.

Equally volatile, Shadbolt and I fell regularly in and out of friendship. With the darkly equable Gee that was not possible. Duggan, ten years older, was a steady comrade, and when he died I edited his *Collected Stories*. When Shadbolt died I lamented missed opportunities.

Simply as writing, Gee's fiction had strength and authority right from the start. Sargeson commended his 'sentences'; and wrote to him later, after reading *Plumb*, 'I kiss your hand if you will let me.' Brasch wrote of his stories, 'the tone is so beautifully judged that form, language and content fit perfectly'. He had made Gee one of *Landfall*'s 'new writers of the '50s'. Robin Dudding, founder of *Mate*, and then Brasch's successor at *Landfall*, helped build and sustain his reputation, which was already solid in the literary community before press and public began to notice him. It seems from the perspective of now that Gee's future was never in doubt. There was nothing else he could do so well as write, and nothing he *wanted* to do, or felt at home doing. Yet he told a PEN group in 1984 that he was 'not a natural writer'. He could construct a novel, write chapters and paragraphs, find words and make phrases, 'but with sentences I just can't seem to get on' – which was why he kept them short.

Was he right – or was Sargeson, who could scarcely look past the excellence of the sentences? Both, I think. Gee had difficulty with sentences because he had to work hard at them to make them not only say what he wanted them to say, but achieve their special tone and flavour. He was conscious of the labour; Sargeson was conscious of the reward.

When, after many vicissitudes, including the long and rocky relationship with Hera Smith, the mother of his son Nigel, and varying employment as teacher and librarian, none of it enjoyed or satisfying, he finally settled in Nelson and began work on what was to be his masterwork, the first volume of the *Plumb* trilogy, it 'felt great,' he told his biographer. 'I felt as if I had come home [...] I felt that at last I was doing what I was meant to be doing.'

Gee's quality as a writer was less in his treatment of subjects (which is what is most noticed and written about) than in the writing itself – both structure and texture. It is as if the sensitivity of the writer mother, Lyndahl Chapple Gee, and the authority of the formidable Chapple grandfather (the model for Plumb), combine there. But there is a downside too. Right from the start he has had to contend with (and has resented) complaints that his New Zealand is joyless and dingy; that he does not love his characters; and more, that he has an excessive appetite for violence. Gee was inclined (understandably) to dispute this. Wasn't it the *real* New Zealand his fiction offered – the same you found in Sargeson and Frame? And wasn't the world full of evil (a word he didn't resile from) and violence?

The murder of the girl in *In My Father's Den* struck me as so horrible when I first read it, I found, on a later, second reading, I had remembered it as worse than it was. There were details I had imagined that simply were not there in what Gee had written. To me this was an illustration of how powerfully suggestive the writing is; and Barrowman offers an example of the kind of extreme reaction his writing can produce, in Janet Paul, thinking of publishing a collection of his stories, but writing to Brasch that 'the violence done to the horse at the end of "The Losers" was so unbearably graphic . . . almost sadistically inflicted on the reader' that she 'wouldn't want to read the story again even in proof'.

There is also Ted's drowning of his pregnant wife and two little daughters in *Going West*; and numbers of other scenes in which, not just the events, but the writing, is electric with vicious and destructive energy. In a 1976 interview Gee told Ian Wedde that he found himself more and more obsessed with 'pain and cruelty and violent acts' to the point where if it were not relieved by family life and the act of writing, 'I could possibly go over the edge.' Writing was 'a way of holding on to sanity'. In conversation once he told me he had embarked on what was meant to be a regular police procedural and felt he had to give it up, his imagination had thrown up such horrors.

I remember discussing this 'Gee problem' with Sargeson and concluding that the word 'sadistic' (the one used by Janet Paul, and she was not alone) was wrong. Gee identifies, not with the perpetrator of violence but with the victim. The feeling is indignation; the intention is protest.

Did that make him a masochist? I wondered. 'Not necessarily,' Sargeson said – 'but perhaps a moralist.' When I last wrote about him I headed my piece, 'Maurice Gee, moralist'. He responded by making the subtitle of his next novel, *The Scornful Moon*, 'a moralist's tale'. I saw this as a kind of shrug – a 'Whatever' – by one who would carry right on doing it his way, however others chose to characterise it. That, it seemed to me, was an example of civilised literary discourse.

James K. Baxter says somewhere that for him (and he thought for most writers – poets anyway) there was a place, a location you had to go back to in your mind to recover lost inspiration. Baxter's was a small cave high above the sea, a childhood memory from South Dunedin. For Gee it was a creek in Henderson (which he calls Loomis in his fiction), west of Auckland. 'It has a life', he told Wedde, 'in a way no other place I've ever lived has.' Barrowman's biography begins there in its opening sentence and ends there in its last. Loomis is the setting for *Plumb* and its sequels *Meg* and *Sole Survivor*. Also of *In My Father's Den*, and of my favourite, *Going West*, in fact a tale of two cities, Auckland and Wellington, but containing the famous account of three kinds of transport in and out to Henderson, rail, bus and car. Others of his novels begin, or touch ground, there, as do several of his stories for children.

Gee's life as told here in effect divides between before and after Margaretha, the woman he married in 1970 at the age of 39. The 'before' includes the somewhat idyllic childhood, the 'agonising' teenage years, graduation from the Auckland University English Department, problems with sex which he blames partly on his mother's puritan influence, and the relationship with Hera Smith. There was also the brief period in London and Europe; and through all of these years there were periods of employment, including teaching, which he disliked and wasn't good at, and library training and work, which he found boring and unrewarding. There is quite a lot of grumbling, mainly on his behalf by sympathetic colleagues, Shadbolt and Kevin Ireland especially, writing one another concerned letters about 'poor Moss'. But somehow, through all of this period, and heroically, he kept writing – not without breaks, doubts and blocks, poverty and bad times, but as if it was what he was meant to do, and must find ways to keep doing.

Plumb gave his reputation the leg-up it needed and deserved, and the beginnings of a living wage for literary work. The fact that it won an international award (the James Tait Black Memorial Prize) was especially important. This had what might be called 'the Booker effect' – always a disruption of the marketplace, and especially so down here in the 'colony'; but it was what he needed – at last he was being attended to and widely read. He had become what Strindberg calls 'a Name'.

It also opened doors to other kinds of earning. He began to write for television, which he did well and, not whole-heartedly but intermittently, appears to have enjoyed. Movie options were taken on his work, and though these did not always lead to a movie being made, they sometimes did, and in either case provided extra income. Children's books – *Under the Mountain*, and later *The Halfmen of O* and *The Fat Man* – widened his readership. His public persona, declining honours and disliking attention, without 'side' or intellectual pretence, must have been at the very least incomplete, but (if Kevin Ireland is right) it has made him 'New Zealand's most loved man of literature'.

In later life he has travelled abroad from time to time, but never, it seems, happily or comfortably, which makes him in one sense the most Kiwi of New Zealand writers, in another the least, since, in the present hiatus (if that is what it is) between colonial distance and whatever climate change may bring in the way of future restrictions, travel seems to be one of the things we do.

Rachel Barrowman is a conscientious and capable researcher. This is a thorough account of Gee's life and work, of considerable interest to those who have read him and already know something about the New Zealand literary scene; but it is hardly a book for the general reader. I admire her diligence and thoroughness; but there is something less than gripping about a solid slog through one book after another, recounting in order the genesis, the problems and how they were solved, and the reception. It is a story Moss, with his talent for narrative, could have told better, though it's clear he would not have wanted to do that for fear of dipping too far and too soon into the memory bank and depleting its savings.

Barrowman's separating characters in the life from the forms they take in the fiction is thorough but sometimes (in effect) tedious; and the difficulties of the task hardly help the quality of the writing. 'When he confided their feelings for each other in Lyndahl – where Plumb confides a mix of confusion and concern: he looks on Wendy as a daughter – Lyndahl warned Muriel off.' This is hardly elegant writing. And later in the book there are sometimes three levels to be distinguished – the facts, the fiction, and the movie version.

Auden has a sonnet that begins

> A shilling life will give you all the facts:
> How Father beat him, how he ran away,
> What were the struggles of his youth, what acts
> Made him the greatest figure of his day . . .

It's a poem, I think, about the pointlessness of biography – how few and small the basic truths can be compared to the welter of detail that makes a life. Gee's story could be reduced to a 'shilling life'. There is the family's intellectual and moral inheritance, the box-er-builder father, the writer mother whose puritanism is blamed for what was probably no more than a genetic quirk; there is Henderson, Falls Park, the creek, sex and death. There is the before and after marker-line of Margaretha who, he said, 'saved him' when he was 'going under'; and there is finally Moss in his trademark cardy, scratching away at the 'intolerable neural itch' (another Auden phrase), avoiding the limelight while half-happily producing a remarkable sequence of light-dark images of New Zealand as we all recognise it, don't want to recognise it, love it and hate it . . .

Stendhal, the realist in fiction, has someone say (roughly translated) 'a novel is a mirror taking a walk down the highroad: if it reflects the mire, don't blame the mirror – blame the road!' There is an entirely relevant truth here; but on the other hand each novelist's mirror has the unique colours and tones of its author's style and temperament. Barrowman's account tells us where and how these characteristics evolved in the man who, if he is not our 'most loved' novelist, is almost certainly our most read.

'Sleeplessness, disquiet, ardour' – Zbigniew Herbert's Grand Claim

From the introduction to this collection one learns that on returning to Poland from France in 1969 Zbigniew Herbert was interrogated. 'There were regular daily "conversations" lasting many hours', he told his émigré friend and fellow poet Czesław Miłosz, 'not at headquarters God forbid but at the top of the Metropol hotel with a window open on the courtyard. I could go out the window and not come back and my friends would say I'd been drunk, that I'd always had nihilistic tendencies, there you go . . .'

He was being quizzed about his Polish friends abroad, with an eye to how they might be enticed home, into the net. He goes on, 'They asked me all about you too [. . .] I analyzed your poetry pretending you interested them as the best living Polish poet. I played the fool, but it was no fun. I was alarmed to find that I wasn't used to it anymore, that I wasn't good at strolling around with shit on my head,

A review of Zbigniew Herbert, *The Collected Prose, 1948–1998*, edited with an introduction by Alissa Valles (Ecco, 2010), published in *Areté* 36, Winter 2011.

and that I'm a coward because I fear for the rest of my life. It made me sick (insomnia, depression) but I'm fine now and working.'

If you grew up as most of us in the English-speaking world did, relatively pampered and never called upon to make a moral choice between truth and what might mean going out the window, I think you have not only to respect this man who calls himself a coward, but suppress the sceptic's questions about how he managed to come and go so freely, writing, as this collection reveals, so much and so often about the cultural sites, the galleries, museums and libraries, of Western Europe and even America. Whatever he said to make himself look compliant, it must have been at least plausible. It left him feeling he had shit on his head, but not enough shit that he couldn't finish the message 'I'm fine now and working'.

In these essays you hear from time to time distant echoes, reminders of Poland under communism, and of the bigger picture in which Poland is the little guy between two bullies who are fighting over who has the right to make him their slave – for his own good of course. But what's surprising is how little that central fact of his life was allowed to figure unambiguously in the writing. It is there, but obliquely, in shadow. One would have a better idea of his life, and a better picture of how it shaped itself in relation to the times, if these essays had any sort of effective apparatus. Only a collection of 'Short Pieces (1948–1998)' are individually dated, and these, as it happens, are the most consistently literary. The other 500-odd pages, dealing largely with European art, artists and cultural history, come without any such assistance – no dates, few notes, no index. This is a book that consistently arouses and frustrates the wish to know more.

Herbert's thinking is full of contradictions. There are, for example, two essays which touch on Van Gogh as painter and romantic figure. In what I assume is the earlier he writes as a cultural tourist, visiting Arles to look for traces of the great artist. In the Café de l'Alcazar, the subject of Van Gogh's *Le café de nuit*, he meets an old man who has childhood recollections of the painter.

The old man asks, 'You are interested in Van Gogh?'

'I am.'

'Why?'

'He was a great painter.'

'So they say. I haven't seen any of his paintings.'

For the price of a drink and a cigarette the old man offers meagre yet vivid recollections. Van Gogh 'lived alone, like a dog'. People were afraid of him. Boys threw stones at him. *'Il était drôle.* His hair was like a carrot. I remember it well. You could see it a long way off.'

The owner of a restaurant recounts how his grandfather's vineyard was visited by the carrot-top who needed money and wanted to sell them a painting for 50 francs. He was driven from the yard, and the local citizens got up a petition to have him locked in the asylum. The restaurant owner laments the family's failure to recognise and grasp an opportunity.

These are travel-writer's tales. But when Herbert returns to this subject (a few years later it seems) his tone is very different. He calls his piece 'Van Gogh's sad popularity', and recalls, first, how in St Rémy 'an elderly nun whom I asked to show me the painter's cell became indignant. "There's nothing to look at. You'd do better to pray for that unfortunate man, who weeps eternally."'

In this essay he reveals something close to scorn for those who form long queues to see the work, and for the cult of Van Gogh the suffering and misunderstood artist, which has 'too much sensationalism and snobbery in it, too little authentic acceptance'. No one, he believes, has been able to 'assimilate' this art.

He finds the comparison of Van Gogh and Cézanne 'fruitful' – Cézanne 'realising his programme with an iron consistency, is a classic, a great analyst of form'; Van Gogh, on the other hand, is 'a Romantic, a Dionysian artist, a visionary running across the fields like St Francis shouting: Love, love'.

But the tune changes, softens, as he acknowledges that Van Gogh never departed from his 'Dutch roots'; that he 'remained faithful to

Rembrandt's country even in his best French period'. And he concludes with another, very different comparison: Van Gogh's *Field of poppies* and a painting of the same subject by Monet. 'The French painter's frothy and terribly superficial joy in colours' seems trivial beside 'the great Dutchman's severe, subdued study, no longer of nature but of reality'. It seems Van Gogh is, after all, as great as we all think he is, but for incomprehensible, or anyway mysterious, reasons. That is why his popularity is 'sad' – because it is focused on the man rather than the work.

Asked to choose one of his own poems and write about it Herbert chooses 'Why the Classics' – not because it is his 'best', or represents a 'poetic programme', but for its 'two virtues: it is simple, it is dry, and it speaks of matters that are truly close to my heart, without superfluous ornament or stylisation'.

The poem is in three parts, without punctuation. Part 1 discovers a minor episode 'like a pin in a forest' in Thucydides' account of the Peloponnesian War, recounting how Thucydides himself failed to bring relief to his besieged native city and, accepting responsibility, paid the price of exile. Part 2 contrasts this with modern generals who 'whine on their knees before posterity' and make excuses for their failures. Part 3 is as follows:

> if art for its subject
> will have a broken jar
> a small broken soul
> with a great self-pity
> what will remain after us
> will it be lovers' weeping
> in a small dirty hotel
> when wallpaper dawns

The third part, Herbert says, 'contains a conclusion or moral, and also transposes the problem from the sphere of history to the sphere of art'. Contemporary literature is full of 'despair and unbelief'; 'fundamental values of European culture have been drawn into question'. Human life has been represented in plays, novels, poems as meaningless, absurd. It is this 'black tone' that 'I tried to attack in my poem'.

One should not ask for perfect logic in literary discourse, especially when it comes in the form of commentary on a poem; and one should not complain of large gaps between the stepping stones, so long as the next in the sequence is somehow there and negotiable; but I find the sequence of thought here only dimly intelligible. He is attacking (he says) 'ostentatious subjectivism' – 'the Romantic poet who bares his wounds, relates his own misfortunes'.

> Very early on in my writing life I came to believe that I had to seize upon some object outside of literature. Writing as a stylistic exercise seemed barren to me. Poetry as the art of the word made me yawn [...] I had to go out from myself and literature, look around in the world and lay hold of other spheres of reality.

Van Gogh in the end is honoured for his 'severe, subdued study, not of nature but of reality'. And here Herbert chooses a poem of his own which he hopes also touches that elusive quality. Yet if it does, it does so, surely, not in the big (and questionable) historical comparison, but only at the last moment, when the undesirable modern romantic is imagined weeping 'in a small dirty hotel / when wallpaper dawns'. If it feels at last like 'poetry', it's only those last two lines that make it so.

★

Herbert writes about two places I have visited – Crete, and the Italian city of Siena. His essay on Crete is 33 pages long. On the first page he arrives, by sea from Piraeus, and on the last he departs by air from Heraklion. In between it's almost as if he was never there, except through the medium of what others have written. Certainly he's hardly there in his own lifetime. His interest is in the distant past, and his route, inevitably, is via what others have discovered and what they have written about their discoveries. I don't mean plagiarism (though this too has been alleged); and there are interesting personal reactions. But this is an art historian's account. It evokes next to nothing of the landscape or the sea, the restaurants and bars, the rafferty buses and chain-smoking drivers, the cheap hotels looking out on a glassy port, the lines of light striking through angled slats of green shutters, the single fisherman standing in his craft and sculling slowly forward; nothing of the vines and olive groves into which Germans parachuted and through which Maori infantry bayonet-charged; of Maleme beach or the headstones of Suda Bay – nothing in other words of the Second World War which still counts for so much among present-day Cretans. Herbert's is a bookish Crete, so that even when it is people that interest him, they are more often than not figures on an ancient fresco.

Siena also gets thirty pages and by contrast one feels he is right there. He goes out early and follows the rule 'straight ahead and third left, then straight ahead and third right'. Eventually and inevitably he arrives at the Campo, the town square which he describes as one of the world's most beautiful, having 'an organic contour resembling the concave of a seashell'. We are soon into the history of the city, and here, if there is plagiarism, or simply borrowing of other people's work (we can't all and always be scholars discovering something new), the quiet wit and the personality have to be all his own. The three principal Sienese families are all descended from German invaders:

Liberated from the pressure of helmets, their heads adapted well to accountancy; the warriors' bronze soon yielded to the precious metals of bankers. These demilitarised merchants undertook long expeditions throughout Europe, surpassing even the Jews in the silver trade. They became the Pope's bankers, which brought them large revenues and useful church sanctions against recalcitrant debtors.

We then receive admirably clear guidance on Guelphs and Ghibellines, and on the long-standing rivalry – indeed war – between Siena and its larger neighbour Florence; and on the changing forms of government (the Twenty-four, the Nine); and then, bringing everything close to ruin, the Black Death of the middle fourteenth century.

Just before this comes the great secular mural, Lorenzetti's allegory of *Good and Bad Government* in Siena's Palazzo Publico. Its merits, however, are disputed by the great historian of the Renaissance, Berenson, whom Herbert describes as a Guelph and an 'ardent supporter of Florence'. But the painter, Ambrogio Lorenzetti, died of the plague, and after that what chance did secularism have? Every brand of propitiatory magic must have been reinforced. Despair and the church flourished together.

So we are into the Renaissance now – but still in modern Siena, and accompanied by the personality of Zbigniew Herbert:

> The sun casts long shadows. The sunset adds fire to the brick houses. The *passeggiata*, a daily ritual, is taking place in the main street, Via di Città.
>
> To say that it is a walk is to say nothing. Every Italian town has a street which fills in the evening with a crowd of strollers, pacing back and forth for an hour or two in a limited area. It resembles an extras' run-through for a gigantic opera. The elders demonstrate their vigour and rehearse their titles: 'Buona sera, dottore.' 'Buona sera, avvocato.' Boys and girls walk separately, communicating only with their eyes. That is why their eyes become large, black and expressive; they recite love sonnets, dart flames, complain, curse.

We will be back in a moment with the art of Florentine Giotto and Sienese Duccio – with the detail of servings of fish, both whole and half-eaten, at Duccio's *Wedding at Cana*, with the varying expressions, from adoration to disapproval, among the Apostles and with the detail of three black sandals lying on the steps in the same painter's *Washing of the Feet*. But let's demonstrate one more time that Herbert is in the Siena we know, and not in a book:

> I eat two portions and order a third. The owner of the trattoria is clearly touched. She says that I am *gentile*. Later she asks my nationality, and learning that I am *Polacco*, she exclaims *Bravo!* with sincere enthusiasm. She summons her sleepy husband and fat daughter to witness our historic meeting. The whole family declares that Poles are 'molto gentili e intelligenti.' Perhaps I shall be asked to demonstrate a Polish dance and to sing an aria by Moniuszko. Unexpectedly the owner enquires if there are divorces in Poland. I lie that there aren't, and bring down a torrent of praise on my head.
>
> Above the Piazza del Campo – *luna plena*. A chord is struck between heaven and earth. Such a moment gives an intense feeling of crystallized eternity. The voices will die. The air will turn to glass. We shall remain here petrified: I, raising a glass of wine to my lips; the girl in the window arranging her hair; the old man selling postcards under a streetlamp; the square with the Town Hall and Siena. The earth will turn with me, an unimportant exhibit in a cosmic wax museum, visited by no one.

In the first of these two paragraphs we are in company with the up-beat Pole abroad. In the next, the drink at his lips is probably well past his second and we are back with the faintly self-accusing survivor of interrogation; the man who attacks 'despair and unbelief' in literature as if afraid he may have been infected by them; the art critic who can't quite decide whether to mock or join those who exalt the romantic greatness of Van Gogh.

★

Herbert's most concentrated statement of literary intent comes in his long essay on *Hamlet*. 'In Hamlet thinking does not oppose itself to life or any other inner powers. He thinks with his whole life and his whole person.' His 'orientation [is] towards the concrete, the thought form that is an immediate reaction to reality [. . . .] That is why the Prince's soliloquies, in which the dramatisation of thought reaches its peak, are as thrilling as the action, if not more engaging. They are woven so subtly of thought's material.' Clearly this owes a lot to Eliot – Eliot not only on *Hamlet*, but on the Metaphysical poets, who (from memory) 'felt their thought as immediately as the odour of a rose'.

There is a digression now to consider the character of Hamlet as Goethe conceives it, which Herbert rejects because Goethe turns him into another Werther, another romantic hero. This is not only wrong; it is also a measure of the greatness of Shakespeare's Hamlet. 'The sentimental gesture of the young hysteric clashes with Hamlet's profound drama [. . . .] One can sympathise with Werther, but one can't feel a deep solidarity such as bonds us to Hamlet.'

'Solidarity' – *solidarnosc* must surely have been the word translated here. How one would have welcomed a date on this essay to know whether he used the word at a time when it could not have failed to evoke the political excitements of Poland in the 1980s. He goes on and concludes,

> Fate is an inexorable alien force that can neither be drawn into a pact or crushed. So heroes rebel and fight. Hamlet belongs to the righteous who do not shake their fists at heaven but grow into their fate. [. . .]
>
> Moral greatness manifests itself in a particular tone, used in the telling by one who has encountered it. When the lights of the procession fall on the sharp profile of the Prince lying prone, we lean over him.
>
> We vow to you, Prince, buried in an interval in the roar of guns and in our silence: sleeplessness, disquiet, ardour. We vow to you Prince, buried in a small gap in the earth and in the deepest site of memory, that

when the time of trial comes, we will choose the sharper rapier and the more difficult death.

He is saying something beyond literature here, surely – something Polish and political, though an interrogator, if one can be imagined looking so closely into an essay on *Hamlet*, could never have been sure. (And neither am I.) Is Herbert signalling to us over their heads? As a conclusion it has a fine ring to it – grandiose perhaps, but bold, noble, heroic.

Did Herbert, like Hamlet, 'grow into his fate'? God knows what a Pole, one of his contemporaries who knew him and his situation precisely, would have made of this. It seems (unless I am letting imagination run away with my reading) to make a great claim for itself – for its author. Let's hope it was deserved.

T. S. Eliot as Letter-writer

A 639-page first volume of T. S. Eliot's *Collected Letters 1898–1922*, edited by his second wife, Valerie, was published in 1988. Now it has been re-issued, revised and expanded to 870 pages, together with a second volume, *1923–1925*, of 878 pages. In addition to Eliot's own letters there are a number by others – mostly by his first wife, Vivienne, but some family members and associates too.

Born 1888, Eliot graduated from Harvard and came to England on a scholarship at the age of 25, right at the start of World War I. In London he suffered what he describes to his friend Conrad Aiken as 'nervous sexual attacks' which made him think 'I should have disposed of my virginity and shyness several years ago'. Then, without anything in the letters to prepare friends or family (apart from one reference to their dancing together and her catching on quickly when he 'dips' into his 'American one-step'), he marries a

---

A review of *The Letters of T. S. Eliot*, ed. Valerie Eliot and Hugh Haughton, vols I and II (Faber & Faber, 2009), published in the *New Zealand Listener*, 20–26 March 2010.

posh young English woman, Vivienne Haigh-Wood. They make a fine pair in photographs, she small, beautiful and stylishly dressed, he tall, with fine eyes and a fastidious mouth.

With a degree in Philosophy, and completing a PhD, Eliot was cruising towards an academic life when his fellow American poet Ezra Pound, already precariously established in London, saw some of his poems and, with the confidence Eliot lacked, became his entrepreneur, ensuring that some of his work was published. 'My meeting with Ezra Pound', Eliot reflected much later, 'changed my life.' As Vivienne says in a letter to his mother: 'Tom is *wonderful*. I have never met a man who gets so much pushing and helping and who impresses people so much that he is *worth* helping.'

Vivienne does a good deal of pushing too, usually for money, which seems to come when needed from his brother and his father. Pound writes an appeal on Tom's behalf to the father, a long letter offering himself as the example of how it's possible, with talent, to live on poetry and occasional literary journalism. Bertrand Russell, with perhaps a predatory eye on Vivienne, provides the young couple with accommodation in London. When Lady Ottoline Morrell urges him not to let Vivienne fall in love with him, Russell replies that his interest in the Eliots is 'purely altruistic'. But Vivienne writes to a friend while Tom is away, 'He is all over me, is Bertie, and I simply love him.'

Tom gives extension lectures to what Vivienne refers to as 'the working people', but soon is settled as an employee of Lloyds Bank, writing essays, reviews and poems in the nights. Vivienne recommends black silk sheets to friends who are getting married ('they are extraordinarily effective – so long as you are willing to sacrifice *yourself*') and celebrates their orange wallpaper. She is constantly ill, and so is Tom – colds, flu, headaches, neuralgia, constipation, indigestion, a hernia (Tom), neuritis (Vivienne), 'exhaustion' (both). Other ailments go unnamed but loom large. At the prospect of having a tooth out with gas she writes, 'I am terribly cowardly . . . I scream the whole time.' But there can be little doubt that her illnesses are not just neurotic. Vivienne emerges progressively as the victim of inventive medicine practised by doctors who lacked antibiotics and had no idea what they were dealing with.

What began as an idyll ('I am having a wonderful life' Eliot wrote to Conrad Aiken, and to his father 'She has been the one person for me . . . I owe her everything') can be seen in these years sliding towards the marriage Eliot later described as bringing 'no happiness' to Vivienne and to himself 'the state of mind out of which came *The Waste Land*'. Yet they are clearly attentive to one another, fond (she addresses him in one letter as 'Dear Wonky-penky') – a *folie à deux*, but possibly a good marriage ruined by ill luck and illness.

Soon Eliot is becoming known as the critic of the moment, and the poet to watch. By 1919 John Middleton Murry, newly appointed editor of the *Athenaeum*, offers him the deputy editorship. He declines, but takes it as another sign that he is being seen more and more as 'the best living critic'. To his mother he reports, 'I really think I have far more *influence* on English letters than any other American has ever had, unless it be Henry James.' He was thirty when he wrote that; and he was not wrong.

As letter-writer Eliot is conscientious, lucid, at times conspicuously intelligent, occasionally playful and even (clumsily) obscene. He is seldom self-revealing except unintentionally. His explanatory mode can be remorseless. Just now and then there is a directness, the prose lights up, there is a sparkle – as when he writes to literary hostess Bridget Patmore and one feels his interest is straying beyond his own self-imposed boundaries of propriety.

He seems aware of the impression he makes of intellectual command. But to Mary Hutchinson he admits, 'I read very little – and *have* read much less than people think.' In another letter to the same trusted friend he writes, 'You know what a slow reader I am.' And he's not above pretending to having read something when he hasn't.

We get a glimpse of the emerging political reactionary when he bursts out, at the prospect of a strike, that his 'hatred for democracy' is 'profound', and that contemporary politics 'oppresses me with a continuous physical horror like the feeling of growing madness'. He finds the rise of the Labour Party 'alarming'; and congratulates the *Daily Mail* for publishing a series in which Mussolini is seen as a hero of 'the war against Bolshevism', and the Fascists as 'the Saviours of Italy'. The conspicuous anti-Semitism seems confined at this stage to the early poems.

Vivienne is clever, amusing, slightly batty – lively on the page in a style not unlike Katherine Mansfield's. Mansfield herself, jealous of John Middleton Murry's interest, refers to Vivienne as 'this teashop creature'. Lady Ottoline Morrell, jealous of her lover Bertrand Russell's similar interest, begins by disliking Vivienne ('such a frivolous, silly little woman'), but later seems to have loved her dearly.

It is at the end of a two-month visit to London by Tom's mother, brother and sister that Vivienne loses control, or feels in retrospect that she did. She tells the brother in a subsequent letter that she had 'found the emotionless condition a great strain. I used to think I should burst out and scream and dance'; and that, saying their farewells, 'I had no idea what I was doing. [. . . .] I was extremely anxious to show no emotion before your family at any time, and then I ended it in a fit!'

The visit appears to leave both Tom and Vivienne depleted and bereft. Home again in America, his mother tells the brother she thinks Tom is sad now because he's missing 'the affection that makes no demands' – i.e. hers as distinct from Vivienne's, whom she believes Tom is afraid of. Pound's view of Eliot's family is simple: they, mother, brother, sister, 'are the absolute punk of punk'. The sister writes that the union of Tom and Vivienne was 'not a eugenic marriage'.

It is immediately after the visit that Tom has his famous 'breakdown'. It must have revealed itself in losses of control (weeping? rage?), but there is no sign of these in his letters. On the recommendation of a famous London 'nerve specialist' he is given three months' leave by the bank, goes first to Margate, then to Lausanne where he comes under the care of a Dr Vittoz. The result of this free time is the first drafts of *The Waste Land*. Eliot takes them to Pound in Paris, who, in two or three sessions, edits them down to the poem we know, and is soon telling everyone it is 'good enough to make the rest of us shut up shop'.

Pound is now hard at work with his 'Bel Esprit' – a scheme to raise an income to free Eliot from employment. Eliot is cautious, secretive, even manipulative, wanting all kinds of guarantees, and not entirely honest. He makes an enormous fuss when an inaccurate report of the scheme appears in a Liverpool newspaper, and writes demanding an apology, assuring the paper that he has 'not received any sum from Bel Esprit'. This comes just four months after a letter thanking Pound for money which a note identifies as 'from Bel Esprit funds'. He plays poor, reminds Pound that Pound's wife has family money whereas Vivienne has not, but appears to keep everyone associated with the project in ignorance of the fact that he is receiving returns on shares in his family's brick company in America.

Meanwhile he has been working to produce his new literary quarterly, *The Criterion*, funded by Lady Rothermere. For his patroness's reaction to the first issue, that it is dull and that she doesn't like its format, Eliot blames Katherine Mansfield, whom Lady Rothermere has described to him as 'one of the most intelligent women she has met'. It is of course possible that Mansfield (only a few months from her death) expressed a negative view of the first issue, though there is no evidence that she did.

He continues to labour and complain. Even the ever loyal Vivienne, who is by now (mid-1920s) helping him with his editing of *The Criterion*, and writing for it, records sympathy for him, but impatience too; while Virginia Woolf in her diary describes him as 'peevish, plaintive, egotistical'. The question of whether he will or won't leave the bank is intolerably protracted, the drama of ill health (his own, but more especially Vivienne's) seems as if it will never end. As editor Eliot is industrious, sometimes waspish, but patient, particularly when dealing with his difficult and favoured colleagues, Pound and Wyndham Lewis. As a husband he reveals sympathy for Vivienne, and appreciation of her talents.

In April 1925, there is a crisis in the marriage. Vivienne's decline has been more medical than psychological. She has in effect been very nearly starved to death by her various 'specialists'. Slowly she emerges from this, while over the same period Eliot's financial and employment anxieties are eased by the new publisher, Faber and Gwyer (later Faber and Faber), taking over *The Criterion* and appointing him a director. A few cheerful notes return to his letters; and there are renewed glimpses of Vivienne's warmth and cleverness.

By the end of volume II Tom is on his way to financial security and fame. Vivienne's fate, however, is still uncertain, and there are clear signs that for the marriage the worst is yet to come.

The Trophy Husband

This is 'a mixture of history and memoir'. As a woman in her twenties (probably in the 1980s though no dates are given) Bostonian Christina Thompson, in Melbourne on a postgraduate scholarship, takes a holiday in New Zealand. In a pub in the Bay of Islands she meets a Maori called Seven, misses her bus back to Auckland, and spends a night with him and his cousins in a nearby house. Next day she accepts an invitation to go with them to Seven's parents' house in Mangonui. Soon he and she are living together in a little shack on the beach.

She returns to work in Melbourne, but after a month with no word from him she phones and invites him to visit. He comes, moves in with her, and within a year they are married. At the end of the book, described as 'an unlikely love story', they have three sons and are living in her parental home in Boston.

A review of Christina Thompson, *Come on Shore and We Will Kill and Eat You All* (Bloomsbury, 2008), published in the *Guardian*, 16 August 2008, p. 8.

The book focuses on the fifteen years she spent in the Pacific region, and on the interaction of cultures. What makes it puzzling, however, is its impersonality, the lack of detail about the central relationship, and the lack of a strong sense of the Maori husband. He is described, but not realised. We are told often that he is six foot two, strongly built, with long thick black hair; that he is attractive to women, tranquil, unworried, 'cool' and mostly silent. But he is seldom represented speaking or in action.

I kept thinking of Henry James's injunction, 'Dramatise! Dramatise!' But in one of the very few moments in the book when Seven speaks, he responds to her account of a dream with, 'We indigenous people never have those sorts of dreams.'

'*We indigenous people*'? This is a response I find it impossible to imagine any Maori making, except tongue-in-cheek. Is the author inventing dialogue to sustain a thesis? Or is Seven giving his wife what he knows she wants to hear?

This abstract, or illustrative quality is increased by the fact he is seen as a representative of Polynesia, and even likened to Omai, the young Tahitian brought by Cook to London where he was paraded as the Noble Savage.

The book opens with New Zealand examples of what anthropologists call 'contact encounters'. The first of these, described in the opening chapter, is Abel Tasman's 1642 attempt at a friendly meeting with Maori and the murder of four of his sailors, which caused him to name the place Murderers' Bay, declare 'the inhabitants of this country as enemies' and sail away. There follows, still quite early in the book, Jean de Surville's 1769 encounters with Maori in the north of the country, which began very amicably but ended in the theft of one of his boats and his kidnapping of a Maori (who died at sea) and setting fire to thirty houses, by way of revenge. Next comes another Frenchman, Marion du Fresne, whose five idyllic weeks (1772) among the 'Noble Savages' of the Bay of Islands (Fresne was a Rousseau-ist) ended in his murder and that of a number of his crew and to the kind of bloody revenge Tasman had declined to attempt. Finally, on this theme, there is a deadly encounter between Cook and Maori, also in the Bay of Islands, in which the usually sagacious Cook, on shore and threatened by a haka and a hostile armed crowd, was saved only by the firing of a ship's cannon, an event which foreshadowed the circumstances of his murder in Hawaii ten years later.

The point of these 'contact encounters' is not so much the murder, cannibalism and revenge but rather the misunderstandings on both sides which led to them. But what is their relation to the central narrative? The author represents herself as Europe to her husband's Polynesia; and there is even the suggestion that theirs is a latter-day 'contact encounter'. But since their interactions are either harmonious or unexplored, it's hard to see why all this rather familiar history is deployed, unless as a hopeful attempt to lend weight to what is otherwise blandly domestic. The impression, indeed, is of an academic attempting to make something significant of cultural differences which are not in fact creating difficulties; none, anyway, for her Maori husband. Often, as she acknowledges, he seems only to confirm what she has been taught are popular and largely groundless stereotypes about 'easy-going' Polynesians.

At times the emphasis on his appearance, and the lack of much else, makes him seem like a trophy daringly brought back to cultured New England from the wilds of the South Pacific. To one who lives in what is frequently referred to as the world's largest Polynesian city (Auckland), where intermarriage is commonplace, this aspect of the book seems at the very least naive.

But there is another undertone throughout which becomes specific only in later chapters. The author is from a sophisticated, affluent, well-educated family; Seven is a minimally educated Maori manual worker. For most of the book they move about as she gets postgrad grants, editing jobs and research work that can be combined with motherhood. He finds work, but often with difficulty, and it is poorly paid.

It is when Seven takes a job as a door-to-door salesman that 'for the first time in our marriage I despaired ... ',

> ... [it] forced me to acknowledge the issue of class. Of course I had always known it was there between us, but I never paid it much atten-
> tion .... it was easier for me to think of the differences between Pakeha and Maori than about those between the privileged and the poor.
> But there were moments – days when I would come home from the university to find Seven and Kura [his sister] stretched out on the floor watching monster trucks on TV – when I would look at them and think *you people*.

This brief moment seems to cut closer to a world of difference than a lot of the book's lucubrations on Europe and Polynesia.

In the end their money problems are solved by returning to Boston and her parents: 'my mother could cook, I could clean, my father could pay the bills, Seven could do the heavy lifting'. The tone of this explanation is light; but in a book full of unsatisfactory analogies, we might see ourselves here on the brink of another kind of 'contact encounter' – that between the generations.

The Sky is Falling

Hope Paterson has a more than reasonable expectation of salvation. She is a diligent Christian with a lot of the self-satisfied, busybody qualities that usually implies. When she sees a child fall into a water-filled hole outside Crystal Lakes Mall she gives only a moment's thought to her new suede jacket, prays 'Oh Lord, make me brave', and plunges down. She saves the child but there is for her a painful irony in this: the great sadness of her life has been the loss of a son, Brandon, in infancy.

Only a few days later the Rapture occurs. The Rapture is the fulfilment of Paul's prophecy (Thessalonians 4:16–17 and elsewhere) that Jesus will come with a shout and trumpets, and 'in the twinkling of an eye' true believers will be lifted bodily into the skies 'and so shall ever be with the Lord'. On earth (but who cares?) seven years of Tribulation will follow; the Antichrist will rise and sinners will

A review of Tim Wilson, *Their Faces Were Shining* (Victoria University Press, 2010), published in *Landfall* 221, May 2011.

be destroyed. It's the ultimate winnowing – sheep from goats, saved from sinners.

Hope tells her own story. She, surely, should have gone up, but she has been left. Not only that but her husband, Wade, who always accompanied her to church under protest and joked about her faith, is missing. Has he been raised – and if so, how could that be? What has become of Wade, and why, will be unravelled as the story goes forward. Some gay clergy have gone up, along with anti-abortion campaigners – so is God being even-handed? The Dalai Lama has been seen rising above Fifth Avenue, laughing. The Pope is missing, but not the Queen. Children under the age of seventeen have all been taken, including the child whose life Hope saved, and her own lost child Brandon, whose body has been torn from its grave. A sixteen-year-old condemned for a vicious murder escapes the death penalty: up he goes to be with Jesus. One of Hope's most serious fellow parishioners, Dr Wright, a dentist, believes he and she have been left by Jesus to do some kind of finishing work. He rapes her on the floor of their old church, now abandoned, and feels bad about it. Hope, who tried to fight him off, half-believes she is half to blame. Late in the novel Dr Wright opens the Forgiveness Foundation, begins to identify himself with Christ and Hope with Mary, and becomes a dominating and dangerous presence in Hope's family life.

Wilson amuses himself with a lot of the ironies his initial idea makes possible. He has an intelligent sense of humour, and his prose is sprightly. His father (he recounts in an article about the novel in *Booknotes*) was a Presbyterian minister and young Tim has clearly been an observer. 'During my Christian life', Hope reflects, 'I've had six ministers; only one of them was in any way comfortable with other members of the human race.' And how about, 'The seats were comfortable in a way I can only describe as *secular*'?

But this is not a satire; not even an exposure of false faith or foolish beliefs. It is, rather, an exercise of the imagination: a *what if*? It is also an American novel, not only in setting but in language (gotten, defenses, mortician). It draws on Wilson's experience as television correspondent there – the cities and suburbs, the dingy motels, the behaviour of crowds, the modes of public discourse: self-important, moralising, mad America, land of the free and home of the brave.

At first the Rapture causes fear and disorder. The homes of those who have 'gone up' are looted. Banks totter and foreclose. There are flagellants and 'ash-heads' in the streets (hoping to make it on to a late list?). Then, as life settles down, there are the beginnings of a reaction against belief itself. In a society where religious observance is required of those hoping for public office (think of Bill Clinton carrying that enormous Bible to church after his naughtiness with Monica) it is now required that such aspirants affirm the reverse – a lack of any religious taint.

I find all this credible – enough at least to be entertained (both senses). But at the same time it forces us back to what I will have to call 'reality'. Our disbelief has been duly suspended, as any fiction requires; but how is the story to end? This one ends in a way that is rather conventional. After a failed suicide attempt Hope is forced, mainly through conflict and peace-making with her estranged daughter, and reflection on her marriage to Wade, to recognise that she has loved God more than anything, and at the expense of her husband and family.

In my last year of university teaching, 1986, Tim Wilson was in my creative writing class. I have a photograph of him with his class-mates, one of whom is the poet Andrew Johnston. Tim's hair is enormous, piled up in a sort of bouffant style. I thought he was brilliant and didn't think I could teach him anything. Of all my creative writing students during those final three years he was one of four or five I felt certain I would hear more about. Three are now very well-known. Tim vanished until he materialised on TV One with his mown hair and fluent, clever commentaries from America. So I have been waiting a quarter of a century to hear from him, either as poet or fiction writer.

In his *Booknotes* article Wilson quotes approvingly Marilynne Robinson's rejection of believer/nonbeliever dualities as 'absurd': 'all the beautiful movements of mind', Robinson writes, 'over the range of thought and feeling, the tides and currents of the felt life, are lost entirely when people speak in these terms'. This is, or seems to be, an argument for open-minded agnosticism, or scepticism, from one who is neither agnostic nor sceptic. It is, in other words, disingenuous. Is the same true of Wilson?

Sometimes what seems a great idea for a novel, when it arrives, or is pitched in broad outline, can become a confinement when it has to be spelled out, lived through, in the detail fiction requires. It can set limits from which there's no escape. 'The Rapture' is that kind of idea. It may be only a device for the 'what if?' question; but it's one which closes the door rather than opening it. *Their Faces Were Shining* is intelligent, succinct, and witty. It is also conscientious, following through its initial 'given', and ending in a frenzy of action from which even a moral is extracted. (We are made to love here *first* before we may be 'taken up'.) But we end where we began, in fantasy-land, even if it is one sanctioned by an off-beat tradition within one of the world's religions.

Drawn to the Green Light

I first read *The Great Gatsby* at the age of eighteen and was deeply impressed. I scored marks down the margin of the final three paragraphs of chapter six, in which Gatsby's and Daisy's first kiss is recounted, and put three large exclamation marks after them. When I read it again in my fifties I added (self-mocking) 'These marks were mine in 1951. I thought this marvellous writing, even "the tuning fork that had been struck upon a star"!' Re-reading in 2013 I have added, 'Well OK, but I wasn't wrong to mark this. It's the emotional centre point of the novel.'

So here are three readings: one simply 'blown away', the second reacting critically against the first, the third occupying middle ground, admiring but with reservations. None of these is simply 'right'. Each is a keen reader's reaction, has its reasons, and could be defended critically. I suppose what the third (present) reader particularly admires about the book is its structure, the way it

A discussion of F. Scott Fitzgerald's *The Great Gatsby* published in the *New Zealand Listener*, 14 November 2013, p. A28.

relates a complex set of events through a first-person narrator, giving us as much information as we need, but no more, at the right time. So at first we doubt, even disapprove of, Gatsby and his overblown claims for himself (wealthy family, an Oxford man 'old sport', recipient of military honours); but slowly, as the narrative takes us forward, we learn that some of what he claims for himself is true. He was a major in the Great War; he did take the opportunity the army offered to study at Oxford; and this was the delay in his return which gave Daisy's restless affections time to wander and to attach themselves to Tom – a marriage on the eve of which she had an emotional crisis.

It is learning (in chapter four) about this last-minute panic that causes Nick Carraway, our witness and narrator, to alter his view of Gatsby, and produces one of those ringing statements by which Fitzgerald signals Nick's feelings and influences ours. Remembering his first sight of Gatsby, arms raised, looking out across the water towards the green light at the end of Tom and Daisy's jetty, Nick reflects, 'it had not been merely the stars to which he had aspired on that June night'. And he goes on, 'He came alive to me, delivered suddenly from the womb of his purposeless splendour.' All the apparently pointless lavishness and waste of the Gatsby parties has been part of a grand strategy. Gatsby is a dreamer, almost certainly dishonest in business as well as in his accounts of himself; but he 'believed in the green light'. He is a romantic on an American scale, the scale of twentieth-century America.

But it is also in making known to us this fact about Daisy's crisis on the brink of marriage that the constraints of first-person narrative almost break down. This has to be something Jordan told Nick, because he wasn't there and can't otherwise know it. But Fitzgerald cannot put so many facts, such a story, into speech reported at second-hand. So for four pages the 'I' of the narrative is Jordan. This is quite a radical breach of the novel's own narrative limits, and one a purist like Henry James would not have allowed himself. But it was necessary, and though there are signs of authorial anxiety, I think he gets away with it.

Late in the novel Fitzgerald has to contrive a situation in which Myrtle Wilson will be run over and killed in such a way that her grieving husband will believe not just that Gatsby was the driver but also the lover Wilson knows she has but whose name he hasn't been told. I think the management of this difficult stuff may strain credulity slightly, but again it works. If other things about the novel (atmosphere, narrative momentum) are retaining your goodwill, you will read on, absorbed. These are elements the novelist must constantly weigh up, and I think Fitzgerald gets the balance right.

The other quality this novel is notable for is its atmosphere, its sense of place and of contrast – the cool elegance of Tom and Daisy's mansion (and of their slightly dishonest golfing friend Jordan), the frenzied opulence and bad taste of Gatsby's parties, the wasteland of the ash heaps overseen by T. J. Eckleburg's eye-advertisement, where Wilson has his gas station. These are three very American social layers – old money, new money, and no money. The Wilsons are so dingy one wonders what attraction Myrtle holds for Tom, who hits her and breaks her nose when she dares to assert her right even to mention Daisy by name. Only when she is lying dead we are told 'Her mouth was wide open [...] as though she had choked a little in giving up the tremendous vitality she had stored so long' – the significant word there matching one used of Gatsby: 'the colossal vitality of his illusion'. Those who lack something – money (Myrtle), a love object (Gatsby) – are capable of this 'vitality' by which rich Tom, with his bulging thighs and racist ideas, and charmingly dizzy Daisy, are each briefly captivated. Jordan, on the other hand, 'unlike Daisy was too wise to carry well-forgotten dreams from age to age'.

There is a kind of rhetoric in this novel which impressed me deeply when young – 'So we drove on toward death through the cooling twilight'; or that passage I marked at the end of chapter six – 'He knew that when he kissed this girl, and forever wed his unutterable visions to her perishable breath, his mind would never romp again like the mind of God.'

Now I am more critical, cooler, more detached, not so easily played upon. Yet if the writing teeters now and then, it does lead us on with Nick towards the steady tone of a youngish man acquiring wisdom. By the end we probably feel, sadly, that Daisy, though a divided soul, is back where she belongs: 'They were careless people, Tom and Daisy – they smashed up things and creatures and then retreated back into their money . . .' And we are likely to agree with what Nick shouts across the lawn to Gatsby: 'They're a rotten crowd . . . You're worth the whole damn bunch put together.'

The writing is deliberate, almost too consciously 'fine', faintly tinged with the high-toned and sugary flavour of *The New Yorker*; but it is also a good story, and one of those rare books which catch a time and a place so perfectly they become signifiers of an age.

3.

First Person

My First Book/s

I published two books in 1964 when I was 31, a collection of poems, *Whether the Will is Free*, and *The New Poetic* (in later editions *The New Poetic, Yeats to Eliot*), which was my Bristol University PhD thesis. I don't know which came first that year. During the preceding decade I had been publishing poems and reviews, and had won the first BNZ Katherine Mansfield short story prize, so I had already some kind of presence on the literary scene, and it seemed rather late for a first book. Published by Blackwood Paul, the poems were printed at the Caxton Press by Leo Bensemann, a typical 'fine book' of its time, with thirty-plus well-worked poems. It was a young poet's assemblage in differing styles and forms; a record of finding (and sometimes losing) ways forward. It was full of echoes and influences – Donne, Yeats, Eliot, Pound, Auden, Stevens, Larkin, Hardy, and James K. Baxter.

The New Poetic was a study of twentieth-century poetic Modernism, published first in the Hutchinson University Library, then as a

Published in *New Zealand Books*, Summer 2012, in which two writers were asked to recall their first publications.

Pelican, and in America as a Harper Torchbook. It was a book which revised the standard view of the Georgian poets, dividing them into two distinct groups, and spoke up for Yeats against the Leavisite (negative) view of him. Bristol University's was a Leavisite English department, and I had begun my work on a scholarship there with a graduate seminar paper taking to task my professor and supervisor, L. C. Knights, who in an essay in *Scrutiny* had described the refrain in Yeats's 'Easter 1916' as 'an escape from realization'. I set out to show the poem's strong intellectual framework. Professor Knights, a wonderful teacher and mentor, accepted without complaint or demur that he'd failed to do justice to the poem, and when I prepared that part of the thesis for publication I took out all direct reference to the essay which had occasioned my new reading.

But *The New Poetic*'s most original contribution to Eng. Lit. studies was its reinterpretation of Eliot, rejecting the academic orthodoxy of the time which accepted his own self-characterisation as an 'anti-romantic' whose poems were careful constructs with only 'the suppression of certain links in the chain'. I had re-read, indeed raided, Eliot's early critical writing, and was able to show his best-known poems were in fact the products of indeterminate 'pure' lyric moments, which he then had to labour (or, in the case of *The Waste Land*, Ezra Pound had had to labour) to bring into some kind of imaginative order.

The book's time was right – it said what people were ready to hear. I remember joking that it was 'my first novel', and it's true that it made something of a story, in which the poets were the characters and literary history the plot. It has appeared in many forms since, including, even, in an American academic reprint series, as 'a late classic of Imagist criticism'. Though it must now be well past its use-by date, it is still in print, with a commendation from Seamus Heaney who said in an article that it taught him to read Eliot.

So I would never be out of a job. But it was poetry I wanted most to write, and then fiction. For me, literary criticism was only a natural offshoot of these. As critic and literary historian I would be writing always from the inside, not looking in at the window – always in the role of what Leavis taught us to call 'a practitioner'.

In *Whether the Will is Free* two poems were, for me personally, most important – the title poem, because it found a way, not just to articulate, but give body to, a 'philosophical' conundrum that was something of an obsession of my younger years; and 'Pictures in a Gallery Undersea', in which the echoes of Eliot were clear and, indeed, a necessary part of the poem. That Allen Curnow had already selected both of these for his 1960 *Penguin Book of New Zealand Verse* was a confirmation I was grateful for; and 'Pictures in a Gallery Undersea' had won the *Landfall* Reader's Award, where subscribers had voted for the 'best' poem to have appeared in the journal's first fifteen years. It was a poem that had sprung directly from the exhilaration of being in London for the first time, combined with the excitement of my work in the British Museum (the famous old circular Reading Room, now a tourist site) towards what would be *The New Poetic*.

So those two, 'Pictures in a Gallery . . .' and *The New Poetic*, were more intimately connected than might have been guessed, and I return to the poem after more than half a century always with surprise and wonder. Where did it come from? I know where the material came from; but how or why in that form, in that order, is the kind of mystery that accompanies the arrival of every poem that feels 'new' and not quite like anything its author has done before. It was, I suppose, my *The Waste Land*, an outsider's response to London, the 'unreal city' (as Eliot called it), the mythic place that had been learned first at a distance in childhood when bombs were falling on it, and from books. I think I have described it somewhere as the ultimate 'colonial' poem, unapologetic, self-celebrating.

So that is myself in 1964, author of two new books, a young lecturer at the University of Auckland, recently back from a flying visit to New York where I had given an invited paper about Eliot at a conference. It was also in that year that I wrote a short story called 'A Fitting Tribute', which appeared a little later in the *Kenyon Review* and subsequently in a number of New Zealand anthologies.

I was, you could say, well-launched, but with all the unimagined problems and conflicts of being 'a New Zealand writer' yet to be revealed, yet to be confronted.

Comprehensive:
The Lawrence Jones Interview

1. The Shape of a Career, 1951–2009

Lawrence Jones: *The earliest work in your* Collected Poems *dates from 1951, so it's been a 58-year career thus far. Despite that stroke in 2005, the publication schedule has continued to be pretty full in the last three or four years, with books in your three primary areas – poetry, fiction, and critical and other non-fiction prose. In 2006 there was your eleventh novel,* My Name Was Judas; *in 2007 your fourteenth collection of poems,* The Black River; *and last year there were both* Collected Poems 1951–2006 *and* Book Self: The Reader as Writer and the Writer as Critic, *your seventh book of critical and other prose. With that long publishing past behind you continuing right up to the present, how do you feel about your writing future?*

Interview with Lawrence Jones, 14 April 2009 with follow-up Q-and-As, slightly edited from the version published in *Words Chosen Carefully: New Zealand Writers in Discussion*, ed. Siobhan Harvey (Cape Catley, 2010), pp. 240–61.

C. K. Stead: The writing will continue as long as I'm able to do it. I'm realistic that you can't go on forever, but at the moment it seems to come as easily as it ever did; so, as long as I'm fit and healthy and I've got things I want to write, I'll continue.

LJ: *Do you anticipate more fiction?*

CKS: Well I'd like there to be more fiction, but at the moment, I don't seem to have an idea for a novel; and because of that, in the last eight months I've written what I always swore I'd never do – a memoir – a piece of autobiography, *South-West of Eden*. It was partly because the reaction to the autobiographical sections of *Book Self* was very positive, very warm; and that book has sold quite well.

I conceived of this new book – the memoir – as a whole: that it would start at the year 'nought', as soon as memory, consciousness, set in, and go to the age of 23 when I first left New Zealand; the idea being that whatever has followed really has its genesis in this place and that time.

LJ: *I've made for myself a chronological chart of your books under four headings – poetry, fiction, critical and other prose, and editions – with a line drawn at the mid-1980s, the time of your early retirement from your professorship at the University of Auckland. I did a rough count of books on either side of the line: in the thirty years of preparing for and engaging in an academic career, there were seven collections of poetry, taking up about 220 pages in the* Collected Poems, *three novels and a collection of short fiction, two academic literary studies and a collection of critical essays, and four editions; in the 23 years since early retirement from that career, there have been seven separate collections of poetry, taking up about 300 pages in the* Collected Poems, *eight novels and a collection of short stories, two collections of critical essays and two collections of critical and other*

*prose, and two editions. The striking development post-retirement
is the blossoming of the fiction. The impulse to write it must have
been there early, for your first significant piece of fiction, the novella
'A Race Apart', was published as early as 1958, and the first novel,*
Smith's Dream, *was in 1971, but the full harvest of novels didn't come
until after 1986. You said to Michael Harlow in 1983, 'Maybe if I
found some way of being a full-time writer then I'd be able to say that
I was a paid-up fiction writer as well as a paid-up poet', and obviously it happened.*

CKS: Trying to be a university professor, which I did very con-
scientiously for many years, and continue to be a writer, was
exhausting. In fact I began to ease myself out of teaching around
1979 when I stepped down from my chair for three years to take a
senior research fellowship. Then there were a few years back as
professor, a sabbatical leave in 1984, and early retirement in August
1986 when I went off to teach at the Yeats Summer School in Sligo.
My intention in leaving the university altogether was to give the
writing, particularly fiction, space to breathe and expand. So, yes, it
seemed a slightly risky thing to do, and took some of my colleagues
by surprise, but it worked out well. Writing novels did mean that for
a few years the poetry lapsed. But once I felt I'd established myself a
little more firmly as a fiction writer then I went back and forth more
even-handedly between the two.

LJ: *So this was really the most important development in being a full-
time writer – getting those blocks of time for doing the fiction?*

CKS: Yes. The first draft of a novel might be done in six or eight
months and during that time it'd be extremely unlikely that I'd
write any poetry at all. But I've learned that I can work my way back
into poems. For me now it's always working my way into one mode
or into the other, and then staying there for some considerable time.

2. Some Recent Themes

LJ: *Among the books of the last six or seven years, one theme that leapt out at me, cutting across the genres, was religion. That theme was there in your earlier work, but it seemed to be a special focus in two recent works,* My Name Was Judas *and the poetry collection* Dog *(2002). You said of* My Name Was Judas *that the idea came when you were working on* Mansfield *and faced the question of a how to write on a messianic character such as D. H. Lawrence; you decided that it had to be done not through his consciousness but through the eyes of others – an outside view. And that led to the idea that if you were to write about Jesus, the ideal voice to do so would be Judas, who of all the disciples had some distance on him. So, as it worked out, you've got a kind of double view of Jesus presented by Judas – it's Judas's viewpoint, but long after the events, so he has a retrospective vision of Jesus and the development of his own feelings about him as well as of the biblical events. How do you think this narrative strategy affected your portrayal of Jesus in the book?*

CKS: It gave me distance of course, and I'm writing as a sceptic, a person who doesn't believe that Jesus was divine, or that there is such a thing as resurrection or life after death. This is a story we all know, but in the form in which we receive it it's not a story I can believe. I have that in common with a lot of people. Some can't believe bits of it – the Virgin birth, the bodily resurrection – and lots of people who call themselves Christian can't believe those parts either. But Christianity is a religion which has demanded of its followers belief above all else. You were required to believe even if you didn't or couldn't – as if it could be achieved by an act of will – and if you failed, you were damned eternally. So what I wanted to do was to write the Jesus story we all know, but in terms that I could believe. This meant that I had to think about the psychology of such a person at such a time, the psychology of one who believed, or came to believe, he was the Messiah.

What interested me was that, when I revisited the Gospels (and I made myself a biblical scholar in a very short order), I found there were two Jesuses. There was the gentle Jesus with a message of harmony and hope, especially hope for the poor, the underprivileged, the deprived, the bereaved. And there was the other Jesus, the militant one, who, especially in his final sermons, is extraordinarily violent and threatening, not gentle at all. From the Gospels you don't get a clear chronological development of the character of Jesus; and that's what I gave him in the novel – which I think gives his character psychological credibility. This is Stead the realist, if you like. In the novel Jesus begins as one – gentle Jesus – and ends as the other, demanding, 'Believe in me or you're going to suffer eternal pain'. I then had to create a situation where it was credible that Judas, who is essentially of a sceptical turn of mind, would ever become a disciple. And I did that in two ways. First, since we know next to nothing of the childhood of either, I made them boyhood friends; and second, I had a crisis in the life of Judas, the death of his first wife, at just the moment when Jesus comes back to Nazareth as a charismatic preacher. Those are the circumstances which lead Judas to follow him. But the Jesus Judas follows is the one who gives hope for the poor and disadvantaged. Later Judas is alarmed as he sees, creeping into the message, the implication that Jesus is more than just a prophet and teacher; he is divine, and finally the Messiah. That gave me a better-shaped story, and it gave me the story in a form that I could believe.

LJ: *So you do get a tragic figure in Jesus rather than on the one hand a Saviour and on the other a deluded man.*

CKS: It becomes a human tragedy, not a divine intervention in human history; though it would not be wrong to say that the

Jesus we see through the eyes of Judas seems, in the end, clearly deluded.

LJ: *Is this what differentiates Jesus in the novel from a mad messianic figure like the one in the poem 'Messiah' in the poetry collection* Dog, *who says baldly that he's the son of God and he's the way to be saved?*

CKS: The emphasis in that poem is comic/satiric. The figure in the poem says exactly what Jesus says; but the novel is able to humanise him by showing you a progression towards that extreme position. That in turn makes it possible for the reader to wonder, Were there doubts? Did Jesus actually and consistently believe what he was saying about himself? – questions that make the cry from the Cross, 'My God, my God, why hast thou forsaken me?', all the more human and tragic.

However, you remind me of your own review of that book of poems, *Dog*. To me the emphasis of your review is wrong in that it repeatedly uses the words mocking and mockery and sarcasm. Well, there is mockery, I suppose, but there's a whole lot more and other, if you take that poem 'Creation etc.' as a whole. So I don't think you can say that whereas I'm fairly sensitive towards Christian belief in the Judas novel, I'm totally insensitive in the other. I think there's a spectrum in both.

LJ: *Yes, and in a sense you're pretty hard on the non-theist prophets also as in the poem on Nietzsche and Whitman . . .*

CKS: Oh yes, yes [laughter]. I'm not well disposed towards messianic characters.

LJ: *The idea that all will be well if God is dead [laughter]. Well, figuring strongly in* Dog *is Allen Curnow. In 'His Round' you have a line about him going in a westerly direction, moving to death, trying*

to find his Dog (with a capital D). And then in discussing him you
use a capital 'A' when you say he had a sense of the divine as a great
Absence. All those capitals, are they a way of differentiating Curnow's
religious responses from your own?

CKS: The word 'Dog' there, as in the schoolboy joke between the
two lads in *Talking about O'Dwyer*, is 'God' spelled backwards, and
ascribed divinity only by the addition of a capital letter. Curnow
was brought up in the church. His father was an Anglican clergy-
man and Allen trained for the ministry. And according to the story,
which I never checked with him, he completed his training here
at St John's in Auckland, and was heading back to take up his first
junior post in the church, when, crossing Cook Strait, he realised
he'd lost his faith. Now I don't know whether that was true or not,
but I wrote a poem called 'Between'... Is it called 'Between'?

LJ: *It's called 'Without'.*

CKS: 'Without'. I don't name Allen, but in it he throws his Bible
into the sea, which is my fiction based on that story. But the thing
is that Allen never lost his sense of being of the Anglican community. He didn't believe any more, but for him, as for many serious
non-believing Anglicans, the church was important. It was many
things, including a superior social club. So there was communion
with a small 'c', but no longer with a large one. Allen was excom-
municated in the sense of belief, but still an Anglican – in the way
many lapsed Catholics are still Catholic. He was also very pedantic,
almost snobbish, in knowing the theology and the proprieties, and
I wonder whether, if he'd been alive when *My Name Was Judas*
was published, he might have thought it quite improper of me to be
trespassing on territory that he knew so much about, and I knew so
little. He would certainly have been surprised to find I knew my way
about in that territory.

LJ: *Yes, well in that poem you give him a thought very much like your own in 'What I Believe', except that for Curnow you've got a capital in there: 'God wasn't there, was nowhere, a Word [with capital w] without reference or object.' You also say for yourself, 'The gap isn't there', but you talk about the God gap in Curnow and the ways in which he filled this with his poetry. I thought that was probably a difference.*

CKS: Oh, it's a huge difference. Because for me these questions of theology and faith and intellectual history are very, very important, but they're not personal; whereas for him they were deeply personal – there must have been a lot of personal pain, at least to begin with. I can't say that for me there has ever been any personal pain about believing or not believing. I began as a child believing there was a God because I was told there was; and then gradually, as I got older, and reason and observation set in, the belief, for which I saw no grounds, slipped away painlessly. So the only times I've become impassioned about it have been when I've felt that believers are claiming territory for themselves, being proprietary, claiming rights; and especially when they've inflicted pain, suffering and restriction on others – particularly on children in their care.

LJ: *In 'What I Believe', you add as a postscript a 1987 note where you say that there is a feeling, a kinship of the living, which you say emphatically is not spirituality but is impersonal and transcends the ego and transcends the basic drives. Does this feeling appear much in your work, are you aware of it, this feeling of the kinship of the living on this planet?*

CKS: I think it's there everywhere in my work, isn't it? The farm animals in *The Singing Whakapapa*; the cats Agatha and Christie in *All Visitors Ashore* and the dog Rosh (short for Hiroshima); the poems 'Cat/ullus', 'A Cow is . . .', 'History: the Horse', 'The Season,

Tohunga Crescent', 'the stilts up on their stilts', the vines and olives of the Mediterranean – animals, plants, the seasons, they're everywhere. As a short-cut to answer your question, you could look at the quotation by Dennis McEldowney on the jacket of the *Collected Poems* where he speaks about lucidity and 'an unfailing ear', but then of 'a striking and unchanging element throughout his career' being that 'Stead pounces with delight on particular birds, plants, children, weather and human behaviour'. In both my fiction and my poetry, a huge amount comes simply from observation. And observation comes from being *interested*. That starts when you're a child. It's the escape – the relief! – from the ego. The world around you is what matters. To say it's not spirituality is perhaps a quibble; but if I rejected that word in the passage you refer to, it would have been because I don't like all the accretions that come along with it. The Zen Buddhists say 'everything is spirit' – but that seems to me a quibble too. If everything is spirit then the word cancels itself out – cancels out the need for itself. It's the real that interests me – the phenomenal world and its inhabitants, all of us, plants and animals, all favoured with life and doomed to die.

LJ: *This may be going way off on a tangent, but part of the message of the messianic D. H. Lawrence was that you are at one with the life-force during the sexual act, when you have a sense of unity with life. In the sexual scene in* All Visitors Ashore *when Curl is caught out with Felice, he is described as being the nearest he can come to 'a state of* satori *and of Grace'. Did you have something like Lawrence's attitude in mind without turning it into a religion?*

CKS: The word 'satori' of course comes from my interest in Zen Buddhism. That scene in *All Visitors Ashore* is also comic. It's funny, and it's absurd, but nevertheless, it does express what has been my attitude towards sex in my writing, and in my life. It's the feeling that there are not many situations in which you are behaving naturally, spontaneously, authentically, and where the mind-body dichotomy disappears completely. Not for long perhaps, but there are moments which are (paradoxically) timeless.

3. Fiction

LJ: *In that 1993 lecture in Dunedin, 'Narrativity, or the Birth of Story', when you talked about broad impulses in your fiction, one of them was 'to keep open and faintly ambiguous the degree to which what is offered is seen to be true'. And you went on to say that 'there can be a very fine line between fact and fiction, and to make the reader more or less aware of it, seems to me one of the enriching things fiction can do'. I was thinking that in your novels where you have individual characters based on historical figures or real people, to what extent in any individual novel, is the recognition of and knowledge of the historical person necessary to make that enrichment? You talked about Judas, you expect the audience to know that story and you expect them to know what happened to Judas and have a sense of the characters, but what about Mansfield?*

CKS: Well with Mansfield, I knew a lot about her, and I was quite sure that I shouldn't depart from the known facts at any point. But what you discover, when you write about someone who is well known, is that the difference between fiction and biography is that fiction has to be written as if you know it all. In reality the gaps in our knowledge of even quite famous people are huge. Even when events have been well documented, in fiction you have to know more than that documentation provides. It's an exercise that teaches you how very different fiction and biography are because, if you're writing a scene, you can't say 'It's believed Katherine said such and such, but it's not known what so-and-so replied' – because the moment you do that you're out of the novel-mode and back into biography. So you're creating a world in which the novel knows everything.

LJ: *And so what did you expect the reader to bring to this? I remember having lunch, soon after the novel came out, with an American Mansfield scholar who hadn't yet read it, and his first question to me was, 'What does Stead make of Katherine's relation with Fred Goodyear?'*

CKS: How strange! That's one place where I did invent. I invented a brief affair between Mansfield and Goodyear without knowing whether one occurred. Such letters as existed between them suggest that something was going on. But you see, even when I was inventing, I was only inventing within what the known facts seemed to make possible, and even plausible.

LJ: *Well, here's a question: here was someone, a scholar with a lot of specialised knowledge who would recognise, 'Oh, this is where you're filling in the gaps', and who was interested in the way you were doing it. He could take a kind of professional interest in what you were doing, but that would be a bonus, not something that you expected of the reader. But how much would you expect the reader to know about John Middleton Murry's romanticised view of the spiritual development of Katherine Mansfield? You seem to be opposing this view in the novel, implying that it doesn't explain everything.*

CKS: I wanted to write a novel which would be of interest to someone who knew nothing about Mansfield. It had to be of interest in its own right. When you write a novel about Judas, you can hardly expect that there's any reader who doesn't know the story is going to end with the crucifixion, but that's not the case with Mansfield. There will be numbers of readers who won't know anything about her, and it must be written with them primarily in mind. There will be things of special, extra interest for those who do know something about her – but that's not the primary determinant of what goes in to the story.

There are a few scholarly discoveries however. For example Katherine had put into a letter to someone that when her brother was dying he had said, 'Lift my head, Katy, I can't breathe'. When I looked at the only letter giving an account of his death, no such thing was said. She had re-written the death scene so that she was in her dying brother's thoughts. So there's a little gem hidden in the novel for Mansfield scholars.

LJ: *In relation to* All Visitors Ashore, *someone told me that you were happy that it came out in England before it did in New Zealand because in England there would be people who knew nothing about Frank Sargeson and Janet Frame and they could read the book just as a novel with no reference to specific people, so that if it worked for them, and clearly it did, then it didn't depend on recognition of the models. If there were at least some New Zealand readers who could pick up on Janet Frame and Frank Sargeson as standing behind Cecilia and Melior, would you view this as a kind of bonus that the reader gets, maybe analogous to the implicit allusion to Pound and Eliot in Melior's name, or just an interesting sideline?*

CKS: I think there are two ways of looking at it. One is that it's a distraction and the person who suits the novel best is the reader who doesn't know anything about Frank and Janet. The other would be that awareness of a connection with Sargeson and Frame adds a dimension of interest. But of course those two characters are only partly Frank and partly Janet. I've always thought that in writing characters in fiction, each is in a way yourself. So, yes, that is Frank Sargeson but only in the way that I would be if I were Frank Sargeson; and it's Janet Frame only as she would be if I were Janet. It's a mix of myself and my models – partly real and partly invention. I think it's a rather idealised portrait of Janet. And of course, the Frank character is a painter.

LJ: *With* Talking about O'Dwyer, *would it in some ways be a disadvantage to know too much about Dan Davin? Is this a book in which a real person might have given you some ideas that you could take off from but where there is no advantage to a reader recognising that source?*

CKS: Dan Davin wasn't the primary source for Donovan O'Dwyer. The primary source was a man called Humphrey Dyer. Davin was on Crete but only briefly. He was wounded within the first 24 hours and was taken off – though he did subsequently write the official New Zealand war history of the Battle of Crete. Davin is only in the novel in the sense that the image of Donovan O'Dwyer at Oxford is partly derived from him – the man who hasn't been quite as successful there as he wanted to be. There has been too much booze, and his best days are behind him – a long way behind. But even there there's a lot of invention. I knew Davin but not really well, so I wouldn't say it's a portrait. At the same time, I never met Humphrey Dyer. I knew his son very well, and I did read his own records of his experiences on Crete. So, very loosely, you could say that the character of O'Dwyer is a third Davin, a third Dyer, and a third invention.

LJ: *Yes, so the effect would not at all depend on recognition of sources.*

CKS: Not at all. People who knew and loved Davin have taken offence. And Dyer's son doesn't like the novel either. These connections have taken them away from the novel rather than towards it. Well, you just have to live with that. You're not writing to please them. You're practising the art of fiction, which is always partly an art of voyeurism, spying and theft.

LJ: *I get a sense from* The Secret History of Modernism *that there are probably some real life models there, but I don't know them, except for that sly implicit allusion to Damien Wilkins's review of* The End of the Century at the End of the World. *Such small details aside, you seemed to be simply drawing on people and places and events that you knew – sources, with no allusion, no expectation of recognition.*

CKS: There are elements which come from my first time in England. But one of the things you do when you're drawing on your experiences is that you move them around in time. Insofar as *All Visitors Ashore* draws on actual experience in Takapuna, it moves it back in time four years to 1951 to include the waterfront dispute of that year. *The Secret History of Modernism* is set in the 1950s, but the editor called Marx McClaren, and his off-sider Wilma Marienbad, were drawn to some extent from two London editors I worked for in the 1980s and 1990s. But really this is just a matter of the author keeping himself entertained. It's not relevant to how the novel should be read. We all do it of course – get excited because there's a character 'based on' Katherine Mansfield in a novel by D. H. Lawrence; or one 'based on' John Middleton Murry in one by Huxley – and so on to infinity. This is sometimes significant as literary history and sometimes it's just gossip. But it's mainly a distraction from a proper reading of the novel. It's only critically significant if the character existed in reality and is given his or her own name – as K.M. is in *Mansfield*, and as my namesake Christina Stead is in *The Secret History of Modernism*.

LJ: *Yes, yes. Where was it that you wrote about how a catalogue of books in print got the two of you confused? The computer corrected the Christian to Christina [laughter].*

CKS: She was credited with all my novels along with her own!

LJ: *Then there's the question of Mervyn Thompson in* The Death of the Body. *I sensed in reading that book that there were some parallels with Thompson because his was a dramatic case bringing out some of the things that were happening in our society, but that you were expressing your own views on the issues without reference to specific individuals ...*

CKS: I don't believe Mervyn Thompson was even on my mind when I wrote *The Death of the Body*. I have no recollection of thinking about him. But I suppose the novel does come out of the same nexus of political and academic tensions that the Mervyn Thompson crisis came out of. Poor Mervyn mishandled the whole thing. He was such a devoted feminist, he even put on a revival of that play by Renée, *Setting the Table*, where a woman who has been raped gets her friends to take revenge. And then what happens in the play was done to him in reality. He was kidnapped at night, tied to a tree and threatened with castration. In the fuss that followed he was interviewed on television and asked, 'Have you ever raped anybody?' Being scrupulous, and thinking on his feet, he said, 'No, but I'm sure there have been times when I've behaved insensitively.' In a way he was such an innocent, he didn't realise that this was not the time, and television was not the place, to be agonising over whether he might ever have done anything to deserve what had happened to him. I think that crisis killed him. The theatre community turned against him, and wouldn't put on his plays. It was a very cruel atmosphere. Some of that atmosphere might be background to *The Death of the Body*, but no more than that. My novel is a comedy with elements of thriller.

LJ: *Another trademark characteristic of your fiction which you list in that narrativity lecture was your love of narrative and narrative complexity. When I thought about this, I was struck by how in so many of your novels there's a mystery, a secret, a question to be* *answered. These are traditional novelistic devices, and of course fiction depends on them. Then there are the techniques for dealing with secrets which bring in more narrative complexity: the multiple time levels, the differing points of view, and the playing off of different accounts of the same thing, raising questions as to what is 'factual' within the fictional world. The complexity is part of the fun, the challenge of it. I think you use these devices in different ways in different novels. I think you spoke of* Villa Vittoria *as a kind of thriller where much depends on this revelation of the secret of what happened in the past.*

CKS: Yes, well let's take these things in order. First, story-telling. I like telling stories, and I like getting things in the right order – which means that you don't begin with the punch-line and you don't pay the information out in the wrong order; you withhold, and pay out, in the order that suits the narrative. Some people are natural storytellers and others are not. Critics have puzzled over why Wordsworth's *Lyrical Ballads* were so successful when they clearly don't have the same lyric intensity as 'Tintern Abbey' or 'Ode on Intimations of Immortality'. I think the answer is that Wordsworth was a good storyteller. The *Lyrical Ballads* are very good stories which he happened to put into rhyme.

As to complexity in the narrative: the way I've rationalised it is that for me I want the novel to be a reflection of the human mind; and the human mind doesn't work like a popular novel, going chronologically from A to B to C through to Z and 'end of story'. Our consciousness exists simultaneously in three dimensions. You're aware of the present, but at any one moment you may be more aware of what has happened in the past – or equally of your anticipation of what's going to happen. These time dimensions are there simultaneously, and with different emphasis from moment to moment. The novel which proceeds chronologically, and only tells you things in sequence – I think to an active mind, that's rather boring, undemanding, and not an image of reality at all. So I have argued that metafiction, which people think of in contrast to the realist novel, can be seen sometimes as a further step into realism. Not realism as it's normally understood, but closer to the reality of human consciousness.

LJ: *Yes, you've said that you're sometimes driven beyond realism to get nearer to reality, not to dispense with it. Perhaps an analogous argument can be made about the use of metafiction. To some contemporary readers the convention that the novelist is an historian of the fictional world telling us the 'truth' about something that 'really' happened is just irritating, and the writer can possibly win a willing suspension of disbelief better by a metafictional baring of the device.*

CKS: This reminds me of Shakespeare. I saw *The Winter's Tale* recently – and I used to lecture on it. In a late scene, where the statue 'comes to life', Paulina says, more than once, 'If this were written as a play and performed on a stage it would be hooted at.' You're being reminded that you're watching something scarcely believable, and suspending your disbelief. I think this is what I meant in 1993 when I talked about keeping readers aware of the fine line between fiction and reality. I didn't mean reminding them that there are sources in reality for characters and events; I meant keeping them aware that they are believing a fiction; experiencing it as if true. This has a long and honourable tradition. But one needs to be aware that for quite a number of readers who want reading to be an effortless diversion, such intellectual 'play' can be irritating. You have to recognise there is not one 'reading public', there are several; and you need to know which of these you are writing for. Mine, I think, is fairly select, though not on the whole, or not primarily, academic.

LJ: *In your review-essay of Michael Morrissey's anthology of the 'new fiction' back in 1986, you talked about how you wanted fiction 'to be as complex and as self-conscious as need be to stay alive and fresh' in the present, but you also wanted it not 'to stop doing what it has always done – telling stories, and seeming to convey some truth broader than its immediate subject'. To reject the realist's aim along with the traditional methods might be 'running out of one cage to find yourself in another, even smaller'.*

CKS: I think if you go too far with experimental writing of fiction, as say the French *nouvelle vague* did, you lose one of the advantages fiction has over poetry – that of reaching out to a wider audience. There are certain things you can do in fiction which you can't do in poetry; and in doing them you're writing for a broader audience. That's important economically if you're a full-time writer. You sell more copies, you get translated – the Judas novel was translated into eight or nine European languages – options are taken, and paid for, for possible movies. These things are not unimportant. But above all, you just find a lot more people are reading your books and talking about them and talking to you about them. So it's a matter of striking a balance, and of doing different things for different readers. In the end what matters to me most is poetry; and my poems, though I like them to be read and admired, are really, primarily, a transaction between me and the page. Fiction and social criticism on the other hand keep me engaged in a bigger world, though because of the kind of person I am it's still a distinctly literary one.

4. Poetry

LJ: *In the essay on Baxter's later poetry you talked about 'Night Watch in the Tararuas', your 1954 student poem, as very much*

*influenced by early Baxter and you spoke about how your 'present
discontent with the poem comes precisely from its forced march to a
moral conclusion'. In 'From Wystan to Carlos' you used the poem as
an example of what Modernist structure reacts against. Now, 55 years
since its original publication, and 30 years since your stated discontent, you have included the poem in the* Collected Poems *with some
local revisions. What are your feelings about it now? A good poem of
its kind and its time?*

CKS: Of course! A good workmanlike poem of its kind – though
distinctly youthful. There is no one right mode for one historic
moment – though of course if you write in the mode of quite
another age (Pope, say, in the year 2009) that can only be an exercise
in pastiche. But I think when I gave the 'From Wystan to Carlos'
lecture I had a somewhat clearer notion of where contemporary
poetry was heading than I have now. I suppose that was partly
polemical. Now I don't feel there's any particular axe it's my responsibility to grind, and when I look around at the current scene I'm
glad there's such a variety of possibilities. Some of them I want to
explore and others not. I'm happy to slip back now and then into
formal rhyming poems, if that's what the occasion seems to require.
'Open form', syllabics (which I use frequently these days) – there's
no anxiety. I let the poem tell me what it wants me to do and I try to
do it.

LJ: *I think of 'Night Watch' as a poem in which you were working with
a well-established form and showing that you could operate within it,
but you didn't want to stop there. I was also thinking, when I read it,
of Dylan Thomas, rather than Baxter, but then I thought, well yes, but
Baxter read Thomas.*

CKS: There's much more direct influence of Thomas in a poem
called 'And could he now', written around the same time. The direct

influences on 'Night Watch' would have been Baxter and Fairburn, in the attitudes and structure, and Donne. Particularly in the paradoxes, the Donne influence is hiding away there.

LJ: *Yes, yes, that whole idea of paradox and tension was in the air then. On the other hand, 'Pictures in a Gallery Undersea' clearly has a lot of Eliot there, as you say, and yet it's very much your own poem, and you talk of it as expressing your own sense of being in London for the first time, and how it's a supremely colonial poem, which makes a lot of sense to me. But you also say that it was a poem that almost dictated itself to you; which seems to imply that if the influence was operating on you it was almost at a subconscious level.*

CKS: That's literally how it was. I must have written it – or it wrote itself – over a matter of just a few days. It's full of being in London, my early days there, full of that excitement, together with the discoveries I was making in my PhD, which was ultimately going to be *The New Poetic*. And although the Eliot influence is clear, it's my own poem, a poem Eliot could never have written.

LJ: *So it wasn't, in a sense, a poem to build on, but it happened, and it worked. Interesting that you had to twist the arm of Charles Brasch to publish it, because obviously the* Landfall *readers appreciated it.*

CKS: Yes, he hesitated about it. When I was coming down a couple of years ago to lecture in Otago, the Hocken Library very helpfully sent me my correspondence with Brasch and I rediscovered our exchange there. He did hesitate, and then I sent him an explanation of certain things which puzzled him, and he accepted it. He'd kept all of that, including an earlier draft of the poem.

LJ: *When Brasch put together* Landfall Country, *he chose 'Dialogue on a Northern Shore' rather than 'Pictures in a Gallery' to represent* *your work in* Landfall, *but that is one of the earlier poems that you revised considerably in the* Collected Poems.

CKS: Brasch absolutely loved 'Dialogue on a Northern Shore', he and James Bertram. I was uneasy at first, but it sounded all right on radio. When I went back to it so many years later it seemed to me embarrassing, naive. So it's the one early poem that I allowed myself to completely revise – I don't know if you've checked –

LJ: *Oh, yes, completely revised – different ending, the male spirit becomes the female spirit, and the wording is changed and some passages have been taken out.*

CKS: I simply rewrote the whole thing. I'm sure it's better now, though Charles would be appalled. As a whole I tried to set out in the Foreword to the *Collected Poems* what rules I had made for myself and how I had not wanted to rewrite my past in the way Curnow and Yeats and Auden tended to do. When I did revise I tried to make it a little better but the same poem. 'Dialogue on a Northern Shore' is by far the most revised, and there I did break my own rule. But it was either going to be seriously revised or it was going to be omitted.

LJ: *Oh, it would have been a shame if it had been omitted .The poems we've been discussing came from the middle and late 1950s, but there wasn't a book collecting those early poems until* Whether the Will is Free *in 1964, and then not a second collection until* Crossing the Bar *in 1972. After that, collections were much more frequent, and there seemed to be a blossoming of a different kind of poetry. Were those years relatively less productive of poetry because of the demands of establishing an academic career?*

CKS: I think the sequence after my student and apprentice-poet years was that I was writing in Australia when I was lecturing there, I was writing in England while I was a postgraduate; then I came back here and I felt as if the house fell on me. I'd come back without finishing my PhD, so I had to work on that while preparing new lectures. I've never in my life been as seriously stressed as I was then. By the time I'd finished *The New Poetic* and got the PhD, there was nothing left in the tank. I managed to put together a book of poems. And then there was a delay because Caxton accepted it, but Leo Bensemann was famously dilatory. I grew impatient with Caxton and took it back and gave it to Blackwood Paul. So my first book of poems didn't appear until 1964 – the same year as *The New Poetic*. There was a gap – no new poems from about 1961 until I went on leave in 1965 when, very slowly, I found myself getting back into the poetry mode. And as you say it was a different style, a more mature style. That year in London was where quite a large number of poems that went into the second collection came from.

LJ: *Yes, I can remember reading some of those poems when they first came out, such as 'A Small Registry of Births and Deaths' – which hit me very hard. The Vietnam thing, and the experience of children being born, and that put the war in such a context –*

CKS: It does, doesn't it?

LJ: *And then 'April Notebook' and, published later, those 'Spring 1974' sonnets. I remember especially Sonnet Number 9: a young man knocking on the door, and the Voltairean hedge-clippers and Solzhenitsyn for birthday presents, and that ending: 'The quarrel of sparrows / Fills the silence of God that has lasted forty-two years'.*

CKS: My poems at that time were full of Vietnam. It was my great political obsession for years. It began in England in 1965, when Lyndon Johnson committed troops in large numbers to the war; and it continued right through to 1974, when America was finally defeated. It's a recurring background to my poems throughout those years – and to my first novel, *Smith's Dream*.

LJ: *You clearly were responding to those terrible political times and maybe also to what was happening in poetry. Those 22 unrhymed sonnets: was this late Baxter, or Lowell, or in the air?*

CKS: It was certainly in the air. I read the Baxter sonnets when they came out, especially *Jerusalem Sonnets*; I read Lowell's sonnets; I read Berryman.

LJ: *About the same time you also moved to longer poems than any you had published before, beginning with 'Quesada'. From the first they seem to me more inclusive than your earlier poems, containing long lines and short ones, traditional rhetoric and jokey word-play, with numbered sections with no narrative line or consecutive argument to hold it together. In your interview with Gerri Kimber you put 'Quesada' in your personal top ten. What do you especially like about it?*

CKS: It achieves a kind of free-flowing eloquence which is the vehicle for a lot of real feeling; but at the same time the feeling is controlled and distanced. I suppose in one way or another I think poetry should achieve beauty. Not sugar-cake; but in the sense Keats means when he proposes Beauty and Truth as interchange-able – which means there must be darkness as well as light. I think 'Quesada' achieves that – but with wit, with detachment, with self-irony. There were a number of triggers to the writing of that poem – some very personal, others literary. One of the literary ones was Whitman. Another was my being the supervisor of a thesis by Roger Horrocks – a very brilliant student and a very brilliant PhD. It made certain kinds of familiar Modernist experimentation seem exciting in ways that were new. I found it intellectually stimulating.

Horrocks was briefly Coleridge to my Wordsworth – something like that. Very unusual in a student–teacher relationship. I think Roger made me more aware of Whitman than I'd been before.

LJ: *Yes, well 'Quesada' certainly stands out as something different from what came before. And then the move from there to 'Walking Westward', longer and even more inclusive of a variety of elements, even an attack on the New English Syllabus, a Venn diagram, and Forrest Scott dancing with Iris Murdoch. You say in your note to it in the* Collected Poems *that it was meant to be the first in a sequence of five long poems.*

CKS: I had a plan for five long poems – the description for each was very general but I hoped they would amalgamate into something longer, which I suppose was a Poundian idea; and there's clearly something of Pound in the style. But some of that plan got dissipated into fiction. It never quite came together, but it lies behind some of the long poems, each of which, however, stands on its own. 'Walking Westward' was located in time but not in space – so it ranged freely about the world. 'Scoria' was fixed in space – very much an Auckland regional poem – but free in time. 'Scoria' was Kendrick Smithyman's favourite among my poems, because its region was also his.

LJ: *In the notes to the* Collected Poems *you say that in 'Yes, T.S.' you used up some of the intentions for the long sequence.*

CKS: That's right, and I wasn't sorry about that. It was just one of those times when I was free, alone, and ranged around the world, often miserable, lonely, but exposed and sensitive and reacting vividly. Unhappiness can be a great stimulant – not that I was only unhappy. It was really the ups and downs which were so stimulating that got into that poetry and gave it its peculiar flavour, its lift.

LJ: *As you point out in the notes to your* Collected Poems, Paris *is very different from the other long poems. You also place it on your top ten list, but you go on to say that you also like the very different 'Paris: The End of a Story'. Do you think the elegant form of* Paris *came about because the poem is not inclusive in the way that the other ones are or in the way that the essay 'The Sweetshop Window' is? Does that formal elegance fit a depiction of the 'Paris that's nobody's dream but your own' which must by its very nature leave out 'Deconstructing the Rainbow Warrior' and 'Paris: The End of a Story'?*

CKS: *Paris* is a witty poem – or ten witty poems. It's partly Paris as Paris, but more Paris as style, as 'poetry', as sensibility, as a way of thinking and feeling and being – *une manière de vivre*, very different from the Anglo tradition we inherit in New Zealand. In fact I think it's partly a poem *about* that difference, written in Auckland by a sensibility hard-pressed at work and at home, saying under its breath, 'Help. For fuck's sake let me out of here!' So of course it doesn't strike hard, in the political/philosophical way that 'Paris: The End of a Story' does. But it's not without its stings and its references to the real world. The President whose decision about H-bomb testing affects 'your southern oceans' is there; and the one who is bribed with diamonds (Giscard d'Estaing).

LJ: *A change comes about in* Voices *in 1990 and continues in sequences such as 'Crete' or 'King's Lynn & the Pacific' or 'History'. Instead of the long open form poem made up of 'radioactive fragments' from personal memory and experience, these are sequences, drawn mostly from historical texts and often involving dramatic speakers. Does this form allow you to bring a bit more of the novelist into the poetry without having to supply the continuity of narrative?*

CKS: It does, yes. But *Voices* is the most formal, the most anonymous stylistically, because it was a commissioned poem, and I didn't think my 'showing off' should get in the way of the historical subjects. It's like a return to the style of the 1950s, with plenty of evidence of hard work if you look at the subtle way in which rhyme schemes, for example, are almost invisibly worked into the formal sonnets. Consequently it's more pedestrian than the others you name; but when presented on radio it did work very well. It proved itself dramatic – these are indeed 'voices'. The others are much freer and more inventive stylistically. 'History', though it draws on factual sources as *Voices* does, goes back to the double-margin form used in 'Yes, T.S.' and in my Catullus poems. 'Crete' is a sequence in which subject determines shape. Some sections of 'King's Lynn & the Pacific' use syllabics, particularly the thirteen-syllable triplets I used in the poems at the chapter ends of *My Name Was Judas*, where (incidentally) making Judas not just an old man looking back and remembering, but something of a poet, meant fiction and poetry were brought together in a single work – something new and unusual.

LJ: *'S-T-R-O-K-E': The subjective voice and the radioactive fragments again? I think also of one of the key texts of my literary education, Robert Penn Warren's 'Pure and Impure Poetry'. This poem is certainly 'impure' in his sense, like Donne rather than like Shelley – puns, playful allusions, word games (even with the name of the Australian rugby player) in a poem evoking the extremity of personal experience. Was this 'impure' inclusiveness a conscious aim, a test of yourself?*

CKS: That was just the way it happened. I'd had a stroke that left me – fortunately only briefly – dyslexic (and, incidentally, innumerate). I was just trying to prove to myself, in my head, that I could still make poems, even if I couldn't write them down. Any kind of poem – I was hardly thinking about kinds, just proving to myself that in there the language was still willing and able to work for me. As days passed and the fog began to clear I managed to scribble them into a notebook. It was like writing in the dark. Later again I selected the ones that seemed to work best, and published them. They have (not surprisingly) a slightly desperate quality which I think gives them a real edge. I still think they have a kind of bed-rock quality. They are right down there, the basic person, the basic talent.

5. The Critical and Other Prose

LJ: The New Poetic *in 1964,* Pound, Yeats, Eliot and the Modernist Movement *in 1986 – your two book-length 'academic' studies of Modernism. I think the first has been your best-selling book – rather extraordinary that a critical study should outsell even novels. I've got on my shelf a well-thumbed, much-marked 1967 Pelican reprint. The second, written, as you say, at about the same temporal distance from Pound and Eliot as Arnold was from the Romantics when he wrote his critical essays on them: 'a good distance from which to get a perspective – far enough away to see the whole picture, close enough to see it clearly and as a living, intelligible action'. Both seem to me really important in understanding the nature and history of Modernism, but also, I sense, bearing a significant relationship to your own poetic practice. I get the sense in reading them in the context of your poetry that* The New Poetic *in some ways precedes your own poetic Modernism, maybe providing a poetics for it, while* Pound, Yeats, Eliot . . . *follows your movement to a Poundian poetics in your own poems, especially the long ones, in the 1970s.*

CKS: That's probably right – near enough. And of course the famous – or anyway much discussed – 'From Wystan to Carlos' lecture was simply the application of my thinking, at the time of writing the second big book, to the subject of New Zealand poetry. It gave a fresh picture of our poetry, shifting away from

Curnow's overview. Of those two books, which were, both of them, literary criticism and literary history, the second might be better – more searching critically, more (even more!) knowledge-able, more mature – but it didn't have the impact *The New Poetic* had. I remember thinking when I finished *The New Poetic*, 'People will *read* this!' And telling friends it was really my first novel. The crucial thing about it was that it was *timely*. It said in particular about Eliot what many serious readers of his work half knew and yet hadn't brought to consciousness – that the way his poetry had been written and talked about was wrong; and that this had been brought about by following too slavishly the obvious and deliberate things Eliot himself had said about it, without noticing other things he had, so to speak, 'let slip'. And this was at a time when Eliot was right at the centre of poetic and of critical practice. Everything came back to him. Everyone wrote about him and cited him. So *The New Poetic* landed right in a moment of literary history. It also put Yeats right up there where he belonged, and where the Leavisites, for example, had refused to acknowledge he deserved to be; and it corrected and clarified some matters of literary history – about the Georgians for example. It made a big impression – much bigger than I realised at the time. It has been re-issued many times, both in the United Kingdom and the United States, most recently only two years ago; and I still encounter people in the UK – often poets – who say they were significantly influenced by it. Paul Muldoon when he was here for the Wellington Festival said the same thing – that he'd been a 'fan' for forty years. And famous Seamus, of course.

LJ: *What about literary theory? You seem to have been untouched by it.*

CKS: Yes, in the sense that I haven't tried to adopt that style – which is what it is really; a style, a fashion. There was a period here in New Zealand when it washed over us. If you were young you proved your Eng. Lit. credentials by writing in a professional argot that no one but other like-minded academic pros could understand; and since I had always insisted that there was no excuse for critics who couldn't make themselves understood, this put me at odds with some high-fliers who have since vanished into the sun, or Australia. Critical fashions come and go, like fashions in anything. In the end the writing survives if it's intelligible and contains real intelligence (both senses).

LJ: *On criticism of New Zealand literature:* In the Glass Case *in 1981 and* Kin of Place *in 2002 collect the major essays on New Zealand writers, although there are other reviews and reminiscences included in your more miscellaneous prose collections –* Answering to the Language *in 1989,* The Writer at Work *in 2002 and* Book Self *in 2008. The first discussions of New Zealand writers appeared in the late 1950s, the most recent in 2006 – fifty years of critical writing on New Zealand literature. In his review-essay on* Kin of Place *in* Landfall *in May 2003 John Newton accuses you in your New Zealand criticism of trying to 'prolong [the] nationalist impulse . . . far beyond its use-by date'. What do you see as the shape of your developing attitude over fifty years to the writings of the Sargeson-Curnow-Brasch generation of cultural nationalists?*

CKS: Literary and cultural nationalism was very important because up to, let's say the end of the 1960s, *nationalism* was important. What I mean by that is that we had to break away from cultural dependence and a colonial mind-set, and that required intellectuals and literary people to lead the way – and they did – Fairburn, Glover and Curnow especially. You only have to think back (if you're old enough) to the royal visits of the 1950s. They were demeaning. Pride demanded that we assert ourselves, and that's what the writers did. Once the break was made, nationalism became unnecessary. I don't like nationalism – a lot of the worst in human

behaviour stems from it – but, like a rifle, it has its moments and
its uses. As for my trying to prolong it – that's simply wrong. I'm
probably the only New Zealander who has managed to function
as a critic, mainly from home, but *inter*nationally. And what was
I doing in the 'Wystan to Carlos' lecture if it wasn't shifting away
from the Curnow focus and putting our poetry into an international
frame? In the field of literary criticism I'm seen abroad less as a
New Zealander than as one who has published and lectured over
many years in many places on the subject of poetic Modernism.
I notice, for example, that a recent article in *Viaggio in Liguria*,
on English-language poets who have written about the Ligurian
region, I'm described as '*uno dei piu noti critici letterarari anglosas-
soni*' – no reference to New Zealand at all. How can I be described
as New Zealand's super-nationalist critic, even outstripping
Curnow in this?

LJ: *Since the early 1980s a very visible portion of your writing has
been cultural criticism. The passage in 'From Wystan to Carlos'
about 'a certain flow of the tide' in a literary movement that cannot
be turned back has been turned back on you in relation to both your
literary and your cultural criticism. But in 'The New Victorians' in
1984 you referred to a different metaphor that Curnow had used: '. . .
we are subject to waves of intellectual fashion which strike us after
they have abated at source, and there is not, here, the conservative
inertia that operates as a safety drag mechanism in larger, longer-es-
tablished societies'. If this is the New Zealand situation, what do you
think your role has been in the culture debates of the last 25 years?*

CKS: What I had to say was often striking and provoked debate.
It could have been put more obliquely, and mildly, and might
have passed unnoticed. Would that have been better? A lot of
what shocked at the time now looks inoffensive. Think, just as an
example, of 1980s feminism, which I sometimes dared to question:

the idea that girls and boys were essentially the same, and that,
apart from physiology, it was only cultural conditioning made
the differences. Modern studies have proved exactly the reverse,
that the differences are largely in the genes – as common sense
and observation told one at the time. What I resisted in that area
was the politicisation of relations between the sexes – one of the
most fraught, delicate, subtle and complex areas of human experience, while politics, of necessity, reduces and simplifies these
matters to slogans. This politicisation still goes on, but much less
bullishly than twenty years ago. In matters of race I think I have
tried to put a Pakeha view which is reasoned and thoughtful and
which avoids the red-neck racist mindless ahistorical opposition
to every advance Maori make and every claim that is made by or
for them. I still think that Pakeha view is needed, perhaps more
than ever, but it calls for steady nerves and I'm probably too old
to engage any more. I would like reason and justice to prevail. I'm
still keenly aware of the Maori at the bottom of the heap, and so
many in jail on brutal, ever longer and ever more counter-produc-
tive sentences, who have not been helped in the least by the way
Maori at the top have been often artificially advanced. This is an
area of our lives in which there is so much hypocrisy and pretence
I find it painful. I don't spend a lot of time looking back, but when
I do I find very little I've written in these fields (racism, feminism,
the culture debates) that isn't carefully thought out, rational, and
clearly expressed. There is always another point of view; but why
my having my own should have provoked quite the heat it did for a
time is . . . I don't know. Just a measure of New Zealand's smallness,
I suppose. One lives with it.

My Parnell

I have lived in Parnell (with intervals away overseas) for the past half-century, but my family connections go back much further. My understanding is that when my great-great-grandfather, Church Missionary Society catechist and subsequently gardener, John Flatt, moved with his wife and two children from the Bay of Islands, driven out by Hone Heke's attack on Kororareka, he came to live in Parnell. That was in 1845.

The next family connection with Parnell that I'm aware of comes when my seafaring Swedish grandfather (from whom my two first names, Christian Karlson, are derived), and his wife Caroline Karlson (née Flatt), set off for one of his periodic expeditions into the Pacific, they left their only daughter, my mother Olive Karlson, in the care of another seafarer's family, the Quelches, who lived either in Brighton Road or Lee Street. That expedition lasted three years, and during that time my mother used to play with the Quelch children in and around Hobson Bay, where my own children and grandchildren

A foreword to the first issue of Parnell Heritage's *Journal*, September 2011, pp. 2–3.

have played. She also, as they did, attended Parnell School, though its location in those days was not where it is now but (I think) in Fraser Park on the harbour side of Parnell Rise.

So although I grew up a Mt Eden boy, I am able to claim connections with Parnell School that began long before my time and continue right up to the present, with one grandson still a student there.

In 1963, when my wife Kay and I bought our house in Tohunga Crescent it was small, run-down and ridiculously cheap. Over the intervening years I have thought of it as a kit-set house, subject to expansion and re-arrangement according to the needs of the family. It has been widened, lengthened (including a two-level addition at the front), a double carport has been added, the fibro shed on the back lawn has been replaced by a Lockwood office connected to the house by a deck. Two bedrooms became three, then four, then shrank back to three when an extra bathroom was added – and so on. It has never been large; but wooden houses can be as adaptable as their occupants.

The Scottish immigrant from whom we bought the house in 1963 told us that 'colour was creeping in at the top of the street' but assured us it would stay there. By this he meant, we assumed, not just Maori but Pacific Islanders, and his 'thus far and no further' opinion was meant to be reassuring. We neither believed it, nor cared. Soon Parnell School was 50 per cent Polynesian, and richer for it; and then, alas, as the decades ticked over, a certain familiar pallor began to pre-dominate once again, as Parnell became middle class and property values behaved accordingly.

For us, indifferent to colour-shading of neighbours or neighbour-hood, we were glad to be in a quiet corner of Auckland so close to the city, and particularly to the university where both Kay and I worked, and where our three children would all, over time, be students and graduates. We have always had one car, and often two; but all the family have been walkers as well, to and from the university, around (and across) the Bay, through the Reserves and the Domain, in and out of town. Swimmers too, sometimes at Judges Bay, sometimes at the Parnell Baths, though more recently Kay and I have made a habit of swimming at Kohimarama.

Immediately round about us there has been surprising stability. The neighbours at the back have remained the same all the time we have been here, with a change only of generation not of family. The neighbour on the eastern side, who was an Elam student when we first arrived in the street, is still there, now head of the art department at an Auckland secondary school. Across the street since 1965 lived my university colleague and fellow poet Allen Curnow and his wife Jeny. Until he died aged ninety in 2001 Allen and I conducted an on-going literary conversation, both oral and written, exchanging poems and ideas across the street.

In the time we have lived here Parnell has changed in many ways. In the 1960s it still had the aura of the old, unfashionable, inner-city suburbs, with many small workers' cottages in the hollows, and bigger houses on the ridges. As the suburban fashion for living away from the centre of Auckland changed over the years, every small cottage became a valuable property. If we had chosen our dwelling place with a view to long-term gain (we did not) we could hardly have done better. We have had a secure home base and have travelled abroad frequently, sometimes for extended periods.

In Parnell in those early years there was money to be made from property, as there was to be later in Ponsonby. One person who recognised this was Les Harvey (popularly known as 'the mad millionaire'), who bought up declining buildings along Parnell Road and refurbished them, creating what is now known as Parnell Village. Although Les's taste for adding bow windows, stained or art nouveau glass, decorative bridges, finials and other 'period' signifiers was somewhat random, even occasionally bizarre, it has to be acknowledged that something of the past was preserved which might otherwise have been replaced by the characterless anonymity usually favoured by developers.

In our early years there was still a fire station on Parnell Road with an English-looking terrace of small houses for the firemen and families. The station itself is now a private house, and the terrace-houses privately owned. The lovely old wooden cathedral was still on the west side of the road; and the shift across on mammoth rollers to its present site was a classic piece of Kiwi 'house-moving'. Placed beside the new brick cathedral, which still at that time lacked the Dick Toy-designed front it has now, may have been a way of freeing up the old site for real estate development; but it had the effect of making the contrast – the modest and elegant nineteenth-century wooden structure and the rather gross twentieth-century brick one – more than ever obvious and painful.

Down the road, the little wooden Catholic church remains unchanged and, in its modest (basic) way, not unattractive. In the early 1960s the priest there was Father Forsman, who liked to drink and talk with Jewish doctor George Andre, whose home and practice were on the corner of Maunsell Road.

Spear fishing at night was not uncommon on Hobson Bay (one neighbour had a set net, probably even then illegal); and I have a distinct memory, from the time when we all used the old sewer pipe as a causeway for walking, of seeing large kingfish at high tide patrolling up and down in the pipe's shadow, and making lightning raids on flounder out where the sun was shining. When someone walked along the pipe the gulls would rise ahead and settle behind so from a distance it was like a white ribbon gracefully rising and falling. At times the gulls would use the pipe as a roosting place and the noise of their quarrelling and fighting for space carried on even after dark. The Bay of course is still an annual autumn staging post for migrating seabirds, including, possibly, godwits.

Those were pre-supermarket days, when a village of small shopkeepers flourished. There was even a cinema on the corner of Gibraltar Crescent, converted briefly to become the Danish embassy, and now housing gift- and tourist-shops. There were some nice old-fashioned pubs and seedy rooming houses; and still some factories – Heards on the main road, and Nestlé down in the gully of

St Georges Bay Road, whose employees lived round about in the old cottages, or in places like Avoca House.

Twice in our time here Hobson Bay has seemed to come under threat. The first was the plan in the early 1960s to reclaim it as a new site for Auckland University. Allen Curnow and I were among the most vigorous opponents of this plan; so was John Morton, Professor of Zoology, who argued passionately that the few remaining of Auckland's tidal bays should be preserved for the health of the harbour and for their intrinsic beauty.

The next threat appeared roughly two decades later in the form of the plan for the Eastern Corridor, a motorway that would have cut right across the Bay. When I heard it said how little damage this would do to the Bay I remembered hearing, decades before, that a motorway down Grafton Gully would scarcely change the lovely bush there. One only has to look at Grafton Gully now to know such palliative assurances were dishonest.

The Eastern Corridor battle was hard fought and involved many people willing to give time and money to preserve the Bay. It was the issue that cost John Banks the mayoralty – a fact he seemed to have taken to heart when, after a gap of three years, he became mayor again. But there are lessons to be learned from these episodes, and not to be forgotten. Once bays are 'reclaimed', or motorways built, there is no going back, even when it becomes apparent that what has been lost was priceless.

Dear Chris

I suppose it was some time during World War II that Allen Curnow wrote the now famous lines

> Not I, some child, born in a marvellous year,
> Will learn the trick of standing upright here.

Looking back now it seems to me by the time Curnow wrote that, the 'marvellous year' had already happened. It was 1922 – post-World War I, and eleven years after Curnow's own birth. An extraordinary group of our most talented literary and academic people were born in 1922 – Keith Sinclair, Bob Chapman, Kendrick Smithyman, Maurice Duggan, Bill Pearson, Hone Tuwhare, W. H. Oliver, Ronald Hugh Morrieson – and of course Christine Bull whom we're celebrating and farewelling today as Chris Cole Catley. Very soon after would come James K. Baxter, Janet Frame, Dave Ballantyne.

A eulogy given at the funeral of publisher Chris Cole Catley,
University of Auckland Chapel, 27 August 2011.

In a way Curnow was right. It's as if no Pakeha born before World War I could stand upright here. Curnow made great poetry out of that insecurity – that uncertainty about who we were; and strangely the new confidence that followed the war was caught most simply and directly in a few lines of Curnow's contemporary Denis Glover:

> I do not dream of Sussex downs
> or quaint old England's
> quaint old towns –
> I think of what may yet be seen
> in Johnsonville or Geraldine.

Chris, of course, knew all of the people I've mentioned. When Dave Ballantyne moved to Wellington to work on the *Southern Cross* he was Chris and John's next-door neighbour in Willis Street. When Maurice Duggan ran away from Auckland, it was to the Willis Street house he went – but not before checking out that it would suit a one-legged man of liquid habits: 'Do you have to climb to reach your place', he asked first, 'and how far are you from a pub?'

Willis Street was flat, and there were plenty of pubs.

I got to know Chris through Frank Sargeson. I heard about her long before we met; and she said she'd heard a lot about Karl and Kay Stead. Frank's conversation had that effect. There are some of his friends I feel even now I know well though I never met them.

To jump forward: Frank made Chris not just his literary executor, but his heir. There were three small bequests to others, and then the rest was all Christine's. He told her to spend it all – go on a world cruise; but of course, cunning old Frank knew she wouldn't do that. She was too scrupulous. She was conscientious, she was efficient. He teased her about that, 'the head prefect' – and she would ruefully acknowledge that she had indeed been a head prefect – but he depended on it. He must have known she would do something to honour the man and protect and preserve his work. I doubt that even Frank could have guessed how thoroughly she would go about the task.

When Frank died Chris was living in Picton, so she set up the Sargeson Trust, herself as chairperson, myself, Dave Ballantyne, Michael King and Nigel Cook as the ones on the spot here in Auckland who could help her arrive at decisions and carry them out in her absence. As you all know, the Sargeson house was preserved, but alas at the cost of most of the surrounding land that had been Frank's garden. No matter – Chris was determined it should be saved. Wordsworth's Dove Cottage in Grasmere had become a shrine, a place of literary pilgrimage. Very well, our place of New Zealand literary pilgrimage would be not a stone cottage but a fibrolite bach.

> I do not dream of Sussex downs
> or quaint old England's
> quaint old towns –

– I dream of a fibro bach in Takapuna.

But she wanted more than that. She wanted a place and a stipend so writers could come and work. We set our sights on the stables on the edge of Albert Park – now the Frank Sargeson Centre and the George Fraser Gallery. We raised money, some from the sale of the Esmonde Road land, some from Auckland City, and some from PEN, to set the thing in motion. PEN in those days was run from Wellington by what I used to call *droit de géographie*. They'd asked for a grant to establish a writer's retreat, but typically, when they received $30,000 from the Government, they realised they had nowhere in mind to spend it. We suggested it be given to the Sargeson Trust, and to our surprise (I hope I'm remembering this correctly) we got it.

I wrote to Chris after the meeting:

> I think most people didn't realise that you are the beneficiary [of the Sargeson will], not just the trustee . . . I made it clear at the meeting

that that was so, and asked that your generosity be noted, because I
remember Frank telling me (and I recounted this) that he'd told you
when he died you were to take a world trip on the proceeds!

In her reply Chris said:

Thank you for telling PEN about Frank's idea that I should go on
a world cruise with his money. Not a trip – a *cruise*. You can well
imagine those eyes snapping and twinkling as the connotations of
'cruise' were evoked.

In the same letter she wrote, 'I shall duly butter up the Hon Minister,
as I found Keith Sinclair dutifully doing after the funeral. Ministers
need a lot of butter.'

Soon the Sargeson Trust was expanded to include Dennis
McEldowney, Elizabeth Caffin, Kevin Ireland, Graeme Lay, Gordon
McLauchlan. Chris moved up here, to Devonport, and it seems to
me these final years, continuing as publisher, running the Sargeson
Trust, setting up the Michael King Trust with its writers' centre on
Mt Victoria, were a marvellous rounding out and completion of a
wonderful life.

Chris has been the ideal literary executor – not precious, or protective, or greedy – entirely lacking in the unhelpful qualities outlined
in Ian Hamilton's book *Keepers of the Flame*. Recently I made this
point on a public occasion, comparing her to another literary executor
who has behaved like an illustration of the dire Hamilton thesis. After
that event I emailed Chris to say I hoped I hadn't embarrassed her
by making the comparison so explicit. The superb diplomat emailed
back to say she was having trouble with her hearing aid that night and
hadn't heard me say anything of the kind.

Chris was full of enthusiasm and energy – but it was enthusiasm
with discrimination; energy with intelligence. She was a woman of
liberal conscience. She was keenly and comically aware of human

folly, but also kind, generous and compassionate. She was fun to be with. I admired her, enjoyed her company, felt immense fondness for her. I feel grateful for the good luck of having known her, and honoured – thank you Martin and Jenny – to have this opportunity to speak about her.

One Thing Leads to Another

In preparing this lecture I decided to forgo the temptation, and the attendant risks, of elderly reminiscence. Rather than an account of 'How it was in my day' – which could equally have been the 1960s and 1970s when I was a professor in the English Department, or the early 1950s when I was a student, I thought it might be of more general interest to offer an impression of my life as a writer in the decades since I left. So I've prepared a narrative which I'll call 'One Thing Leads to Another'.

I've always regarded myself as a writer first and an academic second. Teaching was my profession, writing my vocation. Of the three literary modes, poetry, fiction and criticism, poetry was for me the most important, the most demanding and satisfying, but also the most mysterious and ungovernable. I taught myself the basics very early, and I was a competent technician. But poems – real poems as distinct from verse exercises – came and went according to determinants

A lecture delivered in the Maidment Theatre, University of Auckland, to mark my receiving the university's Distinguished Alumnus Award in February 2008.

which could seem almost independent of the will. I used to describe poetry as a welcome visitor which made its own decisions about when to come and how long to stay. The process doesn't seem quite as unfathomable to me as it once did; but the various myths about the Muse and the Aeolian harp are not based on nothing. They express the poet's feeling that poetry comes partly from forces that are not fully explicable, or available to consciousness.

Literary criticism was part of my work as an academic. I was trained in it and practised it successfully, both in New Zealand and beyond. But fiction, which I also wanted to write, I found hugely demanding of time and energy. While I was lecturing I sometimes wrote short stories; but when I tried to combine writing a novel and teaching, I became exhausted, depleted and depressed. Clearly if I was going to have a better shot at being a novelist I had to stop being a Professor of English.

I left the university finally in 1986, but in fact I'd been easing myself out of teaching for some time before that. I'd held the Arts Faculty Research Fellowship for three years, and had taught in only four of the preceding eight years.

I had a small Lockwood office built in the back garden; my books and files were transferred there from the university, and my working habits as well. Leaving the security of university employment was liberating, but also slightly scary. As I say in the introduction to my recent collection of essays, *Book Self*, 'I went without regret. Not, however, without fears for my future. It was like stepping off a secure academic perch into nowhere.'

I remembered my old mentor Frank Sargeson's warning that writing was a full-time job; you had good days and bad days, but if you let yourself off because you didn't feel 'inspired', or because your mood wasn't right, you would soon let yourself off again, and yet again, until you were one of those people who talk constantly about 'my *writing*' but never appear in print. So I kept at it, and kept office hours. I worked really very hard. For the nine or ten months of the year I was in New Zealand I worked from 9 to 5.30, Monday to Friday. I managed to get away at least once each year, usually to England and France, sometimes to the United States, often at someone else's expense, but if not, then at my own. That way I kept contact with publishers and editors, but also extended the stock of experience and the range of locations I could draw on as fiction writer. And even while away I was usually working on something.

It was only while thinking about this lecture that I did a survey of my publications over the sixteen years from 1984 to 2000 and recognised how many there were. I worked hardest at fiction; but I also wrote quite a lot of literary journalism for papers here and in Australia and the United Kingdom; and at intervals which for the first few years were spasmodic, I wrote poems. The novels were *All Visitors Ashore*, 1984; *The Death of the Body*, 1986; *Sister Hollywood*, 1989; *The End of the Century at the End of the World*, 1992; *The Singing Whakapapa*, 1994; *Villa Vittoria*, 1997; and *Talking about O'Dwyer*, 1999. In addition, during that period I published my last big academic book (done while I held that Arts Faculty Research Fellowship), two collections of essays, one of short stories, and four of poems. Together with the novels I think it made a total of sixteen books in as many years.

I was making up for lost time. I was also getting myself into a certain amount of trouble by engaging in public controversy – not that that was new, but I no longer had the faint aura of respectability and authority a university chair had seemed to provide. I was living 'the life of the writer' which Frank Sargeson, all those years ago, had urged me to do – but in a way that was headlong and occasionally bruising.

If I had done that survey from 1984 to the present rather than to 2000, there would have been no difference before and after the turn of the century. The apparently smooth and uninterrupted production line has continued. But in fact an interruption occurred which is part of the narrative I'm constructing here. In 1996–97 Kay and I were in Oxford for eight months where I was Senior Visiting Fellow at St John's College; and following on from that came a new collection of poems, *The Right Thing*, and the novel *Talking about O'Dwyer*.

Once those two things were done I felt emptied out. For the moment I couldn't think where my next novel was coming from, so I passed the time bringing together a collection of essays from recent years, published in 2000 with the title *The Writer at Work*. But when that task was done there was still no new idea for fiction, and I began to feel anxious. I was used to having ideas and no time to make something of them before they went stale. This was different – a sort of dryness and blankness. It was my first real experience of what's called 'writer's block'. I knew I was as fluent as ever on the page; I'd learned a great deal about the art of fiction simply by doing it; the brain seemed as clear and sharp as ever; but the idea, the germ, the *donnée*, as Henry James liked to call it, was missing.

In a state of mind that mixed amusement and anxiety in about equal measure, and absolutely lacking anything better to work on, I began to write a story in the persona of an elderly New Zealand fiction writer suffering from writer's block. 'Where do your ideas come from?' is the most frequently asked question at literary festivals. Clearly this one came from desperation! It was a shot in the dark. This is how what was to become the novel called *The Secret History of Modernism* began:

> My name is Laszlo Winter. I'm a novelist, and for the purposes of this identification we will begin in Auckland, New Zealand, at the beginning of the new century, a time when I'd been experiencing, for perhaps three months, perhaps six, something new for me, an obstacle commonly called writer's block. Maybe my writing life was over. Maybe it, and I, belonged to the old century, and could be rounded off with a retrospect, some sort of autobiography – or 'memoir' as some of my similarly-placed writing colleagues [. . .] had lately been calling their books of recollection, a description used, I'd begun to think, as an excuse for invention, inaccuracy, and the settling of old scores.

Or perhaps I might let myself off writing altogether, and simply close up for ever the room in the back garden where my work has been done, the structure I refer to mostly as 'the shed' (humbler than it deserves), but also as 'the studio' (pretentious), 'the office' (too businesslike), and 'the Lockwood' (name of its manufacturer).

Sometimes I thought of joining a gym, losing the weight gained, and regaining the muscle lost, in the past ten or fifteen years. Sometimes of buying a piece of cheap land and building a kitset house (a Lockwood, perhaps). Then there was the thought of slugging my way through all the unread books I knew I ought to have read, and still wanted to read. Or of giving in entirely to my passive addiction to movies. Or of travelling all over New Zealand on a bicycle. Or of accepting Louise's idea (Louise is my wife, and French) that we should sell everything and decamp to eat and drink ourselves to death in the French countryside . . .

But at the same time that I thought up these schemes for a new life I was listless, lacking the purpose and energy necessary to make them more than whimsical dreams. I was always picking up a newspaper or magazine, which was really an excuse to lie down. When I lay down to read, I slept. When I woke I was tired. I knew (or thought I knew) I wasn't ill. It was, I supposed, a mild depression. I felt healthy, discontented, exhausted.

Any of these plans of action might, if there were ever an objective measure of better and worse, be better than telling yet another story, or another (as mine tended to be) story-within-a-story within-a . . . (and so on), my narrative habits tending to the structural character of a Russian doll. (1–2)

All this was a direct transcription from what was happening to me. As this passage goes on Lazlo drifts into a discussion of the nature of narrative. He reflects that all of Shakespeare's dying kings and tragic heroes leave instructions about how their *stories* are to be told – Richard II's 'tell thou the lamentable tale of me'; Hamlet's 'absent thee from felicity awhile / And in this harsh world draw thy breath in pain / To tell my story' – and so on. And then he reflects on his own novels:

> When at this time [. . .] I cast my eyes over the books I had written,
> I began to notice that if they had a single subject it was the century just
> ended. They appeared to be about many different things, but were really
> about just one: the fifty years of human history I had lived through
> with an adult consciousness, and how the earlier fifty, which I knew
> by reading and report, bore upon them. Perhaps that (I began to think)
> explained my writer's block. My time was up. The story I'd made it my
> business to tell had come to an end, not quite with a whimper, but only
> with the bangs of the millennial fireworks. (3–4)

Soon I began to feel that by writing about writer's block I was writing myself out of it. I still had only a very general notion of what the story was going to be, but by the end of the first chapter I'd created a character, a voice, and a situation. Laszlo Winter was not C. K. Stead. But clearly he was in some ways a projection of myself, with the same temperament and stylistic inclinations, amused by the same kind of jokes, given to similar behaviours, good and bad, and currently facing precisely the same problem – how to begin a new novel.

Laszlo finds his subject by an accident which is also taken from my own experience right at that time. A German academic with whom I'd had distant connections many years before visited Auckland and got in touch with me. I met him, and with the ruthlessness of a needy author I 'borrowed' him, renamed him Otto Stiltz, and put him into the novel.

Beyond that point the invention begins. I made it that this Otto Stiltz had been briefly married to a young Australian woman with whom Laszlo Winter had been in love as a young man when he was a postgraduate student in London. That sets off a process of reminiscence by Laszlo which takes us back to London in the 1950s, and a great deal of the action occurs there. But to complicate the story, and to give it a deeper and darker historical undertone, this Australian woman, Samantha, or Sammy, was herself at that time having an affair with a Jewish journalist whose parents were refugees from the Nazis, and some of whose relatives had not escaped. So indeed the opening pages' suggestion that Laszlo's fiction has been, in one way and another, a review of the century just past, is ratified by the novel that follows. The story of Laszlo and Sammy in London of the 1950s is inter-cut with the story of the German Jewish family of Sammy's lover – a story that ends in the gas chambers and crematoria of Auschwitz. As all novelists do, Laszlo Winter is repeating himself. He is writing his prototype novel, but hoping (again as all novelists do) to do it better this time.

Among my novels *The Secret History of Modernism* is one of my favourites, but also probably my least successful if success is measured by sales, book tours, translation rights and the panoply of awards and prizes. Here in New Zealand it didn't even make the short-list for the Montanas. You could say with only slight exaggeration that at home it sank without trace. Abroad it had a quiet *succès d'estime*, so I hope you will forgive me if I quote briefly from some of the reviews that were *not* seen in New Zealand:

'C. K. Stead is challenging, fun, urbane and brilliant. Read him!' – John de Falbe, *Spectator*. '. . . the narrative is dynamic, the prose limpid. I can't enthuse too much' – S. B. Kelly, *Scotland on Sunday*. '. . . grippingly intelligent' – Michael Thompson-Noel, *Financial Times*. 'Engrossing yet delicately understated . . . fiction of the highest order: gracefully intelligent, emotionally probing, politically sharp . . .' – Rosemary Goring, *Dublin Sunday Tribune*. 'Inspiring . . .' – Ruth Scurr, *The Times*. '. . . a remarkable novel . . . beautifully written . . .' – Barry Forshaw, *Good Book Guide*. '. . . intricate, keenly felt . . . Stead is one of the finest novelists writing in English . . .' – William Tanner, *Hampstead & Highgate Express*. '. . . humane, intelligent, often funny, and very accomplished' – Alan Massie, *Scotsman*.

'. . . as subtle as Jane Austen and as fatalistic as Thomas Hardy . . . .
a minor miracle of a novel . . .' – Eileen Battersby, *Irish Times.*

I wish I could say these accolades meant a popular success, but as I've indicated, they didn't. Literary reviewers (including, I should mention, Iain Sharp and Michele Hewitson in New Zealand), and friends like Mac Jackson, gave the novel a warm welcome. Book buyers on the whole avoided it. I felt I'd never written a better book to worse effect. I was disappointed, of course. But it's also true that the only real satisfaction in writing is measuring up to some internal quality monitor; and by that measure I did feel as if I'd turned water into wine. I'd made something witty and complex out of nothing. I'd made writer's block the key to its own door. And no one, looking at my list of publications, would see the least sign that there'd been a crisis.

But the title I've proposed for this occasion is 'One Thing Leads to Another'; and as it turned out, *The Secret History of Modernism* not only cured a bad case of writer's block; it also, in passing, gave me a subject for my next novel. Here's how it happened.

While Laszlo Winter and his Indian friend Rajiv Battacharya are working as postgraduate students in the London of the late 1950s, the character of the Australian girl, Sammy, is represented as pursuing her own researches into the lives of modern writers, which she's planning to turn into a book called *The Secret History of Modernism* – hence the title of my novel. Her discoveries are somewhat random, somewhere between scholarship and gossip (always a fine line!). One fact she discovers (and this is indeed a fact) is that Katherine Mansfield and T. S. Eliot attended the same dinner party in Hammersmith in June 1917, and their encounter on leaving the party goes into her book. Late in the novel Laszlo gets hold of a copy of her manuscript (which has never been published) and reads her description of that encounter.

It was this small item that reminded me I knew a great deal not only about Katherine Mansfield but about the literary milieu in which she operated, and that it was a subject that offered a *story* – full of extraordinary characters and dramatic events. Katherine Mansfield could be my next subject for fiction!

I decided I would cover just three years of her life, during the First World War – before she became disabled by ill health. This was a period that included her affair with the French writer Francis Carco; her friendships with D. H. Lawrence, Bertrand Russell and Lady Ottoline Morrell; her relations with John Middleton Murry; and the death of her brother Leslie that pitched her back into writing about her childhood in New Zealand. The war would once again give the fiction a larger perspective, making the big picture of twentieth-century history a backdrop to the miniature and personal dramas of the foreground story. And I decided to make that scene from Sammy's *Secret History of Modernism*, where Mansfield and T. S. Eliot encounter one another coming away from the same dinner party, the opening scene of the new novel.

But the scene had to be recast. If this was a more technical, 'lit crit' kind of lecture, I would show how the scene in *The Secret History of Modernism* is written as an account of something *read* – expository prose, with elegant periods and balancing statements – and in the Mansfield novel the same event has to become something that *happens*. It has to be *dramatised*. We have to be inside the experience, rather than seeing it from the outside.

Here, anyway, is a sample of what it becomes. These are the opening paragraphs of the novel I called *Mansfield*:

He must have heard her coming after him. She guessed he would want to escape; yet part of him (a large part) would feel he should not, that it would be a rudeness; and another, smaller, part would be curious, would want to wait for her, walk with her. His shyness might win out if she did nothing but clatter along behind losing ground, so she called: 'Oh Mr Eliot.'

She panted up to where he stood awkwardly, leaning to one side. She put a hand on his lapel, as if steadying herself. In fact steadying herself. But it was a mistake and she removed it. 'Mr Eliot,' she breathed.

'Mrs Murry,' he breathed back. And after that, while she was wondering whether she should explain that she was not yet Mrs Murry, only soon to be, and that she was, meanwhile, Murry's mistress and handmaiden (the thought of saying it amused her), he said: 'So you decided to leave too.'

'I took my chance. You made an opening.'

'Oh dear.' His concern was real. 'I do hope I didn't break up the party.'

'No fear of that. Captain Graves is in full flight.'

There was an awkward moment before he said, 'It's such a lovely night I thought I might walk for a while. But you will be wanting . . .'

'You want to be alone. You're a poet, after all. There might be poems out there.' She waved at the night sky, briefly clear over the river.

'Not at all. If you would care to walk with me . . .'

She was not sure in what spirit this was uttered, but she responded: 'I should like nothing better.'

So they turned and walked through the faintly misty night under alternating light and shadow from the street lamps. Below the parapet on their right, the Thames made the quiet but forceful undertone of river-flow and tide moving in unison. Ahead, a pattern of not altogether distinct lights sketched the Hammersmith Bridge.

'I felt I just had to escape,' she said. 'Captain Graves has so many opinions; and they come at one so hard.'

'He's been wounded,' Eliot said.

'And won medals,' she acknowledged. 'Or *a* medal. An important one. MM. Or MMM.' She hummed it, 'Mmmmmmm . . .' but Tom Eliot didn't smile.

'I think it was the MC,' he said.

'And you think his MC excuses . . .'

'I'm sure he wouldn't think he needed excusing.'

'No of course not.' She looked at him resolutely. 'And I don't.'

'You don't . . .'

'Excuse him.'

'Oh . . . I see. No, well . . .'

Graves had been loud, argumentative, dogmatic, disagreeable. She said, 'I disliked him – *so* much.'

She felt Tom Eliot wince at the intensity of it, but she carried right on.

In this opening passage we're seeing T. S. Eliot through Katherine Mansfield's eyes, and hearing about him as if in her voice – but we're also seeing her through the eyes of C. K. Stead. That, in fact, was to be the technical discipline I imposed on myself. The whole novel was a very conscious exercise in what's called in film-making POV – point of view. Each chapter was to be seen through the eyes of one of the characters. About half the chapters would be seen through Katherine's eyes. The other half would be shared among the other characters.

Mansfield was published in 2004. It was welcomed by reviewers. It sold well – well enough, anyway, to keep my publishers, both here and in the UK, satisfied. Everyone was prepared to forgive *The Secret History of Modernism* – forgive and forget, alas, because, as I've said, it's a novel I'm rather fond of.

'One thing leads to another.' It took a while, but by an oblique route, and after another bout of new poems, the Mansfield novel gave me the subject for my next. I was talking to Kay about writing it, and said that one of the difficulties I'd faced was how to deal with the character of D. H. Lawrence who was for a time such a powerful presence in Katherine's life. I said his messianic temperament was so different from my own he had to be seen from the outside. This is once again a POV problem. I couldn't *be* Lawrence; but I could be someone *seeing*

Lawrence, observing him. I said, 'It's the kind of problem you'd have if you were trying to write about Jesus Christ.'

That chance remark planted an idea, which developed into a series of questions. How *would* one, how would *I*, a person of my temperament, an unbeliever, go about putting Jesus of Nazareth into a work of fiction? – that was the first question. As with my D. H. Lawrence, my Jesus would have to be seen from the outside. It would need to be up close, so the view would probably have to be that of one of the disciples – but a sceptic. A sceptic among the disciples? That, surely, would have to be Judas. So Judas entered the equation.

At first it was just the fascination of a set of puzzles. As I thought up a possible solution to one problem another presented itself. For example: I would want my Judas to be a man I could identify with in the writing, a Judas of mature years, looking back over a significant gap of time, sufficient for him to have understood both the reasons for his following Jesus in the first place, and in the interim to have settled firmly and finally into his unbelief. This meant that the story of his suicide after the crucifixion would have to be untrue. But there are, I found, two quite different accounts of his death in the Gospels, so one must be wrong. If one is wrong, they can both be wrong. I would make it that my Judas had gone away after the crucifixion, started a new life, left the years of his discipleship far behind, but had gone on thinking about that dramatic time.

As for his betrayal of Jesus – this, I decided, would not be as in the Gospel account, which in fact makes little narrative sense. (Jesus hardly needed a betrayer to be identified and arrested.) My Judas's betrayal would simply be his inability to believe, and his refusal to pretend to believe, that Jesus was divine, the son of God, the promised Messiah.

So my mind went on playing with the idea, developing it, at the same time that another part of me was saying, 'You are not the person to write a novel on this subject. Stop wasting time and intellectual energy. *Drop it!*'

The Mansfield novel had indirectly planted the Judas idea, and now, by another accident, it helped to confirm it. I was invited to Wellington to give a lecture in a series about the men in Katherine Mansfield's life, and I gave mine on the fictional strategies used and the POV problems encountered in representing John Middleton Murry, Bertrand Russell, Francis Carco and Katherine's brother Leslie. Afterwards I was taken to dinner at a Wellington restaurant and found myself sitting next to Paul Morris, Professor of Religious Studies at Victoria, whose wife had organised the lecture series. I was still rather secretive about this Judas idea – in fact embarrassed by it; but after my tongue had been loosened by a few glasses of wine, I outlined it to Professor Morris. His response was immediate and emphatic. 'These are our stories,' he said. 'They must be constantly re-told.'

Previously the Judas idea had been like a tune on the brain I wanted to be rid of. From the moment of that exchange I stopped trying to get rid of it. I went on thinking about it as a set of fiction writer's problems, but now I intended to find ways to solve them. And I embarked on a course of reading that turned me, in a few months, into a passable biblical scholar – sufficient anyway to do the job. I re-read the Gospels with great care and attention. I read a certain amount of modern commentary on them; and I read enough Roman and Jewish history to give me a view of the biblical story in the context of its time. On that basis I was able to write the first half of the novel, inventing a childhood and young manhood for my two main characters, Jesus and Judas – something which the Bible itself doesn't provide. After that first hundred or so pages, the story had to follow the narrative path of the Gospels – but the Gospels reinterpreted by Judas, the survivor and sceptic.

What I found myself doing was retelling a story we all know, but in a way that would make it intelligible and believable to myself and to people like me – unwilling to keep faith in a compartment separate from modern scientific knowledge. 'These are our stories.

They must be constantly re-told.' Re-told from a twenty-first-century perspective, it becomes, not a story of divinity triumphant through pain and death, but of human aspiration, delusion and consequent tragedy.

To give a flavour of the novel that resulted, and how it re-interprets – indeed subverts – the Gospel story, I'll read a few pages that come very near the end. Judas, remember, is re-telling the story forty years after it happened. At this point in his narrative the crucifixion is just over and the body is being taken down from the cross:

Mary Magdalene came to speak to me; greeted me, in fact, as if I had been the mourner at a funeral and she a representative of the bereaved family. I had the impression that she was acting on Jesus' behalf; that she might say, 'Thank you for coming.' I saw again that expression I'd noticed at a distance and hadn't been able to interpret. Her eyes were shining. She was not unhappy. She was exalted.

My anger came back. I remembered a conversation when I'd wanted her to help me persuade Jesus to go back to Galilee, and she'd said his destiny might be to die. 'You're pleased?' I said. I pointed at the crumpled naked bleeding white body in the arms of the sweating Roman soldiers. 'He's dead. You're satisfied with that?'

She was unnaturally calm. 'He's dead. He will live again.'

When my frown, my anger, didn't abate she explained more clearly, as to a child. 'Jesus will walk the earth again. You'll see, Judas.'

I couldn't speak. I had to turn and walk away. When I'd calmed myself and came back, a man was explaining to the three women and to Simon Peter that he had permission from the Roman authorities to take the body. He was a wealthy trader who had heard Jesus preach and had been persuaded of his divinity. He came originally from Arimathea, but lived now in Jerusalem. He'd had a tomb made for himself, a sepulchre carved in rock in his garden in the city. It would be a fitting place, he said, for the body of the prophet; and he would make another for himself so that one day, in death, he would lie beside the great Jesus of Nazareth. (232)

After the crucifixion Judas has no friends, no money, no occupation. His fellow disciples – all except Peter – have run away. He's at a loss what to do. For a few days he's taken in by his uncle, one of the Temple priests. It was because Jesus was a threat to the authority of the Temple that the priests persuaded Pilate to crucify him rather than Barabbas. The uncle knows that Judas has been a follower of Jesus but he's indulgent to his nephew. He knows nothing of Judas's doubts about his friend's claims to divinity, and sees his discipleship as the consequence of misplaced youthful idealism.

He knew that I had watched the crucifixion and that I was distressed, and he was not so insensitive as to show satisfaction at the death of my friend. But it was not difficult to see he thought Caiaphas had scored a great victory over the Roman prefect in having Jesus crucified instead of Barabbas; and when I told him, that first evening, that a wealthy businessman was going to inter Jesus in a sepulchre somewhere in the city, he said at once, 'That can't be permitted.'

I asked who would prevent it. 'This man has authority from the prefect.'

My uncle smiled and nodded. 'Of course,' he said. 'That's it, then. Nothing to be done.'

But it was clear he didn't – not for a moment – think there was 'nothing to be done'. And when I heard, two days later, that the stone had been rolled away from the mouth of the tomb in the night, and that the body was gone, I knew this must be the work of the Temple priests and the Sanhedrin – or must have been done at their behest. It's one of the ironies of the story, as I look back on it, that this piece of grave-robbery by the priesthood, intended to prevent a cult of Jesus growing around the site of his burial, had (from their point of view) the worse effect of fostering the much more powerful myth that he had risen from death.

Of course his followers 'saw' Jesus after the crucifixion. I'm always hearing stories of these sightings, which were many and various. He was seen near the tomb, he was seen in Galilee, he was seen on the road to Emmaus – sometimes by one, sometimes by three, once, even, by five hundred. He was changed, he was unrecognisable, he was the same, he was unmistakable. He talked, he was silent. He told one person not to touch him, another to finger his wounds. Ptolemy tells his faithful crowds a moving story (hearsay, of course) of Jesus, dressed in white as at my wedding, rising into the sky, taken up into heaven by the Father – growing smaller as he ascended until he was just a point of light, fading and vanishing.

I too saw Jesus after his death. In those first few days, especially, while the memory of the crucifixion tormented me and kept me awake at night, I saw him in the street, caught sight of him in crowds, heard his voice coming from an open window – just as I'd seen and heard Judith after her death. I still see them in dreams – both of them, though never together. Our dead are always with us. But they are not alive. That's the nature of being dead, and it's best we accept it. (234–5)

A novel of this kind is not going to be reviewed simply as a literary document. What the reader believes in relation to the Jesus story and the Christian religion can't but affect the response. There were a few (surprisingly few) angry responses from the faithful. The angriest came in New Zealand, in the Presbyterian magazine *sPanz*, where the reviewer explained that she had stopped reading after only two thirds of the novel, but nonetheless wrote her review. 'In the Gospels', she wrote, 'Mary and Jesus enjoy an ideal mother-son relationship. But here', she continues with heavy irony, 'Stead sets us right; in fact Jesus hated and resented his mother.'

I wrote a reply in which I said 'hate' was too strong a word for what Jesus displays towards Mary in the novel, though it was not too strong a word for Jesus himself. And I quoted Luke 14:26 (the Devil can always quote Scripture), where Jesus says 'If any man come to me and hate not his father and mother, wife and children . . . he cannot be my disciple'. But further, I pointed out that in the very few interchanges between Jesus and Mary recorded in the Gospels, Jesus is either impatient, or indifferent and dismissive. And I suggested the reviewer's reading of the Bible was perhaps as incomplete as her reading of my novel.

There were many positive reviews; and of course a lot of those were written by non-believers who found it not only moving as a story, but also helpful, because, quite simply, it's *plausible* – much easier to believe than the Gospel account. One woman sent me an email that said, 'For me from now on yours is the Authorized Version.'

But what surprised me most was the number of Christians who were *not* offended; who were in fact fascinated by the novel, and in varying degrees even persuaded by it. Respectful sermons were preached about it in Auckland and Hamilton. The retiring Dean of the Auckland Anglican cathedral, Dean Randerson, sent me the script of his sermon and insisted we meet over coffee and talk about it. A group called the 'Sea of Faith' invited me to talk to them in Hamilton. In London I was interviewed on Christian Radio about the novel, and asked to come back to join a panel discussion on the subject of Judas. I had a letter from a retired Presbyterian cler-gyman, David Simmers, who had been our Auckland University chaplain when I was a young lecturer in the early 1960s, who said, 'I have spent a fair amount of time trying to understand the Jesus and Christian phenomenon, but the material has always seemed irre-trievably inadequate and puzzling. You have shown that it is possible, with imagination, to create a plausible story.'

What became clear was that for many reasonable people for whom the subjective experience of religion has been important, our knowledge of ourselves, our psychology, our evolutionary history, not to mention the physics of the universe we inhabit – all of this makes belief in things like the miracles, the Virgin birth, the resur-rection, very nearly impossible – yet they don't want to give up the comfort zone of faith. These people constitute, I think, the parish of Lloyd Geering. Everything is gone from Christianity except

Christ – except that he is not 'the Christ' any more; not the Messiah. He is Jesus of Nazareth, the ultimate Good Man, surrounded by the light of the unspecifically numinous.

But what had struck me in re-reading the Gospels, and even more in the process of turning the Gospel Jesus of Nazareth into a believable character in a human story, was how much of what's in the Gospel record is deleted or overlooked by this ultimate Good Man image. If Jesus was not born of a virgin; if he did not walk on water, feed five thousand with two loaves and three fishes, and turn water into wine; if he did not rise from the dead and is not going to open the door to his father's 'many mansions', then in making the claims he does for himself, and *especially* in uttering threats of dire and eternal punishment for those who don't believe him, he is (even allowing for the times in which he lived) showing clear signs of mania. That's how my Judas character comes to see Jesus; as a man who begins with a message of peace and love and comfort for the poor, the sick, the grieving and dispossessed, but who is carried away by his own success as a preacher, and begins to believe what his followers want to believe, that he is indeed their Saviour, the Messiah promised by the prophets, who will deliver Israel from the Roman yoke. My novel (as Michele Hewitson said in the *Herald*) is partly a story about friendship. Judas tries to save his boyhood friend from himself, and from the consequences of his claims for himself – tries and, of course, fails. That's the nature of the tragedy.

The novel came out towards the end of 2006 in paperback here, hardcover in the UK, and was well received. Towards the end of 2007 it was re-issued in paperback in the UK. It was again very well reviewed there, and is just now reprinting; and in the meantime it has appeared in French, Spanish, Portuguese, Croatian, Hungarian and Polish, with Romanian coming soon, and others (including Serbian) to follow.

'One thing leads to another.' As I've explained, all of this came from a simple remark to my wife that writing about D. H. Lawrence would be like trying to write about Jesus of Nazareth. One never knows where the next idea will come from, or where the next thought may lead. One must simply stay alert, and wear a hard hat.

Sylvia and her Editor

C. K. Stead: *I thought I'd begin with a general approach to the subject of your role as Sylvia's editor. In fact we had one very interesting paper yesterday by Dr Judith Giblin James who has read some of your correspondence with Sylvia and she had also read an interview with you in the* Paris Review. *She had extracted some editing principles that were clearly yours and she advanced the interesting idea that since you were very young and you were Sylvia's editor very early in your career, you may in fact have formulated some of these principles in editing her work. And she gave examples. One was that a book can be improved simply by changing the title – which is a narrower application of your idea that the central part of the editing process, the most important part, was the work on the beginning and the ending of a book. Another was that editing is just the application of the common*

This interview took place by video link on 10 August 2008 between C.K.S., at an international conference on Sylvia Ashton-Warner at the University of Auckland's Epsom campus, and Robert Gottlieb, Ashton-Warner's American editor, at home in New York. It was published in *The Kiss and the Ghost: Sylvia Ashton-Warner and New Zealand*, ed. Alison Jones and Sue Middleton (NZCER Press, 2009).

sense of any good reader, and I thought the crucial word there was
good, not the common sense of any reader, but any good reader, and
that an editor should save writers from themselves. First of all, do you
recognise these principles; and can you tell us something about how
you applied them in editing Sylvia; and maybe did you extract some of
those principles from that early experience?

Robert Gottlieb: Well you have to remember this all was fifty years
ago. I first encountered Sylvia in 1958 and a lot of water has passed
under my dam since then. At that point in my life I didn't have
any principles. In fact I never had any principles until the inter-
viewer from the *Paris Review* asked me for principles. . . . I'm not
an abstract kind of person. I just react and respond and say what I
think. Not just in editing, but in life. I don't formulate. So anything
I said to this very bright woman who interviewed me was what
she forced me to think about. With Sylvia, the first book that we
did together was *Spinster*. That book was already edited and published in England before I ever saw it. It was not an easy book to sell
in America. . . . I don't have the correspondence in front of me so I
can't tell you for instance what I said about *Spinster* or *Three* but I
can tell you about Sylvia and me and how we worked and how we
came together and in one particular case, which is *Teacher*, I can say
a great deal because I essentially made that book, created that book.

CKS: *I think everybody wants to hear what's of interest to you and*
what you remember most vividly and clearly.

RG: OK, let me give you the background. I was essentially a kid
although I didn't think I was. I first must have read *Spinster* before I
was 27. I had published a wonderful novel, Sybille Bedford's *Legacy*,
which was very, very successful, and I was looking for another
book of that quality that I could respond to very personally because
publishing is just making public your enthusiasm – so you have to

have the enthusiasm before you can do it well. One day I was having lunch with a literary agent named Monica McCall. I didn't know her very well. We had been thrown together in a highly tense and emotional situation involving a Broadway play and a writer who was insane, a producer who was insane, so since she was a very sane, canny Scots woman in her sixties and I had always been realistic, we met. I remember it was lunch at the Plaza Hotel so our meeting was already very glamorised and I adored her on sight and she me. So we were talking, talking, talking and she said to me, 'Would you by any chance be interested in a novel about a school teacher in New Zealand?' And I was about to say 'You've got to be kidding' because why would I be interested in publishing a novel about a school teacher in New Zealand, when I remembered that I had already figured out that it wasn't the subject of the book that was important, it was how it was written and what it had to say. And I said 'Sure, I'd love to read it'.

She sent me the next day a finished copy of the hideous English edition of *Spinster* which I immediately read because I always read everything immediately. I read it overnight and I called her and I said 'This is absolutely wonderful and I would love to publish it'. So my colleagues agreed and we published it. And we worked very, very hard to bring it to the attention of book reviewers and book review editors because again I was then working at Simon and Schuster which was known as a commercial rather than a literary publishing house. Although they published a number of literary books, it was essentially commercial and they were not likely to think that a novel about New Zealand from Simon and Schuster was something they had to pay attention to. But somehow we captured the attention of the critical apparatus in America at that time. It got wonderful reviews and it actually crept on to the bottom of the *New York Times* bestseller list, which was a highly unlikely thing to have happen.

Meanwhile Sylvia and I were in correspondence and it was a very heightened correspondence. I was susceptible to the charm and intelligence of her writing and she clearly needed a lifeline to the outer world because she didn't have any. You know the English publisher and she had no relationship – and even with Monica McCall, her purported agent, they had never really had anything to do with each other. Monica got this book because she was representing the English publisher. But I was the first person, I think, in the outside world who connected with her and responded to her and so she invested a great deal in this correspondence. I did too, because from her writing, from her letters, I loved her and was fascinated by her. So this correspondence quickly became quite personal.

In all her letters to me, up at the top where you would have the date and whatever town she was living in, they all started 'From behind the woollen curtain'. That was essentially the way she saw her life. It was clear to me that she felt trapped behind the woollen curtain, and frustrated. However, the fact that her book was being published in the outside world when she felt, as you know, that New Zealand had no use for her, was a tremendous boost for her psyche and for her ego – whatever you want to call those things. It was wonderful because suddenly she was internationally, if not nationally, known. I don't mean on a vast scale, but it was real and as you know *Spinster* was chosen by *Time Magazine* as one of the ten best novels of the year. That was extraordinary.

By then she was writing *Incense to Idols* and that's when we first started having an editorial correspondence. She was very, very available to the editing process. I mean very rarely did she take exception to things I suggested because the things I suggested were sane. She on this level was totally sane. The only problem we had was about the embryo and the wine glass, because as I remember it, this was an embryo when it was aborted, a couple of months old. But she had it in her book as this perfectly formed little person in the wine glass and I remember pointing out to her that as far as I knew, anatomy in New Zealand was the same as it was in the rest of the world. Babies at that age were like a little . . . toenail of a shrimp. They were not little replicas of you and me. So then she wrote me back with a wonderful little drawing of a martini glass which would have a tiny little baby in it. Common sense finally prevailed, although she did stick at it. But maybe she asked a doctor she knew.

CKS: *I don't know whether you remember but she did . . . she wrote you a very funny letter, clearly not to be taken seriously, in which she said that foetuses behind the woollen curtain clearly advanced much more quickly than in New York . . .*

RG: Exactly.

CKS: *. . . which was putting your image of the metropolis and the provinces in reverse. In fact we're much more advanced . . .*

RG: That was not a real issue, it was just funny. That's my real memory of *Incense to Idols*. The book did well, but not as well as *Spinster*. It was a more difficult subject. One of the things that can make a book as we say 'work' is if it reveals a new world to a readership, but not every great book does that. There are great books made up of common matters everyone is aware of. But when you come to a new world, some place that nobody knows anything about, the exotic aspect can really help launch a book, because it gives reviewers something to write about. You know, what do you write about novels? This is somebody's eleventh novel and it's a little bit better or a little worse than the last one.

But if suddenly you're in a world of Maori school children and a beleaguered teacher who is coming up with the theory and it's very emotional and there's a love interest, and it's New Zealand . . . there's a subject that reviewers can get their teeth into! So that was very helpful. I think people like books that give them an entrée to a new world. *Spinster* did that for a number of people including me.

I was partly drawn to it because – what was this all about? I didn't know. I knew there were Maoris. I didn't know anything more than that they were an indigenous people in New Zealand.

When we got to *Teacher*, this was a completely different experience, one unlike any I have ever had – and by this time I had probably edited over a thousand books. She wrote to me and said out of the blue, 'I'm sending you all of my papers, diaries, letters, etc. about my teaching experience. They're all in boxes and there are cut outs from magazines and there are things that the children in school did and I can't live with them any more and I've got to get them out of my garage and they've got to go somewhere, do something, make a book or throw them out, I don't care.' So they arrived in my apartment in New York, several boxes filled with not disorganised material, but utterly unorganised material. She had just taken everything and flung it into cartons and posted it off. I had a long, narrow living room at that time. It's all completely visual memory: a long, narrow living room that for some reason I don't recall, pretentiousness no doubt, was painted a kind of dark blue enamel. So I took all this material and I just put it in piles on the floor, which my then-wife wasn't too happy about. But nevertheless I prevailed and slowly over a period of about six months I sorted it and tried to figure out what the hell I had. Now you have to understand that a great deal of that material was duplicated. But it wasn't duplicated word for word. You know we didn't have Xerox, we didn't even have copying machines. She certainly didn't. Everything was typed with carbons and there would be ... I would find three pages, pages 8, 9 and 10, on a particular coloured paper. There didn't seem to be anywhere in this mass of material a 1 through 7 or 11 through 45. They were just three isolated pages and they seemed to be the same material that was in a whole other piece of material that was pages 36 through 45. But they were all different. Clearly she worried at this material and went over and over and over it, but she threw nothing out. Then there were the photographs. You all know the photographs that appeared in *Teacher*. A lot of them were coiled up, splotched negatives, others were splotched snapshots. They weren't in very good condition because I don't think the garage was air-conditioned. It had been hibernating there, so it was one great big mess. But the more I penetrated it and read, the more I thought it was wonderful. It was wonderful, wonderful material. So I started doing what you do.

It was like a giant jigsaw puzzle, except that with a jigsaw puzzle you know there is a real picture you're supposed to be achieving. Here there was no real anything. It was just what we made of it and I couldn't let anybody else work on it because it was too complicated and had to be in one person's head. Anyway, very slowly I figured out the structure of this book and sewed it all together. I chose the pictures and worked very closely with a designer I trusted and with a jacket designer I was very close to. The jacket by the way was based on the dust jacket for *Born Free*. That was the look I wanted because it incorporated block type colour and small photographs. She had said 'Don't show it to me, I don't want to know, I may never even look at the finished book'. I knew that was ridiculous and I said 'I need a short introduction from you or foreword, so I'll send you the galleys'. Of course she had things to say about what I had done but they were very modest and totally reasonable. And she did write something.

So we put this book out. And by an extraordinary piece of luck – I didn't quite know what this meant back then – it was reviewed on the front page of the *New York Times Sunday Book Review* which was the number one launching pad for a major book. Anything reviewed on the front page of the *New York Times Book Review* was an immediate signal to all of *New York Times'* readers and to the whole community this was something you had to pay attention to. A very sympathetic person who had been involved with poetry for children was given this book to review and just said this is the greatest thing ever, this is a revelation, this is an astonishment, the world has to sit up and pay attention! So the world did, because it had been told to by the *New York Times*.

So this book had an immediate success, not so much that it sold millions of copies, but that it appealed to educators across America – remember this was at a new period, a kind of revolutionary period, in America, the late 1960s and 1970s when everything was supposed to be new and untraditional. You were no longer allowed to learn reading by the way things sounded; you had to learn combinations of letters. It was completely hopeless; nobody could learn it. Educators were waiting for something new, and they found it in this book and this book was picked up by experimental educators all over America. It was a great thing to have happened. Of course, her theory when applied sometimes worked and sometimes didn't work, because you can have wonderful ideas but unless you're brilliant at deploying them, it's not going to work in the same way. This would be true of almost anything, anything about which you can develop theories. I'm sure Sylvia was a genius of a teacher, and when she then came up with her theories, she was a genius at applying them. I'm not sure that you or I could apply them to equal effect. That made no difference to all the people who thought they'd found the Holy Grail. So they all started to apply Sylvia's ideas, and then when Sylvia finally came to America and she started to apply them ... I wouldn't say people were disillusioned, I think by then people were wary; they understood that they couldn't be her. Who could be her? Who would want to be her?

So that is the story of *Teacher* as I remember it. It was thrilling for me because it was so interesting. The material was so interesting and doing it was so interesting. You know I'm a puzzle solver. And it was a unique experience in my life and then it was a success too and it made her very happy.

CKS: *When* Teacher *appeared there was this image of a book that had been rejected in New Zealand, that Sylvia wanted this book published,* she wanted her theory published and revealed in New Zealand, but she hadn't been able to achieve this. And then it was published in New York and part of the success of the book was not only that it was excellent in itself but that it was the book of a prophet who'd been rejected in her own country.

When Lynley Hood's biography of Sylvia appeared, we had a new story: that a book (to be called Organic Teaching) was submitted to a publisher called Bill Moore of William Heinemann Ltd in New Zealand. He spent a great deal of time on it, and with Sylvia, going backwards and forwards between Wellington and wherever she was – and working with typesetters – and then at the last minute, when he wanted her to sign a contract, she said 'Go away, I've got a publisher in New York.' When you read this in Lynley's book* there's a disparity between the book that's about to be published in New Zealand and the story which you've just told about these boxes of material that went to New York being spread over the floor for months and gradually assembled into a book. Clearly there are two truths here. In reality they can't be irreconcilable, but they're not easy to reconcile.

And we know from Geraldine McDonald another story, another element, which is that everything that occurs in the first half of Teacher, with just a few exceptions, appeared in sequence in a periodical called National Education in New Zealand.

RG: Well, that's certainly possible. Remember a lot of what I got was tear sheets of pieces, articles, reproductions of articles, and there was nothing that was a manuscript, but there was material from all kinds of places. Now for all I know Sylvia had shown a lot of material, offered a lot of material, to a publisher in New Zealand.

---

* Lynley Hood, *Sylvia! The Biography of Sylvia Ashton-Warner*, Penguin, 1988 / 2008, pp. 170–2.

That could very well be. I can't believe it was organised in a full manuscript because she would have sent me that. There was nothing organised in what I saw. What I saw was scraps, some of them had been published in I assume the kind of magazine you're talking about. I don't really remember what those pieces of paper were but they were not in an order. There was nothing that was coherent in terms of the structure of the book. Everything was coherent in itself and she could easily have shown that material to who knows who, I don't. I don't know about New Zealand educational publishing.

CKS: *Everybody acknowledges your great role with Sylvia . . .*

RG: I don't want my role acknowledged . . . I'm just trying to get to the reality of the matter.

CKS: *Well, it is acknowledged whether you want it or not. I'm an academic, but I'm also a fiction writer, and I really prefer this story according to the fiction writer to the story according to the academic researcher. I prefer the simple story. But it seems to me my role at this moment is to get somewhere in between.*

RG: I can offer nothing but what I experienced. Certainly she never told me that she had been or was in discussion with a New Zealand publisher. 'I can't deal with this any more', she said, 'so you have to deal with it.' Why I assumed that because she couldn't deal with it I had to deal with it, I don't quite know. She had that effect on me.

CKS: *The other thing before we move on to your late work with her is that you said you were the first person she had connection with outside . . .*

RG: As far as I know.

CKS: *There she was behind the woollen curtain and it's certainly true, Lynley Hood makes a point that there were only two people with whom she had a long ongoing and important correspondence, you and her son Elliot. All other correspondence is somewhat fragmentary and that in itself indicates how important the relationship was. But it's also true with Sylvia that everybody she had anything to do with was made to feel they were the only one, and without them she was just isolated, neglected. She had a tremendous talent for making people feel she needed them and life would be impossible without them.*

RG: Also she romanticised, because she was a romanticist if not, to put it politely, a fabulist. She needed to believe in ... look at that time I wasn't thinking about what this correspondence was or what this relationship was. I was writing letters and she was writing letters. I didn't know anybody forty years later would be interested and I'm still not sure why. She wrote me, I wrote her, it was very interesting, very touching often, and I felt I was giving her something I guess that she needed. And she must have been giving something I needed. It certainly wasn't for professional reasons. I had vast professional relationships. Part of it was the distance. If she were a writer in America or England, where I went every year, I would have known her very well. We would have seen each other all the time, we would have had lunches, she would have come to my house for dinner, there would have been intercourse. Here there was nothing but a lifeline of correspondence, so we were abstract for each other. I discovered that when I read the manuscript of *I Passed This Way*, her autobiography. The most work I did on that book was to cut out probably 50 per cent or more of what she wrote about me, almost all of which was fantasy. She had created a 'me' and that's what she thought I was. We all do that to a certain extent but not on paper. A number of times I had to edit books in which I appeared and it's always hilarious. But this was over the

283

top, and she had made inferences etc., etc. that just ... so I said 'No, no, no, no you've got it all wrong. I don't care what you say about your husband, about your children, about your country, about your teaching, but you can't tell these fantasies about me, because they're just not true.' None of it was derogatory; it just wasn't true. So I dug my heels in there. So I was an invention in her head, and she being a novelist, I was a character in her novel. I am not a novelist. I have no creative impulse and I'm not a romantic nor a fabulist. So for me she was a wonderful writer who lived in New Zealand whom I was in close touch with.

CKS: *A lot of the other parts of the book must be fable as well but ...*

RG: She was more in touch with the rest of her life than she was with me. I was an invention and I fed that invention because I wrote to her very directly and somewhat intimately so she had material there and she used it to the best possible advantage but not mine.

CKS: *There was a period, particularly when she was in Vancouver when it seemed she was unwell and she was writing below her best. You were always very frank and diplomatic but honest with her. There were two books in particular which weren't published. One was called* Barren Radiance *and one was called* Tenth Heaven. *Apparently she asked did you think that* Barren Radiance *was suggesting that the basic relationship was lesbian. You said yes. And this terribly stirred her and she abandoned the book. The only reference I've been able to find to* Tenth Heaven *is that it was her favourite. Do you remember anything about those at all?*

RG: I wish I did, but I don't. *Tenth Heaven* – and this is just a wild guess – could part of that have eventually become *Greenstone*? That's my hunch. I loved *Greenstone*. So I can't imagine why I would have rejected a book that then became a book I loved.

CKS: *You just rejected it in its initial form I suppose.*

RG: There's something in my very vague memory that suggests that those two books are linked.

CKS: *Judith Giblin James suggested that an example of the editor saving the author from herself was your saying a very firm no to Sylvia's initial end for* Three *– which is the novel about her self-imposed exile, essentially. In the first version of the novel she had the son-in-law race on to the tarmac, and tell his mother not to leave, that he wanted her to live with him, that she was the only woman in his life and nothing . . . This is clearly fantasy and you said no to this and then she ended it in a way which matched the direction of the novel up to that point. Do you remember that?*

RG: Now that you mention it, I do remember it vaguely. I remember thinking it was such a great example of wish fulfilment but it was clearly not an example of good novel writing and it never would have passed. It wouldn't have passed this way and it wouldn't have passed that way.

I wish my correspondence with her exists. Her letters to me and probably carbons of my letters to her exist, I know . . . With all the early letters I was at Simon and Schuster. In early 1968, I went to Knopf which is the premier of literary publishing houses. When I left I had files as big as this room. I only took two folders of correspondence with me. One was Sylvia's and the other was Joseph Heller's because it covered *Catch-22* and all sorts of other things. But that correspondence was not as full because Joe lived in New York so we worked together editorially in my office. There would have been memos; there would have been some correspondence, but it wasn't the back and forth I had with Sylvia. I know I have that correspondence. In fact the last few days knowing I was going to be doing this, I have been looking through my house but it's

a four-storey house in New York and I've been in it for 35 years.
You can imagine the accumulation of material that both my wife
and I have in that house, so I haven't come upon it. If I come upon it,
I will alert whoever you want me to alert.

I do want to say something about the strangeness of the relationship we *didn't* have, which was the person-to-person relationship.
When she was in New Zealand and I was in Manhattan, there was
never even a notion that we would ever meet. When Keith her
husband died, that was the first time I tried to speak to her. We had
never spoken. I'm a telephone guy and I'd be very happy picking
up the phone and calling New Zealand even back then when
long-distance calls were serious. But it never happened. When
he died, I called her home to speak to her and she was not able to
speak. I don't know whether she was asleep or unable to talk to
anyone, but I spoke to one of the boys for five minutes or so and sent
my love and attention, etc. That was my first attempt to encounter
her directly.

Many years later as you know she came to America. I'm not a
flyer. I fly a lot more now than I did then. Back when I was flying
around the country it somehow never crossed our minds to divert
our two itineraries so we could encounter each other. At one stage I
was in London and she was in England with Elliot and we realised
we were in the same country. And England is not big. It would have
been very, very easy to meet and I think I wrote to her and said
'OK here we are. Twenty-five years have gone by and shouldn't we
take advantage of this?' She wrote back and said 'No I don't think
we should. It's been very, very real the way it has been and I don't
think I'm prepared at this point to actually meet you.' Whether she
was nervous that she wouldn't like me or whether she felt it would
be too emotional or whether she wasn't happy with the way she
looked, I don't know. Since I'm married to an actress wife I can well
believe the latter. I don't know why it was, but that was her choice
not mine. I guess we came that close and then it didn't happen.

Why Catullus?

Maxine Lewis: *Your poetry shows your familiarity with many writers from the Classical tradition but the interest in Catullus seems particularly persistent and wide-ranging across your poetry. What factors drew you to using Catullus in particular? What made you want to construct a 'Catullus' voice rather than say a 'Virgil' or 'Propertius' or 'Ovid' voice?*

C. K. Stead: There is probably an element of chance in this but also there is the particular appeal of the personality of Catullus, his freedom, directness, seeming indifference to proprieties, irreverence – I think he let loose the same elements in my own personality while not making them my own in reality and in every detail. Catullus became a persona in my poetry, close to myself without being me – and where the line between what was me and not-me didn't need ever to be clear. I am not by nature a 'confessional' poet;

Questions put by Maxine Lewis, lecturer in Classics, University of Auckland, in December 2014.

but the Catullus persona liberated certain aspects of self and certain autobiographical elements.

ML: *In an interview with Fleur Adcock you talked about knowing French but not Latin ('I can't pretend to know Latin'), yet I'm struck by how closely some of your poems reflect or capture Catullus's vocabulary and tone. With that in mind I wanted to ask some questions related to resources. What translations, editions or commentaries on Catullus have you used over the years?*

CKS: On my shelves I have translations by C. H. Sisson (given to me many years ago by Maurice Duggan, and much used); Carl Sesar (Latin and English on facing pages, and falling apart through constant use); Charles Martin; Reney Meyers/Robert J. Ormsby. I've borrowed others from the AU Library – but my own are the most used. There's also a little book *Reading Catullus* by John Godwin.

ML: *Did you have any exposure to Latin at school?*

CKS: Alas no – greatly lamented.

ML: *If certain editions or translations have particularly appealed, can you explain what you appreciate about them?*

CKS: The most useful was the parallel text so I could attempt to *hear* the Latin. I enjoyed Sisson, and began there, but preferred a freer-flowing line, a more Modernist flavour. But really I relied on myself for the stylistic quality.

ML: *Given that Catullus's own collection seems to invite readers to read the poems intra-textually, one of the most striking aspects of your 'The Clodian Songbook' (and its successor) for me is that it seems*

*at points to invite cyclical or intra-textual readings. Figures such as
Catullus and Lesbia appear in multiple poems. Did you intend for
the recurring names to create a sense of stability of character across
multiple poems? Did you intend for the poems featuring similar
themes or featuring the same figure to be read intratextually, or do
you view them more as stand-alone pieces?*

CKS: I certainly intended Catullus to be one person, and to be
involved in a colourful and often painful affair with the woman I
called Clodia (based on things in the scholarship you will be aware
of, and to avoid the confusions suggested by the name Lesbia).
My Catullus is the same person, with the same friends and enemies
from poem to poem. That doesn't mean absolute consistency, but a
fair degree of it.

ML: *This question can be broadened to Part II 'From the Clodian
Songbook', since some figures appear across the two songbooks, such
as Suffenia. Did you anticipate that the reader would read the songbooks in tandem?*

CKS: Well, I suppose when I wrote the second set I thought readers
might well look back at the first and make the connections. But the
poems vary from being almost translations from the Latin, to being
an idea taken from one of the Catullus poems and sent off in a new
direction, to having no connection except the continuity of personality. This latter is what should hold it all together.

ML: *Although you don't adapt each of Catullus's poems, those that
you do adapt appear in the same order that they do in modern editions
of Catullus. Your notes point the reader to the Catullan sources.
Did you envisage the reader reading your poems in order in tandem
with Catullus' own work?*

CKS: I'm not sure what I intended or supposed to begin with.
Now Catullus is just an aspect of my poetic persona, and people can
take the poems in whatever way they choose. For example, when
I decided to write a poem for the Hippocrates poetry prize [for
Poetry and Medicine] I tried first to write about a recent (2005)
stroke I'd had, and I couldn't seem to make it come out well. Then
I decided Catullus should suffer a stroke and write a poem about
it as he recovered and his powers returned. That worked, and the
poem won the first Hippocrates poetry prize in 2010 – £5,000 – the
most I've ever earned for a single poem. There are references in it to
characters who appear elsewhere in Catullus – but clearly there's
no Catullus poem in which the poet suffers a stroke – or any other
major ailment. I don't know whether you've seen Anna Jackson's
new collection just published by Auckland University Press (*I,
Clodia, and Other Portraits*) in which she assumes the voice of
Catullus's lover, Clodia. In her acknowledgements at the end of the
book Anna thanks 'Karl Stead, whose translations of Catullus into
a New Zealand idiom first gave me a Catullus I could feel at home
with'. I value that of course – the knowledge that one has taken
something from the ongoing stream and fed something back into
it – the feeling of the continuity of literature itself: to me that is mysteriously exciting.

ML: *In your interview with Fleur Adcock you touched on the relationship between CKS and the 'Catullus' voice; the distance between the
voices shifts depending on the poem. I noticed that Charles Croot's
review of* Between *interpreted the 'Catullus' voice as essentially
CKS's voice, a proposition that you challenged in your correspondence
to the editor* (Journal of New Zealand Literature, 1991). *It struck
me that being a poet who had adopted the persona of a poet (called
'Catullus') you faced a problem that Catullus himself dealt with;
writing in the persona of 'Catullus' he was (erroneously) taken completely autobiographically.*

CKS: I had completely forgotten Croot's review and that I replied to it. I've now looked it up and I'm not sure that my reply helps much because my Catullus is often very close to CKS, and the poem about positive discrimination [which Croot refers to] did have NZ (and hence I guess CKS) in mind. The self and not-self in poetry is always a fine line. When I was young, academics used to insist that the Donne of the *Songs and Sonnets* was not the real Donne, but a sort of fictional invention. I never quite managed to believe that.

ML: *Looking back how do you feel about the relationship that you established between Catullus and yourself? Have you ever felt constrained by how readers might interpret a 'Catullus' poem (as being more autobiographical than you intended)? Does the 'Catullus' voice still allow you the freedom to fuse personal experience with fiction, poetic references, etc.?*

CKS: For many years the 'Catullus' persona was a liberating identity – a voice which was my own and yet could be disowned as autobiography – a sort of mid-point between myself and the Roman poet. And it worked because it did seem there was a temperamental similarity, a kinship, between Catullus and CKS – a tendency to mock, to challenge, to resort to jokes; not quite one of whom T. S. Eliot would say *'il est un homme qui sait se conduire'* – and yet with a distinct streak of romanticism, lyricism, delicacy ... I certainly found it a free space and was glad to be that self-and-not-self, with no one but CKS (or 'Catullus') knowing (if even he knew) where the line between the two was drawn.

Poetry: Formalists and Freedom Fighters

My first recognition of poetic form came, while I was still at secondary school, simply from reading traditional poems and noticing how metre and rhyme scheme and stanza pattern were all part of my sense of each poem's particular 'feel' and identity. It came from liking poems enough to read and re-read them, taking note of these things. I was not a particularly industrious student, but a young reader hooked by something mysterious and, to me, absolutely fascinating; and soon a writer – or trying to be.

Form, I soon discovered, could be very tight (Pope's rhyming couplets) or relatively free (late Shakespeare). It could be intended to be heard, imposing itself on your ear (as in nursery rhymes); or written so that a normal reading would ride right over it (the *Songs and Sonnets* of John Donne). I don't know when I learned that Ben Jonson had said, 'Donne, for not keeping of accent, deserved

Published in *Booknotes*, issue 178, Summer 2013, p. 7.

hanging.' He meant that the way Donne's lines sounded, and the way they looked on the page, didn't match. So there was dispute between formalists and freedom fighters; and ferocity in these matters was the norm.

Yet if Donne was a freedom fighter, he was also, in his own way, an amazingly exact formalist. His poems allowed you to ignore the form and read them according to the run of meaning; but if you stopped to analyse, what you found was astonishing. His 'Nocturnal upon Saint Lucy's Day', for example, has five nine-line stanzas, each rhyming abbacccdd, and with iambic counts per line of 5/5/4/4/3/5/5/5/5. If you tried to read the poem aloud so as to make that form and its rhymes audible, it would sound artificial; yet Donne had imposed it on himself in the writing, as a discipline.

But then there were also 'free verse' poems that had no measurable form, yet seemed by no means formless. The 'form' was whatever shape the poem took – unique to itself. So you had to have the courage of your own critical recognitions and say a poem was beautifully formed if it seemed so, and if not, that it was formless, perhaps a failure. This was no science; it was a skill that no one but yourself could teach you, and only by continual reading, observation, comparison and reflection. It was the poet's (and incidentally also the critic's) apprenticeship.

I was in my last school year when I encountered T. S. Eliot's *The Waste Land*, with its beautiful variations of form and tone. I soon discovered that Ezra Pound, the eccentric, erratic, irascible fellow American who had helped Eliot edit *The Waste Land* into its final shape, and whom Eliot called '*il miglior fabbro*' (the better craftsman), had declared, 'to break the pentameter, that was the first heave'. He meant that the five-beat line – either iambic (de-da de-da de-da de-da de-da), or simply the count of five speech stresses – had come so much to dominate the ears of poets in the English language a way had to be found to change it. It was a habit that needed to be broken.

Pound broke it by spending more than half his life writing a rambling disorganised poem, 'The Cantos', which he could never finish. It had moments of great lyric beauty interspersed with vast formless prosy historical meanderings and political harangues. This was the freedom fighter run riot, and there had to be better ways.

The battle with the pentameter went on throughout most of the twentieth century. There were periods when traditional form reasserted itself, as in the British poets of the Movement in the 1950s; other times (and especially in America) when freedom from 'form' was propounded as if it were one of the Rights of Man. But there is no escape from form – only from whatever current fashion has set, like concrete, into convention. When Pound demanded poets 'make it new', he was wanting, not newness for its own sake, but a break from what had become simply fashionable and repetitious – poetry imitating itself. The same impulse had motivated Wordsworth a hundred years earlier, when he broke with the eighteenth century's 'poetic diction' and insisted poetry must be written in 'the real language of men'.

One method, introduced by Marianne Moore in the middle years of the twentieth century and taken up by W. H. Auden in his later work, was the counting of syllables rather than either metrical feet or speech stresses. This is something previously known in English only through the Japanese haiku; but Moore and Auden, and many poets since, have pursued it into longer forms. The lines tend to run on like prose, yet the difference from prose is marked by the sense of linguistic economy and precision, intensity and discipline. Well done, it can bring the best out of skilled practitioners, whose attention to the requirements of the chosen syllable count ensures every word is thought about, every alternative considered, every choice a conscious one.

Fashions change from one decade to the next, but there are no rules except those you impose upon yourself. Maybe, in rare moments, the Muse will take the pen from your hand, the poem will come (as Keats said it should) 'like leaves to the tree', and you won't have to think about any of these matters. The measure of success is like Woody Allen's – 'whatever works'.

Poetry is an art with a history, and the poet needs to tap into that without being overborne by it. You are on your own; but it's best if the poets who have gone before are looking over your shoulder.

Small Talk Questions

Who is your perfect reader?

Someone who is well-read, untheoretical, open-minded but not without opinions, sensitive to language, unsnobbish, interested in varieties of human behaviour, intelligent. 'Literary', I guess would sum her up.

What books are currently on your bedside table?

The cat is on the bedside table, the books are on the floor. They are the just-published edition of Frank Sargeson's *Selected Letters*, Ian McEwan's *Sweet Tooth*, and the current issue of *Areté*.

What book changed your life?

No single book has changed my life – I'm not that kind of person, subject to sudden transforming revelations. Many books have

---

An interview with Anna Metcalf published in the (UK) *Financial Times*, 3–4 November 2012.

influenced me, especially as a writer. In fact I must be in part what a lifetime's reading has made me.

What is the strangest thing you've done when researching a book?

I borrowed the house and car of a friend's friend in Los Angeles when I was writing a novel that took place largely in Hollywood, and lived the life of an Angelino for a few months, which was only 'strange' because it was so different from the life I usually lead; but I do look back on it as 'another life' rather than part of my own. And I quite like the book that came from it – *Sister Hollywood*.

What do you snack on while you write?

No, I'm boringly disciplined about food. I have a cup of coffee mid-morning but try, and mostly succeed, not to eat anything until lunch; and nothing in the afternoons until dinner.

Which literary character most resembles you?

Couldn't think of an answer to this. I asked my wife and she said at once, Don Quixote.

Who would you most like to sit next to at a dinner party?

Katherine Mansfield would be good. I know so much about her, have read her letters and journals, and even written a novel about her. I would like to ask her whether I got anything wrong; and to tell me what it was exactly that drew her to John Middleton Murry.

Who would you like to be stuck in a lift with?

Groucho Marx. Or Barry Humphries. Or (even better) both.

Who would you choose to play you in a film about your life?

I assume this would be my younger self, and thinking of my personality, not my 'looks'? – in which case the younger Jeremy Irons would be satisfyingly flattering; as would Ralph Fiennes.

What are you scared of?

Not much really, though since the Christchurch earthquake I've felt a kind of 'future anxiety' that Auckland is built on a currently inert but not extinct volcanic field. I think the only real fear I have is of not dying quickly enough and becoming a helpless confused unhappy undignified incontinent old vegetable. I think an easy exit pill should be available to all of advancing years who want it.

What keeps you awake at night?

See my new novel *Risk*: it's usually a mix of embarrassment at any thought of my own behaviour, and concern about the fortunes of family and friends. There need be no real cause for this, and often I find it hard to think up reasons for feelings which seem to persist without any. I have to search back into my past to find something to be embarrassed, or anxious, about. I have come to see it as a kind of depression, often induced by alcohol, and one reason why I drink so little.

When were you happiest?

When I felt I had written a good poem. When I was younger it would have been while having sex with someone I loved.

When do you feel most free?

I feel pretty free all the time these days. But there is a special freedom about swimming far out from the shore in Auckland when

the temperature is mild and the seas moderate – and then turning
on my back, staring up at the cloud formations and watching the
gulls drifting up there.

How do you relax?

Swimming, walking, listening to classical music, reading good
poems, watching movies.

What is the best piece of advice a parent gave you?

I've tried, but honestly I can't remember any advice they gave me,
except a very few things I didn't agree with or abide by. If they
taught it was by example; and I was very selective about what I took
note of.

When did you last cry?

At the Globe after a performance of *Richard II*, not because it
was 'sad' (though I suppose it was) but because it was beautiful,
especially the dance the cast ended with. I took my daughter and we
had to sit separately. When we found one another afterwards it was
obvious we had both wept, I think for the same reason.

What would you go back and change?

I might be tempted not to return to New Zealand after completing
my postgraduate work in England. But I was tempted then to stay
and didn't, so I suppose I might make the same choice, and be left
with the same doubt about whether I had done the right thing – or
alternatively with the regret that I could have chosen to make wonderful Auckland my home and chose not to!

What would you change about yourself?

I would let more things pass without comment or objection; without input from 'C. K. Stead'. I would try (in Eliot's words) to teach myself 'to care and not to care', and 'to sit still'.

If you could own any painting, what would it be?

Apart from the ones I own now (all by New Zealand painters and none of which I would give up) I would like a Matisse done during his period in Nice; or a Picasso dating from around 1945.

What book do you wish you'd written?

Donne's *Song and Sonnets*; Grass's *Cat and Mouse*; Moravia's *Conjugal Love* (for example) . . . And so on and on.

What are you most proud of writing?

Particular poems from various times in my career, including some quite recent. A few short stories including the one that won the 2010 *Sunday Times* EFG Prize; and novels *All Visitors Ashore* (for the energy of its sentences), *The Death of the Body* (my cleverest), *The Secret History of Modernism* (for depth) and *My Name was Judas* (for lucidity and rationality on the subject of religion). My book *Pound, Yeats, Eliot and the Modernist Movement* probably contains my best literary critical writing but I'm not sure of that because I haven't re-read it since it was published in 1986.

How would you earn your living if you had to give up writing?

There has always been employment to go back to if needed in a university English Department. If I could begin right back at the beginning, however, I would train as a singer and see how far I could go.

Where is your favourite place in the world?

Apart from Auckland, New Zealand, which I am passionately attached to, it would have to be the French Côte d'Azur, or south-west France, the River Gardon in the region of Uzès, Avignon and Nîmes. But then I have to add that I love London and consider it my second home.

Can you remember the first novel you read?

Yes it was a boys' historical adventure called *Young Jack* by someone who went by the name of Herbert Strang, but that, I discovered when I was an adult working in the British Museum towards my PhD, was really (and bizarrely) a pseudonym for someone who wrote in conjunction with another pseudonymous author called Richard Stead. Before that my father read me *Treasure Island* and I re-read it many times. *The Wind in the Willows* also came very early, though I always got stuck on a chapter called 'The Piper at the Gates of Dawn'.

What does it mean to be a writer?

It's an occupation, a form of self-employment, but more satisfying than most probably, and rather more conspicuous at times.

The Case of David Bain

Associate Professor Ken Palmer's letter to the *Herald* was so emphatic in his support of Canadian judge the Hon. Ian Binnie's report on the Bain claim for compensation, and so (it seemed to me) immoderate in its rejection of QC Dr Robert Fisher's response, I felt to have an opinion on this currently 'talking' topic one must read both, which I have now done. This has not altered my view (a layman's not a lawyer's) of David Bain's likely guilt, but it has added a new perspective. It is only reading Judge Binnie's report that I recognised how clumsy and less than competent the police enquiry, and consequently the first Crown case were, and how much of the subsequent drama sprang from those initial errors.

Reading through the detailed forensic analysis, and the challenges to it which have accumulated over the years of Joe Karam's crusade on David Bain's behalf, it is easy to imagine how the second jury might have grown weary of detail and focused instead on the

Published in the *New Zealand Herald*, 5 January 2013, pp. A18–19.

drama and the rhetoric – in particular the defence lawyer's boldness in 'standing up to' the trial judge, his 'courage' and his outrage. It would be tempting, in that second jury's shoes, to think, 'This is such a mess. The first Crown case has been full of holes and has had to be re-patched. The Law Lords have said the first conviction was a mistrial. Why should we struggle any further? Let's say at least that the case hasn't been proved, and acquit. If he's guilty, well, he has served his time anyway.'

I have an impression that in some degree Judge Binnie may have entered the fray in the same spirit, seeing himself as someone called in to 'right a wrong'; though he is certainly not, I should add, one who is impatient with the facts or unwilling to wrestle with them, one at a time.

But that 'one at a time' is part of the problem. As Dr Fisher points out, a circumstantial case depends on the strength of a single rope made up of many strands, any one of which may be insufficient. Judge Binnie's method is to begin with the Luminol footprints, the weakest (at least in the sense of being the most technical and therefore technically arguable) strand, declare it favours David Bain, and then bring each of the other strands in the case up against those footprints and find it wanting. And it is to the footprints he returns first in his 'Summary and conclusions as to factual innocence' (p. 138).

Yet even Binnie admits '"luminescence" in the dark does not exactly give rise to laser-like accuracy', and agrees 'there must be some room for error in the Luminol measurement' (p. 79/257). It seems strange, therefore, that he has 'no hesitation in recommending that the Minister accept the results of the tests of Mr Walsh' [for the defence] (p. 77/251), and proceeds from that point in a manner which suggests the case for innocence has been made and needs only to be demonstrated by reiterating the defence argument against each of the other strands.

His consequent bias is apparent in statements like the following: 'It is only the fingerprint blood that can tie David Bain rather than Robin Bain to the killings.' *Only?* And there is nothing at all that can tie Robin to the murder weapon except that he was killed with it!

Another example of this bias: 'Nothing has been established beyond a reasonable doubt. Nevertheless, the cumulative effect of the items of physical evidence, considered item by item both individually and collectively, *and considered in the light of my interview with David Bain*' [my italics] 'persuade me that David Bain is factually innocent' (p. 139/463). But why should items of fact, none of which, Binnie concedes, is 'free of difficulty', be considered 'in the light of' the accused's own testimony, which is more likely than any other to be false?

A further example: 'If David Bain's recollection [. . .] is accepted, and I do accept it, then the force of the prosecution's argument [. . .] is much diminished' (p. 38/124). But of course if we only have to go to David Bain for the truth then the prosecution's argument is not just diminished – it's dead! What kind of source is the accused for the truth of the matter in a case of murder?

And that brings me to what appears to be the real weakness in Judge Binnie's argument: his naive (as it seems to me) acceptance of David Bain's truthfulness in interview, and his (Binnie's) reliance on 'innocent openness' as the explanation where the accused's testimony seems to aid the prosecution rather than himself. As a 'final word' to the executive summary of his report Binnie quotes David Bain's ringing statement of complaint that he has not only had to mourn for his family and spend thirteen years in jail, but has had to live with the labels of 'monster' and 'psychopath' – all true of course, but only relevant if he is innocent, and that is still the question. If David Bain was not the killer his case is a sad one; but if he is, then he has had many years to go over his innocence story, so many that he must very nearly believe it himself, at least sufficiently to make it sound indistinguishable from a truthful statement. As Dr Fisher says, any number of studies have shown that 'none of us has the ability to decide whether or not a witness is to be believed based on watching and listening to that witness in person' (p. 9/18).

Predisposed as he is, Judge Binnie is able to wave away David's brother's blood on his clothes; the broken glasses at the murder scene which were of use to David but not to Robin; David's fingerprints on the murder weapon and his handprint on the washing machine; David's admission that he heard his sister gurgling and that he alone knew where the trigger key to the rifle was hidden; the blood on David's gloves – and many other finer strands in that rope of circumstantial evidence. Instead of David Bain as the killer Binnie offers us (since there is no third alternative) a murder by the father, Robin, who must have worn gloves (why?) while killing his wife and children, then changed his clothes and put the blood-stained ones in the washing basket (again, why?) before killing himself, still with a silencer on the rifle (why?), and having first turned on the computer to write his confession rather than writing it by hand. Binnie dispenses, it seems to me almost casually, with each of these elements, as with David's strange behaviour subsequent to the murders.

Signs of extreme stress would be expected; but what state of mind was David in that he made detailed plans for the victims' funeral; specified what lingerie his deceased sister Arawa would be dressed in; wanted the pop song 'Who wants to live for ever?' to be played for Laniet; told his aunt she was not to wear black at the funeral 'Because we see death as a celebration'; wanted to hold a posthumous party for Arawa on the Sunday after the murders; and spoke of 'black hands' taking his family away? To me all this suggests a state of disconnection from the reality – a state of mind in which the crime itself might have been committed – as if the one who had taken responsibility for that (by every report) disastrously dysfunctional family was now ready to tidy it all away with a tasteful funeral.

In every case where the original police enquiry failed to preserve, or to look for, evidence – Robin's hands which should have been checked for gunshot residue, and finger-nails for any signs of a fight with Steven, the bloodstained carpet, the whole house which was allowed to be burned down – the David Bain team has used this failure as if here was a piece of evidence that would have cleared his name; and Judge Binnie has tended to follow them in this. But in each case it could be (and in my view equally, or more likely, was) the destruction of an incontrovertibly damning piece of evidence for the prosecution. There are certainly no grounds at all for saying, or implying, that these pieces of 'lost evidence' lead one to the conclusion that David Bain is 'factually innocent'.

One final word against the payment of compensation: to say, as Binnie does, that the 'factual innocence' of David has been established clearly implies the 'factual guilt' of the father, Robin. Yet no case has ever been made against him, except by implication. And if the case were made it would be so much weaker than the one against his son, it would not stand inspection for more than a few minutes. I don't think a decision by the New Zealand Government should be allowed to label Robin Bain the murderer of his family.

That the second jury found the guilt of David Bain had not been proved 'beyond reasonable doubt' does not mean they would have affirmed that his 'factual innocence' had been demonstrated; but that is what the case for compensation requires, and what Judge Binnie affirms. It does not surprise me that when she received his report Judith Collins felt another opinion was needed, either for confirmation or rebuttal. It does not surprise me, either, that Dr Fisher did not confirm, but found serious fault in, Judge Binnie's report.

Postscript: It seemed to me that the Privy Council's ruling was based on weaknesses in the way the police case was prepared and on the police/Crown's subsequent carelessness with evidence, and was therefore correct; but that (for the reasons given above) the second trial should have resulted in a second guilty verdict. But there have been a number of other New Zealand cases where a clear injustice has been corrected by the Privy Council's ruling, and the question of what we are losing by giving away this avenue of appeal has to be asked.

Since I tend to be a republican, and in constitutional matters think it absurd that we should still have a head of State and a final Court of Appeal 12,000 miles away in a country currently a member of the EU from which we are excluded, I should, and in principle do, approve of our taking final responsibility for our own judicial system. But the fact remains that cases like that of Teina Pora, who spent twenty years in jail for a crime of which he was clearly innocent, demonstrate that there is a kind of dumb (and sometimes unscrupulous) intransigence about the way our police conduct such matters, and worse, an inexplicable willingness among senior New Zealand judges to permit them to have their way. Until we have a review panel of the kind currently proposed by Labour, and I think the Greens, and opposed by National, Act and (probably) the misnamed 'Sensible Sentencing Trust', we will continue to be in danger of such injustices, and with nowhere to go as a last resort for their correction.

Just before this book went to press, a report in the New Zealand Herald *claimed that the Australian judge called in to review the matter further has advised the government that it is not possible to conclude that Bain is factually innocent. If correct, this would confirm what my piece argues.*

A Talented Transient

When I was a young writer in the 1950s there was a certain mythology emanating from Frank Sargeson and reflecting a phase, and a literary world, already passing. This was the period of the Second World War when Sargeson himself, and others like Curnow, Fairburn and Glover, who had established their presence in the 1930s, were beginning to dominate the literary scene. It was a period of literary nationalism; but there was still a high regard for anyone who had work published in Britain, either whole books (Robin Hyde, Sargeson, D'Arcy Cresswell), or in periodicals like *Penguin New Writing* (Sargeson, Curnow, Glover). The attitude to British writers who came here to live was faintly ambiguous, but mainly positive, so long as they were talented, 'modern', and interested in local writing and writers. Two notable examples were Greville Texidor and Anna Kavan. Texidor became for a time part of the literary scene. Kavan was more distant, mysterious, but

---

A foreword to *Anna Kavan's New Zealand: A Pacific Interlude in a Turbulent Life*, ed. Jennifer Sturm (Vintage, 2009).

her association with Ian Hamilton, admired for his courageous pacifist stand during the war, and her rather 'posh' *façon de vivre* (i.e. dashing, and carelessly beyond her means) made her a figure of gossip and interest. After she had returned to London the interest deepened when it was known – or believed to be the case – that she was working with Cyril Connolly on *Horizon*, the major literary periodical of the time.

Kavan only (and very briefly) became known in New Zealand beyond literary circles when she published her article about us in *Horizon*, 'New Zealand: Answer to an Enquiry'. This appeared to be largely negative and was therefore largely unwelcome. What the literary community made of it is less clear; but if Bill Pearson's reaction in his essay 'Fretful Sleepers' is typical, there was more interest than hostility – not surprisingly because, although full of contradictions, some of her negative views (for example, of the division of male and female roles in our society) were common currency among writers and intellectuals when I was young.

To me at this distance in time the article has the feel of something that might have developed into a distinguished piece of writing. Her representation of New Zealand as a 'strange lonely dream scene full of lovely sadness. The dream without a dreamer' seems deeply felt, and owes something to Curnow's 'land of settlers / With never a soul at home'. Her 'That's what I see in New Zealand. Always the desolation, always the splendour' directly echoes his 'O splendour of desolation' from 'Landfall in Unknown Seas'. Other things – 'no music, no theatres, no pictures . . .', 'null', 'dull', 'tepid', 'mediocre', 'the down under of the spirit' – again seem to derive from a common intellectual currency, but needed stronger illustration, more analysis, to carry much weight. In the end she may have given up the attempt to be serious and taken the easier path of entertainment for her British readers.

What the present collection, together with Dr Sturm's commentary and editorial work, shows is that New Zealand had made a deep, complex, and largely positive impression on Kavan. It had helped to form (or reform) her as a writer, and for some time after returning to London she tried very hard to get back. I am struck especially by how 'New Zealand' these fictional pieces are, not only in their material, but in their manner and language. By this I mean not just the free use of Maori words and place names, and the widening of human interest beyond the solipsism that characterises much of her work before and after – all noted by Dr Sturm. There is also a style, a flavour, a turn of phrase that suggests now an influence of Sargeson's fiction, now a sense of Fairburn's expository prose, and now a Curnovian overview of 'island and time'. This is work by an Englishwoman who, though already in her forties, went back to school here and became for a time a 'New Zealand' writer.

In a very revealing opening piece to 'Five Months Further', Kavan distinguishes two kinds of dream, one full of anxiety, the other producing a state of 'superior composure'. She describes lying awake at Waitahanui (Torbay) 'in the silent New Zealand night' asking herself why, if the anxiety-dream can impose itself on the waking self, the same should not be true of the dream of 'non-attachment'. This proposition grows into a dialogue with the morepork she can hear outside her window:

> To fight is to invite madness and destruction, I said to the morepork. To keep any claim to sanity one must simply submit and record what happens.
>> Submit and record, I said. It's the only thing left.
>> More pork. More pork. More pork, said the morepork.
>> Submit, record, I said. Submit, record.

Later in the same story, and in the stories that follow, we find the products of this decision that to 'submit and record' is her role as a writer and her salvation as a person. It is a kind of realism, a kind, even, of nationalism; it is a moment in our intellectual history, registered by a talented transient, sensitive to the New Zealand literary climate, and willing to submit to, and record, the facts of place and people as she found them.

Even when she spends three days in New York on her way back to London, the most vivid (and best-written about) experience is with the Kiwi sailor she refers to alternately as the first officer and the mate – the slightly reluctant bed-mate, who has declined to go drinking. Here for a moment it's as if she assigns them symbolic roles, she the Old World lying in the arms of the New, refreshed and renewed by the knowledge she has brought with her of Waitahanui.

She was to move on in the years that followed to other things – a species of substance-induced, or heroin-enhanced, fantasy, which would make her a cult figure a world away from Auckland's North Shore. But what Dr Sturm has done in the present book is to make available for the first time, with commentary and notes, an essentially 'New Zealand' work, previously lost to us – a piece of recovered history.

The *Takahē* Interview

Patricia Prime: *You have had a life-time's career in teaching, editing and critical writing that does not seem to have diminished your productivity in creative writing. Which of these genres do you find most congenial?*

C. K. Stead: Each has its satisfactions and frustrations. But the creative writing, poetry first and then fiction, is what matters to me most. When I was young it was not possible to make a living out of serious creative writing in New Zealand. It hardly is now. You need an overseas publisher because the NZ market is so small. If you want to live here and be a serious writer you need, at least to begin with, to teach or find some other means of earning a living. I regarded university teaching as my livelihood, writing as my vocation.

PP: *In your career as teacher, cultural commentator, critic, author (translated into many languages), poet and person, you use a diversity*

Interview by Patricia Prime, *Takahē* 68, Issue 3, 2009.

*of 'voices'. The forthcoming memoir perhaps concentrates a little
more on yourself as a person. This glimpse into your life is one that I
am sure readers will find enlightening. Could you tell us some common
problems that you see in writing a memoir?*

CKS: I have written about using my own voice in *Book Self*, and
about trying to keep the presence of the critic, his personality, his
'self', in critical writing, rather than using the impersonal voice that
is common especially in academic writing. In fiction of course one
uses many voices, most of them in some way false, yet all of them
also one's own. Writing an autobiography is simpler, at least in the
sense that the voice is entirely one's own. One difficulty is to tell the
truth and get the facts right. I know there are currently NZ writers
who say this doesn't matter – autobiography is only another kind
of fiction. There's a small element of truth in that, because you have
to choose which facts, and what tone to use – how to tell each story,
and with what special emphasis. That is, so to speak, the 'colouring',
and engages your skill as a fiction writer. But it is quite different
from inventing things that didn't happen, or consciously distort-
ing facts, 'sexing up' the account. I am trying very hard to tell it as
I remember it, so if there are inaccuracies they will be failures of
memory, not deliberate falsifications.

PP: *Your memoir has been described as possessing 'a poetry of innocence, but also the clarity and wisdom of introspection, recollected in
mature years'. The excerpt in this issue serves not only as a mini-in-
troduction to the chapter and the wider memoir, but also adumbrates
a child's powerful sense of observation and recall. Have you always
been a keen observer and commentator, and have you always been
enthralled with the communicative possibilities of language?*

CKS: I think yes to both these questions, and especially to the first.
People have expressed surprise that I can write a book of 100,000

plus words that only goes up to the age of 23. But this is possible because I have always observed closely and consequently the memories are well imprinted. I think interest in the world outside self is the protection of sanity against solipsism and the ravages of the introspective ego.

The interest in language is basic to literature, and especially poetry, because language is what distinguishes us on our planet. Writing, published work, which does not in one way or another come from an interest that penetrates below its 'subject', its occasion, its genre, to language itself, is not 'literature'. I make that distinction in my own mind – an unfashionable one in a time when anything that smacks of 'elitism' is frowned upon.

PP: *Your creative and critical work is undoubtedly a source of academic interest. If you were to be approached by a writer or a post-graduate student, would you be open to or well disposed towards someone writing a study of your work, or indeed a biography?*

CKS: Yes and no. I have had theses done on my work without knowing about it, and later had the interesting and (on the whole) pleasant experience of reading about myself from a new per-spective. But I'm not so keen on the idea of someone writing my biography. One person began, and I co-operated at first because I thought I should be grateful for the interest in my work. But then I felt I was becoming involved and would soon be almost co-au-thor, and so withdrew entirely and would have nothing more to do with it. This was not because the writer's 'take' on my work was unfriendly – quite the reverse. The writer then turned the work into a biographical/critical study, which I think may soon be published, neither with my assent nor, on the other hand, disavowal.

PP: *Regarding, in particular your novel* My Name Was Judas, *could you tell us why you brought together prose and poetry in the novel?*

CKS: I wrote the novel at first without the poems. Once the first draft was complete I felt it needed something extra. The character of Judas echoes my own views on religious experience and the notion of the Divine – he is, or has become over the years, the complete sceptic. And yet there is a power in the figure of Jesus, which explains how his followers, and in the end Jesus himself, are deluded. I reject the Divine, the supernatural, yet I wouldn't want to be called a materialist either. What then for me represents the further reaches of human experience, the dimension beyond the material? Clearly it is in language itself, and in its most complete expression, poetry. (If I were a scientist I suppose I would have to add mathematics.) So the idea came to me that in the second draft Judas would be a poet. Each chapter would end with one of his poems, partly summing up, but also adding something that was not already clear. These poems would represent that further realm, beyond the material. This meant, incidentally, that for the first time I had found a way of putting my two writing selves together, poet and fiction writer.

PP: *One review I've read of the book suggests that 'confession finds its best expression in the poems that end each chapter: intended to deny the truth of Jesus' ministry, they do so in the form of a prayer' (James Wood, Telegraph, 2006). Do you believe that Judas denies Jesus, or that he is simply recalling in old age what he thought at that time of uncertainty? How else might his poems be called 'prayers'?*

CKS: That review by James Wood* gave me huge pleasure because I had often said that he's the best reviewer of fiction in the business at present. It was great that I had said it before he had ever reviewed a book of mine, and that when he did he was so positive.

---

* See p. 145 for a review of Wood's *How Fiction Works*.

But no, I hadn't thought of the poems as prayers. I suppose they might be, but to whom? Judas doesn't deny Jesus the brilliant child and youthful scholar, the great preacher of compassion, the inspirer of his people, the daring moral innovator; but he denies his divinity throughout, and is appalled towards the end as Jesus becomes crazed with the sense of his own power, threatening and violent in his last preaching. This contradiction between 'gentle Jesus' and Jesus who 'brings not peace but a sword' is given a time dimension in the novel – he moves from one towards and into the other; but all its elements are there in the Gospels.

PP: *I particularly enjoy the humour you bring to this novel – for example in the poem which occurs at the end of chapter fourteen:*

> *Lying by the lake,*
> *once on a summer's*
> *night I heard*
>
> *Andrew recount*
> *how, at the baptism*
> *of Jesus*
>
> *a dove appeared*
> *in a beam of light*
> *and a Voice said*
>
> *'This is my beloved*
> *Son in whom*
> *I am well pleased.'*
>
> *Did I believe*
> *this? No. I'd been there*
> *at the ford and*

seen no dove, heard
no voice. Yet it's true
I was perplexed

not that God's grammar
should be perfect
but that it seemed

beyond the
reach of fisherman
Andrew to invent.

Judas appears to have a spiritual affinity with Jesus, although he is an outsider, and his inability to believe in Jesus' divinity, presents the problems many of us have. Do you believe the poems present a different side to Judas?

CKS: This is quite a subtle joke, and allows a tiny space for doubt by Judas – Judas doubting his own doubt. I suppose I thought a man of those times would not be quite so certain as my Judas is that Jesus was NOT divine; and so here he asks how could the simple fisherman Andrew recall hearing a divine voice speaking with a formal grammar he would not himself be capable of? It makes a small point, without deflecting the overall direction of the book. But it's there mainly for the pleasure I found (and hoped the reader would find) in the joke itself, i.e. it is more a part of the characterisation of Judas than an indicator that he has any serious doubt about his doubt.

The poems by the way are all in thirteen-syllable triplets – each three lines exactly thirteen syllables. I did think at one point of putting a sort of clue to why at the front of the book in the form of one more self-explaining triplet, but decided against it. It would have read simply

> Thirteen syllables
> because there were
> thirteen of us.

Meaning of course there were twelve disciples and Jesus.

PP: *Has your critical background influenced your poetry writing and vice versa?*

CKS: My knowledge of the processes of writing, and in particular my understanding of the writing of poetry, made me a better critic. A lot of my literary criticism springs directly from that knowledge and would have been impossible without it. I don't think it works much the other way; though perhaps writing criticism forces things to become conscious that might otherwise have remained intuitive.

PP: *Your critical writing has been a major part of New Zealand's contribution towards understanding of Modernism. Could you perhaps explain why you were drawn to poets such as Yeats, Pound and Eliot?*

CKS: Yeats and Eliot, and to a lesser extent Auden, were regarded as the major living (or very recently deceased in the case of Yeats) poets when I was young. Pound was a crucial, but more complex case – a mixed blessing, but important in terms of the development of open forms and what came to be called the process poem. Also as midwife at the birth of Eliot's *The Waste Land*. When I first wrote about them I was writing about the great English language poet-figures of the time.

PP: *I'm wondering how these various genres of academic writing, creative and critical writing have fed off each other. How does the interaction, if any, work?*

CKS: Literary criticism is partly a matter of persuasion. If you are a real writer rather than just an academic, you write more persuasively, readers enjoy what you have to say and are more inclined to listen. Reading academic writing can sometimes feel like eating blotting paper; and there was a recent fashion for literary theory which substituted wallboard for blotting paper.

PP: *As the author of thirteen novels, how does the prose writer C. K. Stead get on with the poet C. K. Stead? Do they co-exist in harmony or do you consider yourself primarily a poet?*

CKS: The poetry is what I value most; but there are things you can do in fiction which can't be done in poetry; and fiction reaches out to a wider, less purely literary, audience. There's no reason why one should not go back and forth from one to the other.

PP: *While you operate on a global and cultural sense, what lay behind your decision to remain a 'New Zealand' writer rather than live overseas as other New Zealand writers have done?*

CKS: When I was young I was inspired and encouraged in particular by Allen Curnow and Frank Sargeson, who were both, in their very different ways, literary nationalists – and I became one myself, because that was what the time seemed to call for. It all seems long ago and rather remote. I can't say I regret making the choice I did; but I'm glad to have been able to spend regular and significant periods outside NZ. I haven't found it a consistently warm or welcoming environment for the kind of writer I happen to be. But I'm not complaining – the truth is I've had a very good run.

PP: *Coming to your poetry, it's clear that poetic technique matters greatly to you. Do you enjoy equally work that is 'freer', less obviously engaged with the issue of poetic craft?*

CKS: There has been a slow development away from regular metrical and rhymed verse towards freer forms; and then in more recent years quite a lot of syllabics. But I like to feel free to go back as well as forward, since the only 'progress', if there is any, is in your skill and control and the sense of knowing what you want to do and how to do it. I tend to think of myself as a musician, sometimes writing symphonies (the novels, I suppose), sometimes quartets or trios, sometimes works for a solo instrument. Why should there not be variety? I think a poet who writes one kind of (short) poem over and over again for a lifetime can be interesting, but I wanted a wider range to suit different moods, occasions and experimental possibilities. I would say by the way that my poetry was improved by the long hard grind of writing fiction. Simply by having to write a great deal you get better at writing of every kind. I am an Arthur Lydiard kind of writer. I believe the more you run/write the better you are at it.

PP: *One does not always realise whom one has been influenced by and many of the writers we most admire seem to leave no trace in our work. When you started to write who were the poets you admired? Have these admirations lasted?*

CKS: I have been through so many phases – beginning when I was about fourteen with Rupert Brooke, followed by Keats and Wordsworth, going on to the great Modernists and beyond, but also John Donne and the Metaphysicals – not to mention New Zealanders, Curnow, Baxter, Mason, Smithyman, bits of Fairburn – and too many others to acknowledge sensibly. I think you begin by imitation and gradually find your own voice, though that voice is there right from the start. That's the normal process.

PP: *How do you approach criticism of your writing?*

CKS: Criticism of my work or of anyone else's needs to persuade me it is written by someone who has real literary intelligence; otherwise it doesn't, or shouldn't, interest me. Not a huge amount that is written about literature seems to me to pass this test. Of course if it's my own work that is being discussed and that quality of literary intelligence is lacking, then there's an added irritation because one is interested for the wrong (i.e. egotistical) reason. I am not immune to this failing.

PP: *What do you think of the quality of contemporary poetry reviewing and criticism and its influence on what gets written?*

CKS: There are always, everywhere and at any time, very few good critics of fiction, and even fewer of poetry. Real critics are rare and deserve to be valued and celebrated more than they are. We have very few because they are rare everywhere and our literary scene is small. Because it's small it's also somewhat repressive.

PP: *What does the prize culture, the rewards and reputations, mean to you?*

CKS: The literary prizes and awards culture is almost totally geared to commerce; it distorts literary values, creates false reputations, and is pernicious – here and overseas. Judge Time (as Martin Amis – who has never won the Booker – says) will sort it out; but meanwhile too many readers let the literary judges (always a mixed bag) do their thinking for them. If there had been a Booker Prize in the first half of the twentieth century, would Henry James, or D. H. Lawrence, or James Joyce have won it? I doubt it. Yet the winners would by now be forgotten. Bill Bryson, in his recent book on Shakespeare, points out that the greatest writer in English only seems to have rated third or fourth in his own time. He adds: 'This shouldn't come entirely as a surprise. Ages are generally pretty incompetent at judging their own worth. How many people now would vote to bestow the Nobel Prize for Literature on Pearl Buck, Henrik Pontoppidan, Rudolph Eucken, Selma Lagerlöf or many others whose fame would barely make it past to the end of their own century?'

So we need not worry, if we take the long view. But to some extent we all live in the moment, and in the moment the prize industry is somewhere between a distraction and a pain in the neck for anyone serious about good writing.

PP: *What thoughts do New Zealand journals and magazines provoke in you?*

CKS: Literary journals have been very important, especially to the young writer looking for recognition, a launching pad, a platform, a forum for literary discussion. But they should be quarterly. *Sport* has become annual – or occasional; *Landfall* six-monthly. These gaps are too long. And the *Listener*'s recent announcement that it was discontinuing publishing poems was a very bad concession to commerce.

PP: *Would you like to say something about New Zealand and its move towards cultural confidence (in life and whatever expression this takes in the arts)? For example – when the London flat for New Zealand writers was first raised all those years ago – you were the only one who saw its purpose. Could you say why this was so important to you?*

CKS: I wasn't the only one who saw the value of the writer's flat in London; but there were those who opposed it on the grounds that it was a return to Mother England's apron strings. This is the reverse of confidence. If you are confident of your country and its culture you will go anywhere, taking them, country and culture, with you.

The recognition that 'a NZ writer' does not always have to have a 'NZ subject' represents progress.

National confidence has grown enormously since I was young. The independence of our foreign policy under Labour has been good for us all, but is sometimes undermined by National's decisions when it returns to government. We should become a republic soon, and have a new flag – maybe the one Helen Clark suggested, the Southern Cross on a blue background – grab it before the Australians do!

Beyond the arts, collectively as a nation, we need to be confident without constantly telling ourselves we're marvellous. We're not marvellous. We're just enterprising and industrious like the human species (and the ant) everywhere, and with the good luck to be born here and not in, let's say, the Warsaw ghetto of the 1940s, or the Gaza strip in 2009.

PP: *In terms of academic teaching and writing you have been inordinately innovative and brave – never hesitating to question yet always with a mind as to what New Zealand is and its relation/position to the wider world. You are totally aware of world literature but have consistently sought for your own voice and encouraged this in others. How far have you succeeded in imparting your wisdom to your students and to young writers?*

CKS: Thank you for those kind words. As to the question, only they can say.

World War I –
Close Up from a Distance

For me it was in childhood the Great War – that's how it was referred to in the family, and it figured especially because my grandmother's half-brother, with the wonderful name of Owen Vincent Freeman, had been killed fighting with the New Zealand forces in France. The grandmother, who lived with us (or we with her), had been deeply attached to her only male sibling, and still grieved, reproaching herself for having encouraged him in his youthful eagerness to 'join up' for war. As next of kin she had received a finely engraved bronze plaque which hung on the dining room wall and which I still have, with his name inscribed and showing Britannia and the British lion, with the inscription 'HE DIED FOR FREEDOM AND HONOUR'.

Of course I knew about Gallipoli, which was somehow 'glorious' though a defeat (a word that wasn't used). But a cloud hung over

Written for *How We Remember: New Zealanders and the First World War*, ed. Charles Ferrall and Harry Ricketts (Victoria University Press, 2014).

all talk of that war because of 'Uncle Owen' whose head, my grand-mother told me once with self-punishing brutality, had been 'blown off'. He was buried in France and no one from the family had visited his grave, or ever has.

But the Great War figured more generally in the popular mind because it was so clearly remembered by my parents' and grandpar-ents' generation as a time of shock and disappointment. Its onset had been almost welcomed as a glorious assertion of British grandeur, an opportunity and an adventure which would be quickly and victori-ously over; and had turned, instead, into the grinding horror of the trenches, with its pointless and self-destructive attempts at gaining ground, its stalemate and climbing death toll. The only way it could be coped with had been to describe it (using H. G. Wells's phrase) as 'the war to end wars', and now, only twenty-one years later, another was upon us.

Pakeha New Zealand in 1939, though physically so remote from its British origins, and though priding itself on difference (and even a kind of provincial 'superiority'), was in effect, in its actions and affec-tions, still a part of Britain, so there was no question of our opting out or even hanging back. If Britain was at war again, and with the old enemy, so were we. And as I saw my father's younger brother go off to it, I wondered whether he too would die, as my great uncle had, and whether we would have another plaque to hang on the wall. In fact he survived, but as a POW. We 'won' of course; it had never occurred to me as a child that defeat was possible. The celebrations were wild, followed by something like a faint but distinct collective depression.

Our World War II soldiers were not referred to as the ANZACs. They were 'the boys' mainly, or more specifically 'the NZ Div', 'the 3rd Echelon' and 'the Maori Battalion'. ANZACs were survivors of that other, earlier, and as time went by it seemed, even worse one, the First World War, the Great War – worse for the military anyway, because of its death-dealing stalemate. Hitler's war while it was hap-pening seemed not so terrible, simply because in Western Europe he had won it so quickly. What was going on in occupied Europe would not be fully known until it was over; and the worst of the bombing happened to Germany, which was (the child thought) just 'getting what it deserved'.

But gradually World War II, with all its differences from the one before – the complexities of the Russian front, Pearl Harbor, Japan and the war in the Pacific, the tough but relentless slogs across Europe and up through the Pacific, the carpet bombing of Germany and the atomic raids on Hiroshima and Nagasaki, the revealed horrors of the Holocaust – all of this, though it didn't eliminate the Great War from our collective consciousness, seemed finally to supersede it, rendering it only the overture, 'unfinished business'. By the time World War II was over and I was at secondary school, the Great War seemed 'old stuff': it was history. It seemed further in the past than it really was. It was to come back into my consciousness but in a new way – through the medium of literature.

At the age of about fourteen I borrowed from my sister, who never asked for it back, a copy of *Rupert Brooke: The Complete Poems*, sent as a present by her English 'pen-friend' to whose family our wartime 'food parcels' had gone. It was the first time I had owned a whole book of poems by one author and I read it assiduously, and read about Brooke in books borrowed from the library, excited to learn that he had even visited 'the South Seas' (including New Zealand), and that among the funeral party burying him on one of the Greek Islands had been our own Bernard Freyberg, winner of the VC on the Somme. My own family had close emotional attachments to the Pacific islands where my Swedish grandfather had been a sea-captain and layer of deep-sea moorings, and where my mother had spent much of her childhood. So Brooke's Pacific poems, with their glamour and exciting undertones of sexual experience, went together in my mind with another of my youthful heroes, Robert Louis Stevenson.

The frontispiece to that collection of Brooke's poems was the British Museum holograph manuscript of his sonnet 'The Soldier', with its cancelling of the first two words of the sestet, 'Think too', replacing them with 'And think'. I must have been already writing poems myself; and this evidence of the poet's hand making a late change was a peculiar excitement; a reminder that even important and historically durable poems were written by real people who changed their minds about the words they wanted.

Brooke became, after his death, and had remained, a symbol of young British manhood lost in warfare. His physical beauty was always remarked upon, but this aspect – which I was to discover later had been enormously significant to the New Zealand critic and biographer Eric McCormick, who had developed a sort of youthful crush on the poet – didn't interest me. In the photo at the front of that *Complete Poems*, I thought his eyes were too small, the eyebrows too pale, and there was a sort of shine about his skin, so there was no temptation to linger on the face rather than the poems. And the war poems – not about fighting, because he died unglamorously of septicaemia from a mosquito bite before reaching a battle[1] – but about the call to arms, and national glory, and the romantic possibility of warrior death, were not to me his most interesting. I still have 'The Soldier' by heart, not intentionally but because I read it often and have that kind of memory. I don't think the incipient critic was sufficiently alive in me to quite turn thumbs down on lines like (from another sonnet) 'Now God be thanked Who has matched us with His hour / And caught our youth and wakened us from sleeping'; but certainly I turned away from those to his other poems; and soon to other poets, and other styles. So I would remain grateful to Brooke for waking me to poetry, as he was grateful to God for waking him to war – but I'm sure in both cases it would have happened without the intermediary.

World War I now reverted in my consciousness principally to its secondary place as the overture to World War II, except when it popped up, in school History studies, and then in my undergraduate years, as an event which had had complex 'causes'. 'What were the causes of the First World War?' was a puzzle to which a great deal of intellectual energy and research had been applied. In my novel *The Singing Whakapapa* my principal character, Hugh Grady, is an historian of only moderate success, always slightly uneasy about the notion of causation; but happy enough with the narrative which relating these 'causes' required. The novel's tone lightly mocks the idea of historical causation:

certain things happened, and then certain further things, followed by more, and others, and yet more; and at the end of all this a war was declared, men and guns were mobilised, many, and more, and other, and further (including his great-uncle Vincent Flatt) were killed, and then it came to an end. How many (Hugh was to wonder) of those things listed as 'causes' would need *not* to have happened for the First World War not to have happened either? Or for it to have been so different as to have been something else? And what were the causes of the causes?

In fact I was 'good at' History, and very nearly made it my major subject – in which case I might have become one of those narrative historians who are enjoyable to read and often derided by the unreadable ones. World War I was now a story with a complex plot, many strands of cause, and many consequences. And though the emphasis has changed it seems the subject of 'cause' has never entirely gone away. Even as I write, the current issue of the *Times Literary Supplement* (15 March 2013) is reviewing a book by Ian Beckett called *The Making of the First World War*.

I did not, however, stick with History; and so it was literature again which returned me to the subject. By the time I came to do my PhD (this was in Bristol on a scholarship from New Zealand) I knew what might be called the authorised twentieth-century Modernist literary history in which Rupert Brooke figured hardly at all. Poetically he was a 'Georgian'; more broadly, he had become a minor literary figure representative of British self-adulation and military delusion, blamed by association, and as much for what was made of him posthumously as for what he wrote. In literary terms T. S. Eliot was now the dominant figure of the century, both as poet and critic. Ezra Pound, the firebrand who demanded poets 'make it new', and who knocked Eliot's great poem *The Waste Land* into its final shape, was hardly more than Eliot's lieutenant, excused the folly of his late enthusiasms for Social Credit and Mussolini, not to mention his virulent anti-Semitism, and taken seriously as poet and literary critic, only because Eliot himself insisted he must be, and even called him *'il miglior fabbro'* – the better craftsman.

But the poets of World War I – the real ones who really fought, and recorded the horrors of the trenches, and in many cases died – though they were not accorded the primacy of being true 'Modernists', were given an important place, especially in the British heart and mind. One enormous emotional element in the reaction to these poets was guilt. The poems were either directly or by implication full of reproach, and the reproach was accepted as deserved. Owen's cry 'The poetry is in the pity', and titles like 'Anthem for Doomed Youth', struck home.[2] The war was something that had been done to the young by the old – a cruel trick that had been played on them, on their emotions, their sense of loyalty and duty. If you could have seen the soldier 'guttering, choking, drowning' from poison gas, Owen says:

> My friend, you would not tell with such high zest
> To children ardent for some desperate glory,
> The old Lie: *Dulce et decorum est*
> *Pro patria mori.*

My grandmother's reaction to the death of her brother was something that must have been felt by people similarly placed throughout the Empire (as it then was). There had been such enthusiasm, in retrospect such an embarrassing *appetite*, for the war, that inevitably what followed, as its horrors and its sheer waste of life were revealed, was shame – and for those who fought in it and lived at least long enough to tell its story, special honour. So I think few if any literary critics have ever written with cool precision about these poets. It's as though to mention their occasional (and perhaps frequent) ineptitudes, would be dishonouring 'the glorious dead' – something which may not be done. Their poems are sacred memorials. I don't mean to suggest they were not, many of them – Wilfred Owen, for example, Siegfried Sassoon, Edmund Blunden, Isaac Rosenberg, Charles Sorley, Robert Graves, Herbert Read – talented poets and worthy figures in the history of literature in English; only that they have seldom been viewed with what might be called critical detachment and discrimination.

So I had come back to World War I through the study of literature; and that would happen again, some years later, when I studied Katherine Mansfield, and even more when I wrote a novel about her which I decided should cover just three years of her life – 1915 to 1918. Mansfield was one of those who had encouraged a brother's warrior inclinations, and then suffered anguish and guilt when he was killed. He had spent his last leaves with her in London and they had re-established their old bond, playing a game in which they went endlessly over details of their childhood in Wellington. This renewed her attachment to family, childhood and New Zealand, and became the basis of the new fiction she would write which is still by general consent her best – stories like 'Prelude', 'At the Bay', 'The Garden Party', 'The Doll's House', 'The Wind Blows'. There were also stories and accounts in letters and journals in which the war plays a direct and important part – 'An Indiscreet Journey', for example, describing her successful attempt to visit her French soldier-lover in the war zone. 'The Fly', clearly based on her father, deals with a heartbroken parent trying to find ways of coming to terms with the death of a loved son, killed in France and buried there, in whom the father's hopes for the future had been invested.

The brother, Leslie Beauchamp, became Mansfield's ghostly prompt, as if she had made a promise to him which must now, because of his death, be honoured:

'Do you remember, Katie?' I hear his voice in the trees and flowers, in scents and light and shadow. . . . I feel I have a duty to perform to the lovely time when we were both alive. I want to write about it and he wanted me to. We talked it over in my little top room in London. I said: I will just put on the front page: to my brother, Leslie Heron Beauchamp. Very well: it shall be done.

He was killed in France giving instruction in the use of hand grenades. One exploded in his hand and killed him; but he had a few minutes of dying consciousness, in which Katherine invented last words about her – 'Lift my head, Katie. I can't breathe' – which until very recently scholars saw no reason to disbelieve. It was one of the minor discoveries of the research I did for my novel that, though Leslie did say something about not being able to breathe, he did not mention his sister. But she needed his dying words; his last thought had to be of her, so she invented them.

Mansfield's case is just another example, but a good one because so acutely felt and vividly recorded, of the intensity with which that war was experienced – its shock, its horror, and the awful lesson it taught about the difference between idea and reality. It was a war, one might say, experienced in the first person. In World War II, by contrast, the scale was so large the individual tended to vanish into the statistics – which may be why the first produced much notable poetry, the second relatively little.

Mansfield lived the war to the full – as much, anyway, as a woman of the time, and one who was ill, could. Her brother came to London and spent that important time with her, and then was killed shortly after departing for France. Her close friend, Fred Goodyear, with whom she made secret plans for what they would do, and where they would go together, when it was over, was also killed. Rupert Brooke had been a friend and died on the way to Gallipoli. She was offered a re-issue of her first book of stories, *In a German Pension*, which might have gained her instant applause because of their strongly anti-German flavour, but declined because she thought them immature. She became part of the Garsington set, where conscientious objection was honoured, and COs given recognised work and in effect a place to hide. She was close to D. H. Lawrence and his wife Frieda, who suffered suspicion and hostility because Frieda was German. She was for a time friend, possibly more than friend, to Bertrand Russell, famous and loathed for his pacifism, and sentenced to jail for speaking against the draft. Her husband (as he became late in the war) John Middleton Murry was conscripted into war work, as was her friend Ida Baker. After her early adventure with the French soldier-lover, she was in Paris when it was bombed; and she continued to move to and fro between France and England, avoiding the war zones, but experiencing the deprivations of the time – more acutely because she was suffering, as it went on, from tuberculosis and seeking warmer climates for the winter. It is not possible to deal with those years of Mansfield's life without encountering the war in many of its aspects.

Mansfield of course was not alone in this. Hermione Lee in her biography of Virginia Woolf writes:

The First World War as a catastrophic break, and as the event which shaped the twentieth century, overshadows Virginia Woolf's work. In her novels there is often a violent moment of destruction or obliteration. All the lights go out, there is a roaring blackness and a sense of 'complete annihilation'. Her own apprehension of and attraction to death creates the private psychodrama behind these frightening patterns. But personal feelings are translated into history. Her books are full of images of war: armies, battles, guns, bombs, air-raids, battleships, shell-shock victims, war reports, photographs of war-victims . . .

It was a war that got deeply into the European consciousness, and so into ours as well – 'the event that shaped the twentieth century'.

I have said the war poets were somehow exempt from critical rigour; but there is an exception to this, and rather a shocking one. W. B. Yeats in his 1936 *Oxford Book of Modern Verse* slighted them,[3] excluding entirely the one he acknowledged (without naming him) was by now the 'best known', Wilfred Owen. He says he has a 'distaste' for these war poems, and explains that they have been rejected because 'passive suffering is not a theme for poetry. In all the great tragedies, tragedy is a joy to the man who dies; . . . If war is necessary, or necessary in our time and place, it is best to forget its suffering as we do the discomforts of a fever . . .'. This lack of 'tragic joy' had turned the war into something philosophically meaning-less: 'some blunderer has driven his car on to the wrong side of the road – that is all.'[4] Worse, in a letter he might well have anticipated would fetch up in the public domain, he said Owen was 'unworthy of the poet's corner of a country newspaper'; 'he is all blood, dirt and sucked sugar stick'.[5]

The question must be asked: which is more foolish – Brooke's heroic pose, or Yeats's intellectual one; or are they equal in silliness? Brooke had at least the excuse of ignorance of what the war would bring, whereas Yeats must have known very well, by the time of editing the anthology, that Owen and his like had been reporting it as it was. For a (perhaps *the*) major poet of the time to have so dispar-aged a younger and well-respected one who had written vividly and movingly of the horrors of the war in which he was killed, is surpris-ing – more than just extreme bad taste – and I think any explanation must bring us back to the complex allegiances the war sometimes invoked.

Yeats himself wrote about a young friend, the son of his mentor and patron Lady Augusta Gregory, killed in World War I, and at the same time that its argument arouses difficult questions, it is a poem that shows him in many ways at his best, or anyway his most adroit:

An Irish Airman foresees his Death

I know that I shall meet my fate
Somewhere among the clouds above;
Those that I fight I do not hate,
Those that I guard I do not love;
My country is Kiltartan Cross,
My countrymen Kiltartan's poor,
No likely end could bring them loss
Or leave them happier than before.
Nor law, nor duty bade me fight,
Nor public men, nor cheering crowds,
A lonely impulse of delight
Drove to this tumult in the clouds;
I balanced all, brought all to mind,
The years to come seemed waste of breath,
And waste of breath the years behind
In balance with this life, this death.

It is beautifully turned, probably more perfect, simply judged as verse-making, than anything Owen wrote, or could have written: a perfect poem in its way, but (and this is no small matter) almost certainly untruthful in what it claims for its subject (and by implication for its author) – that Major Robert Gregory, being Irish, cared nothing for the cause of England against Germany, didn't mind which side won the war, and was motivated only by 'a lonely impulse of delight'. Yeats here is imposing retrospectively on his patron's son the 'joy' with which, according to his theory, the tragic hero meets death, and which Owen's poetry, with its emphasis on suffering, lacks.

One of the memorable things Owen said about poetry was 'The true poets must be truthful.' He meant if war is sordid, ugly and randomly wasteful, we must not lie and pretend it is glorious. His poems are, accordingly, truthful: they give us 'the facts'. In 'An Irish Airman Foresees his Death' by contrast, Yeats, I think it is not too much to say, is exercising a brilliantly expedient and beautifully turned mendacity. Major Gregory didn't care whether he lived or died; didn't care who won the war; knew the war's 'outcome' would make no difference to his people whichever side won: it is hard to accept any of these assertions and, worse, very difficult to believe that Yeats believed them. 'Truthfulness', of course, is not the beginning and the end of how we arrive at a 'value' for any poem; and one does not forget that Shakespeare has one of his characters say 'The truest poetry is the most feigning'.[6] But one can say at least that Irish allegiances were making the war a subject Yeats might have done well to avoid.

It was a problem for him because it divided Ireland – the Nationalists opposed any Irish participation, and the Unionists supported Britain against Germany. Yeats had too much of a stake in literary Britain (and, one might add, in the English language and its literature) to want to see Britain defeated. Privately he wrote:

I have friends fighting in Flanders, I had one in the trenches at Antwerp, and I have a very dear friend [Maud Gonne] nursing the wounded in a French hospital. How can I help but feeling [sic] as they feel and desiring the defeat of Germany.[7]

But he favoured Irish independence and did not want to do or say anything that would appear to side with the Unionists. This, I suspect, must go some significant way towards explaining the vehemence of his rejection of the British war poets. So he invoked an elaborate theory about tragic poetry to explain his avoidance of what could have been a political embarrassment.[8]

In fact I have found literature has taken me back again and again to that war the end of which preceded my birth by fourteen years. There are not just the war poets but the important memoirs of survivors – Graves's *Goodbye to All That*, Sassoon's *Memoirs of an Infantry Officer*, Blunden's *Undertones of War*, Vera Brittain's *Testament of Youth*, and novels like Richard Aldington's *Death of a Hero*, of which Maxim Gorky is said to have remarked that he 'would never have thought that the English could produce a book like it',[9] and Ford Madox Ford's masterful tetralogy *Parade's End*. Then there are single items not easily classified, like American poet E. E. Cummings's novel *The Enormous Room*. Fitzgerald's narrator in *The Great Gatsby*, Nick Carraway, has 'participated in that delayed Teutonic migration known as the Great War', and Gatsby himself has risen to the rank of major; and it is similarly in the background of Hemingway's *Fiesta*, in which Jake Barnes has been wounded and left impotent. As a subject for fiction it has never entirely gone away, and has been revived in recent years by Pat Barker's *Regeneration* trilogy, including *The Ghost Road*, which won the Booker Prize. So when I came to write about it in my novel *Mansfield* I felt I was on entirely familiar ground. It was a subject that had become part of the common mind.

In New Zealand we had our own literary soldier-survivor, the writer, politician and MP John A. Lee, who lost an arm in the war, earned a Distinguished Conduct Medal and recorded his experience in *Citizen into Soldier*. I remember Lee as a political orator; and, after his expulsion from the Labour Party and hence from Parliament, as a striking figure always *marching* to and from the bookshop he kept in Mt Eden, with his hair done 'switchback' style, and the empty sleeve pinned to the shoulder of his jacket.

Ormond Burton wrote an outstanding memoir of his experience of the war, *The Silent Division*; and in an unpublished autobiography claimed that New Zealand became a nation 'somewhere between the landing at Anzac and the end of the Battle of the Somme'.[10] John Mulgan's character Johnson, hero of *Man Alone*, is a 'returned man' from World War I. But probably the single most significant New Zealand literary outcome of that war (leaving aside its powerful effect on Mansfield) is Robin Hyde's faction *Passport to Hell*, which drew directly on the memories of Private J. D. Stark ('Starkie'), survivor of both Gallipoli and the Western Front.[11]

Hyde caught something that seemed characteristically 'Kiwi' in Stark – the quality of the larrikin, the rebel, the 'natural man' who rose in war to become at moments heroic. That was clearly what she felt, and she was able to use his voice and go at times beyond it into an eloquence which was her own. In the Gallipoli section Stark is still the larrikin; but in the battle scenes in France, as real as, and more detailed and terrible than, those in the poems of Wilfred Owen, he becomes the hero:

> The dead in No Man's Land had not even the dignity of death. Their nugget-blacked faces made them look like limp and shattered Christy minstrels. Yet grotesquely he remembered a high room in Gladstone School, and a school-teacher with blue eyes and fluffy hair leaning over a desk repeating poetry.
>
> Baldur the beautiful is dead, is dead.[12]

Throughout the novel Hyde conveys the sense in which what a man such as Stark does, at times violent and extremely anti-social, at others noble and selfless, is always the spontaneous outcome of man-and-circumstance. Carrying a wounded comrade to safety under withering fire, punching an officer in the face, shooting a German prisoner – none of these is a considered action. It is what is required of him being the man he is. It is what he *does* – and so is he. When he finds young Jackie MacKenzie, whom he has been trying to keep safe, shot through the heart, he slings the dead boy over his shoulder and walks seven miles back to Armentières, where he finds an undertaker to provide a coffin, and buries him at night in the local cemetery. In a landscape littered with tens of thousands of shattered and rotting corpses it makes no sense, especially from a man who has just come from killing three Germans with 'a great axe-handle with an iron cog nailed to one end.' But it is what feeling demands of him; and it might have happened in a story by Frank Sargeson.

1   Though he had taken part in the retreat from Antwerp in October 1914.
2   I notice the *TLS* review referred to above says that Ian Beckett 'was one of the first historians to challenge the persistent view in Britain of the First World War as nothing but a charnel house to which the only reaction is pity'.
3   Of the war poets Yeats gave the biggest representation to Robert Nichols, who had been, immediately after the war, considered, with Graves and Sassoon, one of the three really important survivors. Yeats gives him nine poems, but none from his experience of the war. An excellent account of Nichols's brief fame and subsequent eclipse will be found in Harry Ricketts, *Strange Meetings: The Poets of the Great War*, Chatto & Windus, 2010.
4   *The Oxford Book of Modern Verse*, ed. W. B. Yeats, Clarendon, 1936, Introduction, pp. xxxiv–xxxv. Yeats lets Herbert Read's 'End of a War', 'written', he points out, 'long after', represent the subject.
5   *Letters on Poetry from W. B. Yeats to Dorothy Wellesley*, Oxford University Press, 1964, p. 113.
6   *As You Like It*, Act III, Scene iii.
7   Quoted by Elizabeth Cullingford in *Yeats, Ireland and Fascism*, Palgrave Macmillan, 1981, p. 87.
8   The poem he called 'Nineteen Hundred and Nineteen' gave him similar problems. See my 'Yeats the European' in *Yeats the European*, ed. A. Norman Jeffares, Colin Smythe, 1989, pp. 119–30.
9   *Richard Aldington: An Intimate Portrait*, ed. Alistair Kershaw and F.-J. Temple Southern Illinois University Press, 1965, p. 147.
10 Quoted by Keith Sinclair in *A Destiny Apart*, Unwin, 1986, p. 171.
11 Published 1936 and reissued by Auckland University Press in 1986 with introduction and comprehensive notes by D. I. B. Smith. Hyde echoes Brooke's famous sonnet when wounded New Zealand soldiers steal orchids from an English peer's garden: 'There was some corner of his greenhouses that had been for ever England. . . . That corner was now, without prayer or pardon, hopelessly colonialized' (p. 190).
12 *Ibid.*, p. 130.

Hawke's Bay Answers

Q: *Why, as an English literature student, was I of the impression you were the grumpy old man of New Zealand literature?*

C. K. Stead: I'm certainly old now. Was I already old when you were a student? But I imagine you're more interested in 'grumpy'. Over the years I have been involved in some literary and political debates and have argued quite fiercely, and with a clarity that people sometimes find alarming. No masking of the intent or gilding of the lily. But I have wondered occasionally whether this reputation has to do partly with my bony face and the tendency my mouth has to pull down at the corners whenever a camera is pointed at me. I would have to say that anyone who has this impression hasn't looked very closely at my work, or known me personally. The author of *All Visitors Ashore* 'grumpy'???

These were my replies to questions sent by a local Hawke's Bay paper in March 2009, in advance of my appearance at a festival there.

Q: *If there was/is an undeclared war between C. K. Stead and the Kiwi literati, could this explain why you've yet to be crowned New Zealand Poet Laureate?*

CKS: How decisions are made on things like the Poet Laureateship, the PM's Awards, and the Montana Book Awards is as mysterious to me as it is to most people. Often they seem inexplicable. Maybe there is, as you suggest, an 'undeclared war'; but questions of this kind are an invitation to paranoia so I avoid giving them serious thought. On this subject, however, I should mention that an article in a recent *Metro* said that I had not been sufficiently acknowledged by my own city. This is quite wrong. I have received awards and honours from my old school, Mt Albert Grammar, and from my university (Auckland); I was made a Laureate of Waitakere City (on the basis of having a bach at Karekare), and in 2007 given Auckland City's annual Distinguished Citizen award.

Q: *A Victoria University professor once told me he found most contemporary New Zealand poetry overly introspective, 'too much navel gazing going on'. Is this a fair comment on modern New Zealand poetry?*

CKS: It's probably true of most poetry everywhere, always – which is only a way of saying that poetry is extremely difficult to do well, and that using it as a vehicle for therapy or a form of self-medication is just one of many traps everyone who tries to write it has to look out for and guard against.

Q: *Who's your most admired New Zealand woman writer? Why?*

CKS: Living: Charlotte Grimshaw. (Well, she is my daughter. But she also has a huge talent.) Elizabeth Knox – for the quality of the writing rather than for where her imagination takes her. Keri Hulme (when she's doing it). Michele Leggott.

Dead: Katherine Mansfield. She died young, but she not only wrote fiction, sparkling with intelligence and insight, which took the art of the short story in English forward to a new level; she also left such a treasure trove of letters and journals – a wonderful record of the writer at work. Sylvia Ashton-Warner, Robin Hyde, Janet Frame . . . Really it makes more sense to ask about admired books than admired writers, because they're all so uneven (as writers always and everywhere are) and have highs and lows.

Q: *Were you ever one of the famous literary drinkers?*

CKS: No, but I've known some of them.

Q: *In your book* The Writer at Work, *you wrote that your sense of what is local in writing is something always fitted into a larger picture. What do you mean by this?*

CKS: The local is very important, especially in poetry. But I think there should be consciousness, somewhere implicit in the work, of a larger world – of history, of literature at large, of politics – otherwise the work is provincial.

Q: *An ex-editor once told me the idea of writing schools is absurd, i.e., that you can't teach someone to write creatively. Thoughts?*

CKS: I agree on the whole, though I did run a Creative Writing course at the University of Auckland in my last three years there – 1984–86. But I think there is much more for a writer to learn about writing by studying great literature than by attending writing classes.

Q: *You once agreed that all art aspires to the condition of music.
It struck me as a brave stance by a staunch man of letters . . .*

CKS: I think this is a way of saying that literature doesn't succeed
or fail by what it means, but by being a work of art. It has meaning
of course. But what makes it a poem or a story or a novel is the art
of poetry or of fiction, which depends as much on shape, structure,
sound, mellifluousness, tone, grace – and so on. In other words it is
like music: this is more a metaphor than a statement of literal truth.

Q: *During his visit last year, Irish poet Paul Muldoon said 'poets dis-
improve as they get older'. Do you know what he's saying / is this the
same for C. K. Stead?*

CKS: There is a freshness and vividness of feeling that is lost,
I suppose. But I feel more that there's a loss of self-consciousness,
and consequently a freeing up, a greater ease. I find as I get older
that poetry comes more readily, not less. But I do admire Muldoon,
and respect anything he has to say on the subject.

At the Molino a Sesta, Gaiole, in Chianti

The house is ancient (I think Michael [Seresin]) said the oldest part dates from the eleventh century), spacious and beautiful, and has been lovingly tended over recent decades. In the usual, largely pointless way in which one tries to hang on to the moment, I find myself photographing its spaces and accidents of light and shadow. We eat out on a terrace overlooking the lower garden and a clear stream with many fish. When I go down there the fish panic and race away in all directions, like a schoolyard clearing at the sound of a bell. In a moment there is not a fish in sight. Maybe they think I am the elegant heron I saw this morning roosting in the trees over the stream. Later, when I throw bread into the stream from the balcony, there is the reverse, lolly-scramble effect – fish racing in from all directions, fighting for scraps. Beyond the garden are deep

---

I was awarded the Landfall-Seresin Residency in Gaiole in Chianti in 2009, and one condition or understanding of acceptance was that I would keep a record of my stay there which would be offered for publication in *Landfall*. This appeared in *Landfall* 219, May 2010.

woods, and beyond again the lights of some kind of house or chateau shine down through the trees at night.

The stream has been dammed to create a millpond which must once have fed out in the lower part of the house to drive the millwheel. No sign of that exit now, and the pond, though still a millpond full of fish and frogs, is used as a swimming pool, with even a tall fountain shooting up 15 or 20 feet from its centre. Kay and I were slightly reluctant at first; but, keen swimmers, and having been assured by Michael that his whole family swim there, we tried it, and enjoyed it. As long as the weather continues as now (very warm) so will the swimming. The fish there are smaller than the ones in the stream and rather beautiful, green grey on top and silver beneath; but I'm told there is also a giant carp there. We have yet to see him. I have said there will be a prize for the first to catch sight of him: the Molino Medal for Carp Sighting.

When, looking down from the terrace, I first saw the fish I felt at once what I would have felt as a child – a hunter's excitement and the wish to catch some. Whether for eating or just for sport would have made no difference. That feeling was once so strong I'm sure it's atavistic, the genetic inheritance of the hunter-warrior male. Now the idea of catching them seems wanton; I wouldn't do it – though I do eat fish caught 'professionally' by other people. That second impulse – the protective one, a sort of altruism – is also part of the genetic inheritance. It's there to protect, in the first instance, the family, then the tribe; but intellect extends its application outward, riding over boundaries of tribe, nation and race, and in the end even over species, becoming a desire to see not only the race survive, but the planet and everything that lives on it. This is the basis of Green politics, sound, though incapable ever of perfect reconciliation with the fact that in 'the state of Nature' the species (including the human) are constantly eating one another.

I look at the massive stone structure and enormous horizontal beams, built before the Maori came to Aotearoa/New Zealand, and find myself wrestling with ideas of time and human history – as I did earlier in the year when I became obsessed (not for the first time) with the Pont du Gard near Uzès, built a thousand years before this mill. It's not just the giant scale of that famous triple aqueduct that captures imagination, but the ingenuity that found a way to bring water from a spring at Uzès, *across* – i.e. over the top of – a valley (itself containing a river) and down to the Roman camp at Nîmes, a distance of 50 kilometres and a fall in height above sea-level of only about 11 metres. Of course the water from the river would have been more abundant and convenient; but there was no way of pumping it out of the valley; so water from a spring up and beyond was given a path along appropriate contours and then, so to speak, airlifted on that immense stone structure (a second bridge erected on top of the first, and a third on top of the second) across the intervening river valley. In 1972, when we were first in that region, it was not the tourist attraction it is now, and one could walk over the top layer from one side of the valley to the other.

In terms of human history the Maori are very recent arrivals; yet they reached our shores without a written script or numbers, without the wheel, without the ability to cast in metals or even to make earthen pots; and if they had ever had the ability to record a sea-route and navigate *back* to a point of departure, they had lost it. But those skills were long-possessed by Asian cultures whence they appear to have come. Does human history, then, involve instances of recession – loss – as well as gain? If yes, what are the implications for our future? And setting that question aside, there is the thought, inevitable here where sheer *ancientness* presses upon one's consciousness, that the claim to special status as 'indigenous' doesn't mean much more than 'we got here a bit before you'. Pakeha roots may be shallow; but Maori roots are hardly deep. In New Zealand we are all, Maori and Pakeha, inheritors of the gains and losses of dislocation.

Yesterday we went to the village of Radda for supplies from a little *alimentari* which we were later told was the Fortnum and Mason's of the area. Just as well it was, and that we were buying a lot, because I dropped a cloth bag containing a bottle of olive oil which broke and spread over the floor. I was full of *Scusi*s and *Mi dispiaci*s to which the response was an unfailing and clearly genuine *Nienti*. (If this account gives the impression I am even slightly competent in Italian, it is misleading. I'm not.)

30.8.09: Margaret, Guy and the children are here, staying a few days on their way back from Cantona to London. I have awarded myself the Molino Medal for Carp Spotting. It's a large fish indeed (there are photos of it held by Ivo the gardener when they last drained the pond to clean out silt). In the water it looked yellow. I went back later to get a photograph, but it sank away into the depths, camera shy. We climbed through the vineyards to the castle this morning, and later drove no great distance to a modest restaurant for what turned out to be Sunday lunch with the locals. The grapes are a few weeks short of the *vendange* (what do they call it here?), small black sweet and edible – real grapes, with pips, as distinct from those artificial 'eating' grapes sold in shops. There are low electric fences around the vineyards to keep out the wild boar, but the wild visitor I'm afraid just steps over. The hillsides hereabouts are beautifully ordered, vines laid out in straight rows, trees likewise, and garden plots. I am swimming every day, doing 'lengths' – from the house to a far tree, five double lengths this morning and yesterday, which would be 100 metres, or at least 100 yards, per double length. I am still swimming mostly backstroke and occasionally breaststroke, reluctant to take into nose and mouth the amount of water I do when it's the crawl. There's something terribly satisfying about swimming on one's back and seeing the trees passing by overhead against the sky.

31.8.09: I keep up each day my work at *South-West of Eden*, as it is now called – one final run-through from start to finish, adding and subtracting and polishing in preparation for the press. The contract was signed before I left Auckland, and the plan is to launch it next May at the Auckland Festival. I've had word that I'm to receive the PM's Award for Fiction in October and a date has been fixed, 28th, before which it's not to be mentioned. Today after my morning's work we drove to the Museo Civico in Siena especially to look at one work there that Margaret wanted to see – a medieval mural representing good and bad government, remarkable in quality and in the fact that it is entirely secular. We had lunch there, mine a pasta with spinach, unusual in that it was flavoured with peanut and fennel. This evening Kay and Margaret combined to do an Italian meal which we finished with Siena cake (heavy, sweet, almost like toffee, and full of nuts) with a dessert wine and macchiato coffee. There is some confusion about whether I have in fact won the Molino Carp Spotting Medal. I have now located a very large pale fish with a bright orange splash, and a large silver-grey mottled fish, neither of which looks quite like that very dark fish Ivo the gardener is cradling in his arms in a photograph of the pool-cleaning. Seven double lengths in the millpond this evening.

5.9.09: Guy went back to London on Tuesday and Margaret and the kids yesterday. We got up very early and drove them to the airport at Pisa. I have today given up the ban on the crawl-swim (freestyle) and now alternate it with backstroke and breaststroke. And we have identified four large fish – the three described above, and the biggest, the one in the photograph, large and dark brown, almost black. The three seem to hang out more or less together along the race some way from the mill. The big one is seen, solo, at evening from the upstairs windows, cruising around the base of the fountain. My work on *South-West of Eden* continues daily. I have included a new piece, quoting Conrad's *Lord Jim* about the search for guano (used for phosphate fertiliser), and the dangers of extracting it from islands with no moorings. This gives a fuller context for the work my grandfather and namesake, Christian Karlson, did in the islands, and which in the end cost him his life. The last night Margaret and the kids were here we ate at Radda, and the bigs had wild boar stew with white beans – delicious! Last night there was a full moon, a clear sky, and just one huge star (planet), which has been visible in varying positions for the past week or so. I know that we see more stars in the southern hemisphere – something to do with our position in relation to the Milky Way – but an apparently clear sky with only a single planet visible is a puzzle. I suppose the brightness of the moon must wipe the others out, as if in daylight. The terrace, garden beyond, the stream, and beyond again the woods – it all looked wonderful; and a single owl took off from the woods on one side and did a swoop-glide right across to the other, catching the light as it went. I thought earlier I had heard foxes barking, but, uncertain of the sound, couldn't be sure. The people in the village continue to be very friendly and welcoming. I'm ashamed of my almost total lack of Italian. Constantly in France one feels frustrated and incompetent; but I have to come here to discover what a difference there is between having a working knowledge of a language and having none at all.

6.9.09: Progress continues with *South-West of Eden*. I will probably send off the first batch of revisions in a day or so, and at this rate will be finished my final run through before we leave here for the Mansfield-fest in Menton. Most days we get up quite early, have breakfast on the terrace, and I go to work for a couple of hours. Then into the village for the day's shopping and coffee in the square. Then a swim in the millpond, lunch, a siesta and reading the English (*Guardian* mostly) newspaper; after which I go back to work. Then an evening walk, up around the castle and through the vineyards, and a meal, followed by serious reading and music – though last evening it was a DVD, *The Bourne Supremacy*. I've just climbed to the single bedroom above the floor with the main bedrooms and bathrooms. I keep being struck by how personal, particular, everything in the Molino is, how it's full of the fingerprints of one family, people of individual, and good, taste. Just inside the door there is a sort of vestibule with many straw hats in many styles around the walls. Someone must have had a taste for *putti* – sort of cupid-angels beloved of (eighteenth-century?) Italy – and has found examples which surprise one from walls and shelves, and from behind little open cupboard-like doors in the walls [see 14.9.09 below for more on this]. Someone had a taste for floral paintings, and there are many – possibly thirty – in the kitchen. One alone might pass unnoticed, or signify a rather conventional taste – but so many, and all originals, make you look and discover when they were done and by whom, and consider the styles. There is a fine collection of jugs, bowls and vases along the sill under the curved windows of an extension to the main sitting room, that part furnished in cane with pale green cushions, while the main area around the enormous fireplace has two couches, both capacious and soft. The taste in books is again slightly unusual, not, anyway, simply conventional, but there's absolutely no crap. The same with music. All of this makes the opportunity to live here for a time seem generous, a special favour, even almost as if one is intruding on a space that should be private.

I feel I've established beyond doubt that the fish in the lower stream are used to being fed. When you look down from the terrace they are cruising, drifting, as if sun-bathing. But if you say one word that's audible down there, or wave an arm, they rush about hunting for the scraps they clearly expect to come raining down from above. I now feed them bread twice a day.

9.9.09: All the nines. Yesterday I sent a large batch of *South-West of Eden* to the publisher (AUPress) and we went to Firenze (i.e. Florence) for the day – drove to Montevarchi and took the train. I realise that I will be pleased to be done with the memoir, but sorry not to have it to play with any longer. We lunched at a place called Gozzi Sergio's recommended by Margaret, close to San Lorenzo, one of those authentic family businesses with marble-topped tables, no fuss, and good cooking. I had *trippo* with a delicious sauce of tomato and basil and some other mysterious ingredient. We had not been in Firenze since 1972, when we drove there from Menton with the children aged two, five and eight, with a pushchair on the roof-rack and camping gear in the boot, and managed to find the Uffizi Gallery and see the Botticellis which had been the object of the exercise. Once the pushchair flew off on to the autostrada, and I managed to park on the shoulder and walk back for it where I found it guarded by a police car and two cops who admonished me but allowed me to reclaim it. In Pisa, while Oliver, Charlotte and I climbed the leaning tower (you could do that then) and Kay entertained Margaret on the greensward below, a gypsy woman stole the pushchair, but Kay managed to reclaim it and wrestle it away from her. From there we drove on to Firenze (must have found a camping ground), and then to Venice, where we camped on the Lido and were in St Mark's Square for May Day. Now you have to buy tickets for the Uffizi and then, later, join a long queue at a designated time. And you pay to go into the churches. But the city is no less remarkable and if tourism, and tourist money, is preserving and even restoring it, then one has to be pleased. But pleased to have seen it when everything was simpler and more accessible, and when the Arno appeared to be yellow. Yesterday it was green. Since coming here I have read James McNeish's biography of Paddy Costello, which doesn't entirely escape his old journalistic habit of gilding the lily, but is very well told and essentially convincing about the man himself and the wrongful accusations of 'spying' made against him. Now I'm reading one of Michael's books, Ingmar Bergman's autobiography, a narrative of extraordinary immediacy and painful frankness.

10.9.09: An owl in the woods last night; and, earlier, a very large hare among the castle's grape vines – had probably got under the electrified wire where the land has fallen away on a steep slope leaving a gap. We are working our way through Beethoven's late quartets – four CDs bought in London – on Michael's wonderful new-looking machine. Thinking again of 1972: I have in front of me a little booklet of my poem done for the Mansfield conference last year, which has Marti Friedlander's photograph of me standing at the door of the Isola Bella room in Menton where the Mansfield fellow works – paisley-pattern shirt, trousers tight but flared, sandals and copious beard: such an image of the time. Auden says somewhere 'We are lived by history'!

11.9.09: (Nine eleven!) Last evening there were swallows in the open space over the stream between the house and the woods – the first time I've seen them here. Could they be en route somewhere, heading south for winter? Not quite the same species as we see in Uzès – paler on the underside – but with the unmistakable forked tail and sharp wings, and the evening aerobatics, swooping and diving and stalling like Spitfires and Messerschmitts in WWII dogfights. I don't know how to distinguish the types – swallows, house-martins, swifts – not having grown up with them (though there are often some up the road near the top of Tohunga Crescent). I am still swimming – five double lengths, the last over-arm – but the water is distinctly colder than when we were first here.

12.9.09: Charlotte will at this moment be in the air somewhere between Auckland and Singapore, heading for Cork where she's once again short-listed for the Frank O'Connor Prize for short stories. Winner gets 35,000 euros. Last evening I got quite close to the big carp, which Michael tells me is at least forty years old – got a shot with the flash, which may come out. Then while we were eating quite late on the terrace we heard something in the undergrowth down below, and in the stream. It was quite a large deer – saw me in the half-light and took off into the woods. We are going in to Firenze today and will 'do' the Uffizi if all goes well. Last night's movie was *Burned by the Sun*, a recently made Russian story of the terrible times under Stalin – an atmosphere of Chekhovian summer idyll with the blow waiting to fall, and falling horribly and tragically at the end.

14.9.09: To continue with the nature observations – the swallows were there that one night only so they must be in transit south. One swallow doesn't make a summer but many departing make an autumn, and I feel it in the millpond which is beginning to be cluttered with fallen leaves, and small gaps are appearing in the trees that previously shielded the nearest hill-slope. (Eliot: 'The river's tent is broken: the last fingers of leaf / Clutch and sink into the wet bank.') One other observation: a bushy dark red tail, seen from the terrace. It seemed too big for a squirrel, too low to the ground for a fox, but must have been one or the other, and it was gone in an instant. The red squirrels have been mostly driven out of England by the American grey, but I've seen them in France occasionally, so why not here? But I like to think it was a fox, and only appeared low to the ground because the grass is long. On our second Firenzi expedition we drove again to Montevarchi, missed the train by three minutes and had to spend an hour and a half there. Couldn't help comparing it with Radda, which is spruce and perfect and full of tourists ambling about 'looking lost and lame' like the dog in Curnow's poem. At Montevarchi, which is ordinary-to-dingy, with some faint signs of recent affluence, there are only Italians looking as if they have reasons for being there and something to do. At Firenze we bought our ticket to the Uffizi for 3 p.m., had lunch at a trattoria in an alley just off the Piazza della Signoria, the square with all the extraordinary giant statues, including Michelangelo's *David* (with the big left hand – it must have been the one that threw the deadly stone). David is now the giant, which doesn't seem quite right. Then the Uffizi and a slow cruise down the Primo Corridoio, slowly in and out of the rooms, lingering longest (as we did all those years ago) with the Botticellis, as waves of Japanese, Germans, even Italians, arrived in groups, hovered, ear-plugged to their talking guide, and passed on. I have finished Bergman's autobiography, *The Magic Lantern*, a vivid, brilliant book by a man who, by his own account, appears half mad and all genius. I have learned from a book on Michael's shelves that in this small area, Gaiole, Radda and Castellina, known as Chianti *storico* [historic], the symbol for its Chianti Classico wine since 1924 has been the black cock on a gold background; and for the nearby region of Rufina, Montalbano and the hills north of Florence, the symbol is a pink angel on a light blue background – those wines referred to as Chianti 'Putto'. Also that their word for the grape harvest is *vendemmia* (French *vendange*), and that since the Middle Ages the rule has been that it must not take place before 29 September. One seldom sees a bottle of Chianti with the traditional raffia surround any more. When I was young there was a fashion for decorating interiors with them; and the people who did that often liked also to pin travel posters to their bedroom walls, not horizontally and vertically but at odd angles, as Maurice Shadbolt, when young, did with the jackets of his novels.

15.9.09: Eldest grandchild Isaac's 21st birthday. I was almost on my way to the airport for an overseas flight when Virginia rang from National Women's to say he had been born. There was just time for a quick visit. Oliver was there, and newborn Isaac Stead, all three looking in very good health and good spirits. I have just read the following opening sentence in a book (another from Michael's shelves) by Arthur Koestler: 'A writer aged seventy-six has only two prospects before him: to be forgotten before he dies, or to die before he is forgotten.' It's a striking statement, especially since he committed suicide a year later, and even more so for me in that I'm seventy-six, seventy-seven next month; but I don't really believe wanting to go or to stay will have anything at all to do with being remembered or forgotten as a writer. I said to my GP recently, 'The

time must come when one has to think about finding the door.'
She said, 'I suppose so, but it must be the right door.' A discreet and
intelligent young woman!

16.9.09: Rain. It's been coming and going in light showers for the past
few days but now it's here and feels rather familiar and comfortable.
It will be 'good for the garden' and swell the grapes. The stream is
up, and cloudy. The occasional gardener, Ivo, has stopped by to
check on the footbridge over it which I noticed is chained to a tree –
must sweep away in flood time. The work on *South-West of Eden* is
finished at last (and alas?) and I must now get on with preparing
something for my 'plenary' presentation at the Mansfield-Menton
Fellowship forty-year celebrations at the end of the month. I should
stop agreeing to do these things because I don't have much that's
new to say about her. I'm going to focus on her presence in my fiction
and occasionally in poems – that at least is 'different'. But I hope
there's a chance to mention Sheilah Winn, who largely financed the
first Menton fellowships, and especially Celia and Cecil Manson,
those grand old Mansfield enthusiasts who first floated the idea.
Without those three it would never have happened, and they are
seldom acknowledged.

17.9.09: The rain turned into a mighty electric storm which put out
the power at the Molino. We had our friends Roger and Joselyn
Morton visiting – they are New Zealanders, theatre people, now
living in France, and were in the area to visit a cousin. The rain was
huge, the stream turned briefly into a brown torrent, the lightning
and thunder cracked almost simultaneously overhead, the phone
gave a dying peep, the power went off with a sharp crack and the
fountain died away. Roger and I, after some hunting, found the fuse
box and the way to restore the power. Today the sky is watery, but
there's some sunshine. The stream is up and brown, but no longer
racing. The fish are no longer visible. Are they swept away – like

humans in a hurricane? Probably not, but they must have had to work hard to stay in one place. The inhabitants of the millpond and millrace of course are unaffected. I swam yesterday before the storm but will miss today because we are going to Siena.

18.9.09: Yesterday at Siena. This time we went into the *duomo* and spent an hour taking in the astonishing detail and the scale, marvelling at the thought of so many talented craftsmen working at once, and of the massive scaffolding that must have been needed to do the extraordinary decorative work on the inside of the dome. Also puzzling at why Christianity has persisted as a faith when its whole cosmology represented in the paintings – earth at the centre, heaven up above (saints are always pointing there, and one, S. Giuseppe da Copertino, even taking off bodily) and hell below, and the sun circling a stationary earth – has been shot down over the centuries. Belief is so often more compelling than the evidence, and details which once seemed crucial, and even worth killing or dying for, can be shrugged off as insignificant compared to the central Truth which becomes even more numinous as reality forces it to become more diaphanous, un-pin-down-able. Such structures built on ancient and now discredited tenets are anthropologically interesting and often artistically wonderful in their consequences; but to see people fervently crossing themselves and putting themselves on the rack of prayer is, I think, to a clear mind, sad and even deplorable – like a bad habit, sucking the thumb. There was one chapel that appeared to be given over to mementos of dead children – many crash helmets, a bridle, a picture of a motorbike, baby photos, bibs, booties, rattles. Today the stream is very brown, though now moving quite slowly. But when I threw bread down where all those fish had been, none came – not one. I can't believe they don't survive a storm like that, but they must have other less turbulent places to go, quiet chapels for deep prayer and meditation. I saw one red squirrel this morning, and then, an hour or so later, a second, smaller, and I now think the tail I saw a few days ago was also a squirrel, not a fox. The usual swim today, was bracing but very good for the spirits.

19.9.09: Last day at the Molino. We will be away first thing in the morning tomorrow, drive to Pisa and return hire-car, train first to Genoa, then on to Menton. Today the sun is shining, the stream still slightly murky but the fish are back from their retreat – back and feeding. The village is full of police cars and motorcycles, cops in jackboots, a television team, an enormous balloon advertising HSBC, the sponsoring bank, and the word ARRIVISTA on an inflated yellow arch over the main street – and many cyclists, multi-coloured, readying themselves, the occasion a race between here and Siena. This evening a last glimpse of the big brown carp, an elderly creature of habit never seen at any other hour of the day. So the month has passed and the main purpose, final work on *South-West of Eden* has been done – in such a congenial setting. *Arrivederci, Molino a Sesta!* And thank you Michael Seresin.

'Yes T.S.'

'Yes T.S.' was one of several poems I wrote in the 1970s and 1980s which were attempts to enlarge the frame of poetry beyond the tight well-made poem, often with traditional forms and rhyme schemes, which had dominated British and New Zealand poetry in the mid-century. Various names were given to poems which experimented in this way – 'open form' was one, 'the process poem' another. There was a feeling that the 'long poem', which had been declared a contradiction in terms in the early years of the century (because *real* poetry was by its nature lyrical and therefore brief), could be brought back, not as a vehicle for conventional narrative or the exposition of ideas, but as it had been in some of the best work of T. S. Eliot, Ezra Pound, and William Carlos Williams – as an aggregation of moments of sufficient intensity to create a force field binding disparate elements into a single work of art. This was something in the air of the time, not radically

Written for *99 Ways into New Zealand Poetry* by Paula Green
and Harry Ricketts (Random House, 2010).

new by the time I was doing it, but nonetheless demanding – difficult to do well.

'Yes T.S.' kept me company on a literary/academic tour which took me around the world. It kept me occupied, focused on myself in interaction with changing scenes and circumstances. Though I had various purposes for this travel, places to visit, people to see, lectures and readings to give, the poem became the real, the secret, purpose. Often I was reacting to being unfamiliarly alone in foreign places, but the reaction had to have a justification beyond any interest in myself, or in the poem as 'confession': it had to have verbal life, wit, some special interest, some kind of originality as *poetry*. There could be rhymes if that seemed to be what the moment required; there could be quotation, reportage, jokes, anecdotes, juxtapositions, puns – anything which contributed to the life on the page and was consistent with what preceded and followed. Whatever the changes of mood, place and circumstance, there had to be a continuous thread, a stylistic unity. Here style and personality are almost interchangeable: *le style, c'est l'homme.*

So, for example . . . the lonely poet buys himself a kettle which dances and sings on the hot plate and becomes his friend, his travelling companion. He sends a sad message home, and in doing so, catches the passage of time in shifting moon-shots. A conservative poetry editor talks about 'the return to form', while the poem, recording him, gently mocks. A quotation from the poet's reading of Van Gogh's letters seems to catch a parallel between the life of poetry and the life of painting. The poet crosses the Channel on his 48th birthday and hears his age in the repeated sound of the wheels' clatter.

The sample offered [i.e. in the Green and Ricketts book] is a small one from a work that runs on over 32 pages – my longest single poem – and really to 'get' the full sense of how it works one needs to see it all, in all its variety. Everything is 'taken from life', 'caught on the wing', and the skill the poet requires of himself is partly opportunistic – to have eyes open, to be looking out much more than in (a very male mode of consciousness), and to see and grasp the chances while they are there. Opportunistic, but also stylistic – to know how to make verbal use of what is seen, heard, overheard, to make words of it, and good words.

What's Going On Here?

Matthew Harris: *Firstly, do you see your novels (such as* The Death of the Body) *as fitting into the mode broadly described as 'meta-fictional' or 'self-reflexive'?*

C. K. Stead: In widely varying degrees, though this is not something that has greatly concerned me or been a motivating element.

MH: *If so, how would you distinguish your use of the metafictional mode from 'realist' modes so often discussed as the staple of the literary tradition in New Zealand?*

CKS: I think my notion of realism may be peculiar to myself. I think of myself as a realist in fiction, and don't see that as being at odds with metafiction. When I began writing I had in mind something I thought of as 'conventional fiction' (characterised by

---

These were answers to questions put to me in December 2008 by a PhD candidate, Matthew Harris, working at Massey University under the supervision of Dr Jack Ross on the subject of modern fiction techniques used by New Zealand writers.

the work of my contemporary Maurice Shadbolt) which I wanted to avoid. I thought of it as a mode one could easily slide in to – a kind of cruise mode written by, and for, habitual readers of the same conventional stuff. A self-consciousness about the process was necessary to avoid this. I used to worry a lot about 'provenance' – what was the (fictional) source of the 'knowledge' the story contained, whose was the 'voice', etc – and I paid a lot of attention to the work of Alberto Moravia. Some of the outcomes (mine, that is) are, I suppose, though without the support of any specific theory, correctly described as 'metafiction'. To consider this development in my case you would have to look at my short stories as well as the novels. They were very important work-outs. Also if you look at what I write about Maurice Duggan you will see (slightly concealed but clear enough to the careful reader) that I am impatient with a lot of his later work, but see 'Along Rideout Road that Summer' and 'Riley's Handbook' as his late breakouts from conventional fiction – by far his best work – after which he fell back into the old habit.

One other point: people like Lawrence Jones tend to conflate a writer like Sargeson with one like Shadbolt under the heading 'realism' – whereas to me they were quite distinct. Shadbolt was the writer of conventional middle-class marketable fiction; Sargeson was the self-conscious literary artist.

MH: *Yes, your story 'A Quality of Life' seems a precursor in some ways to* The Secret History of Modernism, *housed as it is in the backyard studio?*

CKS: And isn't there a similar crux about a pregnancy (to the wrong person)? 'A Quality of Life' was close to autobiography. But 'concealed' (not very well) by the mechanics of Nova and the grandfather famous-author narrator, written when I was much younger than the narrator and relatively unknown.

MH: *You have spoken of discarding realism to get closer to reality. Is there any specific way you envisaged your metafictional works as developing realism, as opposed to discarding it altogether?*

CKS: When I've said this I suppose I've meant discarding realism as a set of literary conventions that tend to become more literary the more they imitate themselves and what has gone before. To get a sense of the 'real' one must shake off the merely conventional. This is the Wordsworth principle. He wanted to be rid of 'the family language of poets'. I wanted to be rid of 'the family language of novelists' – or rather, I didn't want to fall into writing it myself.

MH: *In that context, Wordsworth gave an example or two of stylistic conventions that he thought were trite, such as 'personifications of abstract ideas'. Can you pinpoint any popular fictional devices you've felt the need to do away with?*

CKS: Well, do you know the often-referred to 'Pass me the butter' chapter of *All Visitors Ashore?* – chapter five. The way all that is spelled out makes the point very clearly.

MH: *On the topic of breaking with conventional 'realism', it could be said that your novels illustrate how unrealistic it is to exclude the authorial presence from the story. Do you feel that including a writerly presence in the diegesis [meaning, I think, the events of the story – CKS] can sometimes create a greater impression of reality?*

CKS: It's something I suppose I fall in to easily because of the kind of person I am, and that helps to make it sound 'natural', authentic.

MH: *Writers such as Lawrence Jones and Michael Morrissey have claimed that postmodern fiction here is (or was in the 1980s), to use Morrissey's words, something of a 'neglected phenomenon', and*

that its neglect is due to the dominance of the realist tradition here.
Do you agree?

CKS: I'm not much interested in the kind of literary schools
paranoia (Loney is an example in poetry) that argues it is the 'fast
track', or the 'front of the wave', and only ignored because it is *avant
garde* – meaning that in time everyone else will catch up. But in
fiction there is always the commercial imperative. Unconventional
or innovative things sometimes get overlooked because they are
not saleable, or because publishers fear they won't be – and this
becomes more acute in a society the size of ours, where the market
is small and consequently the minority market is unsustainable.

MH: *Your metafictions, particularly* The Death of the Body *and* The
Secret History of Modernism, *might be seen as bringing to life the
so-called 'dead' author, particularly in the way they foreground the
authorial process (for example, when Winter describes his narrative
habits as resembling Matrioshka dolls, and when the narrator of* The
Death of the Body *discusses the difficulties of narrative's linearity).
Do you see them in this way? As re-assertions of authorship?*

CKS: I take it your question means something about literary theory
and 'the death of the author'. If so, I suppose a correct answer
would be that I don't find it uncongenial or 'wrong' to see those
fictional personae of mine in that way. But I didn't write those
novels with that in mind. Literary theory would not have been even
remotely in my thoughts in embarking on those novels, though a
reader might see theoretical implications in what I found myself
doing. From the inside it felt more like proceeding guided by
instinct, or stylistic intuition.

MH: *I raise that possibility because you seem to have been as under-
whelmed with twentieth-century French/American critical theory as*

you were with certain strands of feminist thought that accompanied it. Your take on the extremist feminism of the 1970s and 1980s is pretty apparent in The Death of the Body, *so I wonder if, with hindsight, you see in your 'metafictional' novels an implicit response to some of the theory you encountered around the time?*

CKS: I can only repeat what I said above: I don't mind if they're seen in that way, but I don't think that's how they came into being. The representation of militant campus feminism in *The Death of the Body* is more just a realistic representation of how it was.

MH: *How useful was the metafictional mode in helping to revitalise your writing practice, especially following what you described, in your recent address at Auckland, as a severe bout of writer's block?*

CKS: Well if I used the metafictional mode at that point, and I suppose I did, then it was very useful. But I didn't think, 'I know – I'll use the metafictional mode!' That kind of thinking would not have helped at all. I don't think about these things in abstract, except perhaps in looking back afterwards and recognising how what I've done might be described. I doubt that any fiction writer does. The problems present themselves in practical terms.

MH: *You commented recently that you wanted, especially in your early work, to make 'the voice which gave the story its authority a part of the fiction' – a statement I assume is tied in with what you've just said about 'provenance'. Why is/was this such a point of interest?*

CKS: I was fascinated early on by the fiction of Alberto Moravia which is almost all (with only one or two exceptions) in the first person. I think in his essays, which I read with admiration some long time ago, he proposes this problem of provenance: in a world where there can be no 'eye of God' narration (because there is no God) it was a matter of primary importance. That was how I felt in writing fiction. Who knows these (fictional) 'facts'? What is the authority for them? Moravia confirmed that anxiety and seemed to give it intellectual respectability.

Even in a novel like *Sister Hollywood*, which is much less radical – less clearly 'metafictional' than *The Death of the Body*, or *The End of the Century at the End of the World* (an interesting case which we haven't mentioned) – there is still a character, Bill Harper, who is the source of the story's 'knowledge'.

MH: *I guess 'provenance' is important to your critical work as well? There seems to be a link between the way you've handled writing fiction and writing criticism: in both cases you've often been careful to place yourself (or a fictional version of CKS) in context, in relation to the text. Is this a matter of transparency in both cases?*

CKS: I hadn't thought of connecting them but I think the answer has to be yes.

MH: *In* The Secret History of Modernism, *your narrator raises some interesting questions on the relationship between fiction and autobiography. 'Did changing people's names make autobiography into fiction? Did real names [. . .] make autobiography any less fictional?' (pp. 212–13). I wonder if you have any further thoughts on those questions?*

CKS: The idea is there, clearly implied in the question. Stories are stories and create their own reality – and we need stories for our sanity, create them and live by them constantly. It's true, as everyone knows, that for fiction and autobiography very different rules apply. But they are nearer to one another than we usually acknowledge. There's a sense in which both have to be 'constructed'.

MH: *Your fiction could be seen to have contributed to the growth of an 'internationalist' perspective in New Zealand writing. Do you see it in this way?*

CKS: Again, not as an intention – but if as an effect, then I'm pleased.

MH: *Internationally-oriented or not, your narrator in* The Secret History of Modernism *acknowledges the importance of New Zealand to his writing, saying that his perspective has been 'determined by what was for me home base, Auckland' and that it is as if his 'feet were planted somewhere on the Tamaki-Makau-Rau, "the Place of a Thousand Lovers" . . .' (pp. 47–49). How autobiographical are these passages?*

CKS: I think that's pretty much CKS speaking – for that moment. He might contradict himself the next, of course. Personality (and therefore thoughts/ideas) are never entirely stable. But there's a perhaps relevant comment by Hilda Tapler in *The End of the Century at the End of the World* when she's asked why a novel of hers which is not set in NZ and has no NZ characters is a NZ book and she says 'Because I'm a NZer and I wrote it.'

Twelve Questions

C. K. (Karl) Stead, ONZ, has been called New Zealand's greatest living writer – and also our most controversial. His new book of poetry, **The Yellow Buoy,** *was launched last night.*

1. Is poetry the most satisfying of your writerly arts?
Yes, it's what makes the greatest demands, gives the greatest feeling of satisfaction when it goes well, and disappointment, or emptiness, when you have periods of drought.

2. Is its small audience a source of frustration?
Not at all. Either Keats or Milton said he wanted 'fit audience, though few'. And the other (whichever it was) said he wanted to leave 'great verse unto a little clan'. And Auden said 'our [i.e. poets'] readers may be few, but at least they can rune'. I write for real *readers*, not for 'everyone'. I don't think I'm in the least snobbish about this, but I'm a realist, and an élitist.

Published in the *New Zealand Herald*, 21 February 2013.

3. As a young man you were a protégé of Frank Sargeson: which young writers would you consider protégés of yours?

Well, Greg O'Brien, Andrew Johnston, Chris Price and Tim Wilson – three successful poets and a fiction writer now – were in the Creative Writing class I ran in my last three years at Auckland University, so I suppose there's a sense in which I could claim them. But would they want that? Only they could say.

4. You joined the Labour Party aged seven – what's your view on its current state of health?

I was (and am) a great admirer of Helen Clark and still support the Labour Party, and I'm generally 'left-liberal', further left of the party on many issues, wishing it was more radical, less cautious, less pragmatic, though I know politics is the art of the possible. The Greens have lost most of their earlier dope-smoking dottiness and now often appear as another party of smart ideas and sound policy, so I think a Labour–Green coalition would be good for us. I find it really dumb that a population which didn't want public assets sold elected a government committed to selling them.

5. It seems a while since your last literary feud. Are you going soft in your old age?

Oh there's a wee scrap in the new book if anyone is keen to hunt for such things.

6. Did you ever reconcile with Keri Hulme?

Did she reconcile with me? I never had any grudge against Keri. I said *The Bone People* was a work of genius but I found the nature of her focus on violence against the child troubling; and I also questioned (unforgivably, it seemed) whether having only one of eight great-grandparents a Maori was enough for her to qualify for a prize that was for writing by Maori. It's a long time ago, and one has learned to accept the conventional wisdom that this was a question

I should not have asked – though it must have lurked, unspoken, in many minds. The real question about Keri is when will she stop murmuring imprecations online and produce another novel?

7. What compelled you recently to speak out about Justice Binnie's review of the David Bain case?
It seemed to me such an injustice was being done to the father, Robin, who was being used as a posthumous lever to get the son off the hook.

8. Is there a novel in that ongoing drama?
Certainly, but I won't be the person to write it.

9. What's the most surprising thing about being eighty?
Being eighty is the surprise – the fact of having survived so long.

10. What's your favourite low-brow pursuit?
Is swimming low-brow? I'm addicted to that. And to movies – not just art-house stuff (including French and Italian), which I love, but thrillers, especially if they can be done without an interminable and unbelievable car chase.

11. What, in your opinion, is the most over-rated aspect of modern life?
Modern life at its worst is four people, two couples, around a table having coffee (with a glass of water of course), each of them reading text messages on a cellphone, and occasionally looking up to tell the others what he/she is finding there.

12. You've written about the stroke you suffered and how it left you terrified you wouldn't be able to read or write again. If that happened again tomorrow, what's the thing you would most like to say today?
Make sure the plug is pulled on the life-support. And thank you for having me.

Only Connect...

Anthony Rudolf has been for many years a London publisher (the small Menard Press), as well as translator, poet and critic. At the suggestion of Michael Schmidt of Carcanet, he got in touch with me when he was about to visit his daughter in New Zealand. He would be spending two nights in Auckland on the way to Dunedin, and hoped we might meet. I asked how he would like to spend the time and he asked might it be possible to pay his respects at the grave of the German Jewish refugee poet, Karl Wolfskehl (1869–1948). So I met him at the airport, jet-lagged from his 24-hour flight, and took him first to deposit his bags at the B&B he had booked, close to Eden Park. Because he has trouble sleeping he wanted to try to stay awake now, during the daylight hours, so it was agreed we should go at once in search of the Wolfskehl grave in the extensive West Auckland cemetery of Waikumete.

Although Wolfskehl died when I was fifteen, I had heard a lot about him from Frank Sargeson. Wolfskehl was a poet, philologist, translator and literary personality of considerable distinction in inter-war

Published in *Areté* 46, Spring/Summer 2015.

Germany, who had left behind wealth, comfort, family and reputation to escape the Nazis, first in Italy, then in New Zealand, which he
reached in 1938, aged 69, with his much younger companion, Margot
Ruben. Sargeson met him in the early years of the war, was impressed,
and offered to read to him in English once or twice a week. This was a
kindness all the more important as Wolfskehl's sight was failing; and
Sargeson was able to provide literary and intellectual conversation,
gossip, amateur (but extensive) scholarship, and information about
the anglophone writing and publishing world. It's not surprising that
for quite some time their friendship flourished.

Sargeson's memoir, *More than Enough*,[1] has some marvellous
accounts of the two men, the Pakeha New Zealander and the German
Jew, crouching over a gas ring for warmth in the wooden shack that
was Frank's home in those days, sharing the wonders of Gibbon's
prose, or talking about Kafka – this, for example, on a rainy night
when the old man arrives with wet feet:

> I chafed his feet before wrapping them in old pullovers: there were rugs,
> blankets and overcoats to wrap him in until he began to assume the
> shape of a gigantic ball: his shoes were tied by their laces to the length of
> string above the heating kettle where, on wet days, I dried my tea-tow-
> els. I had done all I could do. I hoped he might be feeling a little more
> comfortable. He was comfortable. Was there anything more I could do
> for him? He apologised, could I please close the window? I apologised
> for the draught, the windows were shut but alas, there were so many
> chinks and crannies. He apologised, he understood. I arranged a light
> rug over his head and quoted, 'Flower in the crannied wall . . .' I had
> read him patches of Tennyson. I don't think at that time I knew Cyril
> Connolly's [in fact James Joyce's – CKS] joke: Lawn Tennyson: if I had I
> would have told him and he would have chuckled.

Frank loved to find people in need, and mother them, so this continued for some considerable time. Gradually, however, he began to feel

overwhelmed by the immensity of Wolfskehl's personality and scholarship, his intellectual energy, his seemingly boundless knowledge. Even his physical presence was daunting, and Frank spoke of being crushed by the weight of European civilisation. Effortlessly, and without any such intention, Wolfskehl made him feel insignificant. New Zealand itself seemed to shrink. Sargeson's belief in himself, and in the possibility of being in any meaningful sense 'a writer' in this country, faded in the great man's presence. In the end he made a decision: he must cut himself off from Wolfskehl.

It is still not easy to understand this. It is largely a matter of personality; but also of its time and place, when the colonial cringe was not far under the surface. Sargeson, when he spoke of it, conveyed the sense that the ending of the friendship was both necessary and terrible.

Wolfskehl was lonely and intellectually deprived in the New Zealand of the war years, and though he had, by now, other friends in Auckland, there can only have been one or two as lively, intelligent and interesting as Sargeson. Sargeson's biographer, Michael King,[2] reveals there was a final spat which my guess is Frank allowed himself to use as the trigger he needed. There was an arrangement that Wolfskehl would visit on a particular day which turned out to be extremely windy and wet. Sargeson had no phone, so Wolfskehl could not ring to say he would not be coming. When he did turn up, two or three days later in the morning, which Frank always preserved for his writing, he was turned away.

Some days passed before Wolfskehl wrote: 'Don't you think it is silly not to meet more? Indeed my longing overcomes my presumption, and yours also, I hope. Will you kindly give me a wring [sic] . . . Looking forward . . .' Sargeson did not call, and their friendship ended. Wolfskehl was puzzled and deeply hurt. He had other friends; his time in New Zealand (the last ten years of his life) was not all poverty and loneliness. It produced what are widely acknowledged as some of his finest poems. He was grateful to the country and people who had given him quarter. When he received New Zealand citizenship he wrote that it reassured him, having been stateless for eight years, to have received acceptance and hospitality in a decent and truly humane society. When the war ended he declined to return to Europe. But the wounds of his exile were deep.

Sargeson reproached himself. To Helen Shaw, who was collecting memories of the poet after his death, he wrote, 'Perhaps some of his friends might be charitable enough to think I did my best for him according to my lights – but if they should go on to think my lights weren't very bright I just haven't got an answer.'[3]

So for me to visit Wolfskehl's grave was to remember two remarkable men, as well as being a way of helping a distinguished visitor pass part of his short stay in Auckland profitably.

We had difficulty at first finding the grave. We were directed to the Jewish section but could not find Wolfskehl until it was suggested the date (1948) was early enough for him to have been buried in another, earlier Jewish part, beside the World War II (Pacific Theatre) graves – Americans and New Zealanders. There we found what we were looking for, a plain granite slab, with no dates, a Hebrew text, the name, KARL WOLFSKEHL, and the inscription EXUL POETA. Poet in exile – or banished? Both, I suppose, as he was indeed, that great receptacle of German and Jewish culture and history, major poet, grand and tragic figure, whose last poems are full of the pain of distance.

The evening of the day after our visit Tony Rudolf came to dinner with a couple of our friends and at some point the conversation turned either to Balzac or A. S. Byatt, one or the other, leading to what follows.

During 1977 I had been a visitor in the English Department at University College London, and was one of the lecturers in Professor Karl Miller's course on twentieth-century Modernism. A. S. Byatt was another and we became friends. We were both writing poems at the time. Antonia was working on *The Virgin in the Garden* and she is one of those rare novelists who like to tell the story as it evolves. I had time on my hands and became her willing listener. This telling her books was something that was to continue at intervals over many years, usually in London when I was visiting, now and then when we have both been in France.

At some time in the 1990s, when I was visiting London, Antonia and I together attended a seminar/lecture about a story by Balzac, 'Gillette, or The Unknown Masterpiece'. It had been newly translated and published in a booklet together with an introduction and notes by the translator who offered his own interpretation. The story begins in December 1612 and is about a (fictional) great painter, Frenhofer, who has been working for ten years on a portrait of a woman which is going so to exceed anything he has done before, it will be 'life itself'. He has continued to work at it, often announcing to his friend and fellow artist (non-fictional) Frans Porbus that it is finished, and then always deciding that there is yet more to be done. He is jealous, possessive, and will not allow others to see the work at least until it's complete; but, as the story goes on, he is persuaded (by a slightly improbable bargain) to allow two fellow painters, Porbus and the young Poussin, to view the work. What these two see is something so over-painted nothing can be recognised but paint, with the single exception of 'a bare foot emerging from the chaos of colours, tones and vague hues. [...] The foot seemed to them like the torso of some Venus in Parian marble rising from the ruins of a city destroyed by fire.'

While Frenhofer draws attention to the wonders of what he has done, his visitors at first hide their dismay, until Poussin, unable to contain himself, says that sooner or later Frenhofer must recognise that 'there is nothing in the canvas'. Now the spell is broken. Frenhofer raves at them, then seems briefly to recognise the truth: 'Nothing! Nothing! The work of ten years.' He weeps, despairs, rallies and sends his visitors away saying they are merely jealous of what he has achieved. That night he burns the painting and dies.

The issue about Balzac's story amounts to this: did Balzac mean his readers to see the painting as Poussin and Porbus see it, as a mess, a failure, an incomprehensible and meaningless work? Or was

Balzac foreshadowing (as some, including Cézanne, had suggested) the future in which non-representational abstraction would take art and history forward into new and hitherto unknown realms? It is the latter view the translator took in the essay accompanying his translation, and the lecturer agreed with him.

I had bought and read the booklet in advance and so was in a position to offer a firm opinion – which I did at question time. I disagreed with what was being proposed and said so, probably not tentatively. It seemed to me that Balzac had presented Frenhofer quite unambiguously as a man driven, by the relentless search for perfection, into delusion and madness, and the work he had laboured over so long had been painted to death.

While I engaged in this debate with the speaker I sensed Antonia's embarrassment. It was not disagreement I registered, but disapproval. When I mentioned this afterwards she didn't deny it, but said, looking severe, how distressing she found male competitiveness. I didn't argue – clearly I'd said more than enough already; but, while embarrassed by my own tendency to be over-emphatic, I knew my response had been nothing to do with competitiveness and everything to do with impatience that something simple and clear had been made needlessly complicated. It was a case of 'cleverness' misapplied, and I felt I had been defending Balzac (whose work I loved) against marauding intellectuals.

While I was recounting some small part of this to Tony and the other guests I drifted from the table to the book shelves and found among the Balzacs the item that had been the subject of the lecture. To the astonishment of all, including myself, and creating the sort of quite unplanned *coup de théâtre* that can make dinner parties memorable, Tony Rudolf was the translator and author of the accompanying essay with which I had so staunchly argued.[4] At the back were my pencilled annotations, indicating my disagreements.

Tony was glad he had found support from whomever the lecturer was; and he didn't seem to mind that I had disagreed so strongly.

Before the evening was over he inscribed the little book, 'For Karl and Kay / Tony / who was amazed and enchanted by the circumstances. April 2011.'

I should say at this point that my view has not changed. It seemed to me that one element in particular had been left out of Tony's discussion of the story: money, one of Balzac's great themes. Frenhofer is rich. Poussin's poverty is made clear. It is mentioned in the story that Mabuse (also non-fictional), whom Frenhofer acknowledges as his teacher, had painted a masterwork, 'Adam', 'to buy himself out of prison where his creditors had enforced a lengthy stay'. Even before the great painting/great disaster is finally revealed, Porbus tells Poussin that Frenhofer is 'as much a madman as he is a painter. A sublime painter indeed, but who had the misfortune to be born rich, which has allowed him to stray. Do not imitate him!' At the end, when the truth of failure is revealed to him, and Frenhofer cries out that he has nothing to show for ten years' work, he says 'What a crazy old fool I am! [. . .] I am nothing but a rich man who, while walking, can only walk. In the end I shall have done nothing!'

In a work of such intensity everything comes back, not without complexity but often with little or no subtlety, to the author; and it seems to me that in this story we see Balzac, the man who was always poor and in debt, famous for endless corrections at proof stage which cost him the profit he so desperately needed, telling himself, 'This is what I might have done to my own work if I had been rich – corrected it into oblivion.' Frenhofer is himself, Balzac, without the constraints and necessities of poverty; with enough money to be self-indulgent. The idea that Balzac is looking into the future, foreseeing where art will travel, through Impressionism and into Abstraction, is, it seems to me, absurd. Why, if he had had any such idea, would he have set his story back almost two centuries in time rather than squarely in his own century? Of course history can nudge the meaning of a work of literature in new directions; but this is more than a nudge – more like the shove of a bulldozer.

That conviction was the source of my bad behaviour eliciting A. S. Byatt's reproach.

After our dinner party, when Tony had flown off south to visit his daughter, I emailed asking Antonia whether she remembered the occasion and her displeasure. I told her about Tony's visit, and that he had not seemed to mind my objection to his reading of the Balzac story – indeed was delighted to hear that it had occasioned a lecture from someone who agreed with him. She replied to my email that she remembered the occasion 'vividly'. She went on 'I think you were saying that it was clear the painting was simply a mess and a failure and I agree with that but there is such a strong tradition of painters – impressionists – excitedly thinking that the painting was a proto-Cézanne or Monet that we have to be careful.' In particular she was struck by Cézanne's dramatic self-presentations – 'I am Frenhofer' – and felt that had to be part of the discussion.

She had herself written about the story, and might even have looked again at Tony Rudolf's translation and essay.[5] If she had she was not persuaded by his argument: 'Is the portrait a disintegrating disaster', she asks, 'or do the younger painters not know how to look at it? My own view is that a close reading suggests that the painting was a disaster – one step too far in the arduous and sensuously obsessive process of constructing women out of paint.'

In recent years Tony Rudolf has been known as the companion and principal male model of Dame Paula Rego. When Kay and I were in London the following year he took us to visit Paula in her extraordinary studio in Camden Town, after which we all went to dinner. There was at this time a Paula Rego show at the Marlborough Gallery, 'Balzac and Other Stories'. It was a show that contained all the well-established (often Goya-esque) elements of horror and humour that have characterised her work in recent years, and in which the face of Tony Rudolf was a number of times clearly detectable. Paula has cartooned, or lampooned, the Iberian dictators, Franco and Salazar, and she is much honoured in Spain and her native

Portugal, as well as in Britain. In person she is full of humour, fantasy, mockery and mischief; but under it all there is, as Matthew Arnold said of Keats, 'flint and iron' in her.

But how did Balzac figure in the show? Though one of the works is called 'The Balzac Story' its connection with 'Gillette or The Unknown Masterpiece' is remote. Four women painters – a child, a young adult, a mature adult and an older woman – are all at work. Two are doing self-portraits, so perhaps they all are. There are four painters in Balzac's story so perhaps these four are the originals converted into women; or perhaps they are the four ages of Paula Rego – or both. Perhaps there is no connection with the Balzac story and the title is meaningless.

But there was also in the Marlborough show a painting called 'Mary of Egypt', and this may be the real connection. In the Balzac story a canvas of 'Saint Mary the Egyptian' by Porbus is described and criticised because, though much in it is 'praiseworthy', it is impossible 'to believe that the warm breath of life animates that beautiful body'. Paula Rego's Mary of Egypt is being taken somewhere by sea – to Jerusalem, presumably, as in life, where (so the story goes) she planned to exert her sexual powers on Christian pilgrims, for their money. The Mary figure is Rego's usual female model, Lila Nunes, and the fisherman ferrying her is Tony Rudolf. Mary sits behind, grabbing him by the shirt, frowning, commanding, while he appears anxious and ready to obey. This is perhaps the Porbus painting as it should have been. The woman is not beautiful but she is strong, and there could be no doubt about the warm breath animating her frame.

1   *More than Enough: A Memoir*, A.H. & A.W. Reed, 1975, pp. 106–15.
2   Michael King, *Frank Sargeson: A Life*, Viking/Allen Lane, 1995, p. 227.
3   *Letters of Frank Sargeson*, ed. Sarah Shieff, Random House, 2012, p. 197.
4   Balzac, *Gillette or The Unknown Masterpiece*, translated with an essay by Anthony Rudolf, Menard Press, 1988.
5   A. S. Byatt, *Portraits in Fiction*, Vintage, 2002, p. 23.

4.

The Laureate Reflects

Allen Curnow – 'Poet Laureate'?

1.

Before we had our own officially sponsored poet laureate it could be argued that we had an unofficial one in Allen Curnow. Allen died in 2001 before the New Zealand laureateship had been established; but if it had come earlier he would undoubtedly have been our first.

The time I have in mind, however, when Curnow was in his prime as, so to speak, our unofficial public poet was the decade of the 1940s. While World War II raged, and New Zealand played its part in the Middle East and then Italy and the Pacific, we celebrated the centenary of the signing of the Treaty of Waitangi (1840–1940) and commemorated the 300th anniversary of Tasman's voyage of discovery (1642–1942). This was the period when Curnow, who I assume could not be drafted into the military for medical (eyesight) reasons, was writing poems that chose, whether we were listening

First published on the New Zealand Poet Laureate blog (www.poetlaureate.org.nz), 12 October 2015.

or not, to speak for us all. Resonant phrases from these poems entered one stratum of the national consciousness at that time and have remained there:

> Always to islanders danger
> Is what comes over the sea

Or the sonnet about the skeleton of the moa that ends,

> Not I, some child, born in a marvellous year,
> Will learn the trick of standing upright here.

Or 'The Unhistoric Story' with its refrain that New Zealand as it developed

> . . . was something different, something
> Nobody counted on.

'Landfall in Unknown Seas' celebrated Tasman's landing in New Zealand – a beautifully structured sequence which runs through the excitements of preparation for the voyage and anticipation of success ('time / To go and to be gazed at going'), the exhilaration of discovery ('There was the seascape / Crammed with coast'), the violence of the first encounter ('O in a flash, in a flat calm / A clash of boats in the bay'), and the disappointment – followed by a reflection which asks how all this should be remembered and celebrated now that 'there are no more islands to be found'. The conclusion is that what's needed is something more truthful than self-importance and self-congratulation.

> Only by a more faithful memory, laying
> On him the half-light of a diffident glory,
> The Sailor lives, and stands beside us, paying

> Out into our time's wave
> The stain of blood that writes an island story.

All of this, together with the lovely clarity with which Douglas Lilburn's accompanying music catches the poem's moods and transitions, put poetry for a moment right into the public arena. The time was right for this, and Curnow had seen the need of the moment and had seized it memorably.

Only a few years later he edited two anthologies of poetry which are generally acknowledged to mark a point in the development of a mature and independent New Zealand literature. Curnow in those days was a literary nationalist; but he was also a literary realist, in the sense that what he cared most about was that our poetry should be an honest record, not a 'three cheers for us' one; and this meant recognition of deficiencies, lacks, failures, uncertainties. As Wilfred Owen had said, 'the true poets must be truthful'. Rather than national pride, Curnow would offer us, in that resonant phrase, 'the half-light of a diffident glory'.

Possibly the subtlest and frankest of Curnow's statements of his position in these matters occurs in the introduction to his *Penguin Book of New Zealand Verse* when he discusses Katherine Mansfield's poem 'To Stanislaw Wyspianski'. He calls it a 'half-poem', but praises it because, he says, 'it allows us to date as early as 1910 the emergence of New Zealand as a characterizing emotional force in the work of a native poet'. What he finds and admires in the poem is that Mansfield identifies herself as a New Zealander, and that her country, which she appears to have rejected, figures nonetheless as 'a palpable "here", a pressure from within, an antagonist' and so 'anticipates the conflict of spirit' in the poets who followed.

Curnow was wanting to be rid of weak nationalist self-assertions, the 'Kowhai Gold' kind of thing, that offered the picturesque – tui and bellbirds, 'scenic' bush, mountains and seas, and romantic 'pioneering' – rather than the tormented inner conscience of the nation;

and it was this he felt Mansfield caught in her Wyspianski poem, including

> the New Zealand sadness (always there, however deeply buried in the mind) because life here seems a makeshift and reality (still sadder illusion!) lodged somewhere 'overseas'.

So Mansfield's cry from 'a little land with no history' seemed to Curnow truthful and to catch a sad reality.

The point about sad or harsh realities rather than scenery is made also in varying ways by that other literary nationalist of the time, Frank Sargeson. In one of his early stories, for example, 'Chaucerian', the narrator, who has escaped from a narrow upbringing in a churchy family, has discovered the truth about himself, and about life, in Freemans Bay, at that time a central Auckland slum. He writes

> It's a very interesting place. Any New Zealand poet who hasn't dedicated herself to kauri trees and bellbirds couldn't do better than go and live there.

My admiration for the Curnow of that time is undimmed. But what strikes me now is how deeply and indelibly negative his nationalism was ('the New Zealand sadness, always there . . .'). When I was young I accepted this because the poems were so good, so beautifully crafted, so eloquent. Perhaps I accepted it also because I felt that sadness in myself, as something out of the air, in the water, inherent in the sense of place and history. At this distance in time that doesn't seem to me entirely implausible; but if it's true, I was not conscious of it, and if it had been suggested to me, I'm sure I would have rejected it – would have said that the 'sadness' was just part of being alive.

But looked back on, how pervasive the gloom in those poems now seems! It is a collective grief, a loss, a deprivation. One of his sonnets begins,

The oldest of us burst into tears and cried
Let me go home, but she stayed, watching
At her staircase window ship after ship ride
Like birds her grieving sunsets.

'House and Land', a wonderfully managed and memorably lyrical poem, ends

The sensitive nor'west afternoon
Collapsed, and the rain came;
The dog crept into his barrel
Looking lost and lame.
But you can't attribute to either
Awareness of what great gloom
Stands in a land of settlers
With never a soul at home.

We are characterised as an unhappy, in effect homeless, 'land of settlers'. A 1942 verse letter to Denis Glover laments

O I could go down to harbours
And mourn with a hundred years
Of hunger what slips away there.

These are lines that chime with Charles Brasch's

Remindingly beside the quays, the white
Ships lie smoking; and from their haunted bay
The godwits vanish towards another summer.
Everywhere in light and calm the murmuring
Shadow of departure.

It's hard to look at the work of that period from this distance and not see in it the ghostly face of the colonial child weeping for Mother

England – something which, if it had been put to me in those terms at that time, would have appalled me and I would have rejected. My thought now is that there is no escaping from your actual condition (and I include myself in this). If yours is one of colonialism that will show, even in your struggle to reject and escape from it.

It would have distressed Curnow too, probably, if I had written in these terms during his lifetime. I realise that what I am saying here is not unlike William Blake's assertion that 'Milton was of the devil's party without knowing it'. It is like one of those always slightly irritating exercises in literary deconstruction, where the clever critic proves the writer set out with one intention and achieved precisely its opposite. Nonetheless it seems to me looking again at these poems I have known so long and know so well, that they do surrender to their opposites. The poet who aspired to speak for the nation, was telling us we were not a nation at all but a land of sad homeless settlers. And the poet who said others after him would 'stand upright here,' as he could not, was writing poems which stood upright as none written before him had done, and only a few since.

2.

It was not until 1949, aged 37 or 38, that Curnow got out of New Zealand and to London where in November of that year he wrote his 'Elegy on My Father', an untypically awkward poem, as if his current state of mind, and present preoccupations, had no room for, or means of coping with, such an important but distant death. Back in New Zealand the following year he wrote a poem, addressed, it seems, to someone left behind in London, and reflecting painfully on the loss:

> I pray, pray for me on some spring-wet pavement
> Where halts the heartprint of our salt bereavement,
>   Pray over many times,

> Forgive him the seas forgive him the spring leaf,
> All bloom ungathered perishable as grief,
> For the hulk of the world's between

There is something very personal and private here, but it is made public. Perhaps for the last time Curnow is speaking for us all – of our far removal, of distance, of the great, almost unbridgeable gap between *here* and *there*. It is a last look at, or *from*, New Zealand before jet travel became affordable, and e-communication commonplace; before the 'hulk' of the world shrivelled to a manageable and almost frighteningly small nut, and national self-confidence became, if not actually, at least plausibly self-sufficient.

Meanwhile he had moved to Auckland in 1951 where he became, I think one can say, a regional rather than a national poet: less a public eminence, but no less a brilliant poet. His 1955 poems, marking the beginning of his relationship with Jeny Tole, were an enrichment in every way. The emotional range expanded together with the enlargement of scene and reference. Before too long Curnow, with his new wife, would become, like the rest of us, an international traveller; and though England, and London as a centre of anglophone publishing, continued to be important, as it had to be for a son of Christchurch and the Anglican Church, Italy became the place he loved most to visit, an expansion of his poetry's worldly vision. The sequence 'Moro Assassinato', on the murder of the former Italian Prime Minister, Aldo Moro, is a reflection of that expansion, and is one of his finest.

Of the Mansfield Wyspianski poem Curnow wrote, 'Because she addresses a Pole – type-figure of suffering nationhood – she disengages herself from the invidious and belittling contest of England versus "the Colony". Paradoxically, her lines thus dignify the country they reject.' Perhaps Curnow felt his 'Italy' served the same purpose.

It is hardly surprising that some of the poets who came immediately after Curnow, the ones I think of as the 1922 generation, who were perhaps the children 'born in a marvellous year', in the 1960s rebelled against and rejected Curnow's view of our poetry and of the state of the nation. I was involved in that argument, on Curnow's side because he was the Master and, simply as poets, most of his detractors (with the exception of James K. Baxter) seemed amateurs by comparison. Now it has receded into literary history, and like all such stories, calls for retelling as distance alters the perspectives.

Irish Poets and Poetry

I have a large anthology of poems in my head, not because I have set out to 'learn' them, but because when I was young and got attached to a poet's work, and read it often, some of the poems would stick – and have remained there. When Allen Curnow and I lectured on W. B. Yeats at the University of Auckland, he to the MA class, I to Stage I, we used to talk about Yeats and between us could assemble any of the better-known poems without opening a text. This was early in the 1960s, and I suggested he and I should write a book about Yeats by exchanging letters about the poems we were discussing. I was about to publish my first critical book, *The New Poetic*, which had a chapter on Yeats, and I was being urged by a publisher with connections to T. S. Eliot's widow to write an Eliot biography; but I felt too swamped by the business of preparing new lectures to take on anything so large. An exchange with Allen about Yeats, on the other hand, seemed only an extension of our conversations, and not

First published on the New Zealand Poet Laureate blog
(www.poetlaureate.org.nz), 27 October 2015.

too daunting, especially because each reply would at once suggest a direction for the response.

I think it was a good idea and could have been an unusual and valuable contribution to Yeats studies, but Allen was not keen. His private life at the time was complicated; and I had the impression he was nervous about whether he would 'measure up' and which of us might shine brighter. I should simply have sent him the first letter as a prompt. A few years later we were indeed exchanging letters about poetry – our own (more his than mine of course) across Tohunga Crescent, where we were neighbours after he and his second wife, Jeny, moved to live there after their marriage in 1965 – and this kind of exchange was to continue for the rest of his life.

Over the years my view of Yeats became less reverent. I had begun by defending him in a Leavisite English Department (University of Bristol) where I had gone in the late 1950s on a scholarship from New Zealand to do a PhD, and where the view of the great Irishman had been less than wholehearted and unequivocal. Now, while still seeing him as one of the major twentieth-century poets, and admiring his great skill in labouring ideas up from prose drafts into stanza forms (his usual working method), I sometimes felt one was made too aware of the labour: 'hard work' poems, they were. There was sometimes a clumsiness that did not destroy the poem but could make it fall just short of what it might have been. I thought of the Keats precept, 'If poetry come not as naturally as the leaves to the tree, it might as well not come at all.' This was altogether too absolute – 'shoulds' in poetry are seldom wise. But it was clear that whatever the many merits of Yeats's later poems, they did not arrive like leaves in spring.

And it was more than a technical matter, a matter of verse-making. There was also his Irish posturing ('That we in coming times may be / Still the indomitable Irishry'); his glorification of war and his contempt for the poets of World War I who had paraded their suffering; his romanticism about 'peasants' and 'country gentlemen': so much of it was at least ridiculous, and even politically dangerous. Did great verse have to be – could it be – intellectually jejune?

One of his poems that remains in my head is 'Easter 1916', his great (and yes, it probably is great) commemoration of the sixteen rebels shot by the British for their part in the rising of Easter 1916, a poem for which I had written what became pretty much the standard, often reprinted, critical exposition. 'Easter 1916' is in a simple stanza form of four three-stress lines rhyming (and half-rhyming) a, b, a, b, the stanzas running continuously without gaps, and containing passages of rare beauty:

> Hearts with one purpose alone
> Through summer and winter seem
> Enchanted to a stone
> To trouble the living stream.
> The horse that comes from the road,
> The rider, the birds that range
> From cloud to tumbling cloud,
> Minute by minute they change;
> A shadow of cloud on the stream
> Changes minute by minute;
> A horse-hoof slides on the brim,
> And a horse plashes within it;
> The long-legged moor-hens dive,
> And hens to moor-cocks call;
> Minute by minute they live,
> The stone's in the midst of all.

Lovely lines – and the next bring us back to the reality of Easter 1916, and the thought that these brave rebels perhaps died needlessly; that certain qualities of flexibility and patience might have served them as well and saved their lives: 'Was it needless death after all?'

The image of the stone in the stream is beautiful, but 'Too long a sacrifice / Can make a stone of the heart.'

It's when he tries to characterise some among the rebels who were known to him personally that the verse begins to look clumsy, unpolished, laboured:

This man had kept a school
And rode our wingèd horse;
This other, his helper and friend,
Was coming into his force;
He might have won fame in the end,
So sensitive his nature seemed,
So daring and sweet his thought.
This other man I had dreamed
A drunken, vainglorious lout,
He had done most bitter wrong
To some who are near my heart,
Yet I number him in the song.

He wants to say that one of the rebels was a poet, but brings in that tired old trope about the winged horse (which he signals must be pronounced wingèd to get the full three stresses for the line); and then, for the rhyme with horse, says that the poet's friend, another of the sixteen executed rebels, was 'coming into his force'. Dear god! Meaning he was improving, I suppose, maturing, but what a lazy and cluttered utterance it is! And then one feels one knows what 'daring' thought means; but 'so daring and sweet his thought' to my ear is like singing la-la-la to fill an emptiness, as if for a moment he has forgotten what he meant to say next. After that he begins to lay into (without naming him) John MacBride, whose crime (the 'bitter wrong' he did) was that he married the great unrequited love of W.B.'s life, Maud Gonne. But even MacBride is forgiven – 'Yet I number him in the song': all sixteen of them are forgiven their 'ignorant good-will', their shrill speech, their banality which he used to joke about 'around the fire at the Club', because everything has been 'changed, changed utterly' by the failed rebellion. Comedy has turned to tragedy: 'A terrible beauty is born.'

The poem is retrieved and gathers to its great (again yes, I think so, even if the wearing of the green is slightly embarrassing) rhetorical climax:

> I write it out in a verse –
> MacDonagh and MacBride
> And Connolly and Pearse
> Now and in time to be,
> Wherever green is worn,
> Are changed, changed utterly:
> A terrible beauty is born.

So my attitude to Yeats became more complicated over the years. I still admired him, respected his great feats of verse-engineering, and even more his capacity for lyrical delicacy as in 'The Wild Swans at Coole' – but at the same time I felt he sometimes allowed himself to be bullied by poetic form, and in old age became in effect a ridiculous right-wing reactionary. This made, I think, for a richer and more complex view of his work, and it was reflected in my second book on twentieth-century poetry, *Pound, Yeats, Eliot and the Modernist Movement*, which appeared in 1986 in the United Kingdom and the United States, and which, since the year of its release, I have never re-read. (One day I will do that, and perhaps report back on the laureate blog!)

Nineteen eighty-six was the year I left the University of Auckland finally. I had been easing myself out during the previous five years, and was now departing permanently (though retaining the Professor Emeritus title, and a sense of loyalty and gratitude to the institution). I taught for two terms of that final year and then, in August, took off to lecture at the Yeats Summer School in Sligo, the happy place of Yeats's not always happy childhood, where the clear waters of Lake Innisfree rush out into the estuary of Sligo Harbour.

I flew to Dublin and then needed to find my way onward by rail. At the airport I asked how I would get to the Dublin railway station. 'Is it Connolly or Pearse you'll be wanting?' the young woman asked. So I learned that those executed rebels of Easter 1916 are remembered and honoured in the naming of public places.

The one among them 'who rode our wingèd horse' was Thomas MacDonagh, and many years before my Sligo visit I had found and bought a book of his poems, a first edition. Later, I wrote a poem about him:

Easter 1916

(For Seamus Heaney
to whom I gave the book)

Irish Thomas MacDonagh
thirty years ago
in that dusty Oxford bookshop
I found your poems
published by Hodges Figgis
Dublin, 1910.

Songs of myself you called them:
how lovingly
you must have turned
these long-ago pages
dreaming of fame
and your country free.

Alas, Thomas MacDonagh
shot by the British,

it's not your poems live on
in the mind of your country.
It's your dying,
your death.

I gave the little book to Seamus Heaney after hearing his first lecture as Professor of Poetry at Oxford in, I think, 1989. I had gone to hear it with Craig Raine, who had been Heaney's poetry editor at Faber, and a passing reference to MacDonagh gave me the thought that I should do that. I knew as a loyal Irish Catholic Heaney would value the book; but I gave it to him also because he had expressed gratitude to me for that early book, *The New Poetic* – not just for my defence of Yeats and 'Easter 1916' (though I'm sure that was appreciated) but even more for what I had written about T. S. Eliot. As a young man, Heaney told me, he had been unable to read Eliot until he read my book. In the title essay of his book *The Government of the Tongue*, and again in a lecture called 'Learning from Eliot', he goes on about this at some length.

He had sent me a broadsheet of his poem 'The Sounds of Rain', no. 9 of 15 copies, signed and inscribed 'for Karl Stead with "the feeling of an immense debt"' – a line from the poem itself, which was an 'in memoriam' for Richard Ellmann, critic-biographer of Yeats and of Wilde. So in this matter of acknowledgements, I felt my debt was as great as his, and I tried to balance the score with the gift of that rare MacDonagh book. I'm glad I gave it, and still wish I had it – which is as it should be. 'The Sounds of Rain' appeared in Heaney's 1991 collection, *Seeing Things*.

At Sligo I had made some new friends, among them the brilliant Harvard critic Helen Vendler, the Yeats biographer Roy Foster, and the wonderfully sociable editor of the Yeats letters, John Kelly from Oxford, and his clever and beautiful wife, Christine. The following May we all met again, this time as members of an invited group of 'world experts on Yeats', to discuss the theme of 'Yeats the European' at the Princess Grace Memorial Irish Library in Monte Carlo. We presented and listened to papers (mine slightly out of key with the unequivocally affirmative note of my colleagues), did a lot of good eating, drinking and talking, and were taken to see the shell of the soon-to-be demolished Hotel Idéal Séjour, where Yeats had died in 1939. His son Michael, an Irish senator and member of the European Parliament, and his daughter Anne, a painter – both the subject in childhood of now famous poems by their father – were among the delegates; and Michael reminisced about playing in the garden of the hotel during W.B.'s final illness.

Next we were taken by bus to the Roquebrune cemetery where Yeats was first interred. The cemetery is limited in space and situated on a hillside, the graves mostly above ground, so the dead spend a given period in or under whatever tomb or monument is built for them, and are then removed to an ossuary to make room for the newly dead. The body of Yeats spent the years of World War II there and then was disinterred and taken on an Irish warship to be buried, as his poems had instructed, 'under bare Ben Bulben's head / In Drumcliffe churchyard' in the countryside outside Sligo. One hot day during the Sligo summer school I had walked to the grave, and read on it the famous inscription he had 'commanded':

> Cast a cold eye
> On life, on death.
> Horseman, pass by!

So I could say now that I had visited both of the Yeats graves! But could I claim that with confidence? A strange moment early in the Monte Carlo conference was an assurance the delegates received that any stories we may have heard suggesting that the wrong bones had been sent to Ireland were mistaken. The French authorities wanted us to know that no mistake had been made, and that it was indeed the remains of the great poet that had been handed over to the Irish warship for transfer and re-interment. This reassurance only fuelled the rumour, which almost everyone had heard, and fired further speculation.

Disagreement on this matter continues, and it has been suggested at least once, and in the *Irish Times*, that French official papers indicate bones had been taken from the Roquebrune ossuary and 'assembled' by guesswork by officials who had no certainty about the choices they were making. There is even an English family who believe their loved one and not the poet was in the coffin handed over to the Irish ship. Could an Englishman be buried in the grave of the great Irish nationalist? *Tiens!*

One final irony: the Irish Minister of Foreign Affairs who approved the transfer and accepted the bones as those of W. B. Yeats was Sean MacBride, son of W.B.'s great love, Maud Gonne, and the 'drunken vainglorious lout' and Easter 1916 hero, John MacBride. I think I hear someone having the last laugh. The accent is Irish but I can't be sure about whose voice it is.

Ezra Pound:
One to Be Reckoned With

Ezra Pound was an Imagist, later a Vorticist (an Imagist animated, *energised*) who aspired to write a long poem – 'really LONG, endless, leviathanic'. This was a contradiction he thought he could resolve by the method he called 'presentative'. 'Beauty should be presented, never explained.' That's why the early attempts to begin *The Cantos* that occupy the first twenty or so pages of this book were excluded and re-written – because they were explanatory, expository, discursive.

> Hang it all, there can be but one *Sordello*!
> But say I want to, say I take your whole bag of tricks,
> Let in your quirks and tweeks, and say the thing's an art form,
> Your *Sordello*, and that the modern world
> Needs such a rag-bag to stuff all its thought in;

A review of Ezra Pound's *Posthumous Cantos*, edited by Massimo Bacigalupo (Carcanet, 2015), published in the *Times Literary Supplement*, 15 April 2016; after which I have added further comments on the thorny subject of Ezra.

Say that I dump my catch, shiny and silvery
As fresh sardines flapping and slipping on the marginal cobbles?

These sections, addressed to 'Bob Browning', argued at length (against 'sulk[ing] and leav[ing] the word to novelists') the case for 'the long poem'. But Pound didn't want to argue the case – he wanted to do the job, and so these opening Cantos were dropped.

What this collection offers are not strictly speaking posthumous Cantos, but on the one hand, off-cuts, deletions, passages removed from the ongoing, never-ending (except in exhaustion and defeat) work that was *The Cantos*; and on the other hand, passages which popped up in Pound's notebooks, clearly related to the current work, but finding no exact place where they could be fitted in and made to look at home. They are, then, a mixed bag – but so are the 'finished' *Cantos*.

The book's successive section headings show how we move with Pound from 'London 1915–1917', to 'Paris 1920–1922', to 'Rapallo and Venice 1928–1937'; then 'Voices of War, 1940–1945', 'Italian Drafts, 1944–1945', and 'Pisa, 1945'. Section VII, 'Prosaic Verses, 1945–1960', is largely from his period in St Elizabeths Hospital for the insane (Washington DC) where he was committed for twelve years, thus avoiding a trial for treason; and finally 'Lines for Olga, 1962–1972' from his final years with Olga Rudge in Rapallo and Venice. Those headings are also a reminder of how, despite his serious internationalism, and his commitment to history and to the received European culture, Pound's poetry never escaped entirely from place, location, the immediate and particular, and the perceptions of the senses.

Pound's scholarship was always amateurish, excitable, every discovery a gem he felt needed to be made known at once, fitted into the growing picture which, once grasped by someone like the President of the United States, to whom he more than once appealed directly, would save the world – economically, practically and spiritually. But that 'presentative method', which he was quite strict about imposing on himself, meant that nothing could be explained. There is a kind of purity (it could even be called innocence) about this, which works poetically, but can make *The Cantos* seem indeterminate and ineffectual. The discoveries are tossed before us without connecting material or explanatory argument. It's as if he's saying constantly, 'as I'm sure you're aware', or 'you will recall', as he puts down some obscure discovery from the dustiest archives. The nearer Pound was to a major library (the Vatican was a favourite) the drearier the *Cantos* became. The material on Sigismondo Malatesta, fifteenth-century lord of Rimini, intended for one Canto, grew to four; American presidents John Adams, Thomas Jefferson, Quincy Adams, Andrew Jackson, Martin Van Buren, illustrating something economically 'significant' or politically 'important', choke the work like a dust storm in a desert. There are some beautiful reliefs from this tedious excess of fact (Canto 39, for example, and then 47 and 49); but as the years go by they become fewer.

During World War II Pound, still an American citizen but permanently resident in Italy, broadcast on behalf of Mussolini's regime; and it is hardly too much to say that one of the greatest services the advancing US Army did to world literature was to put Pound in a wire cage in their Detention Centre at Pisa (pending trial in Washington for the capital offence of treason) and deprive him of access to books. He had brought with him (being Ezra) his Confucius in a bilingual edition; and he came upon an anthology of English poetry in a toilet block. Otherwise he was on his own. *The Pisan Cantos* are the triumph they are partly because he was all at once dependent on what was already contained and processed in his head (including memories of a rich literary life), together with what was going on around him – the talk of fellow-American inmates and camp guards, the flora and fauna, the skies and weathers, of the Tuscan landscape.

Professor of English and American literature at the University of Genoa, Massimo Bacigalupo, son of Pound's physician in Rapallo and of an American mother, is uniquely qualified to write of, and to edit, Pound, who spent so much of his life in Italy, immersed in Italian language, life, culture and politics. In addition to supplying an introduction, and useful but discreetly brief notes for all sections, Bacigalupo has translated the drafts Pound wrote in Italian which have not been available in English except in scholarly articles – none of them as rebarbative as Cantos 72 and 73, the Italian Cantos which for a long time Pound's executors would not permit to be published in English. (Canto 73 is the one containing Pound's crowing account of the pretty young woman Fascist who led Canadian soldiers – 'canaille' he calls them – into a minefield, killing twenty of them and herself.)

In the present selection the Italian drafts are offered in both languages. Many of the same ideas, images and illustrations that appear in these were to reappear in *The Pisan Cantos*, which helps to explain why the latter came forth so readily, handwritten after Pound was removed from the cage to a tent in the medical compound, and typed up at night when he was permitted to use the camp dispensary's typewriter. The old obsessions, good and bad, are there – usury, the olive groves on that hill-slope above Rapallo, his historical touchstones (including Malatesta), and the darting back and forth between the dark present and its often luminous, or at least illuminating, past.

There is much less of the cranky Pound in this collection, less of the bore, the irrational anti-Semite, the savage, and much more of the aesthete, the man whose editorial skill turned *The Waste Land* (as Eliot said) from 'a jumble of good and bad passages into a poem'; more in fact of the poetic Modernist. Sometimes the dark and the light come mysteriously together:

> Now I remember that you built me a special gorilla-cage
> > and that the foetor of Roosevelt
> > > stank thru the shitpile that succeeded him
>
> > moon bright like water
> > water like sky
> usury, monopoly, changing the currency

More often there is regret for folly, and gratitude to the women who had sustained him, as in these lines recording his return to his beloved Genoa after his twelve-year incarceration:

> The trees in mist hold their beauty
> I have been a pitiless stone –
> > stone making art work
> and destroying affections.
> [...]
> Till suddenly the tower
> > blazed with the light of Astarte
> @ Genova the port lay below us.
> Miracolo di Dio
> > ch'amor riceve
> > > né la calunnia
> > > > né l'invidia te toca.

[O miracle of God who receives love, neither calumny nor envy touches you.]

There are many tributes to Olga Rudge, whose patience outlasted his wife's, and who was the companion of his final years; and the image comes and goes of that 'salita' – the hill path, through olive groves, from Rapallo up to Sant'Ambrogio where Olga's house figures in *The Cantos* as 'Circe's ingle':

> flood & flame
> thru the long years
> > by night & hill path
> great courage in frail frame
> toughened by four decades
> of climbing thru dark
> > on hill paths,
> knowing each stone
> almost as if by name.

[. . .]

> But against the mounting evils
> she held the will toward good
> Her clear lucidity
> that she saw the Duce with level eyes

The book under review contains essentially the same material as Bacigalupo's *Canti Posthumi* published in Italian in 2002. It is a 'selection from [. . .] abundant material, based on criteria of quality, accessibility, and documentary interest'. There is, then, an element of preference comes into the choices made. If you had read nothing of Pound and sampled this selection you might conclude that he was a nature poet, a love poet, a man with some significant and eccentric grasp of history, given to technical experiment in poetry; a loving man of extraordinary sensibility and finesse.

He was all of those things, of course. He was also an exceptional literary intelligence, obsessive, and from time to time more than slightly mad.

★

That was the review.

My interest in Pound's work followed inevitably from my work long ago on T. S. Eliot. You can't study Eliot without considering the hand Pound had in the making of *The Waste Land* and Eliot's continuing loyalty and gratitude to the poet he called '*il miglior fabbro*' (the superior craftsman). You could not be a serious literary historian of poetry in the twentieth century without making room for Pound; and in fact I would add that every serious poet throughout those years had to make some kind of accommodation with his poetry, his poetic theories, and his bossily brilliant critical writings. Yet the Fascist Pound, the Social Credit fanatic, the supporter of Mussolini, the wildly eccentric and madly opinionated letter-writer, and above all the anti-Semite, made it difficult, and sometimes embarrassing.

If you want to get a feel for the poetic precision and delicacy he was capable of, look at his translations from the Chinese, published as *Cathay*, and also in Canto 49; or his Latin translations, *Homage to Sextus Propertius*. In works like that the *material* comes from the poet being translated, and Pound's presence is manifest in getting the language right, quite unaffected by his personal persuasions and obsessions. Of course there is a buoyancy, sprightliness, energy which are recognisably his – but that is in the language and is the best of Pound, while the crankiness is left at the door.

The wind bundles itself into a bluish cloud and wanders off.

With that music playing,
And I, wrapped in brocade, went to sleep with my head on his lap,
And my spirit so high it was all over the heavens,
And before the end of the day we were scattered like stars, or rain.

Those lines are from *Cathay*; and these from *Propertius*:

The twisted rhombs ceased their clamour of accompaniment;
The scorched laurel lay in the fire-dust;
The moon still declined to descend out of heaven,
But the black ominous owl-hoot was audible.
One raft bears our fates
                    On the veiled lake towards Avernus
Sails spread on Cerulean waters . . .

As I say in the review above, there are vast boredoms in *The Cantos*; but there are treasures too, and you have to know where to find them. More than once I have read that massive work right through from beginning to end over several days, not stopping to puzzle over anything, taking it all as it comes, the good with the bad, just to get a proper sense of his 'presentative method' – where it works, where it doesn't, and why. My one book on this subject, *Pound, Yeats, Eliot and the Modernist Movement*, is rare, or was at the time, in the sense that it tried to discriminate clearly between the good and the bad in Pound. Pound studies tended to be conducted by advocates. These good people, most of them serious scholars, usually employed as academics, attended Pound conferences where it was rare to hear a harsh word against 'Ol' Ez', and where references to anti-Semitism and Fascism were muted or absent. Sometimes his daughter, Mary de Rachewiltz, was present; and once the conference was held at her castle in Brunnenburg. The atmosphere was always slightly defensive. Others (outsiders) who spoke or wrote of Pound were mostly detractors. There is, or there used to be, a wide gap in the middle between detractors and defenders, which in my book I tried to fill.

After a period in London and then Paris in the 1920s, Pound, who came from Hailey, Idaho, made his home in Rapallo on the Italian Mediterranean coast – a beautiful location, but somewhat remote from the world he wanted to be part of. I visited it first in 1972 when I held the Mansfield Menton Fellowship, and in the early 1980s when I was working on my book. I attended a Pound conferences there and got to know Professor Massimo Bacigalupo, editor of the book reviewed above, son of Pound's doctor and grandson of his pharmacist. The Bacigalupo family have had a series of small yachts called *Vagabonde I, II* and *III*. Pound was taken sailing on the first of these and Massimo, a teenager at the time, remembers him well. Massimo lives up in the hills just above Rapallo, and commutes each working day along to the University of Genoa where he is Professor of English and American Literature.

Pound had a kind of informal 'son-in-law' (or son-not-in-law) connection with W. B. Yeats, having married Dorothy, the daughter of Yeats's long-time mistress (as she would have been called then), Olivia Shakespeare. In his officious and self-important way the young Pound had 'taken the older Yeats in hand', wanting to 'modernise' him as a poet. Yeats had allowed this just as far as suited him and no further. The influence was significant; but Yeats saw the dangers. With Pound's help he worked on making his tone and language match the twentieth-century world, sweeping away the *fin de siècle* languors and Celtic Twilight vapours; but he always observed strict form and structure, which was where he felt Pound was lacking. In his book *A Vision* he has a section written in Rapallo where he describes Pound as a man 'whose art is the opposite of mine, whose criticism commends what I most condemn, and with whom I would quarrel more than with anyone else if we were not united by affection'.

At some time in the 1920s Pound began his long-term association with Olga Rudge, though the marriage to Dorothy continued. So his life was lived, as he says somewhere, 'between a door and a door' – one door to his top-floor apartment on the Rapallo seafront, the other up the hill at Sant'Ambrogio, where Olga lived in a house that was partly a small factory for pressing olives. The long walking path up to it through the olive groves was (and is) called the Salita Sant'Ambrogio. It's a steep climb, with the view back to the town and the Bay of Tigullio growing more beautiful at each stage. The house that was Olga's is now marked with a plaque that refers not to her but to Pound, and the road up there is named after him. A passageway on the seafront also records his years of living in the town.

Olga and Ezra produced one child, a daughter, Mary. She was bizarrely farmed out to be fostered by peasants in the mountains of the Italian Tyrol; but each summer Pound and Olga would come and take her on holiday to Venice. Mary has written a book about this extraordinary childhood, *Discretions*. I once had lunch with her and Massimo and Angela Bacigalupo in the Bacigalupos' garden and afterwards she drove me, at breakneck speed, back down the winding road into town. I had brought with me a copy of her book which Kay and I had given daughter Charlotte in 1984 (then seventeen, now Charlotte Grimshaw), and I asked Mary, since it was a book about her poet father, to inscribe it. She wrote in it

> Thank you Charlotte for reading,
> and getting your father to read,
> my 'old' book.
> *Mary de Rachewiltz,*
> Rapallo, 14 July 1993.

When the war came Ezra made regular visits to Rome where he recorded his broadcasts in English. They were supposed to be in support of the Axis side, but were so peculiar and full of the kind of political-economic-historical material with which *The Cantos* are over-supplied, some government officials wondered whether he might really be an American spy broadcasting in code. After the Allied invasion of Italy, Pound trekked north to the Tyrol to explain to Mary, now a young adult, about his marriage to Dorothy and his relationship with her mother, Olga. I'm no longer exactly sure what happened next, but at some point late in the war the Germans moved Ezra and Dorothy out of their seafront apartment and, lacking anywhere else to go, they moved in with Olga up at Sant'Ambrogio. There are differing accounts of how this worked. They had very little money and lacked food. Olga records that they were 'civilised' in their dealing with one another; Mary says the two women hated one another. Pound was there when the US forces arrived. Partisans arrested him and handed him over to the Americans, with the consequences indicated in my review. So *The Pisan Cantos* were born.

Back in Washington and arraigned for treason, he was acquitted on the grounds of insanity, and incarcerated. He was not insane of course; but the idea of executing a major American poet was an embarrassment, and Pound had to accept that he'd got off lightly. When *The Pisan Cantos* was awarded the Bollingen Prize there was outrage. Pound went on writing and holding court in his asylum ward and in the hospital grounds for twelve years, still pushing on with *The Cantos*, still making the same old mistakes. Released at last, he returned at once to Rapallo. As the ship entered the harbour at Naples he was photographed giving the Fascist salute. I suppose he didn't want anyone to think he had softened or changed his ground.

I have sometimes sailed with Massimo Bacigalupo in *Vagabonde III*; and together we once hunted for, and found the site, in the countryside outside Pisa, of the US Army detention centre where Pound was held. There is no sign of it now; but an elderly country woman told us how as a child she had seen the American prisoners and their guards behind the barbed wire and heard the shouted orders from the parade ground. In the distance we could see the Leaning Tower. It was here Pound began to learn humility, to recognise fault in himself, and to put it on record.

> What thou lovest well remains,
> > the rest is dross
> What thou lov'st well shall not be reft from thee
> What thou lov'st well is thy true heritage
> [. . .]
> The ant's a centaur in his dragon world.
> Pull down thy vanity, it is not man
> Made courage, or made order, or made grace,
> > Pull down thy vanity, I say pull down.
> Learn of the green world what can be thy place
> In scaled invention or true artistry. . . .
> The green casque has outdone your elegance.
> [. . .]
> Thou art a beaten dog beneath the hail,
> A swollen magpie in a fitful sun,
> Half black half white
> Nor knowst 'ou wing from tail
> Pull down thy vanity

How mean thy hates
Fostered in falsity,
Pull down thy vanity,
Rathe to destroy, niggard in charity,
Pull down thy vanity,
I say pull down.

In his last years Pound lamented of *The Cantos*, 'I cannot make it cohere'. He stopped writing, and for the most part stopped talking. The Beat poet Allen Ginsberg visited him in Venice. In a hesitant conversation he told Ginsberg and his friend Michael Reck, 'At seventy I realized that instead of being a lunatic I was a moron.' He said his whole project had been spoiled by bad intentions. 'But the worst mistake I made was the stupid suburban prejudice of anti-Semitism.'

Of *The Cantos* he said, 'Basil Bunting told me there was too little presentation and too much reference.' If I had read that at the time I was writing my book on him I might have used it as an epigraph, because it is the whole drift of my argument and analysis – that it's the overweight of reference, of research, of 'discoveries', that swamps and conceals the wonderful clarity, the vision and energy, which nonetheless surface at intervals, and not only in the Pisan sequence.

Ginsberg asked whether Pound would accept the blessing of a 'Jewish Buddhist'. Ezra hesitated, but then agreed, and was blessed.

In 1965, when T. S. Eliot died, Pound, who always referred to T.S.E. as 'Old Possum', came to London for the memorial service and was to be seen, old and wrinkled but still bright-eyed, scuttling in and out of Westminster Abbey, where it was held. He asked, 'Who is there now to share a joke with?' By now the marriage to Dorothy was over and he spent his last years with Olga, who survived him. He died in 1972 and was buried in Venice.

'Taddeo Grande' – Ted Hughes

Reading Jonathan Bate's new biography of Ted Hughes has set me reviewing my own encounters with the poet's work at intervals over most of my literary life since I bought his first book, *The Hawk in the Rain*, and gave it to Kay for her twenty-fourth birthday in 1957. We still have that now badly foxed first edition which I had inscribed with quotations from the poems themselves:

> *For* Kay
>
> Who sees straight through the bogeyman,
> The crammed cafés, the ten thousand
> Books packed end to end
>
> *in*
>
> This mildewed island
> Rained on and beaten flat by wind and water.
>
> *From*
> Karl,   Bristol, 24.12.57

First published on the New Zealand Poet Laureate blog (www.poetlaureate.org.nz), 1 February 2016.

At the time I was doing a PhD on poetic Modernism, so my attention was focused on the early years of the twentieth century, on the impact of Yeats, the Georgians, the poetry of World War I, and the arrival of Eliot and Pound on the scene. As for contemporary British poetry of the 1950s, I had discovered two years earlier the poems of Philip Larkin and had been keenly interested and impressed; and now here was Hughes. I soon found him an alien temperament. In the back of the book I noted (as was my habit at the time, thinking always of how many poems and lines my own first collection might have to be) '41 poems, 974 lines' – and put it aside. Larkin was more interesting among British contemporaries; and beyond work on the PhD, my keenest contemporary focus remained always on what was happening in New Zealand.

But Hughes is such a large presence he is not one I could go on ignoring forever. Reading this Jonathan Bate biography, I've felt again that I've been resisting Hughes most of my life. There's an anxiety about this, a habit of critical conscientiousness learned when young, a feeling almost of guilt as if, as a serious reader of poetry, it's my duty to have an opinion. This is slightly absurd; but these literary-critical questions are worth exploring – there's usually something to be learned from them, if not about the poet then about oneself.

Aspects of Hughes's life have been impossible to ignore – most notably his marriage in 1957 to the American poet Sylvia Plath, the birth of their two children, the break-up of their marriage when he left her for the beautiful, thrice married Assia Wevill, Sylvia's suicide in 1963, and then the impact of the post-mortem publication of her poems. I have that first Faber edition of *Ariel*, Plath's posthumous collection which was a sensational public success, with its dark malevolent images of the male, sometimes father, sometimes husband, often both. Ted appears there as 'the vampire' who 'drank my blood' for seven years, and her own suicide is foreseen and celebrated:

Dying
Is an art, like everything else.
I do it exceptionally well.

The two books, his of 1957 and hers of 1963, seem to match one another, both with yellow and blue dust-jackets now, after almost sixty years, falling apart. Whereas my reaction to his poems had been one of failure (his or mine) to engage, with hers I felt the force of them, a sense that it was a raw force, rough, even rough-shod, with an edge of hysteria and self-dramatisation. The sense of immediacy was what was most striking, and that made Ted's poems by comparison seem muffled.

For all of 1965 (the year of T. S. Eliot's death) I was on leave in London and took part in the Commonwealth Festival readings at the Royal Court Theatre. One of the poets I read with was the Canadian David Wevill, whose wife Assia had left him for Ted and had borne Ted's child Shura. Rumour and gossip surrounded him and one looked for lines of distress and thought they were there. His book of poems, *Birth of a Shark*, published only the year before, was dedicated to her. They had not divorced, and the rumour was that he looked after the Hughes child some of the time, and wanted to preserve the marriage. There were eighteen Commonwealth poets at the festival and each was commissioned to write a poem. David Wevill's began

Every man
Carries a scandal
At his heart.

The woodpile hides
A baby, or
A dead wife's bones

And ended

    I,
Down the same darkness,
Retrieve my lost diamond.

The alliance of Ted and Assia (David's 'lost diamond') we now know
went through many ups and downs until 1969 when she too killed
herself. Sylvia in her suicide had taken special care that the gas did
not reach the children asleep upstairs. Assia on the other hand took
her and Ted's little daughter Shura with her – curled up with her on
the kitchen floor so they died together.

When word of this got about, Ted, already in disfavour because of
Sylvia's death, and because of the way she seemed to present herself
as his victim, became the object of a feminist vendetta which over
the next two decades increased in volume and nastiness. He was
reviled, his books stolen and savaged in bookshops, his house set
on fire and archives damaged; he was hounded in public places
and attacked at poetry readings as Plath's murderer. Plath's grave
in Yorkshire, where Ted's family came from, was attacked again
and again and his name chiselled off the stone that identified her as
'Sylvia Plath Hughes'.

Ted's infidelities were indeed multiple and complex – the woman
he was in bed with the night Sylvia died, for example, was not Assia
but another; but he was also by now a grieving father and husband,
and no feeling was spared for him. His life had become, for the time
being, thoroughly politicised; and though there had been no sign of
him at the 1965 festival he continued to publish new work. We lived
on Prince Albert Road that year, in sight of the Zoo that figures in
his poems, and in earshot of the occasional lion roar or wolf howl.
Within easy walking distance was the house, blue-plaqued because
W. B. Yeats had lived there, where Sylvia died. Our GP was Dr Horder
who had described Sylvia as 'a model patient' and who had phoned
Ted with the (surely intended to be accusing/punishing) words,
'Your wife is dead.'

By now my own first book of poems had been published in New Zealand and my first critical book, *The New Poetic*, in the United Kingdom with a US edition pending. Insofar as contemporary British poetry interested me, Auden, the senior figure, was still producing new work, and Larkin seemed the junior, weird and wounded perhaps, but a star. At least equally important, in America Robert Lowell and John Berryman were filling the frame. Lowell, whose *Life Studies* had so strongly influenced Plath, would soon be moving on to the liberation that his sequences of 'open' sonnets represented.

I was conscious of new work by Hughes, but didn't look closely until *Crow* (1970, dedicated 'To Assia and Shura'), whose raw energy I tried hard to like and admire, but which made me wonder sometimes whether he was trying to match *Ariel* for impact. If he was, he was not succeeding. You can't manufacture desperation on that scale. Only circumstances in combination with temperament can give it to you; and though Ted may well have had (indeed had created) the circumstances, his temperament was curiously British and unruffled. The wildness of *Crow* struck me as what the French call *voulu* – willed, trumped up, meretricious.

> Something grabs at his arm. He turns. A bird-head,
> Bald, lizard-eyed, the size of a football, on two staggering bird-legs
> Gapes at him all the seams and pleats of its throat,
> Clutching at the carpet with horny feet,
> Threatens. He lifts a chair – fear lifts him –
> He smashes the egg-shell object to a blood-rag,
> A lumping sprawl, he tramples the bubbling mess.
> The shark-face is screaming in the doorway
> Opening its fangs.

Who was he trying to frighten? Himself perhaps. Now here are some lines by Larkin written around the same time. The poem begins typically, 'Groping back to bed after a piss', and has the poet parting the curtains to look up into the interchanging moon-and-clouds of the night sky. It ends

> One shivers slightly, looking up there.
> The hardness and the brightness and the plain
> Far-reaching singleness of that wide stare
>
> Is a reminder of the strength and pain
> Of being young; that it can't come again,
> But is for others undiminished somewhere.

The writing is not perfect – the movement of the lines, especially the last, is slightly awkward. But in their tentativeness they seem truthful and don't aspire beyond the level of the human and fallible. Craig Raine writes that 'Ted had more charisma than anyone I've ever met', and that he was 'a spell-binding talker'. I never met him, nor Larkin either, so didn't experience the 'charisma' of the one nor the reputed stammering insufficiency of the other. In the end, as always, it's the poems on the page that matter – in Hughes's case so many, and in Larkin's so (relatively) few.

Meanwhile the Plath dispute raged on, clouding the critical climate. Nothing said about Hughes as poet could seem to stand entirely separate from Plath; and Plath the poet was difficult to separate from Plath the 'victim' of Hughes. There were those who took Plath's side, notably the British critic and Hampstead Ponds swimmer Al Alvarez; and those who took Hughes's – including the American poet Anne Stevenson, despite the fact that she had been at college with Sylvia. And then there was Janet Malcolm who stood brilliantly between, striking a balance in her book *The Silent Woman: Sylvia Plath and Ted Hughes*. I once in the 1980s travelled in a tour bus at an academic conference with Anne Stevenson, who turned out to be deaf in one ear – so on the return journey I positioned myself on her hearing side and we had our previous conversation over again, filling the gaps. When I told this a few years later to Alvarez he said (of course) that Stevenson was deaf on the Plath side.

In 1984 the poet laureate John Betjeman died, and it was assumed the post would go to Larkin. It was offered, but poetry had deserted Larkin in recent years and he declined. It was then offered to Hughes who accepted – embraced it with an eagerness many found bizarre. The Plath affair had slowly faded from public consciousness, and the poems he now produced as laureate gave new and quite different grounds for anxious attention. As Bate writes, 'With his belief in the poet as shaman of the tribe and the royal family as embodiment of the land, he took the role more seriously than any of his twentieth century predecessors.' He was soon the Queen Mother's favourite fishing companion, and regarded by Prince Charles as a 'guru'. His 1992 collection of laureate poems, called *Rain-Charm for the Duchy*, had the little rhyming epigraph

> A Soul is a wheel.
> A Nation's a Soul
> With a Crown at the hub
> To keep it whole.

The title poem of the collection had the sub-title 'A Blessed, Devout Drench for the Christening of His Royal Highness Prince Harry'. There was no irony here – this was serious right royal, loyal British stuff.

But while the critics gasped, the wider public embraced him. If he was good enough for the Royals he was good enough for Britain. So now with confidence that many – probably the majority – were on side with him, he began to feel he could return to the subject of that first marriage and Sylvia Plath's suicide. The result was the 1998 collection *Birthday Letters* in which he goes over that painful ground in memory. My feeling when I reviewed the collection in the *New Zealand Listener* was that it was as if we had all been hearing about, and even perhaps attending seminars on, the Hughes/Plath story for two or three decades, and that Hughes had been attending them too – but with the advantage that he had access to the diaries, his and hers, that had kept the record. The poems didn't strike me as sharp new insights, but as pieces written by someone who knew what we all knew, but knew it better, and was versifying. I also had the memory of Verlaine having said, on reading Tennyson's *In Memoriam*, written to commemorate the death of his friend Hallam, 'When he should have been heartbroken he had many reminiscences'. There was good writing, it was accessible, human, sometimes touching, but lacking economy and the intensity economy brings; or perhaps that should be reversed – lacking the intensity that enforces economy. It was auto-biography in verse, on a par with something like Louis MacNeice's *Autumn Journal* of 1939, but without the historical interest.

But the success of *Birthday Letters* with the buying public was extraordinary. It was said a book of poems had never sold in such numbers since the days of Byron's fame. What can match celebrity gossip for attracting public attention? *The Times* greeted it as

The Greatest Book by our Greatest Living Writer

and reported that 'Hughes gives his account of one of the century's most celebrated and tragic love stories.' All around the anglophone world the news was that a great poet had 'broken his silence'. Almost overnight the devil Hughes became Saint Ted, royal favour-ite and sad rememberer. The British poet Anthony Thwaite, who had just published his *Selected Poems,* complained that it received no public attention at all: 'Taddeo Grande [Great Ted] has swept the board.' Once again, and more dramatically even than usual, the 'Faber poet' sucked all the oxygen from the poetry scene and left it otherwise depleted.

Bate acknowledges that critical (as distinct from journalistic) responses were mixed; but his own tone is reverent. He rates Hughes high among the English poets, alongside Wordsworth, sometimes with Shakespeare. One has to take this opinion seriously; but it seems to me there is little or nothing critical, analytical, detailed, to support it. He appears on the whole to be in the grip of a very English kind of nationalistic awe.

Birthday Letters is the collection that gives this biography its shape. Bate takes a line here from Hughes himself – that the whole Plath debacle had deflected him for many years from 'the true voice of feeling'. 'Everything I have written since the early 1960s', Hughes wrote in a letter, 'has been evading. It was a kind of desperation that I finally did publish them. [. . .] If only I had done the equivalent 30 years ago I might have had a more fruitful career.'

So Sylvia figures in the end as both the cause of a major interruption to the career of a great poet; and yet at the same time, as the subject of his major work. Perhaps there is not a contradiction buried somewhere in this, but to me it feels as if there must be. And when Bate, seeming to follow hints from Hughes, suggests 'his infidelity to others was a form of fidelity to [Plath]', I felt there was something shabby either about the poet, or his biographer, or perhaps both. Not that sexual fidelity is a necessary moral principle; but to make it a principle observed by non-observance seems devious in the extreme.

When Hughes died in October 1998 there was a funeral service at which Seamus Heaney, Irish Nobel Prize winner for literature and professional/international charmer, spoke of 'a rent in the veil of poetry'. Hughes was cremated and his ashes scattered in a spot he'd chosen in the Duchy of Cornwall, equidistant between three fishing rivers, where his name and dates were chiselled on a slab of granite. The following May, Bate reports, 'the great and the good of the nation', including Queen Elizabeth the Queen Mother and Prince Charles, gathered in Westminster Abbey where Hughes was to be remembered in Poets' Corner. Heaney delivered 'another silken eulogy, comparing Hughes to Caedmon, father of English poetry, and to Wilfred Owen, to Gerard Manley Hopkins and to

Shakespeare. The Prince of Wales described his poet as the incarnation of England.'

I suppose Queen Victoria might have referred to Tennyson as 'her poet and the incarnation of England', but I doubt there is another precedent.

W.B., T.S. and W.H. –
'Our clients at least can rune'

At literary festivals I've often been asked why my writing name is C. K. Stead rather than Karl Stead, or even Christian Karlson Stead, and the answer is always the same: when I was young the major poets were W. B. Yeats, T. S. Eliot, and W. H. Auden. They weren't Willie, Tom and Wystan. And initials were common enough here in New Zealand – R. A. K. Mason, A. R. D. Fairburn. Nor has it ever gone entirely out of fashion – E. M. Forster of course, but more recently A. S. Byatt, C. K. Williams, J. K. Rowling. I've had to resist several attempts to convert me to 'Karl Stead', not because I have anything against the two monosyllables, but because I don't want to create problems for librarians and bibliographers.

There is, of course, no such thing as perfect safety. Some years ago a book listing paperback fiction in print awarded all of my novels to the Australian, Christina Stead. Since my first name is Christian

---

First published on the New Zealand Poet Laureate blog
(www.poetlaureate.org.nz), 27 November 2015.

it took only a 'correction' by a computer, shifting one letter and Christian became Christina.

Of those three major poets of my youth, I have read them all probably more often and with closer attention than any others, so each must have influenced my style and my idea of the role of the poet. From Eliot came the example of the poet critic – because Eliot had done so much to influence, and even revise, the accepted overview of the history of poetry prior to the twentieth century. There are always literary people, often themselves writers, aspirant poets, who consider the idea of 'criticism' alien to poetry and 'creativity'. The example of Eliot teaches otherwise. The writing of poetry is a constant making of critical choices – this word or that? this phrase or another? is the tone right? Whether or not poets choose to exercise their critical skill publicly on the poetry of others, they are often the best at recognising what works in a poem, and what doesn't, and why. In any history of the best literary critics, it is the poets whose work has lasted – Philip Sidney, Dr Johnson, Coleridge, Matthew Arnold, and Eliot himself.

In my years as a university teacher, those three 'greats' figured frequently in my courses and in my writing about literary history. Auden was the one whose sheer competence always shone. He had such an ear for assonance, rhyme, alliteration, and such technical mastery for putting them to work. He was also a natural 'occasional' poet – a dependable 'laureate' for any and every occasion, public or private. And of course he figures in my memory bank of poems returned to in the night:

> Look, stranger, on this island now
> The leaping light for your delight discovers,
> Stand stable here
> And silent be,
> That through the channels of the ear
> May wander like a river
> The swaying sound of the sea.

It seems so effortless, as if a musician is at work; whereas when Yeats triumphs, as he very often does, over the difficulties of poetic form, you feel that it's more a feat of intellect than of ear and instinct – more like the work of an engineer than a musician. Eliot is different again – at his best lyrically mysterious,

> O City city, I can sometimes hear
> Beside a public bar in Lower Thames Street,
> The pleasant whining of a mandoline
> And a clatter and a chatter from within
> Where fishmen lounge at noon: where the walls
> Of Magnus Martyr hold
> Inexplicable splendour of Ionian white and gold;

at his less-than-best, offering clunky articles of faith:

> Love is itself unmoving,
> Only the cause and end of movement,
> Timeless, and undesiring
> Except in the aspect of time
> Caught in the form of limitation . . .

So why do I feel – and why do many of those who write about Auden feel – that he is a performer of verse miracles, a walker-on-water, but never quite the Messiah? It is partly, I think, because he is such a moraliser – and worse, that when he changes his mind about what he wants to be the 'meaning' we are to take from his latest parable (I'm thinking here especially of his much discussed political shift from Left to Right) he is able so effortlessly to alter already written, and already famous, poems so they tell us something different – indeed often the reverse of what they meant when they were first published. If the changes can be made so easily, does either version deserve to be taken entirely seriously?

One poem he changed his mind about, first making changes and deletions, and finally declaring it to be 'trash' and removing it altogether, was 'Spain 1937'. Since his death editions have begun to appear which restore some of the originals, so it is possible now to reread the poem as he first wrote it. I think it is a great poem, catching what the Spanish Civil War represented to the Left at the time. Auden came to believe that that political commitment, and the enthusiasm which made it out to be a great Cause, were politically mistaken, intellectually naive, even morally deplorable. But even if one accepted those judgements (and I do not – it was a civil war fought in defence of a democratically elected government) they are irrelevant. It is the feeling that matters, not morality or political justice; and 'Spain 1937' catches that feeling with strangely whimsical force and truthful nostalgia.

It's a poem of 92 lines divided into four-line stanzas – long ambling lines, expository, cinematographic, as history closes gradually on the subject, Spain, and the year, 1937. It has been called impersonal, even unfeeling, but to me its rhetorical structure is brilliant and moving. 'Yesterday all the past' it begins, and that 'past' is at first quite random – more or less whatever comes to mind as representing it, until we get to stanza 6:

> Yesterday the belief in the absolute value of Greek;
> The fall of the curtain upon the death of a hero.
> > Yesterday the prayer to the sunset,
> And the adoration of madmen. But today the struggle.

So this is where the lines, and the history, have been leading us – and the 'struggle' was one of those key words in Marxist terminology, signalling where we stood, which side we were on, and in what great cause: the class struggle – the workers, the underdogs, against all who through the ages have claimed privilege and oppressed them.

So now we are in a present in which that conflict is taking place, not just physically in Spain, but everywhere and in everything – in poetry, in science, in nature, in public bars, in ordinary lives: and what all this adds up to is a collective wish, the people asking the Life Force to intervene, 'to descend as a dove or / A furious papa or a mild engineer', and bring it to a resolution.

But the Life Force throws the request, and the responsibility, back on those asking the question:

'What's your proposal? To build the Just City? I will.
I agree. Or is it the suicide pact, the romantic
            Death? Very well, I accept, for
I am your choice, your decision: yes, I am Spain.

Just past half way through quite a long poem, Spain is named for the first time. What happens here and now will determine the future for humankind; and what happens depends on 'your choice' – on what collectively 'you' want.

Now there are images of people who have come to Spain, as Auden did, answering the call of history to join the International Brigades:

They clung like burrs to the long expresses that lurch
Through the unjust lands, through the night, through the alpine tunnel;
            They floated over oceans;
They walked the passes, they came to present their lives.

The poem takes us forward into the future, which can only be whimsically described because no one can know what it will be – except that it will be better if the 'call' has been answered. 'Tomorrow the rediscovery of romantic love':

Tomorrow, for the young, the poets exploding like bombs,
The walks by the lake, the winter of perfect communion;

> Tomorrow the bicycle races
> Through the suburbs on summer evenings: but today the struggle.

There is no escape from the responsibility of now: you have to make a judgement, you have to take sides. Here is the final stanza:

> The stars are dead; the animals will not look:
> We are left alone with our day, and the time is short, and
> > History to the defeated
> May say Alas but cannot help or pardon.

There is something very particular and, perhaps, for readers new to his work, peculiar, about those early Auden poems. It is partly the flavour of its time, and he was one of those who defined it. He called the 1930s a 'low dishonest decade'; but there is a nostalgia goes along with it – like the memory of one's first smell of Paris plumbing and cheap hotels. I find the whole movement of 'Spain 1937' very affecting, especially the way it slowly focuses on its subject, turns it into a question, and departs, rather regretfully, as if the poet knows already, or guesses, that the Cause is destined to fail.

★

After the end of World War II, Auden wrote more poems that were domestic in content and (finding his precedents in the work of Marianne Moore and Elizabeth Bishop) syllabic in form. But here is a poem, a formal Petrarchan sonnet, that belongs squarely in that 1930s Leftist phase. It was at first named as number 12 of a sequence, in the collection called *Look Stranger*, and later given the title 'Meiosis', which the Concise Oxford defines as, '*Biol.* A type of cell division which results in daughter cells with half the chromosome number of the parent cell':

Meiosis

Love had him fast but though he fought for breath
He struggled only to possess Another,
The snare forgotten in their little death,
Till you, the seed to which he was the mother,
That never heard of love, through love was free,
While he within his arms a world was holding,
To take the all-night journey under sea,
Work west and northward, set up building.

Cities and years constricted to your scope,
All sorrow simplified though almost all
Shall be as subtle when you are as tall:
Yet clearly in that 'almost' all his hope
That hopeful falsehood cannot stem with love
The flood on which all move and wish to move.

Here's what I think it means. 'He' in the poem is a nameless male who is having sex with a nameless woman, and the 'you' addressed is the sperm which, released, will fertilise her egg. The 'little death' (as in French) is their orgasm. The sperm ('you') that 'never heard of love, through love was free'. The journey it is freed to take is inside her body (the 'world' held in the male's arms); and its 'set[ting] up building' is the development of the foetus in the womb.

Now the sestet looks forward to a future in which 'almost all / Shall be as subtle when you are as tall' – everything will be as 'subtle', as complicated, as difficult, when 'you' are grown to adulthood. But the hope for the future is in that 'almost', which allows for the idea of improvement. It is a poem against the idealism of romantic love, which still permits the idea of 'progress'.

It's exceptionally clever but by no means perfect. I admire the formal ingenuity without quite conceding that everything he wanted to say is really said. But form, as always in poetry, is important – and you should always read with one eye on that aspect. The poet, especially one like Auden, wants you to see and enjoy what he has done with the language, and if you only read to be moved or excited, you are selling the craft short.

I think it was in the 1970s I was lecturing on Auden and came on the fact that there were some early notebooks of his in the British Museum. I wrote asking whether I could have copies made and was told yes, if Mr Auden had no objection – but I did need his written approval. I knew he had recently moved from what had been his regular summer retreat in Italy (hence the poem 'Goodbye to the Mezzogiorno') to Kirchstetten in Austria, and I wrote to him there. I got no reply.

So I wrote again, this time mentioning (tentatively and politely) what I thought was a grammatical error in the fifth and sixth lines of the poem 'Meiosis': 'Till you the seed [. . .] that never heard of love, by love was freed.' Since the subject of the sentence is 'you', the verb should be 'were'. Of course if the subject was 'seed' then the verb could be 'was' – but (as I read it) it wasn't, and so it couldn't be. This is what I wrote to Auden, calculating (rightly as it turned out) that an accusation of grammatical error would lure him far enough out of his Kirchstetten cave to respond also to my permission request. Here's his reply, which was handwritten:

April 26th 1969

Dear Mr Stead

Your letter of March 15th has only just reached me.

Of course you can have a photo copy of that Notebook if you want it.

Meiosis:

I think 'seed' is one of those nouns that can take either a singular or a plural verb, so was is intentional.

With best wishes

Yours sincerely

W. H. Auden

I had my permission. The grammatical point had only been a means of getting to him and is not important; but I still think the subject of that sentence is 'you', not 'seed', so the verb should be 'were' ('you [...] were free'); and if the subject is 'seed', and he meant it in the plural, as his letter suggests, then again, the verb should have been were, not was ('seed[s][...] were free'). So I suspect his reply was one he hadn't given much thought. The seed is surely the single sperm that fertilises the egg.

Auden's Kirchstetten retreat is the subject of his charming late collection *About the House*, which includes the poem he called 'The Cave of Making', about the room where he did his writing. It is dedicated to the memory of Louis MacNeice (1907–1963), the first of the MacSpaunday group (as the South African Roy Campbell called them) to die, and it contains lines that might be called Auden's 'defence of poetry'.

> ... After all, it's rather a privilege
>   amid the affluent traffic
> to serve this unpopular art which cannot be turned into
>   background noise for study
> or hung as a status trophy by rising executives,
>   cannot be 'done' like Venice
> or abridged like Tolstoy, but stubbornly still insists upon
>   being read or ignored: our handful
> of clients at least can rune.

Big Spender and Little Matthew

The big Spender I have in mind is Stephen, poet and man of letters, international conferencer and literary bigwig; and I call him big Spender, not because he ever had much money, apart from a modest private income on which he seemed to get by without paid employment as a young man, but because of his stature, 6 foot 3 – not so very tall these days, but exceptionally so when he was young. In the famous pictures of him with his contemporaries, W. H. Auden and Christopher Isherwood, he towers over them. My first sight of him was in June 1965 in the foyer of the Globe Theatre in Shaftesbury Avenue, London (not to be confused with the modern replica of Shakespeare's Globe on the South Bank) at a commemoration of T. S. Eliot who had died in January of that year. It was an extraordinary theatrical homage, involving music by Stravinsky, poems chosen by Auden, Groucho Marx reading from *Old Possum's Book of Practical Cats*, Andrei Voznesensky reading his own, Henry Moore represented by an immense marble sculpture creaking

First published on the New Zealand Poet Laureate blog (www.poetlaureate.org.nz), 21 March 2016.

around on a revolving stage, Cleo Laine and Johnny Dankworth doing *Sweeney Agonistes*, readings of Eliot poems by Peter O'Toole, Paul Scofield, Laurence Olivier . . . And there in the foyer was big Spender, his rather fine head above the crowd.

I stared at him because he had figured in my consciousness since poetry had made its surprising intrusion into my life while I was still a grammar school boy. Not that I thought of Spender, in 1965 or even earlier, as one of 'the truly great' (to use the phrase a poem of his had made famous, and slightly infamous); but he had mixed with them, thought about them (he told us) 'continually', had figured in their lives, had always and everywhere seemed part of the contemporary poetry scene; and so it was not just unsurprising but right that he should be present at this 'momentous occasion'. And that's what the death of Eliot was said to be – 'momentous', 'the end of an era'. Eliot had dominated the Anglophone literary world for three or four decades, both as poet and as critic, and there was no one of similar stature to replace him.

As a student I had bought Spender's autobiography, *World within World* (which typically he had written at the age of 42); and I had even bought a book of his poems (I could ill-afford either), *Ruins and Visions*, which recounted the painful ending of his first marriage. He had a talent for representing his own shames and failures, which appealed to a young, shy and constantly embarrassed poet; and humiliation was what he had suffered constantly in the presence of the magisterial young Auden, his contemporary at Oxford. In *World within World* he describes showing some of his poems to Auden and being told that he was now a member of 'the Gang' and that he must write 'nothing but poetry'.

This remark produced in me a choking moment of hope mingled with despair, in which I cried: 'But do you really think I am any good?' 'Of course,' he replied frigidly. 'But why?' 'Because you are so infinitely capable of being humiliated. Art is born of humiliation'.

The autobiography was also unusual in that it was frank about his emotional attachments to men, but without ever suggesting (or denying either) that these might involve physical love-making. So Spender was generally thought of, when he was discussed among literary people, as 'bi', having a foot in both camps – and with his second marriage to the pianist Natasha Litvin and the birth of their two children, Matthew and Lizzie, the 'gay' phase was supposed to be over. That, anyway, was the story that Natasha promoted and Stephen did not discourage, while unsubstantiated gossip constantly suggested otherwise.

Stephen's early fame came as one of the group of new young Leftist poets of the 1930s – the MacSpaunday group the South African-born poet Roy Campbell mockingly called them – Auden, Spender, Cecil Day-Lewis, and Louis MacNeice. They were also known as the Pylon Poets because of the very conscious inclusion in their poems of the 'unpoetic' features of modern industrial landscapes and city-scapes. It was clear to me early on that Spender's talent as a poet was rather fragile, and that the more (in differing ways) robust Auden and MacNeice were more notable. But Spender had that talent for always being a part of the significant scene; and a fellow student and I used to play her 78 rpm disks of him reading some of his early and famous poems – 'I think continually of those who were truly great', 'The Landscape near an Aerodrome', 'The Express', 'Thoughts During an Air Raid'. I liked his delicate, rather posh voice. He lacked the authority of Auden or MacNeice, but he had sensitivity, and sounded like someone you might like in person.

Many years later I did meet him. First it was at lunch with Alan Ross, editor of the *London Magazine*, and later through the Australian comic actor Barry Humphries, a friend of many years, whose fourth wife was Stephen's daughter Lizzie, who had her father's blonde hair, blue eyes and stature. In those years I was a visitor to London, but a frequent visitor, and after the late 1970s a year never passed without my being there for a month or two, sometimes more. The lunches with Alan Ross were very literary, very civilised, pasta usually, and always with an Italian fizzy wine, Lambrusco, which Ross favoured. Two or three times Stephen came too, and Alan asked me to write an essay about him for the magazine. I did that, but found it difficult. How did one convey (to put the difficulty with less subtlety than was called for) that a poet was important even though none of his poems was very good?

What I did was to first tell a (true) story. I described finding myself in autumn in Germany, in the peculiarly redolent literary atmosphere of the forest-park around the tower where the poet Hölderlin had been incarcerated for 35 years, and being invaded there by the feeling that I was 'inside literature'. At first I was not able to pinpoint what this feeling meant.

> Then it occurred to me that what I was feeling was that I was inside a
> poem by Stephen Spender, one which, like the very best of his poems,
> has never been written.

To this I added a reminiscence of walking in a London street with Christopher MacLehose and being stopped by Christopher's friend, the Liberal peer Mark Bonham Carter, who wanted to show us a little book he had just acquired. He put the book down on the nearest car bonnet which at once set off its alarm; but Bonham Carter, undeterred, simply moved on up the street, away from the racket, and tried again. The book was the list of people, drawn up by the German SS, who were to be summarily dealt with when England was invaded; and there, among the names marked for death, in black German Gothic, was 𝕾𝖙𝖊𝖋𝖋𝖆𝖓 𝕾𝖕𝖊𝖓𝖉𝖊𝖗. It seemed to mark out his importance – that even the potential invader should know about him and want to be rid of him. What we learn now, from his son Matthew's book (see below) is that Stephen had anticipated this and had a suicide plan: if the Germans occupied England he would simply swim out to sea until exhausted, and drown.

I don't know what Spender thought of an article which praised him for the poems he had not written rather than those he had, but much worse had been said about him, and my article also acknowledged his affirmative temperament, his humour, above all his honesty and accuracy, equally in describing what he saw and what he felt. Not a great poet, I implied, but an important observer, an identity and a presence for poetry in the world.

The reason for the second half of my title is that 'little Matthew' has long since grown up and is the sculptor Matthew Spender who lives and works in Tuscany, has written an excellent book, *Inside Tuscany*, and has now published a book about his parents, *A House in St John's Wood*. It is a subject which interests me especially because Kay and I spent a few weeks in that house, 15 Loudoun Road, as house-sitters. It was in 1992 when an unwelcome biography of Stephen by Hugh David was published and Natasha rang saying, 'We're having a *besiege!*' and asking would we occupy the house and keep it safe while she and Stephen escaped to their retreat in rural France. The rather dilapidated rented house in Loudoun Road, which they had occupied for decades, had many valuable works of art and famous archives. It had an alarm system linked to the local police station (as I discovered when I accidentally triggered it), but they felt it was safer if there were people in constant occupation, and their usual house-sitters were away. We were glad to fill this role. In fact it was to be my joke that I'd spent the night of my sixtieth birthday in Stephen Spender's bed, but with Kay not with Stephen.

The *'besiege'* Natasha spoke of was by journalists wanting to ask them about this new biography which the Spenders, Natasha in particular, thought had unfairly focused on the homosexual aspect of Stephen's life. In fact Natasha wrote a long complaining piece about this in the *TLS* – a mistake, I suspect, because it only drew more attention to the subject she wanted swept under the carpet, increasing the intensity of the *besiege*; also because the book itself is surprisingly cautious on that subject and pays fulsome tribute to Stephen's family life with Natasha.

Matthew Spender's book is not a defence of family honour on this question, nor an upholding of Stephen's heterosexuality. It is, rather, a truthful account of growing up in a family where the father's more or less continuing homosexuality is denied by the mother, and not to be spoken about. 'Willpower on her part,' Matthew writes, and 'good manners on his, papered over the cracks'. Stephen's sexuality is not the sole subject of the book, which is a broad and honest account of a childhood that was by no mean blighted or unhappy, but was, at least in this respect, distinctly odd. There is much in it that is colourful and full of interesting people – Auden for example, 'oracular' at the dinner table and smoking between courses; Stephen in argument with William Empson and throwing a glass of wine over him; Natasha's 'non-sexual' love affair with Raymond Chandler; Louis MacNeice, 'tall and pale', arriving at the house to meet Auden, who had been waiting for hours; Chester Kallman's 'disbelief in heterosexual love' and its consequent absence from the libretto of Stravinsky's *The Rake's Progress*; Auden weeping as Chester went off in pursuit of a beautiful young man.

The book also reveals a lot about Natasha's life as a concert pianist, its slow decline and gradual replacement, in later years, by her studies in the theory of aesthetic response (aural perception in particular), a subject she became expert in and taught at the Royal College of Art. She also turned their French rural retreat, Mas Saint-Jérôme at Maussane-les-Alpilles, into a thing of beauty and wrote an excellent and beautifully illustrated book about creating the garden there with the necessary assistance of a very deep well and consequent water supply. Matthew reveals how little Stephen noticed or interested himself in these accomplishments. He was the poet and man of letters, and their public world revolved around him while in private he still fell in love with younger men.

Matthew has had access to Natasha's journals as well as Stephen's; and what emerges early is Natasha's naive idealism about their future together despite all that Stephen had told her about his past. This is not so odd in itself as is her persistence with the fiction right through to their old age. Stephen was not gay; or if he was, you shouldn't say so. Primarily he was a loving heterosexual husband and father.

There are also glimpses, and sometimes details, of Stephen's involvement in matters of literary and publishing politics – his editing of *Encounter*, for example, and the scandal when it emerged that it was secretly funded by the CIA as a cultural weapon in the Cold War. Had Stephen known – or not? Matthew appears undecided about this. And the power of Stephen's influence: 'all he had to do was pick up the phone to a publisher,' an aspiring writer told Matthew, 'and a contract appeared.'

The boy Matthew agonised over the question of whether his father was, as his schoolmates said, a member of the British Establishment. Clearly he was, but the young Matthew disliked the idea and wrote Stephen 'a bitter letter' from school when he accepted a knighthood. Stephen wrote 'an extraordinary reply'. Life, he told his son, was 'very much like school. Sooner or later one had to join the Sixth Form. Most of his friends were in the Sixth form already.' And he listed various friends who were knights, and asked, 'What's wrong with that?' – adding (cunningly Matthew says) that the boy should 'think of the pleasure it would give' his mother.

Matthew was still very young when he began living with Maro, daughter of the painter Arshile Gorky, and they moved to Tuscany, so his separation from his parents – from Natasha particularly, who could not get on with or approve of Maro – was considerable. This book is his way, I suppose, of reclaiming them.

I last saw Stephen the Sunday night, 9 July 1995, exactly a week before he died. I had dinner, at a restaurant called Caprice, with Stephen and Natasha, Barry and Lizzie – just the five of us. I was in London on my way to an Ezra Pound conference in the beautiful little medieval town of Brantôme in France, where I would see Pound's opera *Le Testament de Villon* performed in a cave. When Stephen died, suddenly and unexpectedly, Barry rang my daughter Charlotte, who was living in London at the time, asking her to pass the news on to me and suggest I call him, which I did. He no doubt had many people to call, but it was clear he thought I would want to know and to come back for the funeral. I pleaded conference commitments – there were things I didn't want to miss.

Opera or obsequies, Ezra Pound in a Brantôme cave or the funeral of big Spender – it was difficult, and on reflection I think I probably made the wrong choice.

Index